# BLOODTAKING AND PEACEMAKING

# BLOODTAKING
# AND
# PEACEMAKING

FEUD, LAW, AND SOCIETY IN SAGA ICELAND

## William Ian Miller

The University of Chicago Press
Chicago and London

The University of Chicago Press, Chicago 60637
The University of Chicago Press, Ltd., London

© 1990 by the University of Chicago
All rights reserved. Published 1990
Paperback edition 1996
Printed and bound by CPI Group (UK) Ltd, Croydon, CR0 4YY
99  98  97  96    5  4  3  2

For Kathy Koehler
and to the memory of my mother's mother, Bess,
and my father's brother, Louis

# CONTENTS

# ACKNOWLEDGMENTS

Although expressions of gratitude to spouses are so conventional as to be suspect I must run the risk of sounding tritely predictable because the greatest debt I owe is to my wife, Kathleen Koehler. She is the only person I trust to see my writing in its early stages. I rely almost blindly on her suggestions and without her contribution I know this book would not have been written. I also have a long-term debt of gratitude to my friend Stephen D. White. It was Steve who reformed my interests after graduate school, steering them away from literary concerns toward social historical issues. During our four years of teaching together at Wesleyan in the late 1970s and frequently thereafter I learned as much from him as I had in my previous graduate and undergraduate education. There are other people who have given me the benefit of discussions and suggestions, all of whom I wish to thank. First, Carol Clover who gave me especially valuable advice on chapter 2 and many other matters. Paul Hyams and Richard Helmholz also offered valuable critical suggestions, as did Bruce Ackerman. General thanks are also due to Ted Andersson, Sigrún Svavarsdóttir, Tom Green, Rick Lempert, Fred Schauer, Paul Dresch, and Kevin Smith. I must also mention my teachers at Yale Law School: Burke Marshall, and the late Bob Cover and Arthur Leff, both of whom left a world of grieving students who have never quite forgiven them for dying in their forties, so young.

I would also like to acknowledge several journals for permission to reprint material that originally appeared as articles. Chapters 3 and 4 are revised versions respectively of "Gift, Sale, Payment, Raid: Case Studies in the Negotiation and Classification of Exchange in Medieval Iceland," *Speculum* 61 (1986): 18–50 and "Some Aspects of Householding in the Medieval Icelandic Commonwealth," *Continuity and Change* 3 (1988): 321–55. And selected portions of chapter 8 appeared in "Avoiding Legal Judgment: The Submission of Disputes to Arbitration in Medieval Iceland," *American Journal of Legal History* 28 (1984): 95–134.

# SPELLING

I have anglicized the orthography of Old Icelandic names and eliminated the nominative inflection. When, however, for rather arbitrary reasons, I retain Old Icelandic nicknames for certain saga characters they appear uncapitalized in accordance with Icelandic practice. I then give the sense of the nickname parenthetically at its first occurrence. Thorn (Þ,þ) and eth (ð) appear as th and d respectively, vowel lengths are unmarked, and hooked o (ǫ) appears as o, but ligatured vowels have been retained. Þórðr kakali is thus Thord kakali (the chatterer), Guðmundr dýri is Gudmund dyri (the worthy), while Skæringr is Skæring. Icelandic orthography has been retained in Old Icelandic technical terms and for bibliography. Modern Icelandic scholars will thus find their names spelled as they would spell them. This is some small compensation for the fact that I have identified Icelandic scholars in internal citations by their patronym in accordance with standard citation form rather than by their given name in accordance with Icelandic practice. Icelandic scholars are cross-listed in the bibliography by given name and patronym. For purposes of alphabetizing, thorn follows z, eth is ordered as if it were d, and umlauted, accented, ligatured, and hooked vowels appear mingled with their unmarked counterparts.

The translations in the text are my own. In the case of the laws, however, I have consulted and largely adopted the fine translation of Dennis, Foote, and Perkins (1980) for those sections of the laws included in their text (*Grágás* Ia 1–217). Their translation covers roughly one-third of one of the codices, with future volumes promised. *Grágás* is cited in the conventional style by volume and page in Finsen's editions (Dennis, Foote, and Perkins indicate Finsen's pagination). In order to assist those without Old Norse in locating cited passages, I have cited the sagas to chapter as well as page since most English translations of the sagas maintain the chapter divisions of the Icelandic text and most chapters are mercifully short, often no more than a page in length.

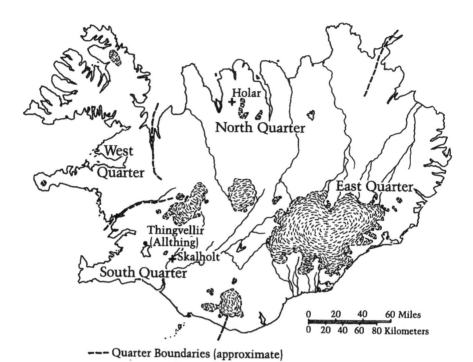

Holar
+

North Quarter

West
Quarter

East Quarter

Thingvellir
(Allthing)
+Skalholt

South Quarter

| 0 | 20 | 40 | 60 Miles |

| 0 | 20 | 40 | 60 | 80 Kilometers |

--- Quarter Boundaries (approximate)

Glacier

+ Episcopal Sees

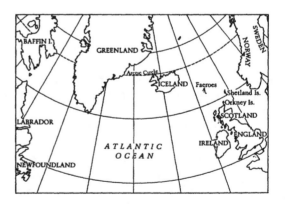

BAFFIN I.          GREENLAND                              SWEDEN
                                                         NORWAY
                    Arctic Circle
                               ICELAND    Faeroes
                                                  Shetland Is.
                                                  Orkney Is.
LABRADOR                                         SCOTLAND
                                                  ENGLAND
                                        IRELAND
                              ATLANTIC
NEWFOUNDLAND                   OCEAN

# PROLOGUE

## "The Saga of Skæring Hroaldsson" (Part I)

Skæring Hroaldsson is an exceed-
ingly minor character in the saga world. He figures briefly in two
incidents, each recounted in a different saga. Part I of his story
is found in *Guðmundar saga dýra* (*The Saga of Gudmund the
Worthy*), a saga recounting local disputes in the Eyjafjord district in
the north of Iceland during the last decade of the twelfth century. It
is in the last chapter of this saga that Skæring is introduced, his tale
providing the epilogue to Gudmund's saga. Skæring, we are told, had
been consecrated a deacon; he was also a kinsman of Gudmund. I
quote the source:

> Some Norwegian merchants chopped off Skæring's hand.
> Gudmund dyri was given self-judgment in the injury
> case. Haf Brandsson [Gudmund's second cousin] and
> Gudmund together adjudged compensation in the amount
> of thirty hundreds, which was to be paid over immedi-
> ately. Gudmund then rode away from the ship.
> But the Norwegians confronted Haf, who had re-
> mained behind; they thought the judgment had been too
> steep and they asked him to do one of two things: either
> reduce the award or swear an oath.
> Haf refused to do either.
> Some people rode after Gudmund and told him what
> had happened. He turned back immediately and asked
> Haf what was going on.
> Haf told him where matters stood.
> Gudmund said, "Swear the oath, Haf, or else I will
> do it, but then they will have to pay sixty hundreds.
> The oath of either one of us will have the same price
> as Skæring's hand."
> The Norwegians refused the offer.
> "Then I shall make you another proposal," said Gud-
> mund. "I will pay Skæring the thirty hundreds that you

were judged to pay, but I shall choose one man from
amongst you who seems to me of equivalent standing
with Skæring and chop off his hand. You may then compensate that man's hand as cheaply as you wish."

This did not appeal to the Norwegians and they decided to pay the original award immediately. Gudmund
took Skæring with him when they left the ship. (G.dýri
26:212)

The scene takes place at shipside where Norwegian merchants
would live during the summer months and Icelanders would come
to trade. The setting allows us to speculate that the reason Skæring
lost his hand had its origins in suspected cheating or thieving. But
the origins of Skæring's misfortune are of no special interest to
either the narrator or his characters. The account has something of
the style of an exemplum and what is important is the existence of
a claim to resolve, not how that claim came into being.

By the time the saga writer focuses attention on this incident it
is not the hand that is the subject of the dispute but the legitimacy
and justice of Gudmund's judgment. The Norwegians think the
award excessive, and not without reason. More than a few men's
lives at this time were compensated for with thirty hundreds or less
(see V. Guðmundsson 1893, 532–35 and Ingvarsson 1970, 353–58,
365–67). Gudmund, however, is able to justify astutely his overreaching by giving these men of the market a lesson on the contin-
gency of value and values. To the Norwegians the award should
reflect the price of a middling Icelandic hand. Gudmund forces them
to conceive of the award in a different way: it is not the price of
buying Skæring's hand, but the price of preserving a Norwegian
hand. By introducing the prospect of one of their hands to balance
against Skæring's, he is able to remind the Norwegians that the
thirty hundreds they must pay purchases more than Skæring's hand;
it also buys off vengeance in kind. He is also able to force them to
take into account the costs of personalizing the injury. Most people,
he bets, are willing to pay more to save their own hands than they
would be willing to pay to take someone else's. The justice of Gudmund's award thus depends on a redefinition of its significance.
Rather than buying Skæring's hand, the Norwegians are preserving
their own, and the price, they now feel, is well worth paying. Fellow
feeling thus comes not in the form of imagining Skæring's anguish
and pain as Skæring's, but in imagining the pain as their own. Gudmund is also able to humiliate them in the process. He reveals them
not only as cowards but as small-minded hagglers unwilling to pay

an award they bound themselves to pay when they gave Gudmund and Haf the power to judge the case. Gudmund, after all, offers to fulfill his own judgment, thereby making, in grand style, a disclaimer of his eagerness for money at the expense of justice. By such indirection the saga writer and Gudmund bring us back to Skæring's misery, even if his misery must take a backseat to the display of Gudmund's virtuosity in the rhetoric of self-legitimation.

This little vignette serves as a reminder of the negotiability of significations, the multiplicity of possible meanings extractable by people from any particular social setting. It also demonstrates that the forcefulness of rhetoric is more than just an internal affair of language and signs; it is about power and violence. Much of Gudmund's wit, clearly, depends on his ability to take a Norwegian hand whether they like it or not. The account is dense with social, psychological, and dramatic possibility, which, if not evident now, will be so to those who work their way through the following chapters. To those unfamiliar with early Iceland the story must be puzzling in many ways. In some respects the case is not typical. The Norwegian presence is mostly responsible for that. The dispute would not have unfolded exactly as it did if it only involved Icelanders. The fact that the merchants were transients meant that the claim had to be resolved quickly if it were to be resolved at all. The parties could direct all their attention to the particular incident at hand since their interaction had not been complicated by extensive past dealings and would not be complicated by future ones. This is one reason why the entire dispute can be so expertly related in such short space and it is also the reason why Gudmund might have felt too little constrained by the norms governing the proper amount to award in such a case. The Norwegians also introduce some technical matters of procedure that were unusual in Iceland. Oaths, for instance, were not an especially important feature of Icelandic law, but, as the passage suggests, they were in Norwegian law. This fact helps account somewhat for Haf's and Gudmund's reluctance to swear an oath unless they were paid handsomely for it. Gudmund also perceives the oath as a dishonor, and we might guess that it would have required that Gudmund swear to the reasonableness and propriety of his original judgment.

In many ways, however, the case is typical or raises questions that involve typical social and legal matters. Why, for instance, does the case fall to Gudmund? Was Gudmund obliged to assist Skæring because they were kin? What is self-judgment? Were all wrongs deemed compensable and, if so, how precisely was the balance struck? Was it always a hand for a hand or were other factors more

crucial? Who was obliged to compensate for harm? Did the source
of the payment matter? (Notice that Gudmund was willing to compensate his kin for his loss just as he proposes the Norwegians do
for the member of their group who would lose his hand.) To what
extent was liability individualized and to what extent was it vicarious? There is, for instance, no concern in this account to identify
and punish the person who actually did the amputation. Are all disputes subject to so much bargaining? What of rules, customs, and
other norms? Were there none that governed this kind of encounter?
If there were ruled constraints, to what extent were they negotiable?
Just what were the expectations of the parties when they met? How
will Skæring requite Gudmund? And what kind of life can Skæring,
maimed, be expected to lead?

These are but a few of the questions suggested by the case. If they
tend to be more strictly legal than social, that is more a function of
the content of an account rehearsing the terms of an arbitrated settlement than of the special focus of this book, which is distinctly
social historical. A significant portion of this book is about the disputing process in medieval Iceland, about how contention was mediated socially, and about how that process impinged on the social
solidarities of households, kin, and Thing attachment. This necessarily involves a focus on obligation, on the types of claims people
made on each other, both on those they considered of their party
and on those they felt hostile toward, and on how they admitted or
avoided those claims made upon them. In short, the focus is on the
micropolitics of social interaction. "Disputes studies" has been in
vogue for nearly two decades among a wide spectrum of legal anthropologists, sociologists of law, and even, lately, historians. I am
deeply indebted to this literature, but a focus on the process of dispute would have been thrust upon me even in the absence of the
vogue simply by virtue of the sources. The relevant written artifacts
of medieval Iceland—sagas and laws—are about what this book is
about: the processing of disputes, bloodfeuds, and the subtleties of
maneuver in social interactions.

Nonspecialist readers will be surprised, I think, to find that many
issues of more general interest to sociologists, historians, legal
scholars, and social and political theorists are raised in a more salient way in early Iceland than they are in medieval England and the
continent, or, for that matter, in many modern settings. Part of this
is due to the remarkable nature of the surviving sources, which allow us to reconstruct the forms and style of face-to-face interaction
and to observe the dynamics within and between small groups (the

saga writers of the thirteenth century anticipated the sensibility and perspicacity of Erving Goffman). Part is due to the simpler state of Icelandic social development when compared with most nonmountainous areas of Europe at the same time. Medieval Iceland, until the end of the commonwealth, ca. 1262, was a society without any coercive state apparatus; it had only a weak sense of lordship, yet at the same time it had a highly developed legal system with courts and elaborate rules of procedure and equally elaborate rules of substantive law. But there was no provision for public enforcement of the law; it was up to the aggrieved party to see that his wrongs were righted and execute the judgments he obtained on his own behalf. This "private" aspect of Icelandic social control and conflict resolution has already gotten the sagas the attention of an occasional Chicago School economist, ever vigilant for real-life examples of theoretical libertarian splendor (see, e.g., Friedman 1979).

Iceland's isolation gives us a society freer from outside impingements than most other European cultures. Its disorders were systemic, not imposed. Isolation relieved the society of the expense of defending against external threat: the North Atlantic was both more effective and cheaper than a system of royal burgs. The objects of fear—the inhospitable environment and the violence of one's own countrymen—were local and familiar. There was also no native population that needed to be subjugated. The land came to its new possessors unembarrassed with prior claims and too far removed for many to entertain seriously making future claims. Partly for these reasons, Iceland was blessed by an absence of a systematic exploitive lordship in the continental style longer than would have been possible had foreign invasion been a real threat. Isolation also delayed and stunted the growth of an exploitive church, although, as we shall see, it was the system of funding the church that ultimately provided the apparatus for some men to skim the production of their neighbors. In short, isolation gave the Icelanders relief from some of the more oppressive social institutions of the continent. And to some extent their relief is also mine, for underdeveloped lordship and a modest church, coupled with the fact that this frontier culture was in no way molded by Roman occupation and administration, make for a neater and cleaner subject than the usual medieval fare. My themes will be uncomplicated by kings, counts, and monks. In Iceland, we actually had a sedentary animal husbandry society, operating in a relative vacuum, which took care to articulate laws and to develop a technique of narration of its feuds and disorders that is the envy of most world literatures. It is as if the universe designed an experiment to test the theories of Hobbes and Rousseau and was kind enough to provide for the presence of intelligent and sophisticated observers, the saga writers, to record the results.

I am primarily interested in social structures and social processes; but I am also in search of the sensibilities of the people who populate the sources. The sagas allow us to observe people living their lives at various levels of competence as they attempt to negotiate and manipulate the possibilities that inhere in the tangle of social networks. The historian is able to discern certain patterns in practical experience of which the natives too, at some level, were not unaware. We can see, for instance, that the Icelanders understood that arbitration was a likely outcome for certain categories of disputes. But the fact that we can, or they could, see pattern or structure at the conclusion of a dispute does not mean that an outcome conforming to the structure was foreordained. There were choices to be made along the route that could delay or rush events to their anticipated conclusion, the very change in the pacing of the events altering both their significance and who ultimately benefited or suffered from the statistically favored pattern. There were also choices that could shift the process into other patterns, choices that could disrupt and thwart expectation. In other words, what looks routinized to the scholar was not necessarily experienced as such. There was always cause for vigilance and anxiety no matter how predictably things were going. In my search for regularity I do not wish to lose sight of tactic, strategy, intelligence, stupidity, fear, anxiety, and grand action.

I have tried to compose each chapter of this book as a coherent and complete essay, but the interdependence of the chapter topics inevitably means that each chapter needs the others to provide closure and nuance to the story being told. Conventionally enough, I begin with a cursory guide to the Icelandic polity, its court system, the juridical ranks of men and women, and its church. It is here that the sense of honor, so crucial to understanding the motivation of events, and intimately connected with rank and status, is dealt with. Chapter 2 is an introduction to the sources—the laws and sagas. My purpose is to lay open for inspection the sources and my methods of dealing with them. I thus present a short but complete saga text and subject it to a rather full explication (much more thorough than our brief acquaintance with Skæring's hand). The choice of text allows me to infuse a discussion of sources—often boring fare for people who are impatient to get down to substance—with substantive issues. The text itself—*The Story of Thorstein the Staff-*

*struck*—recounts a perfectly contained dispute and allows the reader to get grounded immediately in the world that we will reconstruct from the sources. The chapter is a justification of my use of literary saga sources to write social history.

Chapter 3 straddles the world of violence and the world of peace. It lets us glimpse selected aspects of the economy at the same time that it reveals in their clearest form the values inhering in all sorts of exchange: gifts, sales, raids, even the my-turn/your-turn killings of the bloodfeud. Metaphors of exchange and reciprocity were the central constitutive metaphors of the culture, for in this feuding society, paying and paying back, giving and taking, owing and owning were understood in some way to be involved in all social interaction. The chapter is an epitome of the book and its themes reappear again and again.

Chapters 4 and 5 deal with the closely related and rather technical topics of household organization and kinship. I treat these topics in two chapters because of the conventions of chapter length and because of the different scholarly baggage each topic carries with it. These two chapters are about group formation. Without them the discussions of feud, law, and peacemaking are deprived of context and texture. The topics, however, are not without interest in their own right. The household was the basic unit of production and all the evidence suggests it was subject to insistent stresses. Poverty threatened to break up poor households, wealthy households expanded as they attracted servants and poor kin. Movement of people between households was common and we may assume that internal household affairs nearly matched the complexity of the various networks linking individual household units to each other. The discussion of kinship begins with the conventional questions about kinship structures, but the soul of the discussion is practical, not structural. Kinship was a way of talking about rights and duties; it was about the claims people made on each other and how they went about admitting and denying obligation. Kinship, independent of coresidence, was alleged as the grounds of a significant amount of group activity, primarily in matters of vengeance. As such, it serves as a fitting point of entry into the world of disputes which follows.

Chapters 6, 7, and 8 are about feud and the disputing process; they form a tightly knit unit of their own. Each chapter treats a different aspect of the Icelandic feud: vengeance, law, and peacemaking and reconciliation respectively. The culture provided and legitimated several modes of conflict resolution. Vengeance coexisted with law and arbitrated settlement. One could kill his opponent justifiably by self-help or pursuant to a legal judgment. Strangely enough, the formal law was more jealous of extralegal amicable settlement than of blood vengeance, being much less willing to countenance the former than the latter. When a culture provides such a range of option to its disputants, strategy and tactic demand intelligence and the process can become quite subtle and complex. When several of the options put life on the line, the disputing process also requires no small amount of courage.

Chapter 7 not only deals with law as it figures in the disputing process, but also attempts to describe the Icelandic legal style as it appears in the actual penning of laws. The complexity and sophistication of Icelandic law, given the society's weakly differentiated classes and social strata, its utter lack of nucleated settlement, and its undifferentiated economy, is remarkable indeed. Nothing quite like it exists, as far as I know, in the ethnographic record. Even the litigious Lozi (Gluckman 1955a) do not approach the Icelanders' obsession with rule articulation and categorization. The law also bore an enormous symbolic load, independent of its stylistic and practical aspects. More than language, which Iceland still shared with Norway, law was the symbol of Icelandic uniqueness and of Icelandic cultural and political unity.

Chapter 6 and chapter 8 are book ends, the one dealing with the urge to violence, the other with the peacemaking process. The native conception of both of these processes was organized around metaphors and models of balance and exchange. These metaphors structured the native experience of reality. Relations of dominance, politics, were understood in their terms. The Icelandic sources are unsurpassably rich and insightful on the topics of these chapters, and it is my wish that my presentation of the material will kindle in people a desire to have a firsthand acquaintance with the sagas.

This work departs significantly from the issues that have been central to saga studies. It is a work of social history, not literary history. It is not about the sagas, it is about the society in which the sagas were produced. I have envisaged my audience fairly broadly and have consciously written this book to reach social historians in general, not just specialists of medieval Icelandic literature. I have also, in an access of uncharacteristic optimism, imagined law and society scholars, even an occasional jurisprude and political scientist—in other words people like my law school colleagues—as possible readers of this book. The price to pay for casting a wide net is that there will be some additions, differences in emphasis, and occasional repetitions that might annoy or bore the specialist. I have not assumed, for instance, that my readers are familiar with the sources. On the other hand, this work is an in-depth attempt to reconstruct some central social institutions and social processes of a small insular population who spoke a language few have learned; as a result there are going to be many matters of local and special interest that might glaze the eye of a general reader. General readers thus may not wish to immerse themselves in the details of household and kinship in chapters 4 and 5. Some may prefer instead to go immediately to part II of chapter 2—*The Story of Thorstein the Staffstruck* and accompanying commentary—to orient themselves in this strange new world before beginning at the beginning. My hope is that the universals underlying the local and particular will be discernible and that the local and particular ultimately will be engaging. Those not familiar with the saga world will, I think, be surprised at its seductiveness.

My expositional style accords with the conventions of historical writing, except that I have borrowed from anthropological and legal styles on occasion and presented some material in the form of case studies. A significant portion of chapters 2, 3, and 8 adopts this format. My purpose is to give the reader by degrees a feel for the sources, the disputing process, the society, and the culture; case studies provide a convenient way of going about it. They also provide the reader with the means to criticize my interpretations with the materials at hand.

As part of my desire to reach beyond the small and specialized world of Old Norse studies I have made every effort to write readable and unjargony exposition, and with this in mind I made a conscious decision to adopt social science citation style in the text and to locate the notes at the back of the book, limiting them to special points of qualification to the argument, to technical legal matters, and to those bibliographical matters too lengthy to cite parenthetically in the text. I have also tried to refrain from bulking up the endnotes with my debates with the literature. Specialists will easily know the particulars in which my views are different from theirs. For nonspecialists, the internal citations and list of works cited are more than sufficient to guide them to the relevant literature. The internal citations are used to refer to works to which I am indebted or that provide the views against which I am arguing. This mode of citation represents a change from my prior work, which, in keeping with the style of legal scholarship, is almost obscenely annotated, with footnotes threatening to swallow text.

I came to the world of the sagas as an outsider. Although I took Old Norse in graduate school, my area of interest was primarily

Anglo-Saxon and medieval England. It was not until I went to law
school (1978–80), during and after a short career of some four years
as an assistant professor of English, that I turned to the sagas. They
seemed to offer a perfect vehicle for combining my legal education
and my interest in medieval things and I was allowed, even encouraged, to combine law and sagas by my teachers at Yale Law School:
Burke Marshall, the late Arthur Leff, and the late Robert Cover. One
of the costs of being an outsider is that except for a reading knowledge of modern Icelandic (and of course Old Icelandic) I have no
modern Scandinavian languages. This means some scholarship in
the field is not accessible to me. If I were dealing with issues of
literary history this would be a serious drawback, but it is less so in
matters of social and legal history. The bulk of legal and historical
scholarship in the field is in languages that I do read: German, Icelandic, and English. I have been able to get at the most important
Scandinavian literature indirectly by puzzling through it with dic-
tionaries and grammars to get the gist and occasionally by asking
natives to read and summarize articles for me. I am sufficiently well
informed of the Scandinavian literature to know that this book is
not reinventing the wheel.

## "The Saga of Skæring Hroaldsson" (Part II: Conclusion)

We left Skæring riding in the company of Gudmund dyri, his kinsman, with thirty hundreds in place of a hand. We next hear of
Skæring in another saga where he again provides the occasion for
bigger men to confront each other. It is some eight years later
and Skæring is introduced as follows: "There was a cleric named
Skæring, consecrated as an acolyte. He was not very skilled at bearing weapons or in dressing himself—he was one-handed. Some Norwegians had chopped it off at Gasar where Gudmund dyri took up
the case on his behalf." Clumsy though he may have been at getting
clothes on, he was not so bad at taking them off. Thus we learn that
Skæring

> had fathered a child on a woman whose brothers then
> sought out Kolbein to take up their cause. [Skæring], in
> turn, sought out Bishop Gudmund to take his part. Kol-
> bein protested and said he would not accept the bishop's
> judgment in the case.
> The bishop offered to pay six hundreds for the offense,
> claiming that that was more than twice what they were
> entitled to. Kolbein refused the offer saying there was no

point in settling with the bishop because he broke every settlement anyway.

Kolbein had Skæring outlawed, but the bishop put Kolbein along with all those who had been involved in the judgment under interdict.

Nevertheless, two weeks later Kolbein and Sigurd [another chieftain opposed to the bishop] held the court of confiscation for the outlawed cleric and took his property.

When the bishop learned of this he excommunicated them both, because Skæring's property had been assigned to him. (Íslend. 20:246)

That was not the end of it. Kolbein and Sigurd prosecuted six of the bishop's household members for aiding the outlawed Skæring. To make a long story short, matters continued to escalate until, in a pitched battle between Kolbein and the bishop's forces, Kolbein was killed, struck in the head by a rock thrown by one of the bishop's men. Kolbein's death was followed by aggressive action, culminating in an attack on the bishop by a league of seven chieftains. I quote from the source at the point Arnor, Kolbein's brother, had succeeded in surrounding some of the bishop's men in a church:

Arnor and his men went up to the church with their weapons drawn, urging those who were inside and against whom they had the most cause to come out. If they didn't, they said, they would attack them or starve them in the church.

Then Svein Jonsson spoke up. "I will come out on one condition."

They asked what it was.

"That you lop off my hands and feet before you chop off my head."

They accepted his terms.

He and the others then went out, because they did not want the church defiled by them or their own blood. They came out unarmed. Svein was "limbed" as he sang *Ave Maria*. He then stretched out his neck under the blow. His courage was greatly praised.

Skæring the cleric also had his head chopped off there. (Íslend. 24:253)

Thus ends the "saga" of Skæring, a man who, at the very least, had an uncanny talent for being in the wrong place at the wrong time.

He is sagaworthy only because his haplessness provides the occasion for great action on the part of others. The loss of his hand was a mere preliminary to an example of Gudmund dyri's greatness; the bit of pleasure he had with a woman, to his great misfortune, provided a point of articulation for key events in the power struggle between the chieftain Kolbein and Bishop Gudmund; and the loss of his head was nothing more than an afterthought and anticlimax to the incredible death of Svein Jonsson, a person about whom we know even less than Skæring. Svein was a fearless warrior in a modified heroic style, newly affected, it seems, by having heard or having read too much martyrology while serving the bishop's cause.[1] He would die without any expression of fear, but passively, concerned not to defile the church, rather than actively, concerned to take down as many of his enemy as God was willing to grant him. The sagas tend to be much more interested in people like Svein than in people like Skæring. But I thought it appropriate to open this book with Skæring as an example of the little people the sources do not make much of, except to drag them on stage to suffer outrageous fortune. Skæring is a reminder that the heroism of people like Svein Jonsson depended for its effect not only on the fact that it imitated a model of heroic action from the past, but that it was distinguished in the present from the behavior of people like Skæring, neither cowards nor heroes. Without a Skæring, the actions of a Svein are deprived of their special meaning. If the causal chain set in motion by Skæring's fornication seems random and senseless to the reader now, consult his story again after reading the book. Violent as it may be, it is not without its order and its sense.

# Introduction: The Institutional Setting and the Ranks of Persons

Historians of medieval England and continental Europe have the luxury of being able to assume that their intended audience is conversant with some of the basics of their topics. If readers don't know where England is, or the names of its kings and the main incidents of its political history, they blame only themselves for not knowing and not the author for not having supplied the information. But historians whose field is early Iceland are granted no such grace by their audience. Even the few specialists in the field expect to be reminded with each book they read when Iceland was settled and what a family saga is. Except for the Icelanders themselves, who are not a numerous nation, Old Norse scholars, who are even fewer, chess aficionados who remember Fischer and Spassky, vulcanologists, and those people on Greenpeace's mailing list (like my wife), few outside the Scandinavian world know much about Iceland, let alone its early history. To write about early Iceland and intend to be understood is to supply background that would be inappropriate if supplied by the historian whose turf had the (mis)fortune to become populous, powerful, and central to the story western nations like to tell about themselves. What I propose to do in this chapter is to give enough of the nuts-and-bolts history and culture of Iceland for readers to orient themselves; here I provide the broad outlines of the system of governance,[1] the ecclesiastical estate, the rankings of men and women, and the politics of honor. The nuance lacking in the information presented here will be postponed to fuller discussion in the substantive chapters that follow.

According to Ari Thorgilsson (d. 1148), writing in the first third of the twelfth century and the author of the earliest surviving native narrative source, Iceland was settled by Norwegians between 870 and 930, during what has become known as the Age of Settlements (*Íslb.* 1:4, 3:9). The Icelandic sources prefer to explain the settlement by reference to the rise in Norway of Harald Finehair, whose successes were resented and feared by chieftains and local big men. A scene in *Laxdœla saga* is typical:

When Ketil learned that King Harald intended to offer
him the same condition he gave other leading men—to
become his tenant and receive no compensation for
fallen kinsmen—he summoned a meeting of his kin and
announced: "Our dealings with King Harald are known
to you and there is no need to mention them now; it
is of greater import to consider the difficulties on our
hands. . . . It seems to me we have only two choices: to
flee the country or be killed in our tracks. I would rather
have the same end my kin have had, but I do not want to
lead you into such difficult straits on my word alone,
for I know the temperament of my kin and friends: you
would not want to leave me even though it would be a
trial to stand by me."

Bjorn, Ketil's son, responded, "I will reveal my views
quickly. I wish to follow the example of other upstand-
ing men and flee this country. I don't think it's to my advantage to wait for Harald's slaves to chase us from our
lands or kill us off."

People approved of this view and thought it nobly spoken. . . . Bjorn and [his brother] preferred to go to Iceland
because they had the impression that they had heard
many compelling reasons for doing so. They said that
good land could be had for free, that there were many
stranded whales and good salmon fishing, and fishing in
all seasons. (*Lax.* 2:4–5)

The passage suggests that the push of prudence was assisted by
the pull of opportunity. Whatever the validity of these late sources
in preserving reasons for the settlement more than two and three
centuries earlier than their composition, it is clear that the settlement of Iceland was but one consequence of the Viking phenomenon, whatever its causes may have been: land hunger, shipbuilding
technology, political and social transformations in the Scandinavian
homeland, the allure of poorly defended wealth in England, Ireland,
and the continent, or the love of adventure. Other evidence shows
that many of the settlers had previously settled in the Hebrides,
Orkney, Ireland, and Scotland. With them came an indetermin-
able number of Celts, as slaves, concubines, and wives. Strangely
enough, the first Norse settlers to arrive in Iceland were met by
some Irish hermits and anchorites, who, in their effort to achieve
ever greater misery in the service of the Almighty, would sail their
curachs to uncharted seas, trusting in God to care for them.[2] The
Irish presence in Iceland may have anticipated the Norse arrival by
nearly a century (Jóhannesson 1974, 3–7). Ari says that they left

when the Norse appeared "because they did not wish to be here with heathen men" (*Íslb.* 1:5). They might also have been enslaved or killed, since the Norsemen, as we know, felt either alternative a suitable end for Celts.

Besides these Irishmen, the settlers found a land virtually empty: some seventy-five percent of the area was covered with either volcanic ash or glaciers. By 930, according to Ari, the land was *albyggt*, or fully settled, although the sagas provide evidence of continued immigration as well as some reverse migration to Norway. Sometime in the tenth century the basic settlement pattern was fully established. Farms were located in river valleys and in the lowlands along the coast and the few ill-advised attempts to settle at higher elevations were soon abandoned. Bioarchaeological findings suggest that maximum levels of land exploitation were reached sometime in the early eleventh century and began to shrink thereafter as a consequence of poor conservation and deteriorating climate (McGovern et al. 1988).

The basic unit of residence, production, and reproduction in Iceland was the farmstead. Until the end of the eighteenth century, there were no villages or towns, no nucleated settlements at all. Turf, to the chagrin of archaeologists, provided the main building material for housing. What native timber there was, dwarf birch and ash, was unsuitable for extensive use in building and, in any event, was quickly depleted by the early settlers so that by the eleventh century Iceland had become the treeless land it still is. The main crop was grass, which fed the sheep, cattle, and horses the settlers brought with them. During the summer months, sheep were pastured in the uplands where some household members would be assigned to shielings to care for and milk the animals. The sheep were rounded up in the fall and brought back to the farms below. Cereals, mainly barley, were harvested in some areas in the south and west, but the short growing season was precariously close to the minimums needed for the plants to complete their life cycle. Climatic deterioration eventually led to the abandonment of cereal cultivation in many places so that by the twelfth century a certain annual feast in honor of St. Olaf would only be held "*if* two measures of grain were available for purchase at the Thorsnessthing" (*Hafl.* 10:27; see also McGovern et al. 1988; Gunnarsson 1980b). The scarcity of grain meant that the violence of the sagas was usually unassisted by inebriation. Sheep provided most of the calories people consumed and the means to retain them once consumed. The meat and dairy products from the herds were supplemented, as Bjorn heard tell in the passage quoted above, by fish and stranded whales.

But in spite of the richness of the oceanic resources, the social organization of the economy revolved around animal husbandry (Jóhannesson 1974, 288–310; Gunnarsson 1980b, 14–23). The society was considered by its members, and was in fact, pastoral and agricultural, not maritime. The chief sources of wealth were ultimately a function of the control of grazing land and livestock.

Estimates of population size in 930 vary widely from 20,000 to 70,000. By the end of the eleventh century the range shifts upward from 50,000 to 100,000 (Hastrup 1985, 169–71; Karlsson 1975, 5–8; *KLNM* 13:390–92). None of these estimates are any more than hunches. The upper figure "feels" too high, the lower one a little too low and it has become usual practice to split the difference. Circa 1100, Bishop Gizur took a census of the farmers qualified to pay a certain Thing attendance tax, called *þingfararkaup* (see below p. 25). There were 840 so qualified in the East Quarter, 1200 in the South, 1080 in the West, and 1440 in the North. But attempts to construct a total population figure from these very round numbers[3] founder on our feeble knowledge of household size and of the numbers of those households too poor to qualify for the Thing tax.

Whatever the the size of the population there are some small indications that by the twelfth century the land must have been near the limits of its carrying capacity. Just how near can be deduced, albeit by indirection and inference, from the following brief notice: "That summer (1118) thirty-five ships came to Iceland, but only eight returned to Norway that fall after Michaelmas. Owing to this great increase in population there was great famine in many districts" (*Hungr.* 8:71; also *Kristni saga* 14:30). We have no way of knowing the average size of the crews[4] manning these ships, but we do know that the pressure created by more mouths to feed was also exacerbated by substantial losses of livestock that summer in the north (*Hungr.* 8:71). Still, it would seem that a society unable to absorb roughly eight hundred extra adult males for a period five months longer than anticipated was a society shadowed by Malthusian crisis. The prospect of famine must have been part of people's consciousness.

## Courts, Jurisdiction, and the *Hreppr*

The form the new colony took was constrained by the environment and the social and cultural baggage, whether Scandinavian or Celtic, the settlers brought with them. Within these limits they could create their society in their own image. The image they chose was largely taken over from Norway and there is reason to believe, or at least several generations of German romantics and even recent scholars have wished to believe (e.g., Sawyer 1982a, 58), that the Icelandic social arrangements preserved much ancient Scandinavian practice. What formal governance there was was accomplished by a system of annual meetings of free men, called Things, and by the authority exercised by chieftains (goði, pl. goðar) of which more anon. By the early eleventh century a governmental structure had evolved that would remain the model of "public"[5] authority until the demise of what is known as the commonwealth in 1262–64 when the Icelanders surrendered their independence to the Norwegian king and became subject to Norwegian law soon thereafter.[6] The chief developmental milestones were these: the establishment of a Thing for all of Iceland, the Allthing, which was to meet annually for two weeks at midsummer at Thingvellir in the southwest of the country (c. 930); the division of the country into quarters, one for each point of the compass and the creation of Quarter courts (c. 962); the conversion to Christianity (1000); the establishment of the Fifth Court (c. 1005); the institution of the tithe law (1097); and the demise of the commonwealth (1262–64).

Each Quarter, ideally, had three local or district Things, except for the North, which had four. These local Things (várþing, "spring-Thing") met every spring and at them lawsuits were heard and administrative matters were handled. According to the model envisaged by the laws of the twelfth and thirteenth centuries, each local Thing was presided over by three chieftains. They hallowed the assembly grounds and selected the judges who heard the cases tried there. Each householder (bóndi, pl. bœndr) had to declare himself to be "in Thing" with a chieftain, that is, to become his thingman. The Thing attachment of each bóndi's household members followed that of the household head. In theory then, all people belonged to a Thing located in the Quarter in which they resided. A court for each Quarter met at the Allthing.[7] Litigants who belonged to the same local Thing had the option of initiating all but petty cases involving three-mark fines, which had to be tried locally, at either the local Thing or in their Quarter court at the Allthing. The Quarter courts also provided the forum for those cases in which no judgment could be reached at the local Thing, and they served as courts of first instance for cases between litigants who were attached to different local Things. The appropriate venue in such cases was the defendant's Quarter court (Grágás Ia 40–41, II 356). Like the local Things, the Quarter courts were presided over by a panel of thirty-six judges selected by the goðar. Each of the three chieftains at the local Thing appointed twelve judges; at the Allthing each of the thirty-six chief-

tains holding what was designated an "ancient and full" chieftaincy
was to name one judge to the panel.[8]

The Fifth Court served as a court of appeal for cases ending in a
divided judgment in the Quarter courts. Judgments in the Quarter
courts required the concurrence of at least thirty-one judges, but in
the Fifth Court, judgment could be had by simple majority. The
Fifth Court was made up of a panel of forty-eight judges, one chosen
by each chieftain, whether he held an "ancient and full" chieftaincy
or a "new" chieftaincy established at the time of the division into
quarters.[9] These new chieftaincies, three per Quarter, were created
to equalize the representation of the other Quarters with the North
Quarter, whose people had insisted on having four local Things and
hence three more chieftains than the other Quarters. Judgment was
still to be given by thirty-six judges, it being the responsibility of the
litigants to dismiss twelve judges, six by each party, prior to judgment (*Grágás* Ia 82–83; *Njála* 144:401). The Fifth Court also had
original jurisdiction for cases involving harboring of outlaws, runa-
way slaves and churchpriests (see below p. 28), as well as perjury
and offers of bribes that occurred at the Allthing (*Grágás* Ia 78).

The forty-eight chieftains sat as the Lǫgrétta or a court of legislation. The Lawspeaker (*lǫgsǫgumaðr*), and eventually the two bishops, also had a seat. Each member, except the bishops and the
Lawspeaker, was to appoint two thingmen as advisers to sit with
him in the court. The Lǫgrétta made and altered law and decided
what the law was if there was disagreement about a rule. It granted
exemptions from the effects of certain laws, most notably the ecclesiastical prohibitions on marriage within certain degrees of kinship,
and it elected the Lawspeaker (see *Grágás* Ia 208, 211–17; generally
Jóhannesson 1974, 63–66 and Líndal 1984, 124–30).

The Lawspeaker was elected to his position for a three-year term.
It was his responsibility to tell anyone who asked him what the law
was. He was also obliged to recite the law in such a fashion that all
the sections of the law were rehearsed by every third Allthing and
the procedure section was repeated each year. If the oral law was
only one-fourth as extensive as the surviving manuscripts, this task
would require a prodigious memory in addition to expert knowledge. The law obliged the Lawspeaker

> to recite all the sections so extensively that no one
> knows them much more extensively. And if his knowl-
> edge does not stretch so far, then before reciting each
> section he is to arrange a meeting a day before with five
> or more legal experts, those from whom he can learn the

most; and any man who intrudes on their talk without
permission is fined three marks, and that case lies with
the Lawspeaker. (*Grágás* Ia 209)

The Lawspeaker was the only paid officeholder in the system of governance. He was to receive 240 ells of *vaðmál*[10] annually, which was
financed from payments made to the Lǫgrétta to purchase permission to marry within the prohibited degrees. He was also to receive
one-half of the three-mark fines adjudged at the Allthing and in
those local Things in which he happened to participate (*Grágás* Ia
209, 217).

There were also other meetings of formal nature. Two weeks after
the Allthing, assemblies called *leið*, pl. *leiðar*, or *haustþing* (fall
Things) were held locally. Cases were not heard at these convoca-
tions; they were to provide a forum for announcing matters concluded at the Allthing and for reciting the calendar for the coming
year. In addition, ad hoc courts were formed pursuant to various
procedures. Among these were courts called to partition meadows
and jointly owned pasture (*Grágás* Ib 84–86, II 455–60; Ib 115–17,
II 488–94) and *hreppadómar*, courts called an arrowshot from the
home of a defendant who had shirked his responsibilities for supporting dependent kin or the district poor (*Grágás* Ib 174–76, II
252–54), and the *féránsdómr*, a court held to confiscate and settle
an outlaw's estate.

The *hreppr* constituted an administrative unit independent of the
chieftain-Thing structures. It was a local unit, organized territorially, the chief function of which was to arrange for the maintenance
of the poor who fell between the cracks of the kin and household
networks of support (see chapter 5). Each unit was to have at least
twenty households, although smaller units could be established
if the Lǫgrétta gave permission. Business was transacted at regular meetings held three times per year and additional meetings as
needed. It was the *hreppr* that collected and distributed those tithes
and mandatory contributions designated for the poor. The poor
were assigned to various households for differing lengths of time in
proportion to the wealth of the household. The *hreppr* also administered an insurance system. A member who lost more than one-
fourth of his herds to disease was entitled to recover half his loss.
Fire insurance at half the value of the loss was available for three
rooms of the farmhouse: the living room, the kitchen, and pantry. If
a person had both a kitchen and a hall he had to declare in the spring
*hreppr*-meeting which one he intended to have covered. No one was
allowed to draw on the fund more than three times. The insurance

was funded by a maximum assessment of one six-ell ounce per 120 ounces of a member's total wealth (i.e., 0.83 percent). If the fund was inadequate to cover losses, recoveries were reduced pro rata (*Grágás* II 260–61). We are unfortunately without circumstantial accounts to see if this rather remarkable system worked as the laws intended. The origins of the *hreppr* system are obscure, but indications are that it was already in existence before the institution of the tithe law in 1097 (Jóhannesson 1974, 86; *KLNM* 18:287–91).

The preceding barrage of fact can be schematized fairly well in the following diagram (adapted from Njarðvík 1973, 41) if one does not take the initial division into legislative and judicial functions too seriously.

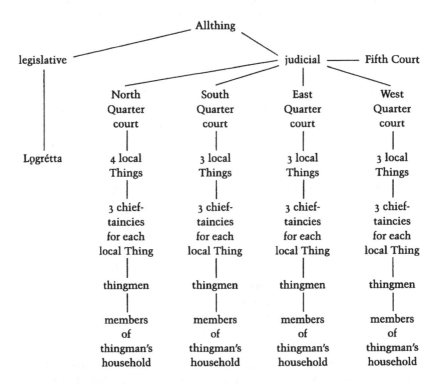

In spite of this elaborate pyramid of jurisdictions and complex scheme of venues and judicial competence, there was no provision for any executive power. It was up to the litigants to serve process on their opponents, maintain order in court, and enforce court judgments in their favor. Ultimately, the sanction behind legal judgment and arbitrated settlement was self-help, most often appearing in the guise of the bloodfeud. There was no bureaucracy, no state apparatus that pretended to enforce the laws, nothing beyond the Things themselves, the annual meetings of free farmers. And although our notion of courts conjures up images of robed judges and pretentious architecture, the Icelandic courts met outdoors, with the judges, it seems, seated on rocks arranged in a circle and apparently drawn not from the body of legal experts who aided the Lawspeaker and pleaded the cases but simply from the farmers in attendance at the Thing. But the lack of executive powers or permanent bureaucratic structures, the absence of indicia of an intrusive state apparatus or permanent legal office beyond the Lawspeaker, should not lead us to underestimate the effects of the Allthing. Political and jural unity was achieved by the symbolic load borne by the Allthing and the law that was recited there. There is no evidence that the various local Things ever developed local law; they applied the law of the Allthing.[11] This fact is all the more remarkable considering the contrary Norwegian experience and the difficulty of communication across harsh country. It would seem that the colonial experience forged a sense of communal identification rather early.[12] The importance of maintaining the unity of the law was the reason Ari, writing in the first third of the twelfth century, attributed to Thorgeir the Lawspeaker (anno 1000) for proclaiming Christianity into the law: "I think it advisable that . . . we all have one law and one religion. For it is true that if we sunder the law, we will also sunder the peace" (Íslb. 7 : 17).[13] The law, the Allthing, the uniqueness of their colonial experience, and the knowledge that unlike all other peoples with whom they had cultural contact, they had no king—these things provided shared symbols and sensibilities.[14]

Even though Thing meetings accounted for but three weeks of the year, those weeks were more intensely lived and more anxiously anticipated than any other random three weeks. These gatherings were a time for making and renewing acquaintances, contracting marriages, and exchanging invitations to feasts. Above all, the Things were the arenas for intensive legal action; they were the locations where successes and failures were unambiguously on display, where prestige and honor was competed for, and won and lost. Reputations, if not exactly made there, were on display there. The Thing was the one place where a large audience was assured and hence the stakes in social interactions occurring there were higher.

Saga sources, however, suggest that the elegant and symmetrical construct of Things and goðar was an ideal whose actualization was often compromised by accommodations to political realities. It is not certain that there were ever precisely three chieftains per local Thing or, for that matter, that all the local Things met annually. One chieftain, Gudmund dyri, was powerful enough to abolish the Vodlathing in the North Quarter in 1190 (*G.dýri* 6:170). In the big power struggles of the last decades of the commonwealth it appears that the number of chieftains had shrunk substantially to about a dozen. It is usually supposed that the model postulated by the laws roughly represented reality until about 1150 (Jóhannesson 1974, 226–39; cf. Karlsson 1972 and Sawyer 1982b, 354–55). The evidence, such as it is, however, does not allow for confident reconstruction. Still, the family sagas and those sagas that describe events in the twelfth century suggest that power then was distributed significantly more widely than it was by the mid-thirteenth century as the commonwealth neared its end.

## Chieftains and Thingmen

Much of the practical activity of chieftains will be discussed in the chapters that follow but some matters should be noted now. The law required a person with property sufficient to qualify as a householder (*bóndi*, pl. *bœndr*) to attach himself to a chieftain for purposes of Thing attendance (see below p. 117). Chieftain and thingman owed each other duties of support and in litigious Iceland this usually meant support in prosecuting or defending legal actions, by providing either counsel and pleading skill or simply the force necessary to ensure the case would not be disrupted or railroaded. The ideal of reciprocal support finds explicit statement in the sagas. In one instance a new chieftain is instructed on how to maintain a loyal following:

> The Thjostarssons advised him that he should be of good spirit, generous, and helpful to his men, a supporter to each of them that was in need. "They would not be men then, if they did not support you when you were in need." (*Hrafnk.* 6:123)

In another source, a chieftain recites the norms of *goði*-thingman obligation when he seeks to obtain his thingmen's aid:

> As you well know, I am considered your chieftain. I judge it to be in the spirit of our relationship that each aids the other in just cases. You should support me against my opponents while I am to be your ally when your needs require it. (*Ljós.* 23:71)

The chieftain-thingman bond had none of the sanctity associated with feudal vassalage or the lord-retainer bond of the model Germanic comitatus. A thingman had no sacred obligation to avenge his fallen chieftain. And though chieftains were expected to take up the legal claims of their thingmen and to aid the kin of their fallen thingmen in getting some redress, the redress that was had was usually legal and not classic blood vengeance. A *bóndi* could transfer his allegiance from one chieftain to another simply by making an announcement of his intention at the Thing, and a chieftain could likewise terminate the bond (*Grágás* Ia 140–41, II 277–78). Several sagas show that chieftains were concerned over the prospect of losing thingmen (*Ljós.* 9:130; *Njála* 107:274–75; *Vápn.* 11:46; *Þorst. stang.* 74). In those districts in which competing chieftains had fairly equal power, the right to change chieftains must have been more than theoretical (*Sturla* 27:102); the sagas, for example, reveal numerous instances of farmers living in the same valley attached to competing chieftains. But a farmer living close by a powerful *goði* must have had little real prospect of freely choosing his chieftain. There is some suggestion in the sources that chieftains expected to have their say in particular territories whether or not all the farmers in it were formally denominated their thingmen; such was surely the case in many districts by the end of the twelfth century. The chieftain Sturla, for instance, bullied a *bóndi* out of the district for having given hospitality to a chieftain with whom Sturla was contending (*Sturla* 23:96). The extent to which chieftaincies were territorially organized, however, is subject to dispute (cf. Karlsson 1972, 28–31 with Byock 1982, 82–86 and 1988, 113–17), but up until the last decades of the commonwealth the territoriality of a chieftain's power was clearly dependent on the energy and power of the particular chieftain rather than on embryonic structures of territorial organization.

A *goði* possessed a *goðorð* or chieftaincy. The *goðorð* was alienable and descendible. It was treated as any piece of property except that it was exempt from tithes, for in the words of the tithe law "a [*goðorð*] is power and not property" (*Grágás* Ib 206). Probably as a consequence of its inheritability, a chieftaincy could also be divided into shares. When a chieftaincy was held by more than one person the laws indicate that the duties and privileges associated with it were to be exercised by only one man:

> If two men own a chieftaincy jointly, the same one of
> them is to act in it for three Things, the local Thing, the
> Allthing, and the *leið* (autumn assembly). They are then

> to change over after the *leið* has been held. . . . It is also
> lawful if men transfer a chieftaincy from one to another
> at a Thing after the courts have been held. If the man who
> is acting in a chieftaincy will not transfer it, the other is
> to summon him to a reckoning and claim he forfeits his
> share and owes a three-mark fine . . . (*Grágás* Ia 141)

The sagas, however, show some evidence that two people might simultaneously share in the administration of a chieftaincy and that the style and rank of *goði* could be claimed by several people owning shares of the same *goðorð* (see, e.g., *Drop.* 4:149; *Ljós.* 4:12) Jointly held chieftaincies must have made for some confusion of loyalty; in any event, they help to explain why the chieftain-thingman relation never attracted the symbolic load that the lord-retainer bond did in Dark-Age England and the continent. The partibility of chieftaincies also meant that membership in the chieftain ranks was open to men of ambition and means who could usually obtain, by purchase or propitious marriage, at least a share of a *goðorð*. In this regard, it should be noted that a chieftaincy could pass to a woman via inheritance; she was, however, disabled from discharging its duties. Should a chieftaincy fall to a woman, she was to transfer it to a male who was a member of that local Thing who was then to fulfill the duties associated with the position (*Grágás* Ia 142).

The chieftain's official duties were relatively few. Some have already been mentioned. They were to convene the Things and hallow the Thing grounds. They appointed the judges to the courts and sat in the Lǫgrétta, and when called on to do so, they were responsible for holding courts of confiscation and for appointing and participating in a panel of twelve, the panel that delivered verdicts in cases of theft and sorcery and certain other select matters. These were, with some minor omissions, the extent of their official duties. Practically speaking, however, much of the responsibility for maintaining order in the districts fell to the chieftains, at least before the turmoil of the last years of the commonwealth period when much of the work of maintaining local order fell to the big farmers (*stórbœndr*) having substantial local power. The sagas show chieftains taking the responsibility for ridding districts of local troublemakers, sorcerers, and thieves (*Eyrb.* 62:166–68; *G.dýri* 4:166–67); chieftains who were lax in this respect lost esteem and thingmen, who might even relocate to other districts (*Sturla* 8:72). From the late twelfth century there are also examples of chieftains who presumed to set policy during times of food shortages, some by distributing their own surpluses (*Hrafn Sv.* 10:655), some by surcharging Norwegian

seamen who were forced to winter in Iceland. Thus Kolbein Tumason claimed a portion of the price he ordered the farmers of Ska-
gafjord to charge for lodging crewmen of three ships that were put
up in a neighboring fjord during a time of severe shortage (*G.dýri*
1:161). Chieftains figured prominently among the men skilled in
law and their knowledge and power made them key figures in the
processing of their clients' legal claims. It is believed that in the
settlement period the *goðar* had, in addition to their secular responsibilities, certain religious responsibilities, such as holding sacri-
fices and maintaining the sacrificial sites. But the evidence for the
early period is sketchy at best. The chieftains of the laws and sagas
are fully secular souls, evincing secular concerns even when they
had taken orders in the church.

The householders obliged to attach themselves to chieftains were
divided into two classes: those of sufficient property to pay an assessment called the *þingfararkaup* or Thing attendance payment
and those of insufficient means. Those required to pay were "those
who for each household member who is a charge on them own a
debt-free cow or its price or a net or a boat and all the things which
the household may [not] be without" (*Grágás* Ia 159, II 320). The
*þingfararkaup* was negotiated between the householder and his
chieftain. It was due from those householders who did not attend
the Allthing to fund the outlay of those who did (*Grágás* Ia 44). The
chieftain was merely a conduit for the payment and he gained no
wealth from the assessment. The liability to pay the *þingfararkaup*
also burdened a householder with the duty to lodge travelers under
certain conditions (Ia 4, II 2) and to make contributions of the food
saved from Lenten fasting to those people of the *hreppr* who did not
pay the Thing attendance payment (Ia 31, II 39). Qualifying householders were eligible to serve on a panel of neighbors in a lawsuit
and obliged to attend the local Things either in person or by sending
a proxy from their households. Allthing attendance was not mandatory, although the chieftain could request his thingmen to accompany him there. The qualifying householders then drew lots or
"determined amongst themselves by other means, but one in nine"
would have to attend (*Grágás* Ia 107). Those who went were also
required to bring cloth to provide roofing for the turf booths the
chieftains maintained at the Allthing and the chieftains were in
turned obliged to provide their thingmen with lodging in their
booths (*Grágás* Ia 44).

There were no regularized mulcts that the chieftains as chieftains
exacted from their thingmen. The chieftain who convened a court
of confiscation for the purpose of disposing of an outlaw's estate was

entitled to a one-mark fee from the estate (*Grágás* Ia 88), but such fees barely compensated the labor involved. In the mid-thirteenth century there are mentions of big men exacting a sheep tax to maintain their retinues (*Þórð.* 37:69; *Þorg. sk.* 14:122, 55:196). These payments could be forcibly exacted and equally forcibly resisted (*Þorg. sk.* 58:200–201, 61:203–4), but they were ad hoc and not a legal prerogative of a chieftaincy so much as an incident of brute power. Only the most rudimentary structures were available to chieftains to mulct the lower ranks of their surpluses. One saga suggests that chieftains made use of forced hospitality by showing up uninvited at their thingmen's farms with a company of men and wearing out their welcome (*Ljós.* 6:117). During the turmoils of the last decades of the commonwealth, the big players in the power politics of the period resorted to raiding. The two most lucrative sources of wealth, in addition to the productive capabilities of their own lands and livestock, were the gains from controlling the access of little people to law (see pp. 239–47) and their own access to tithes, which, as we will see below, was a function of being a churchowner rather than a chieftain.[15]

## Status, Rank, and the Economy of Honor

These classifications—big farmers (*stórboendr*),[16] farmers eligible to pay the *þingfararkaup*, those ineligible to pay it, tenants, cotters, and servants (see chapter 4), even chieftains—were not in the strict sense ascribed statuses. People fell into and out of them depending on the vagaries of fortune. In theory, the laws recognized only two broad juridical classes of people: slave and free. According to the most comprehensive treatment of the subject, slavery in Iceland was no longer common by the middle of the twelfth century and probably nonexistent by the middle of the thirteenth (Karras 1988, 135–36; see also Foote 1977a). *Grágás'* provisions dealing with slavery are not complete enough to provide a comprehensive slave code, although in certain contexts provisions governing debt-slavery appear well-integrated into the regulated scheme of care for dependents (see chapter 5). Saga evidence on slavery is not especially rich and the last slave mentioned in the saga corpus is a late eleventh-century debt-slave. Nevertheless, slave status was still a legal possibility throughout the commonwealth period. The laws also recognized various interstitial statuses tainted by slavery. A freedman was not entirely severed from his manumitter. If he died without legitimate children surviving him, his manumitter or the manumitter's heirs succeeded to his property. The manumitter's right to inherit was offset, however, by his liability to support his destitute freedman should the latter fall on hard times (*Grágás* Ia 227, II 72; Ib 3, II 103). A child born of a free man and a slave woman who was freed while pregnant (*hrísungr*), or of a freedman and the woman who manumitted him for the purpose of marrying him (*hornungr*), or of an outlaw's wife even though she was impregnated by her husband before he was outlawed (*bæsingr*) were all disabled from inheriting (Ia 224, II 68). The status terms naming each of these children look ancient, but if they ever were meant to indicate differing levels of disablement or rank, no such differences were maintained in the Icelandic law.[17]

Several juridical disablements also attended the female sex. In matters of inheritance a woman was postponed to males in the same degree of kinship from the decedant. She was not eligible for Thing participation, and if she headed a household, which, it seems, was not unusual, the laws prescribed five men who could represent the household on a panel of neighbors: her husband, son, stepson, her daughter's husband, and her fosterson (*Grágás* Ia 160–61, II 322). The legal affairs of a woman were to be conducted by her *lǫgráðandi*, or legal guardian. If she was unmarried or widowed the *lǫgráðandi* was usually also her *fastnandi*, the person empowered to give her in marriage and whose agreement was necessary for a valid marriage (*Grágás* II 66). In spite of these rather serious disablements, the Icelandic laws accorded women, both single and married, substantially more rights in property than other Scandinavian or continental codes. And women were more than mere title holders with managerial powers lodged solely with men; women of the *bóndi* class managed farms in their husbands' absence and managed the indoor activities when they were present. Sagas show married women with the power to hire and fire servants (e.g., *Njála* 36:96). And the significant unofficial power exercised by women in the feud and the disputing process is a frequent saga theme discussed in some detail later.

In contrast to the early Anglo-Saxon laws, Icelandic law made no distinction in wergeld values among free men or women. The corpse of a chieftain and a servant, male or female, had the same price. Such was the theory; practice was otherwise. The amount the kin were actually able to collect for the victim of a killing was intimately linked to the social standing of the victim, his popularity, and to the wealth and power of his kin and affines. Nor did the fact that the laws did not distinguish greatly among the ranks of free men mean that all free men had equal access to resources. There were great differences in relative wealth and power among the free. The ability to profit on tithes came to be, in the course of the twelfth century, the chief determiner of economic position (Einarsson 1974). The tithe law provided that tithes were to be divided into four parts. One of these, as already noted, was earmarked for the poor of the *hreppr*, the second part for the bishop, and the third and fourth for the support of churches and the priests' wages respectively. These last two portions ended up in the hands of those *bœndr* and chieftains who owned churches, and they were thus able to benefit substantially from this mandatory transfer of wealth from their nonchurchowning fellows. The direct benefit to the churchowner was augmented by the pathetic legal condition of the churchpriest whose support was the churchowner's responsibility. The lot of such priests was legally little better than a slave's and the laws do not shy away from the comparison. This grim provision is interesting enough in its own right to merit extended citation:

> It is lawful for a man to have a priestling taught for his church. He is to make an agreement with the boy himself if he is sixteen winters old, but if he is younger he is to make it with his legal guardian (*lǫgráðandi*). . . . [In the absence of an agreement to the contrary] he is to provide him with instruction and fostering; and have him chastised only in such a way that it brings no shame on the boy or his kin; and treat him as if he were his own child. If the boy will not learn and finds Latin tedious, he is to be put to other work and chastised at that only in such a way that he suffers no illness or lasting injury, but kept at it in all other respects with the firmest discipline. Should he now wish to return to his studies, then he is to be kept at them until he takes orders and is a priest. . . . If a priest absconds from the church for which he was taught or absents himself so that he does not hold services as prescribed, then the man who receives him into his home or hears services from him or shares living quarters with him is liable to full outlawry. The penalty for sharing living quarters with him is the same as sharing with a full outlaw. . . . It is a case for the Fifth Court . . . and the priest is to be claimed in the same way as slaves. A priest may free himself from a church by teaching another man to serve in his place who seems in every way satisfactory to the bishop who has jurisdiction there. (*Grágás* Ia 17–18)

If slavery was a dead letter by the thirteenth century, its ghost was still stalking about in the Icelandic church.

Perhaps the most noteworthy feature of ranking and class in Iceland was the paucity of objective, external, and unambiguous juridical markers of status and hierarchy. Except for ecclesiastical office, there were no titles beyond Lawspeaker and *goði*, and even the latter was not without ambiguities occasioned by the fractured ownership of the office and the real power of some local big *bœndr*. Wealth allowed opportunities for the acquisition of visible prestige goods, fine weapons and apparel, but there was no necessary connection between wealth and rank. Impressive ancestry and wealth only provided a presumption of deference; people still had to show themselves worthy of their blood and their means. People were thus ever anxious about the state of their own positions and ever jealous of the attainments of others. Such, at least, is the picture the sagas present where so much of the motive and style of discord and dispute is a function of the inherent insecurity of social rank and status. Status had to be carefully maintained or aggressively acquired: one's status depended on the condition of one's honor, for it was in the game of honor that rank and reputation was attained and retained. Honor was at stake in virtually every social interaction.[18] Consider this well-known saga example in which two men, one a powerful chieftain named Gudmund and one a substantial *bóndi* named Ofeig, contend for precedence in seating arrangements at a feast given by a thingman of Gudmund. Gudmund was appointed the seat of honor and Ofeig was given the seat next to him.

> And when the tables were set, Ofeig put his fist on the table and said, "How big does that fist seem to you, Gudmund?"
> "Big enough," he said.
> "Do you suppose there is any strength in it?" asked Ofeig.
> "I certainly do," said Gudmund.
> "Do you think it would deliver much of a blow?" asked Ofeig.
> "Quite a blow," Gudmund replied.
> "Do you think it might do any damage?" continued Ofeig.
> "Broken bones or a deathblow," Gudmund answered.
> "How would such an end appeal to you?" asked Ofeig.
> "Not much at all, and I wouldn't choose it," said Gudmund.
> Ofeig said, "Then don't sit in my place."
> "As you wish," said Gudmund—and he sat to one side. People had the impression that Ofeig wanted the

greater portion of honor, since he had occupied the highseat up to that time. (*Ljós.* 21:58–59)

This is not the only instance in the sagas where offended sensibilities over seating arrangements lead to conflict. The initial incident
in the central feud in *Njáls saga*, eventually leading to the annihi-
lation of both factions, ostensibly had its origins in one woman's
displeasure at her location at a feast. In the same saga, a magnanimous man of honor offered to take a seat of low precedence "because
everyone else would then be satisfied with where they sat" (34:89).
It is not hard to discern why festive meals are charged with such
energized significance. Seating arrangements provided one of the
few occasions in the culture where relative ranking was clearly visible. Of course, clarity could be confused with irony, as in the cases
when magnanimous men made grand gestures in the interests of
festive concord, but irony was only a possible strategy in such situations because they were so dense with meaning.

Breaches of protocol established by past practice or dictated by
norms of politeness and deference were construed as challenges. It
is thus the head of household himself, and not his servant, who had
to invite the *bóndi* at his door to accept food and lodging or risk
giving grave offense (e.g., *Fóst.* 3:129; *Hœn.* 10:28–29; *Vall.* 6:250;
cf. *Þorg. sk.* 19:137). Such sensitivity is not just "greatly to find
quarrel in a straw"; it was not straws that were the subject of contention but honor, and honor was a precious commodity in very
short supply. The amount of honor in the Icelandic universe was
perceived to be constant at best, and over the long run, it seemed to
be diminishing. The men of the present generation were never quite
the men of their great-grandfather's time. Honor was thus, as a matter of social mathematics, acquired at someone else's expense. When
yours went up, someone else's went down. This proposition is self-
evident in the pure case of one-on-one combat, where the honor acquired by the victor is funded almost entirely by the loser. It is less
easily observed in cases in which peacemakers attained honor for
bringing about the amicable resolution of a dispute, but there too
one might see the gains as being funded by all those whose standing
relative to the peacemaker was necessarily adjusted downward relative to him by his gain in prestige. Honor, in short, approximated a
zero-sum game (Gouldner 1965, 49–51), an observation also made
some three centuries ago by Thomas Hobbes (1651 [1841, 5]): "glory
is like honour; if all men have it no man hath it, for they consist in
comparison and precellence." The picture, however, is significantly
more complicated than that which I am painting broadly here. It

was possible, for instance, to circumscribe interactions in such a way that adversaries could both gain honor. We shall have occasion to observe in chapter 2 two men pitted against each other in a matter of honor who both emerge with their honor enhanced. But once we expand the boundaries and look beyond the accounts of just the principal actors to the wider social setting, we see the cost of funding these accounts is the envy elicited among the bystanders. Envy seems to be an unavoidable byproduct of the successful social action of others. In any event, people in an honor driven society tend to act as if honor was a scarce commodity, the supply of which was either constant or diminishing, even if in certain local settings both parties in an interaction could end up looking good.[19]

The game was a laborious one because it demanded the greatest sensitivity to insult and challenge and because there were no intermissions once it started in earnest at the onset of physical maturity. An old man could not relax, nor even the corpse that had suffered violent death, for the final assessment of the victim's honor depended on how much compensation or how great a vengeance his kin could exact on his behalf. The interminability of the enterprise is but one reason why this 'game' needs quotes. It was a game only in the sense that honor necessarily meant competition. There was nothing trivial about the 'game'; it was, for people of self-respect, coterminous with social existence itself.

The state of one's honor was socially determined, as is amply inferable from the importance of seating arrangements. Honor was not just up to the individual. He could not simply maintain it by doing those actions that were prima facie honorable and avoiding those that were not. For the honorable man could neutralize what, in the abstract, were dishonorable deeds, whereas the man of no honor could not acquire it just by performing what, in the abstract, were honorable deeds. The wily and conniving Sturla of Hvamm and his ancestor Snorri goði might occasionally lose honor vis-à-vis their chief competitors, but they never were dishonored by their own deceitful and treacherous actions (see generally *Eyrb.* and *Sturla*). There was thus a kind of inertia in honor. It made for very favorable presumptions in favor of the person who already possessed it.

Honor and reputation were in the eye of the beholder and most beholders' eyes were jealous because they too were competing for the same limited supply. One irony of honor was that it was accorded as much by an enemy as by a friend. And still another irony demanded that it be accorded by people whom one admitted as equals. The 'game' required a competitive field populated by players everyone admitted as worthy of being in the game, all of roughly the same class and status, yet the goal of the game was to surpass the others and create differentiation. Excessive differentiation, however, tended to remove one from the field of play, either toward lordship if positively differentiated, or toward clientage if negatively. A free man did not generally compete for honor with a slave or servant, nor a man with a woman, nor an adult with a child. When the lesser did confront the greater—the slave the master, the small farmer the chieftain, the child the adult—the response was either to ignore the affront as unworthy of notice or to respond by disciplining and "instructing" the offender. In either case, the response denied the existence of a continuing exchange in the field of honor; there was no continuing game with the unworthy, that is, from those who had no honor to lose. This did not mean, however, that honor was not to be gained or lost in specific interactions with lesser people, for honor was always at risk.[20] It's just that as a matter of probability honor was more likely to be redistributed within a class or status than across class boundaries.

Consider, for example, the case in which a man of rank lost two molars and had his jaw broken by a lowly herdsman who was defending his master's household against attack. The injured man suffered loss of honor in addition to his pain, and all those who did not mete out blows as effectively as the herdsman were also the objects of ridicule: "It was people's view that both Gisli's and Eyjolf's men [the two contending sides] had borne themselves most unlike herdsmen" (*Íslend.* 33:266). The "people's view," it should be noted, accorded no special honor to the herdsman; the effectiveness of the ridicule depended on the herdsman remaining indelibly declassé. We may thus presume that the people making the judgment were of the householding class who were able to gain at the expense of Gisli and Eyjolf and those of their followers who were, or pretended to be, men of honor. This instance shows that the honor taken away by a nonplayer in the honor game need not always accrue to the benefit of the nonplayer, in this case the herdsman. Rather, it would go to improve the position of the "people" making the judgment against those whom they had judged. If the herdsmen and servants, however, had had their own saga writers, they would have told a different story, one in which the herdsman had gained glory as against his fellow servants.[21]

A man of rank could take pains to prevent honoring his opponents by refusing to admit they had given him offense in such a way that engaged his honor. When the mighty Jon Loftsson undertook to involve himself in the legal action taken after the chieftain Einar was killed by boys still in their teens of middling farmer rank, he explained his decision in terms that made it clear that the people he must move against were not worthy opponents in honorable competition; the action was simply a matter of good governance:

> My friendship with Einar was such that I feel no obligation in this case. Still it seems to me that it is a grave matter if there should be no correction when inconsequential people kill a chieftain. For that reason I promise you my support in the case. (*Íslend.* 3:230)

Jon's speech is more than just a statement of class interest. By defining his actions as matters of governance and class dominance, he seeks to disengage his actions from the field of personal honor so as not to jeopardize it. Such attempts were not always successful. Jon might not have been competing with the young killers of Einar for honor, but that did not mean he could not lose honor to those with whom he normally would compete, if he should fail in his action against the killers. Or, it might be that people were not willing to accept Jon's characterization of his opponents, seeing it instead as nothing more than a riposte to an affront in the game of honor itself.

If competition within the game of honor produced differentiation, it also worked to level differences. There were forces at play that tended to prevent persons from becoming too powerful so as to be able to remove themselves from the game. The possession of honor attracted challenges, because that was where honor was to be had. And as long as the social organization of the economy did not allow for people to maintain retinues, the basic egalitarian assumptions of the honor system, egalitarian that is within each broad stratum, were reflected reasonably well in reality. I do not mean to suggest that Iceland was an egalitarian society. It was clearly stratified; access to resources was unevenly distributed. But the mentality of hierarchy never fully extricated itself from the egalitarian ethos of a frontier society created and recreated by juridically equal farmers. Much of the egalitarian ethic maintained itself even though it accorded less and less with economic realities (see Herzfeld 1980, 341–42). To be sure, the free had contempt for the slave, those with an impressive ancestry did not hesitate to flaunt it, and the egalitarian ethos, as we have already shown, did not prevent quests for preeminence. On the contrary, it seemed to motivate them. Still, classist claims are surprisingly rare and when made they are mostly ambivalent. When Abbot Brand says that "It is hard for us to bear without amends the killing of our noble kinsmen by the sons of *bœndr*" (*Þorg. sk.* 44:175), the sentiment reeks of a sense of privilege. But when we take account of the fact that the killers were two of the leading men in Iceland at the time, Brand's statement is well within the range of insult that equals might level at each other in the game of honor. The statement does show, however, that by the end of the commonwealth period certain assumptions about class privilege and expectations of deference were already well enough established to have become part of the lexicon of self-congratulation and self-justification.

Our sources do not allow us to reconstruct with much confidence the process of differentiation of classes or of ranks of differing expectations, but they show that by the end of the commonwealth certain big men, although still obsessed with the ideology of honor and still imbued with the heroic ethos, were no longer constrained or constrainable by the leveling mechanisms of the game. The field had grown too small, the players too powerful. Both sagas and laws suggest that by the mid-thirteenth century there had occurred an impoverishment of substantial segments of the farming class, and corresponding increases in the numbers of small holding tenants and cotters, and ever greater numbers of permanent servants and beggars. These people provided a pool for some, notably Bishop Gudmund, to draw on to maintain fairly permanent retinues whose capacity for combat was greater than the traditional groupings assembled on the bases of household, kinship, and chieftain-thingman networks. As noted above, the beneficiaries of the dimming expectations of the multitude were those who had access to tithes, the churchowning chieftains and big farmers, and the church itself. There is no small difficulty in determining the chronology of these developments and the limits of our knowledge in this regard is a matter dealt with in the next chapter when I discuss the nature of the sources.

## The Native Church

The story of the Icelandic church has been told many times (see, e.g., Jóhannesson 1974, Stefánsson 1975), not least by the Icelanders of the twelfth and thirteenth centuries. The conversion figures prominently in Ari's history, in several family sagas, and in the sagas of Olaf Tryggvason. The subsequent history of the church and the lives of its native bishops occupy an important place in early literary production. From *Landnámabók* (*The Book of Settlements*)[22] we learn that a number of the original settlers had already accepted Christianity, apparently as a consequence of their contacts with Christians in the British Isles. A certain Asolf was so serious a Christian that "he wanted to have nothing to do with heathens and would not accept their food" (*Land.* 24:62). Helgi the Lean, however, hedged his bets: "Much mixed in faith, he believed in Christ but prayed to Thor when seafaring and in times of real difficulty" (218:250). But the vast majority of settlers were still pagans. It was not until the end of the tenth century that the Christian cause was significantly advanced. The final impetus toward conversion ultimately depended on the accession in Norway of Olaf Tryggvason, a Christian king, who made it his interest to see that the Icelanders accepted the faith. Christianity was formally accepted into the law at the Allthing in the year 1000 as a result of an agreement by the heathen and Christian factions to abide by the decision of the Lawspeaker Thorgeir from Ljosavatn. Thorgeir, himself a heathen, announced a compromise described by Ari as follows:

> It was then made law that everyone should be Christian
> and those who were still unbaptized in the country
> should accept baptism. But concerning the exposure of
> infants the old laws should stand and likewise concern-
> ing the eating of horsemeat. People could sacrifice [to the
> old gods] in secret, if they wished, but they were liable
> for lesser outlawry if witnessed. But after a few years
> this heathen practice was abolished as were the others.
> (*Íslb.* 7:17)[23]

The new faith was without much institutional support. There was no native clergy and what Christian education there was was supplied by foreign clerics. The first Icelandic bishop, Isleif Gizurarson, was consecrated in 1056; he was a member of a prominent chieftain family and the son of one of the leading champions of the Christian cause at the time of the conversion. Ari tells us that "when the chieftains and other good men saw that Isleif was far more able than the other clergy in the country, they sent him many of their sons to be schooled and ordained as priests" (*Íslb.* 9:20). And by the time his son and successor was bishop, it was observed that "most men of rank were trained and ordained to the priesthood" (*Kristni saga* 13:29). By the beginning of the twelfth century the Icelandic church had become a native institution, assimilated by the upper echelons of the society (Jóhannesson 1974, 152; Foote 1984, 11). The church did not yet stand opposed to secular authority. As in the pagan past, the *goðar* continued to exercise religious as well as secular authority: those who fought were those who prayed. The leading families supplied the leading churchmen and the leading churchmen still lived like the chieftains and leading farmers they were, marrying, procreating, and litigating. Presumably, one welcome effect was a fairly literate dominant male class and it might be that the uniqueness of the native literature owes something to the fusion of letters and axes.

Until Bishop Gizur urged the acceptance of tithing into the law, the native church was funded by privately initiated outlays; farmers and chieftains built their own churches and financed the priests who served them. The tithe law offered the church broadbased, regular, and enforceable funding.[24] The Icelandic tithe was unique in that it was not a tax on yields but a property tax of one percent of a person's worth.[25] Men and women over sixteen years of age were obliged to declare their wealth under oath at a fall meeting of the *hreppr*; underevaluations, needless to say, were discouraged by stiff penalties, as well as by the publicity of the declaration. There were some key exemptions from the tax (*Grágás* Ib 205–15, II 46–57). Chieftaincies, as mentioned, were not titheable, nor was property donated to a church, even if that church was owned and under the sole control of the person making the contribution. This last exemption could be used by churchowners to insulate effectively all their property from tithes. From this exemption, coupled with the fact that one-half of the amount collected from others went to the churchowner for the maintenance of the church and of its indentured priest, we can begin to discern why there is no mention in the sources of resistance to the tithe by the rich and powerful, who in fact recognized and took advantage of the tax loopholes. Bishop Gizur himself endowed the bishopric with lands and moveables, including his ancestral estate at Skálholt, and had the see established there by law. Soon thereafter, in response to the wishes of the people of the North Quarter, Gizur relinquished his claim to tithes from the North Quarter and thereby enabled the funding to establish a second see at Hólar in 1106.

It would seem that the upper-class priests were not sufficiently numerous to care adequately for all souls, and it is not certain to what extent they did. The urge to ordination may have been partly motivated by the quest for accomplishments in the competition for honor. In any event, the provision authorizing the impressment of children into the priesthood and into service in the churches owned by prominent people (see p. 28) suggests that at the time of its enactment there was a serious shortage of priests. There was also a class of priest known as *þingaprestr* or district priest. He had the right to sell his services, although the law limited his wages to twelve marks per annum unless his district was especially difficult to traverse (*Grágás* Ia 20–21, II 24–25). He was often a member of the household of a churchowning farmer and, like other household members, his household attachment was contracted for on an annual basis (see below p. 120). About 1200 Bishop Pal of Skálholt counted 220 churches in his diocese and by his estimation he needed 290 priests to staff them. He made the tally, according to the source, "because he wished to permit priests to go abroad if a sufficient number still remained in the diocese, and he wished also to see to it that there was no shortage of priests in his diocese while he was bishop" (*Pál.* 11:136). The text implies that Pal was close to his needs, but clearly not inundated with clerics. The priests who wished to go abroad might have been seeking to further their education. Clerical education in Iceland varied widely in quality. The churchpriest's education was usually in the hands of the man whom he was schooled to replace. The district priest might have been schooled privately (*Prest.* 4:123) or could have been trained at the cathedral school at Hólar founded by its first bishop, Jon, in 1106–7 (see Jóhannesson 1974, 156–60, 167; Foote 1984, 87–88). We know that some of the priests from leading families were schooled in Germany, Paris, and England.

In the eleventh and twelfth centuries the church was within the purview of the secular law. Violations of ecclesiastical prohibitions were enforced by actions in the same courts at the Things in which purely secular matters were heard with but one exception: a priest who did not obey his bishop was subject to a three-mark fine, the action to be prosecuted by the bishop at the Allthing before a court of twelve priests of his choosing (*Grágás* Ia 21, II 25). The farmers and chieftains who built churches, some of whom may have been in orders, treated these churches as their own, administered the property gifted to the church, named the priest to serve it, and passed on its control to their heirs.[26] The Hildebrandine reforms were late getting to Iceland and late in affecting practice once they got there.

The Icelandic clergy of all ranks behaved as laymen in matters of sex and marriage. One researcher recently found no examples of celibate priests in the surviving sources and only two bishops who abstained of the thirteen native bishops in the commonwealth period (Jochens 1980, 382–83). Priests contracted regular marriages with women of the same social standing they would have married had they not been in orders.[27] The laws regulated clerical marriage only to the extent that a priest fell within the ban on marriages between sponsorial kin. He was not to marry a woman whose children he had earlier baptized (*Grágás* Ib 31, II 158). Sexuality and marriage were a part of the world of manly honor and no one thought to mention that divinity and dalliance need be sundered until the episcopate of

Thorlak Thorhallsson (1178–93). Thorlak zealously attempted to enforce ecclesiastical strictures dealing with sexual practices, but even he did not tackle clerical celibacy, confining himself instead to separating priests and spouses who had married within the prohibited degrees (see, e.g., *Oddav*. 20:284–85) or who kept concubines in addition to their wives. Thorlak's oft told confrontation with the powerful chieftain Jon Loftsson merits repeating. Jon was also a deacon, married, and had had children by several women, one of whom was Bishop Thorlak's sister Ragnheid. "She and Jon had loved each other since they were young" (*Oddav*. 19:282). At the time of the confrontation Ragnheid was living with Jon and his wife. The bishop complained and formally banned their ménage and finally threatened to excommunicate Jon who replied in part: "I shall remain with the woman you are upset about as long as it pleases me and neither your ban, nor other men's efforts either, will make me give up these matters of contention until God inspires me to give them up of my own will" (24:291–92). Some may find irony in the fact that Thorlak's successor as bishop was his nephew, the illegitimate son of Jon and Ragnheid.

Thorlak spent considerable energy trying to establish the church on an autonomous footing. The main subject of dispute was the private control of churches and church property. He had some small successes in wresting titular control of several churches away from their owners,[28] but he foundered again against Jon Loftsson. Jon refused to admit Thorlak's claims even when the latter had the backing of the Norwegian archbishop, whose authority extended to Iceland.

> I am able to understand the archbishop's message, but I
> am resolved to hold it worthless. I do not think he is
> abler or wiser than my ancestors, Sæmund the Learned
> and his sons. Nor will I condemn the example of our na-
> tive bishops who respected the custom of the land that
> laymen should control the churches their forefathers
> gave to God with the reservation that they and their de-
> scendants should have control of them. (*Oddav*. 19:283)

It was not until the end of the thirteenth century, after Iceland had passed under Norwegian control, that the dispute was resolved mostly in favor of the church position. Still, there is evidence that Thorlak's claims discouraged landowners from donating their home estates as churches, choosing to endow churches with outlying lands instead (21:287; Jóhannesson 1974, 186).

By increments the clergy was disassociated from the secular upper classes. In 1173 the Norwegian archbishop forbade Icelandic clerics to take part in lawsuits except on behalf of poor women, orphaned children, or decrepit relatives (*DI* I 222). In 1189, they were forbidden to bear arms (*DI* I 280). And in 1190 the bishop was ordered not to ordain chieftains (*DI* I 291). As to the bearing of weapons, *Sturlunga saga* suggests the ban did not change old habits easily (see, e.g., *Íslend.* 156:462), but there is no evidence that chieftains were admitted to clerical orders after 1190 (Jóhannesson 1974, 190).

Claims for ecclesiastical autonomy continued to be aggressively pursued by the Bishop of Hólar, Gudmund Arason (1203–37). And in these years the unity of clerical and secular authority in the insular church was effectively broken down. After Gudmund, the Icelandic sees were occupied by Norwegians. Until then bishops had been chosen by a consensus of the leading men at the Allthing, with the surviving bishop having the most say in the selection. Scholars, chiefly those associated with the Icelandic school, have been inclined to view the movement toward ecclesiastical autonomy negatively. They often lament the day that Bishops Thorlak and Gudmund were born, believing, not implausibly, that these men served to augment the strife that helped bring the commonwealth to an end. Adopting the argument that the Lawspeaker, Thorgeir from Ljosavatn, made in 1000 (above p. 21), these scholars see ecclesiastical claims for autonomy leading to a sundering of social and legal unity ultimately leading to or assisting in the demise of the unique native social order (see, e.g., Foote 1984, 9–19; Hastrup 1985, 189–96; Jóhannesson 1974, 212–16; Sveinsson 1953, 106–17).

The history of the Icelandic church and the story of the fall of the commonwealth are undoubtedly connected but in no certain way. Our evidence allows us to identify other factors that contributed to the advent of Norwegian rule, but it does not allow us to privilege any one explanation. A confluence of several factors was at work. One of the key changes in the social order during the course of the last half of the twelfth and into the thirteenth century was the consolidation of much of official and unofficial power into fewer and fewer hands. By the 1220s most of the *goðorðs* had come into the possession of five or six families. They were able to rule territories, effectively depriving the *bœndr* of any legal right to choose their Thing attachment. The process by which these families ascended and others declined is obscure. The usual explanations link the process to the greater accumulations of wealth made possible by access to tithes and donations to the church (Jóhannesson 1974, 236–37). Whatever the case, it is clear that the leveling mechanisms available in law—such as choice of Thing attachment—and available in the culture—such as feud, the challenge and riposte of honor—were inadequate to keep accumulations of power within the limits necessary to maintain the leveling mechanisms themselves as viable means of diffusing power. Feud between big families started to take on the characteristics of war, the chief costs of which were not born by the principals but by the people who lived in the territories they controlled. We see the powerful and pretenders to power provisioning themselves by plundering the people they sought to rule. Violence took place on a grander scale, affrays involved numbers measured by round hundreds rather than by single and double digits, and, most importantly, ever fewer people had the means and standing necessary to assume the role of peacemaker. Instead of kin group versus kin group, we have the men of the North versus the men of the Westfjords. In brief, the wars of the big players and the forced contributions they extracted from lesser people to maintain themselves and their followings gave an ever larger segment of the population no special interest in maintaining independence from Norway. If the king promised to make peace, that promise had more promise than a future governed by the big men in Iceland who promised no peace at all.

The extent and scale of change was a good deal more subtle and complex than the broad strokes we are painting here suggest. Some parts of the country, notably the east, remained relatively strife free. Most all of the serious disorder was confined to the north and northwest. Part of the sense of disorder is also a function of the focus of the chief sources of the period—*Íslendinga saga, Þórðar saga kakala,* and *Þorgils saga skarða;* these are stories of big politics, but there is evidence, which emerges almost casually in these accounts, that local disputes of limited scope continued to be processed in much the same way as they always had been.

Norwegian hegemony was assisted by several other factors. Again the church figured prominently. The embattled bishops Gudmund and Thorlak looked to the Norwegian archbishop for backing, and he seldom worked in Icelandic matters at cross-purposes to the interests of the Norwegian king. And it was Gudmund who introduced the idea of submitting native disputes to the arbitration of the archbishop, an idea taken up by powerful laymen in the last years of the commonwealth who submitted their grievances to the Norwegian king for decision (Jóhannesson 1974, 203, 255). In addition, by indiscernible increments over a long period of time, Iceland had become more dependent on Norway for certain provisions, most notably timber and flour. The lack of suitable timber in Iceland meant that control of foreign trade could not remain in Icelandic hands once the ships that carried the original settlers sank into disrepair. Eventually the control of long-distance trade was assumed entirely by Norwegian merchants, thus giving the Norwegian king no small amount of leverage in making his wishes felt in Iceland (Gelsinger 1981, 169–80). This leverage was augmented by the fact that young Icelanders from the better established families often became retainers of the king, bound for life by obligations of loyalty to his person if not always to his interests.

Some amount of credit for the demise of the commonwealth should be given to the uniqueness of the Icelandic social arrangement itself. How strange it must have been to know oneself and be known as a people without a king. In a world in which the peoples one knew about or one heard tell about in legend and holy writ all had kings, some small amount of uneasiness, of self-doubt about the naturalness and propriety of one's uniqueness may have entered the collective consciousness. We know that others believed the Icelandic situation was unnatural. Cardinal William of Sabina, participating in the coronation of King Hakon of Norway in 1247, said so explicitly when he declared that Iceland should be made subject to the king: "for he claimed it was improper that that land should not serve some king like all other lands in the world" (*Hákonar saga* 257:252). If there were doubts, they would have become harder to defend against when things were not going well, when the dominant sense was one of entropy and falling off. In any event, the big players very possibly looked to the example of kinglike power, if not exactly to an idea of kingship, as a goal to be achieved. Such were the pretensions of Snorri Sturluson (perhaps) and Sturla and Thord Sighvatsson and Gizur jarl (see, e.g., *Íslend.* 125:407–8). The idea of lordship was now something within the grasp as well as the contemplation of big men, whereas the prospect of permanent and disabling clientage had become the lot of a large segment of the population. Subservience was an idea whose time had come.

The fall of the commonwealth in 1262–64, marked by the agreement to pay tax to the King of Norway (*DI* I 620), is the usual closing bracket for studies of early Iceland. The conventional practice is not without merit. The demise of the grand saga sensibility occurs soon enough after the political change to suggest some causal linkage. The change in governing institutions could not have had all that great an impact on day-to-day life for the greater part of the population, but the native conceptual universe seems to have soon been transformed significantly.[29] By the early fourteenth century the creativity, the synergistic coupling of the heroic and pragmatic, that produced the sagas was gone.

# Making Sense of the Sources

## Laws and Sagas: Some Problems of Fiction as History

The limits of our knowledge about early Iceland are the limits imposed by the types and quantity of sources preserved from the period. The native written record begins only in the twelfth century and then it only becomes mainly native in focus in the beginning of the thirteenth century. The greater part of the surviving written record from which we can hope to reconstruct a social history is either narrative or normative, that is, either sagas or laws. Neither genre of source is without its own particular problems, and though there is no such thing as a transparent historical source, these are at times especially opaque. First, the laws, which I only briefly introduce here because they are given an extended discussion in chapter 7: the laws of the Icelandic commonwealth, collectively known as *Grágás*, are primarily preserved in two manuscripts—*Konungsbók* and *Staðarhólsbók*.[1] The *Konungsbók* manuscript is dated roughly to 1260, *Staðarhólsbók* to 1280. But, with rare exception, the dating of individual provisions is impossible to determine. We know that a substantial body of law was committed to writing in the early twelfth century and it is thus usually assumed that a good portion of *Grágás* represents the law of the twelfth, as well as the thirteenth, century. The surviving manuscripts are not official compilations and their provenance remains a mystery. Both main manuscripts are imposing codices and one wonders at the motive for their late production. It would seem a reasonable conjecture that their production is related somehow to the same impetus that produced the sagas. The Icelanders, it seems, were anxious to record and preserve monuments of their experience as Icelanders at the very time that the social arrangements enabling that experience were being destroyed or had already been superseded.

The collections of laws are remarkable for their length and their extraordinary detail. They amount to some seven hundred densely printed pages of nonduplicated provisions. In contrast to the barbarian codes, the difficulties of interpreting *Grágás* tend not to involve frustrating ellipsis and terseness so much as the usual vexing problem of how to assess the relation of legal norms to social practice. The sheer mass of the texts creates its own problems. Internal inconsistencies abound and the texts clearly contain provisions of arguable validity. We might guess that some provisions were either obsolete or that others were never fully adopted into law, even though they appear in the text.[2] Some passages have the look of schoolish categorizing for its own sake; but there is no reason to doubt that most of the provisions were available to provide the basis for making claims some time in the twelfth and thirteenth centuries.

The other broad category of source is the sagas, that is, prose narratives. Since there exist several easily accessible and competent literary historical introductions to these sources I limit myself to a few basic issues and relegate more technical supplementary information to the endnotes.[3] Modern scholars have divided the sagas into several genres, of which only two need concern us: the family sagas (*Íslendingasögur*) and the so-called contemporary sagas (*samtíðarsögur*), which are further divided into secular sagas and bishops' sagas.[4] The main identifying criterion of these two genres—family and contemporary—is neither stylistic, nor formal,[5] nor is it based on dates of composition, since the texts of both genres, with little exception, were committed to writing in the thirteenth century;[6] it is primarily a function of the century in which the narrative action takes place. The family sagas are about events set in the Saga Age (930–1030), while the contemporary sagas describe events that took place in the twelfth and thirteenth centuries. There are some thirty family sagas that occupy twelve volumes in the standard Íslenzk fornrit editions. Individual sagas in these editions can occupy as few as nineteen pages (*Þorst. hv.*) or as many as 480 (*Njála*). The contemporary secular sagas, with only two exceptions,[7] are collected together in a single compilation known as *Sturlunga saga*, dating from ca. 1300, although the sagas making it up were composed at various times earlier in the thirteenth century. The notion of contemporariness in these sagas needs some qualification. Some were indeed written by contemporaries of the events making up the narrative. Others, however—those set in the twelfth century[8]— could have been composed as many as one hundred years after the events they portray.

The reliability of the family sagas as accurate chronicles is not seriously maintained. The lag of more than two hundred years between deed and word pretty much concludes that issue, but as this book seeks to demonstrate, the saga sources are admirably suited to certain social and legal historical inquiries concerning the time in which they were written. Strangely, this is a more controversial project than most would guess. The negative judgment of family saga trustworthiness, a view primarily associated with the Icelandic school,[9] coupled with some rather narrow views of what constituted the proper subjects of historical inquiry, led to a general crisis of confidence in the saga sources for all kinds of historical inquiry. One consequence is that there has been little social historical work of importance done on early Iceland since the first decades of this century.[10]

More generally, one still finds among many social historians a resistance to using literary sources in social history. Much of this reluctance is a function of the ways in which we socialize and institutionally constitute our knowledge. Historians of a positivist bent tend to resist elevating works that also get attention in literature departments to the pantheon of "true" historical sources. Historians often come to literature with deepseated suspicion. Literature, after all, is by some estimation nothing but a pack of lies and its interpretation is felt at some visceral level to invite more researcher invention than historians feel should be imposed on sources. Yet one suspects that the reluctance to make use of literary sources has less to do with reason than with the guildish conventions of the historian's trade. "Real" historians look at plea roles and other court records, census returns, cartularies, administrative records, etc. Literature is what you read on vacation. There is also an unspoken sense that the truth value of a source varies inversely with how much pleasure it gives the reader: no pain, no gain. It is thus the case that bad literature has an easier time being seriously considered as a historical source than good literature. Most of the sagas are, by this view, too good to be true. But to reject a source merely because it is good literature is a luxury of those historians who have what, by the custom of the shop, are assumed to be better sources, if for no reason other than that they are duller. The historian of early Iceland has no choice; there are no plea roles or government records and what few charters exist are content to catalog the appurtenances of donations to churches. If early Icelandic social and cultural history is to be written, literary sources will have to be used. This is hardly a revolutionary claim outside saga studies, as the examples of biblical history, Frankish history, or the history of Homeric Greece amply illustrate.[11]

Both genres of saga, family and contemporary, have some extraordinary virtues for the social and cultural historian who is intent on recovering Icelandic society within reasonable temporal distance of the writing of the texts. Besides a host of incidental details, from which we can reconstruct the constitution of households, the practicalities of kinship, and many of the activities of daily life, there is the central subject matter itself—the feuds and quarrels of chieftains and farmers. The sagas, unlike romance and even most heroic fare, are consciously realistic. Their plots, except for occasional trips to the continent, are set in familiar countryside, in familiar interiors, among familiar faces. One of their greatest virtues is that the disputes they relate are presented in the full circumstance of their social setting; litigants have social relations and are situated in networks of support that we can often reconstruct; we can thus discern their strategies, motives, and reasons by social criteria as well as by certain psychological criteria supplied by the author. If there might have been reason for an author to invent a particular character's psychology, there was simply no reason for him to invent *ex nihilo* the social and cultural setting in which these characters moved about. He did not need to, nor did he, invent the norms of gift-exchange, the strategies and styles of dispute processing, anymore than he invented the Things in which the lawsuits of his narrative were tried. These were the givens of his story, provided him by the world he lived in or heard tell about. Fictionalizing dialogue, fictionalizing events, inventing characters and their psychologies might unnerve the political historian, but they need not upset the social historian at all. Even these fictions are constrained by the ranges of the possible in the culture and hence have useful social information to reveal.

The sagas for the most part ring true. Their accounts of disputes rarely exceed the parameters by which we judge plausibility;[12] their narratives fit admirably the limits of social possibility as determined by the large sociological and anthropological literature on dispute processing in cultures at similar levels of material and political development.[13] And this fact provides some control for distinguishing those norms and actions that are aspirational from those that are descriptive. I do not wish to make it seem, however, that the sagas are unproblematic. They are, but not in ways all that different from what medieval historians are used to dealing with in more traditional sources. The fiction of the sagas is no more pernicious to the discovery of what passes for truth than the stock formulas of scribes in penning legal documents, than the partisanship of chronicles, than the categories imposed on reality by census takers and tax collectors. All surviving artifacts, whether art or coprolite, have their tale to tell. And in Iceland the number of surviving written artifacts is too scarce to allow the categorical rejection of a significant portion of them because they do not accord with conventional notions of what a historical source should be. Like the archaeologist, the historian of early Iceland needs to develop sensitivities and techniques that will allow exploitation of the evidence in ways it was never intended to be used. Without the sagas, there is no social history of early Iceland beyond hypothetical constructions based on the law codes.

For all their virtues, the sagas present some nearly intractable problems for the historian. One of these is how to discount for the effects of literary convention. The difficulty is not just a matter of identifying a scene or character trait or a type of behavior as a literary topos. That does not dispose of the question of whether the same behavior is not also conventional in social practice. Art and life, at least in early Iceland, were not autonomous categories. The consciousness of a medieval Icelander was affected by the sagas.[14] It is hardly daring to assume that the saga writers drew on their observations of people's behavior, not merely on their knowledge of other sagas, and people's behavior, if we can trust the evidence of those sagas that show characters concerned to accomplish "sagalike" and "sagaworthy" deeds, was partially learned from the sagas. The literary scholar can confidently recognize in the sagas that dreams that predict ill and the conventional refusal to pay heed to them are the stuff of literary convention. But that does not dispose of the question of whether announcing foreboding dreams had a social function too. It is possible to discern that characters in the sagas manipulated the narration of their dreams to strategic advantage. Can we say that this was not a fact of life (see Miller 1986b)? Some topoi that no one suspected to have been anything but the stuff of literature have been shown to have very probably been matters of lived experience as well. Thus when saga women save the blood or bloodstained clothing of their kin to display to people they charge to take vengeance, we are very probably in the world of performed ritual rather than the world of gruesome imagination (see Clover 1986 and Miller 1983b).

Not all stylization indicates literary invention or literary borrowing. The stylization that accompanies one of the greatest scenes in the sagas is a case in point. When the Njalssons and their chief supporters go from booth to booth at the Allthing in an attempt to muster support for the defense of the suit against them, Skarphedin Njalsson holds his position as fifth in line. In each booth he is uniformly greeted by a query as to his identity, posed in such a way that the query is also a recognition of a special doom that hovers about him. In each case Skarphedin responds with a devastatingly incisive and often vulgar insult of the questioner (*Njála* 119–20:297–306). What is clearly literary in the scene is the compulsion that makes each person visited ask after "the man fifth in line." But that's all. It would be hasty to dismiss everything else as pure artifice. Requests of support from powerful people required some adherence to forms of protocol; we simply do not know enough to dismiss the precisely ordered line as something to make a good story. Skarphedin's insults have a certain ritualized quality to them, but it cannot be certain that this is not a form of flyting that our sources suggest was very much a part of Norse lived experience.

Our way of judging the "literariness" of a particular behavior is subject to error because of the effects of an uncertainty principle. That is, most all our bases of comparison for the ranges of possible behavior from within the culture are infected with the same literary disease. Can we make testable assertions? To a certain extent we can, although not quite in ways that would satisfy the pure empiricist. Each broad class of source—law code and saga—gives us some control on the other, but the test is ultimately one of plausibility. If my accounts of Icelandic households and kinship, feud, law, and exchange make sense of the data—all the data, both legal and narrative—if they accord with the known ranges of human experience in reasonably similar situations and tell a fairly consistent tale, we have indeed constructed a social history.[15] There are, of course, rather obvious limits on the kinds of knowledge the sources will let us produce. The sagas would not be up to the task of determining marriage ages or mortality rates, although even here they might supply some anecdotal evidence. But they are up to the task in certain subject areas. The saga authors, for example, understood the mechanics of conflict resolution in stateless preindustrial societies better than we did until only the last few decades, if even then, and their narrative agenda gave them little reason to misrepresent matters of practical kinship and householding arrangements.

While both the family sagas and *Sturlunga saga* present the same problems when it comes to discounting the "reality" of the account for the effects of literary convention, the family sagas present special problems not as seriously present in the contemporary sagas. There is reason to believe some amount of idealization has occurred in the presentation of the events of the Saga Age, so that it is risky to make too simple an assumption that the content of the family sagas accurately reflects the time in which they were written.[16] But whatever the effects of idealization, they are not enough to prevent the world of the family sagas from looking very similar to the world of *Sturlunga*, especially of those sagas in the *Sturlunga* compilation that deal with twelfth-century disputes. Heusler made fairly careful observations of the matter. He discovered that the general disputing process in the family and contemporary sagas was much the same. The basic modes of conflict resolution—vengeance, law, and arbitration—were selected in the same proportions in both types of source (Heusler 1912, 20).[17] The problem, however, is not with similarities, for that is what we would expect, but with differences. Some of these differences are required by the commitment to realistic presentation that characterizes saga writing. The family sagas thus describe a world without a church and without Norwegian intrusiveness and they do so in a remarkably unpreachy manner. Clumsy anachronism is a rarity; the irreligiousness of the account seems utterly natural, unaccompanied by censoriousness or any great sense that the people of the Saga Age suffered for their lack of acquaintance with the gospel. To adopt a frequent saga topos, we have two choices, neither of them good. We can believe that oral tradition accurately preserved the mentality of the Saga Age or we can attribute the believable secular world of the family sagas to the sympathetic imagination of thirteenth-century authors proud of their land's kingless uniqueness and of their ancestors who made it that way. I am inclined to the latter because original mentalité is one of the things very susceptible to alteration in the process of oral transmission, even if it means we must discount for a certain idealization of the heathen period as it is portrayed in the family sagas.[18]

The family sagas also portray a world with much broader distributions of wealth and power than we find in those contemporary sagas that deal with events of the thirteenth century. To what extent these differences reflect real changes over time or to what extent they represent idealization is not entirely certain. Reasonable inference from the *Sturlunga* sagas set in the twelfth century and from the laws suggests that most family sagas offer a fairly reliable picture of general conditions in the twelfth century and of local conditions in some areas of the country throughout the thirteenth century. Disputes are largely localized and are almost always constrainable by third-party intervention. Affrays generally oppose small forces of less than thirty a side and no one maintains a standing body of retainers beyond the complement of servants needed to take care of the usual demands of household production. Once the effects that Christianity had on the disputing process are discounted, the differences in social control and dispute processing between the family sagas and those contemporary sagas set in the twelfth century are minor. The break in disputing style, and it is still one characterized more by continuity than change, comes with the larger musters and the consolidation of power into fewer hands that characterize the sagas that deal with events in the final decades of the commonwealth.[19]

Perhaps the greatest constraint imposed on the social historian by both the sagas and the laws is identifying change through time. The sagas and all but a few laws are themselves incapable of being precisely dated, although the Icelandic school has succeeded in dating most of the sagas relative to each other. There is also the problem of being able to identify genuine antique material preserved in the family sagas. Some family saga writers are self-consciously antiquarian, making careful reference to the way things were done "then" (the Saga Age) as opposed to the now of the time of composition. Historians, desperate for anything that will indicate change, have been inclined to take the saga writer at his word. *Eyrbyggja saga*, for example, is often cited as a source for Saga Age legal practice, but it could be that the author's antiquarianism was only a pose to lend his imagination the authority of privileged information. It is simply safest to assume that the society of the family sagas is the society that the author knew by experience, idealized somewhat to advance his narrative agenda. He presented his own world adjusted in certain ways difficult to pinpoint to reflect the knowledge acquired from his parents' and grandparents' generations. To this there might also occasionally be added genuine information preserved from the time in which the narrative is set. The family saga world is thus not merely the world of the author's time; it is an amalgam representing the effects of a temporal compression that included whatever the culture knew or wished to believe about its own past. This is not very satisfactory, but, except in certain precise matters that are datable by other means, it is the best we can do. Fortunately some control is provided by *Sturlunga saga*. Its distortions of reality are at least not those that derive from an excessive time lag between the setting of the narrative and the composition of the saga, but rather those that derive from the conventions of the saga style and whatever dissimulations living authors might have to make so as not to offend living *dramatis personae* and their kin.

The problem of poor chronological information in a primitive isolated pastoral community is not as serious as it would be if the period were one of rapid technological change. It is safe to assume that once the dislocation of settlement was stabilized there was little change in the technology of exploiting the environment. People went on farming and herding the way they always had, except that, at the insistence of the Little Ice Age, yields probably started to worsen toward the end of the thirteenth century (McGovern et al. 1988). But there is no reason to assume that the social arrangements for exploiting the environment were as resistant to change as the technology, even on an island as remote from the European continent as Iceland was. Christianity, as we noted in the preceding chapter, did not leave things untouched, although it took some time before it could be said to have altered the basic native social arrangements. Our sources unfortunately relegate us to the "ethnographic present" at a time when it is the vogue for ethnographers to turn historian and abandon synchronic description. The descriptions of various Icelandic social arrangements and mechanisms of social control in the family sagas are applicable, I judge, to a period beginning roughly around the first decades of the twelfth century and continuing through the end of the commonwealth period. Some family sagas seem to raise issues that reflect the turmoils of the later period more than others (e.g., *Njáls saga*), but the general view of the society of the family sagas seems to be more consistent with the world of the sagas of the *Sturlunga* compilation set in the twelfth century than those of the thirteenth. But we are still not entitled to say that society was changing in the same way or to the same extent that those sagas dealing with the last decades of the commonwealth would suggest. To be sure it was changing. Sturla Thordarson, the author of *Íslendinga saga*, was not making up the expansive conflicts of his saga, but some of the appearance of utter turmoil in the last decades of the commonwealth is a function of *Íslendinga saga*'s peculiar style, its confusing mass of names and detail, its length and scope. *Íslendinga saga* is not the whole story of the thirteenth century, for when we see localized disputes in the mid-thirteenth century—e.g., *Svínfellinga saga*—they do not violate the expectations acquired from the family sagas.

## A Case Study of the Sagas as Sources: Þorsteins þáttr stangarhǫggs and the Politics of Accident

What I propose to do in the remainder of the chapter is to provide the reader with some firsthand experience with the narrative sources through an extended discussion of *Þorsteins þáttr stangarhǫggs* (*The Story of Thorstein the Staffstruck*).[20] I have decided to proceed in this fashion because I think it is important to let those unfamiliar with the saga style make their own judgments as to the quality of the sources and as to the plausibility of my way of dealing with them. I put all on a platter for painless sampling. I have selected this story not least because it is short and can thus be presented without guilt in its entirety. It raises nice issues about the intersection of law and society, specifically regarding the social and legal protocols surrounding unintentional harm. A full understanding of the text requires recourse to both saga and legal sources and illustrates how the two types of source often assist each other rather well. Besides other matters of incidental interest it also has much to say about intra- and interhousehold politics as they manifest themselves in the disputing process. As an example of saga style, it is atypical only in a failure to provide its characters with deep genealogies.

The events are set in the northeast of Iceland sometime after 990. The story itself is presumed to have been written anywhere between 1240 and 1269, although the dating is hardly confident,[21] and for reasons to be discussed below there are good grounds for believing that the social concerns expressed in the story are likely to reflect thirteenth-century matters.

## Þorsteins þáttr stangarhǫggs

There was a man named Thorarin who lived at Sunnudale. He was an old man with failing eyesight. He had been a fierce viking in his youth and though he was now old he was still not easy to deal with. He had a son named Thorstein,[22] tall and strong with a tranquil disposition, who worked so hard around his father's farm that three other men would not have done as well. Thorarin was rather short on means but had a good many weapons. Father and son owned some studhorses from which they derived what wealth they had by selling the offspring because their horses never lacked endurance or spirit.

There was a man named Thord who was a servant of Bjarni of Hof.[23] He was in charge of Bjarni's riding horses because he was thought to know horses well. Thord was greatly overbearing and he kept letting everyone know that he was in the service of a powerful man. But he was not any worthier for that, nor more popular either. Two men named Thorhall and Thorvald were also in Bjarni's service. They were great talebearers about everything they heard in the district.

Thorstein and Thord agreed to schedule a fight for their young horses. Once in the bout Thord's horse was on the defensive. And when it occurred to Thord that his horse was getting the worst of it, he struck at Thorstein's horse, hitting it in the jaw. Thorstein saw that and struck Thord's horse an even greater blow. Thord's horse ran and people roared with excitement. Then Thord struck at Thorstein with his goad, hitting Thorstein on the brow ridge so that the skin hung down before the eye. Thorstein ripped off a piece of his shirt and bound up his forehead. He acted as if nothing had happened and asked that people conceal this from his father. Things quieted down, but Thorvald and Thorhall used the incident to make fun and they called him Thorstein Staffstruck.

In the winter, a little before Yule, the women got up to work at Sunnudale. Thorstein got up and looked to the hay and then lay back down inside on a bench.[24] Old man Thorarin, his father, came in and asked who was lying there. Thorstein told him.

"Why are you up and about so early, son?" asked Thorarin.

Thorstein answered, "It seems to me that there are few others to leave the work to around here."

"Do you have a headache, son?" asked old Thorarin.

"Not that I'm aware of," said Thorstein.

"Son," continued Thorarin, "what is there to tell me about the horsefight that took place last summer? Weren't you, kinsman, knocked dizzy like a dog?"

"I don't think there can be any honor in calling it an intentional blow rather than an accident," said Thorstein.

Thorarin said, "I would not have suspected that I have a sissy for a son."

"Say only those things now, father," said Thorstein, "that won't seem more than you bargained for later."

"I will not say anywhere near as much about this as is on my mind," said Thorarin.

Thorstein started up, took his weapons and set out from home, not stopping until he came to the stable where Thord was looking after Bjarni's horses. Thord was out in front and when Thorstein met him he said, "I would like to know, my Thord, whether that was an accident when you struck me at the horsefight last summer, or whether it was intentional. Now are you going to compensate me?"[25]

Thord answered, "If you had two mouths and stuck a tongue in each one, you could use one to say it was an accident, if you wished, and the other to say it was intended. That's the compensation you get from me."

"Then be prepared to accept the possibility that I won't bother to make this claim again," said Thorstein. He leapt at Thord and struck him his death blow. He then went to the house at Hof, ran into a woman outside and said to her, "Tell Bjarni that a bull has gored Thord, his horse-boy, and that he will be waiting near the stable, until Bjarni comes to get him."

"Go on home," she said, "I will tell him when I want to." Thorstein went back home and the woman went back to her work.

Bjarni had gotten up that morning and when he was eating he asked where Thord was. He was told that he was probably out with the horses. "He would be back by now, I think," said Bjarni, "if he were all right."

Then the woman who Thorstein had run into spoke up, "What's often said about us women is true indeed, that where we women are concerned there's not much intelligence. Thorstein Staffstruck came here this morning and said that a bull had gored Thord so that he had been quite disabled, but I was not willing to wake you then and after that it simply escaped my mind."

Bjarni pushed away from the table, went to the stable and found Thord dead. Thord was then buried and Bjarni brought a lawsuit and had Thorstein outlawed for the killing.[26] But Thorstein continued at Sunnudale and worked for his father. Nonetheless, Bjarni let things be.

One time in the fall men were sitting around singeing sheep's heads and Bjarni was laying out on top of the kitchen wall[27] listening to the conversation. The brothers Thorhall and Thorvald were talking. "We never expected when we took service with Killer-Bjarni that we would be singeing lambs' heads while Thorstein, his outlaw, would be singeing the heads of geldings.[28] Bjarni should have been more merciful to his kinsmen at Bodvarsdale[29] instead of letting his outlaw remain at Sunnudale as an equal. But the old saying is true—'All courage drains at the first scratch'; we don't know when he'll manage to erase this mark on his honor."

One man said, "You should have kept silent; it must be that a troll has gotten hold of your tongues. I think Bjarni's unwilling to take the only support away from Thorstein's blind father and the other dependents at Sunnudale. But I'll be amazed if you singe lambs' heads here much longer or sound off about what happened at Bodvarsdale."

Then people went to eat and after to bed and no one could tell by looking what Bjarni had heard. But the next morning Bjarni woke Thorhall and Thorvald and ordered them to ride to Sunnudale and bring him Thorstein's head, chopped off, by mid-morning. "I think you two are the most likely," he said, "to erase this mark on my honor, considering I don't have the nerve to do it myself."

They thought now that they had indeed said too much, but they set out anyway and came to Sunnudale. Thorstein stood in the doorway whetting a short sword. He asked them what they were up to and they said they were looking for horses. Thorstein said they didn't have to look too hard; "they are right next to the fence."

"We are not certain that we can find the horses if you don't give us more detailed directions."

Thorstein came outside and when they were nearing the fence Thorvald raised up his axe and attacked him. But Thorstein shoved him back and knocked him down and then thrust his short sword right through him. Thorhall tried to attack but he ended up traveling the same road as Thorvald. Thorstein tied them both to their horses, set the reins on the horses necks and sent them on their way. The horses returned to Hof.

At Hof servants were outside and they went in and told Bjarni that Thorvald and Thorhall had returned and that they hadn't gone in vain. Bjarni went out and saw the state of things; he said nothing and had them buried. Everything remained quiet until Yule came along.

One evening when Bjarni and his wife Rannveig[30] were in bed she said, "What do you think is being talked about now in the district?"

"I don't know," said Bjarni, "but it seems to me that most people do not have much worth saying."

"The main subject of conversation is that no one seems to know what Thorstein Staffstruck has to do before you think it necessary to take vengeance. He has now killed three of your servants. Your thingmen don't think there's much support to be looked for from you when you leave these things unavenged. You lie still when you should act, and act when you should lie still."

"This all goes to show that few let themselves take warning from another's punishment. Still, I am listening to what you are saying, but Thorstein has killed few without reason." They ended their conversation and slept through the night.

The next morning Rannveig was awakened when Bjarni took down his shield. She asked what he was up to.

"Thorstein of Sunnudale and I are now going to decide this issue of honor," he said.

"How many men are you taking with you?" she asked.

"I'm not going to drag along a big crowd," he said. "I'm going alone."

"Don't do that, don't risk your life against the weapons of that monster," she said.

"Are you going to be like the usual women who bewail one minute what they were inciting a little while before? I am not going to put up with the goading of you and those others any longer. There's no point in trying to prevent me when I am determined to go."

Bjarni went to Sunnudale. Thorstein stood in the door and they exchanged a few words.

Bjarni said, "You will fight me one-on-one today,[31] Thorstein, on that hill there in the homefield."

"I am utterly lacking in everything needed to fight you," said Thorstein, "but I shall go abroad as soon as a ship is available, because I know your character is such that you will provide labor for my father if I leave."

"It's no use trying to talk your way out of this now," said Bjarni.

"Allow me then to go see my father first," said Thorstein.

"Of course," said Bjarni.

Thorstein went in and told his father that Bjarni had come and challenged him to a duel. Old Thorarin said, "Anybody who lives near a powerful man and then contends with him and gives him offense can't figure on wearing out too many new shirts. And for this reason I can't feel sorry for you because I think you've done much to deserve it. Now take your weapons and defend yourself as bravely as you can; when I was young I would never grovel before someone like Bjarni, even though he is the best of fighters. I'd prefer to lose you rather than have a sissy for a son."

Thorstein walked out and he and Bjarni went over to the hill and started to fight earnestly. Soon each had ruined the other's shield. After they had fought for a considerable time, Bjarni said to Thorstein, "I'm thirsty; I'm less used to working than you are."

"Then go to the brook and take a drink," said Thorstein.

Bjarni did so and set his sword down beside him. Thorstein picked it up, looked at it and said, "This couldn't have been the sword you had at Bodvarsdale."

Bjarni did not respond. They walked back up the hill and fought for a good time. Bjarni now realized that this man was quite a fighter and matters seemed a bit harder than he had previously thought. "A lot is happening to me today," said Bjarni. "Now my shoestring is loose."

"Tie it up then," said Thorstein.

Bjarni bent down and Thorstein went inside and brought out two shields and a sword. He went back to the hill and said to Bjarni, "Here is a shield and a sword my father sends you. This one won't get as dull in action as the one you've been using. I am also unwilling to stand any longer without some protection from your blows. I would gladly stop this game because I'm afraid that your luck might well be more effective than my bad luck. Everyone is eager to save his life in the end, myself included if I am able to."

"It's no use trying to beg off," said Bjarni. "We're still going to fight."

"I'm not eager to strike," said Thorstein.

Bjarni then destroyed Thorstein's shield and Thorstein did the same to Bjarni's.

"Now that was a powerful blow," said Bjarni.

"You're not striking weaker ones either," said Thorstein.

Bjarni said, "That same sword of yours is biting better than it did earlier."

"I would spare myself misfortune if I were able to do so. I am afraid to fight you. I would prefer to submit the whole thing to your decision."

It was up to Bjarni to take the next stroke. Both of them were without shields. Bjarni then said, "That would be a poor bargain to trade good fortune for an ill-deed. I would consider myself fully compensated for my three servants by you alone, if you would be true to me."

Thorstein said, "I've had the chances today to betray you if my bad luck were more powerful than your good luck. I will not betray you."

"I can see that you are an exceptional man," said Bjarni. "Give me permission to go in and see your father to tell him what I want to."

"For my part, you can go in if you like," said Thorstein, "but be wary."

Bjarni went up to the enclosed bed in which old Thorarin was lying. Thorarin asked who was there and Bjarni told him.

"What news do you have to tell, my Bjarni?" asked Thorarin.

"The death of your son, Thorstein," replied Bjarni.

"Did he defend himself?" asked Thorarin.

"I don't think any man has ever been a fiercer fighter than your son Thorstein," said Bjarni.

"It's not surprising," said the old man, "that it was hard dealing with you at Bodvarsdale, given that you bested my son."

Bjarni said, "I wish to invite you to Hof. You shall sit opposite me in the other seat of honor as long as you live. I will be as a son to you."[32]

"I am treated no differently than any other person without means. Only the fool is satisfied with promises. And the promises of you chieftains when you wish to comfort someone in a situation like this are usually good for about a month. Then we are honored like other paupers and that makes our grief lessen slowly indeed. But the man who takes a guarantee from a man like you might still be content with his lot whatever the usual example may be. I will shake hands with you. But come over to me by the bed. Come near, for an old man is shaky on his feet, what with age and sickness, and it's true that my son's death has affected me."

Bjarni went to the bed-closet and took old Thorarin by the hand. He noticed that Thorarin was reaching for a short sword hoping to impale him with it. He pulled his hand away and said, "You cursed old fart.[33] You will get what you deserve from me. Your son Thorstein is alive and he is going back with me to Hof. You will be given slaves to work the farm and have no want as long as you live."

Thorstein went home with Bjarni to Hof and served him until he died. He was considered the match of anyone in character and courage. Bjarni maintained his honor and he grew more popular and even-tempered as he grew older. He was the most reliable of men and in the last part of his life he became a very devout Christian. He went abroad and died while making a pilgrimage to Rome. His body is in a town called Vateri,[34] a big town not far from Rome.

Bjarni was blessed with great descendants. [There follows a tracing of some of Bjarni's descendants running down to people alive in the first four decades of the thirteenth century. Among these are numbered the Sturlusons who are descended from Bjarni on their mother's side. The six generations needed to get from Bjarni to them include only one male link.]

The unknown author of this text was a master of his art and western literature would be hard-pressed to find a piece of short fiction any better. There are delicate touches. Thorstein's stolid peacefulness contrasts with his father's obstreperousness. Somewhere in between these types is Bjarni, who shows a movement, although mostly through actions that have taken place "off-stage" (the battle at Bodvarsdale, his devoutness late in life) from kin-killer to peacemaker. The casual observation in the opening paragraph, that Thorstein "worked so hard around his father's farm that three other men would not have done as well," initially appears to be nothing more than the blandest of stock metaphors until at the story's end we find that Thorstein is literally worth three men when Bjarni values Thorstein's service at the price of the three servants Thorstein killed. Bjarni transforms an initial cliché into a nice ironic touch that makes the settlement between Bjarni and Thorstein satisfy a cultural predisposition for balance and equipoise in dispute resolution. This is not only the stuff of art, it is the stuff of a confident art that needs no instruction in sophistication. Nonintrusive figures and symbols are frequent features of the best saga style.

No less deft is the economy with which believable characters are sketched. A person is generally introduced with a description of his main character traits and situated geographically and socially. From then on, characters are developed through their own actions and the reactions they generate in others. The author informs us of the obnoxiousness of Bjarni's servants, Thord, Thorhall, and Thorvald, at the outset. His view is more than confirmed by their own actions, but not until we see the black-humored way in which their fellow servants react to their deaths do we get any sense of just how annoying Thorstein's victims were.

There is no remorse at Hof when Thorvald and Thorhall come home dead strapped on the back of their horses, only a wry comment attributed collectively to a group of servants that "Thorvald and Thorhall had returned and that they hadn't gone in vain." There is also no doubt that the woman servant to whom Thorstein announces the slaying of Thord understands that Thorstein has killed him in spite of his indirection: "Tell Bjarni that a bull has gored Thord, his horse-boy, and that he will be waiting near the stable, until Bjarni comes to get him." He is after all standing before her with a bloody sword and she is most likely more than sufficiently competent in saga convention to know that a killer often makes his announcement with some disparaging euphemism intended to show contempt for his victim.[35] To her mind, Thord's death is not sufficient cause to wake Bjarni, and in her answer to Thorstein's announcement—"Go on home . . . I will tell him when I want to"—we even get a sense of her character. She is a person resentful of her structural situation as a servant and as a woman, which puts her in a position to be ordered about by a male, especially one from a nearby impoverished farmstead; she is also someone who, like the Wife of Bath, is able to draw from the stock of antifeminist clichés to deny accountability for a decision she alone has made not to inform Bjarni of Thord's death. In such short space we get enough sense of this woman to see that she is too smart to have forgotten about Thord's death. But in claiming she has forgotten, she is able to make an announcement of her own assessment of Thord's character to Bjarni. He was not worth remembering. Such elaborate indirection might tell us something about the necessary protocol within the household when a woman servant seeks to counsel her master. And it also serves the added purpose of allowing her to sidestep her own responsibility for making sure no immediate vengeance would be taken for Thord.[36] Bjarni, after all, could not have spared Thorstein had he caught him red-handed. Unfortunately, it is often only in such seemingly insignificant details that we can hope to recover internal household politics.

One of the few resistances an initiate to the sagas experiences is the names. Thor is an element in so many names that non-Icelanders often have a hard time keeping them straight. At some level the story owes its initial fillip to one of the consequences of an impoverished name pool: the conferring of nicknames. Then, as in modern Iceland, a person was identified by a given name and secondarily by a patronymic, or in cases where one's father died young, by matronymic. Male names were likely to be repeated in alternate generations, since it was usual for a newborn to be named after some close dead relative. Thorstein Thorarinsson of our story is likely to bear the same name as his paternal grandfather. Such reduplication might cause problems in locating points on a genealogy when enumerating kinship between collateral branches.[37] The small name pool also meant contemporaries might share a patronym in addition to their given names.[38] Some clarification was achieved by fixing names to places. Thus Bjarni is Bjarni from Hof and Thorstein appears once as Thorstein of Sunnudale. But the effectiveness of identifying someone by fixing him geographically would depend to some extent on a relative permanence of residence which, as we shall see, was not always the case in medieval Iceland.

More precise identification was achieved by nicknames.[39] But because the conferring of a person's nickname was not always controlled by people of his or her party as were given names, nicknaming provided the possibility for insult, an insult made all the more pernicious for being recalled every time the person was referred to. The laws are aware of the possibility and penalize the conferring of nicknames with lesser outlawry—three years banishment and loss of property—if the named person should take offense (*Grágás* Ib 182, II 391).[40] In *Thorstein the Staffstruck* nicknames not only serve as identifiers of people, they also serve to connect a person with some ambiguously shameful event in which he was involved. The fact that Bjarni attacked and killed some of his own kinsmen at Bodvarsdale (see *Vápn.* 18:63) is recalled by Killer-Bjarni. This name shows that not all nicknames need be strongly bonded to their vehicles. Bjarni is mostly identified by his farm (Hof), but he can be Killer-Bjarni when it serves the rhetorical purposes of a speaker who questions Bjarni's present refusal to proceed as aggressively in the defense of his household members as the speaker would wish: "We never expected when we took service with Killer-Bjarni that we would be singeing lambs' heads while Thorstein, his outlaw, would be singeing the heads of geldings." On the other hand, Thorstein's nickname redefines his identity, at least among the members of Bjarni's household. Both the servant woman and Rannveig refer to him as "staff-struck." And there is some indication that the name had a wider currency; presumably it was the way old Thorarin came to learn of the injury since his blindness prevented him from seeing the effects of the blow.

## The Politics of Accident

The passage in which Thorarin reveals his knowledge of his son's injury merits some comment. What could it be in old Thorarin's "Why are you up and about so early, son?" that provokes the mild-mannered son to respond by chiding his father's poverty and invalidism? ("It seems to me that there are few others to leave the work to around here"). There would seem to be little in the father's question to indicate hostility unless we understand that in the sexual division of labor it was the women who got up early to work, as indeed the introduction to this colloquy takes care to point out. The sagas are in general silent about disputes arising from mismatching sex and type of task. In one saga a husband orders his wife to milk the animals, which she refuses to do unless he mucks the pen (*Bjarn.* 12:139).[41] Some tasks were not gender specific. Both men and women participated in mowing and one scene even shows an eminent warrior helping his mother dry linen (*Bjarn.* 11:137). But as Thorarin's subsequent remarks show, he is suggesting his son's effeminacy at the outset and the son seems to have picked up on the subtle hint right away.

Thorarin soon abandons indirection and goes right to the events of the horsefight: "Weren't you . . . knocked dizzy like a dog?" Thorstein's response is to claim there was no wrong to avenge. "I don't think there can be any honor in calling it an intentional blow rather than an accident." It is these words that provoke Thorarin to abandon obliquity completely and move to unmitigated calumny. He calls his son *ragr*, which I have inadequately rendered "sissy." The laws inform us that *ragr* is one of three words that privileged their target to kill the insultor (*Grágás* Ib 184, II 392). To translate it as "coward," as is often done, understates the constellation of values comprised in the term. To be *ragr* was to be effeminate, it was to be a man who was sodomized by other men.[42] In its sexual association, it is of a piece with Thorarin's opening line of dialogue suggesting his son was doing woman's work when the man's work of taking vengeance still needed doing. *Ragr* is the word that sets Thorstein, armed, on his way to see Thord. Once there he again takes up the issue of accident that so infuriated his father. And once again there is an unwillingness to make use of the concept.

A rather strange passage in the laws declares, "It is prescribed that there shall be no such things as accidents." This uncompromising hostility to the notion of accident, however, is less than categorical. The very section that begins with that passage goes on to provide that there was to be no punishment (that is, no outlawry or forfeiture of property) when one man stumbled into the weapon of another, if the weapon was held still and the latter was found by a panel of neighbors not to have intended the other to have been scratched (*Grágás* Ia 166–67, II 334).[43] This is expanded upon in a second manuscript, where the neighbors must also find that no one else intended the injury either (II 334). Further still, a person assumed the risk for injuries in wrestling matches or other games, as long as his opponent did not intend to do him harm. Yet another provision, in which damage to livestock is discussed, allows certain bumblings to be deemed accidental if compensation as assessed by a panel of five neighbors was paid to the victim within two weeks:

> If a man does worse than he intends to do and damage
> results from his clumsiness that is not punishable at law
> and he shall make amends for the damage within two
> weeks time as it is evaluated by five neighbors. Other-
> wise it shall not be judged an accident. (*Grágás* II 208)

The implication of the final proviso is reasonably clear. If the bungler does not pay, he is liable to prosecution for fines or one of the various degrees of outlawry.

What we might discern from these passing comments in *Grágás* on accident is that the idea of accident, of inadvertent and unintended harm, was familiar, but the category had a very short half-life: two weeks according to one law and one nanosecond if we are to take "there shall be no such things as accidents" literally. After that, intention was either presumed or, in the language of lawyers, liability became strict or absolute.[44]

*Thorstein the Staffstruck* shares with the laws a relatively restricted view of accident. The reluctance in the laws and the saga to characterize certain harms as accidental seems to have reflected a rather broad-based cultural norm, although neither saga nor legal account is unambiguous on this score. The saga writer, for example, is clearly unsympathetic to Thord, old Thorarin, and the gossiping servants, that is, to all those who wish to confer intentionality on the event. And we have already observed the apparent contradiction in the *Grágás* section both denying and affirming the concept of unintentional harm.

For the sake of clarity we should return to the horsefight where the conflict that sets the events going arose. Horsefighting, according to saga evidence, was a very popular sport and it seems fairly clear that Thorstein's household is engaged in breeding fighting horses. The horses were accompanied into the ring by their masters, who goaded them on and apparently not too infrequently goaded each other as well. To credit the sagas in this matter, it was not unlikely that the horses would end up spectators as they watched their masters go at it.[45] What is unusual in this account is that the victim of the first blow is willing to make peace on his own motion, uncompelled by bystanders. The injured party, Thorstein, prefers to characterize his wound as an accident. This is manifested initially by his making nothing of the incident. Apparently a significant number of spectators were also willing to accept this view, hence the reference to things quieting down after Thorstein asked that people keep this from his father. Two observers, however, think otherwise. Thorvald and Thorhall grace Thorstein with an insulting cognomen. To be called Staffstruck suggests status degradation (accepting beatings is a marker of slaves and animals). It also hints at deeper insult. Thorstein's nickname (*stangarhǫgg*), derives some of its shamefulness from its verbal and substantive similarities with *klámhǫgg*, a legal term meaning "shame-stroke" (*Grágás* Ia 148, II 299). The shame-stroke was the intentional stabbing or cutting of a man's buttocks and the shame of the stroke was clearly the shame of *ragr*, the shame of being sodomized. And if the nickname stuck, as it did here, it meant that the incident and the shame would not be forgotten. The name also fixes Thord as the striker, the one who made Thorstein "staffstruck" and hence confers a certain intentionality on the action. Recall that one version of the laws made lack of intention contingent not only on the state of mind of the wrongdoer but on that of others too. Even supposing Thord's act had been unintentional, Thorhall's and Thorvald's maliciousness could have been imputed to Thord.[46]

Thorvald's and Thorhall's view is shared by others. Thorstein's father refuses to accept his son's characterization of the injury and calls him *ragr* for trying to play down the affair by so interpreting it. In one respect, even the sagawriter concurs: he appends no mitigating circumstances to his account of the fracas. Thord clearly acted intentionally. And remarkably, even Thord refuses to claim the blow was accidental when given the chance to do so by Thorstein. Surely he must have suspected that his surly refusal to offer compensation to an armed man might bring those arms to bear upon himself. But Thord's insulting refusal to compensate Thorstein rather vividly illustrates how little fear and respect Thorstein inspired and we can only assume that this was related to his willingness to classify his wound as an accident, to his failure to follow up his injury aggressively. Public displays of nonassertiveness and forbearance, while not always status-degrading occasions, had to be cleverly and carefully orchestrated not to be so.

There are two technical issues to discuss: the matter of a right to compensation for accidental harm and the formalities of labeling the incident as accidental or willful. Our story indicates that the way Thorstein revealed that he was willing to treat the whole matter as an accident was to make no claim on Thord. Yet the laws and other sagas confirm that a claim of accident did not mean that the injurer was excused from paying for the damage. He was to be spared from liability for outlawry and fines in excess of the amount of the harm actually caused, but no more. He still had to make restitution.[47] Compare, for instance, an account of a horsefight in *Reykdœla saga* in which A, in trying to strike B's horse, had the blow glance off the horse and hit B in the shoulder. The saga describes the ensuing negotiations (*Reyk.* 23 : 222−23):

> A went up to B and said that this had turned out worse than he intended. "I shall prove whether this was accidental or not. I will give you," he said, "sixty sheep so that you do not blame me for this. You might then realize that I couldn't have intended the results." B said he himself was only a little less responsible.

But lest we think that the only impasse in Thorstein's case was Thord's unwillingness to offer compensation, we observe that the good intentions of the principals cannot always survive the opinion of third parties or other members of their households. For when it came time for A to give B the sheep, A's father, the injurer's father this time, couldn't resist a disapproving wry comment intimating that manhood was being commuted to money and a little too much money at that. B killed A's father for his wit.

One way of reconciling *Thorstein the Staffstruck* with this account on the issue of whether a claim of accident excuses liability altogether or whether the damage must still be compensated for, is to note that "accident" (atburð, váðaverk) seems to mean different things depending on who raises the issue. The example from *Reykdœla saga* suggests that when the wrongdoer raises the issue of accident it is up to him to illustrate his lack of intention by offering some compensation, either in the form of a gift or a formally denominated payment.[48] But when the injured party claims accident it is nothing more than another way of saying, "let's forget it," that is, there was no wrong.[49] And both cases we have seen suggest that it was up to the injurer to clarify his state of mind. Thus it is that, when Thorstein goes to confront Thord, he asks Thord to describe his state of mind when he struck him the previous summer and, in the other example, A moves first to prove his lack of hostile intention by offering B generous compensation. The injurer's responsibility in this respect is largely supported by the *Grágás* provision which allows the injurer to treat the injury as accidental if he makes good the damage within two weeks. If an agreed private characterization of the incident was not forthcoming it could be ascertained judicially when the injured party prosecuted for an *intentional* wrong.[50] It does not appear that there was any way to prosecute for an accident. Once the dispute went to law, the issue of accident could only arise by way of defense. The defendant could answer a charge of intentional wrong by asking the panel of neighbors to make a finding about his intentions. As a matter of legal procedure then, the issue of accident could only be raised by the wrongdoer.

Did the neighbors called as a jury really look into the defendant's state of mind or did they look more to certain objectifiable and observable facts, such as whether he had tried to pay compensation within a fortnight? We do not know for sure on what criteria the finding was made. But, as we shall have occasion to discover, a multitude of considerations not strictly relevant to the suit at hand, like the relative popularity of the parties, the history of their prior dealings, the injured party's own carelessness, might enter into a determination of intent. Both laws and saga agree that Thorstein was not the person who should have raised the issue of accident. It was Thord's responsibility to suggest the categorization by making an offer of compensation or it was his right to raise it as a defense if prosecuted for an intentional wrong.[51]

We are now in a better position to make sense of *Grágás'* "there shall be no such thing as accidents." This does not mean, as von Amira thought (1895, 2.405), that in matters of doubt a wrong should be deemed intentional. It simply means that accidents are not to provide a basis for a cause of action. The claim of accident is a defense to an action for an intentional wrong. This is confirmed by the rest of the same provision which states that the people to decide on the defendant's submission of lack of intention "are to be drawn from the prosecution panel with which he [the wrongdoer] is prosecuted, and five neighbors are to be drawn from it" (*Grágás* Ia 166). Thus informed we are able to surmise that Thorstein must have sought out Thord intending to kill him, which is what we would expect given the purposefully inflammatory incitement that sent Thorstein, armed, on his way. The very fact that it was again he who had to take the initiative must have fanned the flames. Thorstein's request to Thord that he clarify his prior state of mind must have been made in a tone designed to elicit the hostile response he in fact received. The tone is implied by the inappropriately familiar "I would like to know, my Thord, ... " And it would not be overreading to see in Thorstein's announcement of the killing a classic case of *níð*, or sexual insult. Thorstein likens himself to the bull who has used this horseboy rather disgracefully.

There is a nice conjunction of legal and literary source on the issue of accident that suggests this was one of those instances when the laws were confirming fairly widespread social norms. Neither law nor society was especially amenable to claims of accident when made by the injured party. The proper procedure, in court and out, was for the wrongdoer to come forward and offer amends. But when the wrongdoer did not come forward, law and society, though not inconsistent, may have parted company on the degree of action that should be taken. Some saga instances confirm what the laws prefer: suing for an intentional wrong;[52] a greater number of saga cases, however, including examples from both the family sagas and *Sturlunga*, suggest that blood was an appropriate response (*Íslend.* 5:233; *Njála* 53:135; *Reyk.* 23:221; *Vatn.* 32:86).

Our story shows rather clearly that it was more than a misfortune to be a victim of an accident, it was also a dishonor. And the dishonor need not all be the victim's. Both sides might look weak if they were too eager to define the affair as unintentional. The crucial and constant readjustments of prestige that attended all social interaction in Iceland strongly militated against "accident." The concept was there to be used, but many seemed reluctant to avail themselves of the opportunity, at least without first taking counsel with a fairly wide range of people. This is perhaps somewhat of an exaggeration. Both our cases show that the principals (both of them in the case from *Reykdœla saga* and one in *Thorstein the Staffstruck*) wished initially to dismiss the blows as unintentional. The pressures toward conferring intentionality did not come from them, but from their fathers, their fellow servants, kinsmen, and household members. It appears that even before the issue of intention ever would get put formally to a panel of neighbors in a legal action, the determination of accident for purposes of concluding a settlement was already communalized. It was not just an affair to be resolved by two people.

Anthropologists have noted and the sagas confirm that the imputation of intention to misfortunes varies with the quality of relations between the parties and the social distance between them (e.g., Peters 1967, 270; Black-Michaud 1975, 112). Close friends and kin have accidents, enemies do not; a hostile intent will be supplied. Children, women, old people have accidents, men of majority do not; a hostile intent will be supplied. In Njála (53:134–35), when Otkel's horse bolts out of control and runs into Gunnar, the injury is perceived to have been intentional because the two men already have well-established hostile relations. But, when Einar cuts his nephew's saddle girth so that he falls off his horse, the incident passes without mention (Ljós. 26:86), and when old Thorbjorn bumps into the painfully infected leg of another man, his age ultimately excuses him (Hrafnk. 4:113).

As long as the burden of categorization fell to the wrongdoer, there was no way the horsefight incident would ever be processed as an accident. The brief character introduction of Thord suggests why. He was an ójafnaðarmaðr ("a man of no measure,") a word used to describe those who refuse compromise and deny others their rights. He was also pompous, complacently believing himself invulnerable because he was the servant of a powerful man. He intended the harm he inflicted and no amends could be looked for from him. But why should this be dispositive? Why couldn't Thord's master and head of household have taken over the claim and settled on behalf of his servant, whether the blow was intentional or not? The short answer is that he could have and the sagas show many examples of householder responsibility for the delicts of household members. But the same sources also show that servants were sued in their own right and had to answer for their own wrongs (e.g., Sturla 23:95; Gunn. þ. 1–2:198–99). To explain why the head of household would intervene in one case and not the other, the source must be fairly circumstantial as to the relations between the master and the particular servant, and as to the strains the servant's actions create for the master in his dealings with the other household the servant has offended. Bjarni's initial refusal to intervene makes good social sense and some of his reasons are firmly suggested by fair inference from details in the story. An answer will depend on a rather detailed discussion of the particular progress of this dispute.

## The Progress of the Dispute

The dispute at the outset pits the servant of a substantial and powerful household against the head of a small and impoverished household. The power differential between the two units affects the course of the dispute in fundamental ways. In the previous paragraph I resorted to Thord's personality to explain why he did not show a willingness to make amends. But Thord's personality is situated in a social setting that allowed it free rein. There could be no doubt that, if Thord had offended a person attached to a household more the equal of Bjarni's, attempts would have been made to arrange a settlement. Bjarni would not have left the matter up to Thord. He would have intervened and substituted himself for Thord earlier in the process, while Thord was still alive. Only Thord's death elicits Bjarni's involvement against such small fry as Thorstein and then only in a perfunctory manner that is dissatisfying to substantial segments of Bjarni's clientele.

The setting and shape of this dispute also prevented the emergence and intervention of third parties to counsel or even impose peace on the principals. Third-party intervention is a crucial feature of Icelandic conflict management meriting a chapter of its own (see chapter 8). But something in this dispute failed to provide sufficient cues to the uninvolved to get involved. The reasons seem to be these: Nothing meriting intervention occurred at the horsefight where numerous bystanders were present because Thorstein himself dampened hostilities by refusing to act as if he had a claim to make. For the same reason there was no impetus for go-betweens to arrange a settlement once the horsefight broke up. There was also the fact that the principals, a servant and a poor householder, were of insufficient status and commanded inadequate resources to turn the district upside down if they were to pursue hostilities. A breach in relations between such little people threatened no one outside the households involved. If conflict was to break out, the next move was Thorstein's and it was highly unlikely he would or could move against the powerful Bjarni, Thord's master, and likely also to be his own chieftain, in any substantially disruptive way. If he moved against Thord alone, as indeed he did, this would hardly be a matter to attract the attention of independent intervenors since it would be expected that Bjarni was more than capable of taking care of such a matter without third-party intervention. Geography made third-party intervention unlikely also. Bjarni's and Thorstein's farms seem to share common boundaries. In any event they are so close together that hostile encounters between them need alert no other people. They could get at each other without much possibility of third parties being there to intervene.

The people who do emerge then are, not surprisingly, members of the households and clientele of the principals and they have a different agenda than would truly independent intervenors established in different households. It would be misrepresenting their structural association with the dispute to call them third parties. The servants, the women, the old men, all those whose juridical life is mediated via the household unit to which they belong, can never be detached from the disputes of the household leadership. Thorhall and Thorvald, and indeed Bjarni's wife Rannveig also, know that their sense of status and security relative to their counterparts in other households depend on the figure the householder and his sons cut in the world. And in Iceland, in the short run at least, looking good meant acting tough.

_Thorstein the Staffstruck_ gives a keen sense of just how intimately internal household affairs affected inter-household relations. In fact, a significant portion of this story details the remarkable and skillful maneuvering that the two principals, Bjarni and Thorstein, must engage in both to satisfy their household constituencies and then to free themselves from them. How they accomplish this is worth looking at in some detail.

After Thorstein, incited by his father, kills Thord, Bjarni has him outlawed. Because of the weakness of Thorstein's household the lawsuit could be processed routinely without great expenditure of resources or energy, and hence can be disposed of by the author in less than a sentence. Getting someone outlawed obliged the person who got him outlawed to carry out a court of confiscation (_féránsdómr_) two weeks after the judgment and then, as the source makes clear, to hunt him down and kill him (_Grágás_ Ia 189). But Bjarni lets Thorstein remain at home. Not being able to get your man once you got him outlawed was a matter of disgrace, and Bjarni's behavior was so interpreted by his servants, Thorhall and Thorvald. Another unnamed servant is more politic and more astute.[53] He attributes Bjarni's passivity to sensible district management. Thorstein keeps his household productive; without him, its members would become a charge on the district and, as we shall see in chapter 5, this was a burden most would prefer not to assume (_Grágás_ Ia 115). Bjarni's course of action reflects a compromise. Thord was hardly the kind of man for whom his master was going to undertake the risks and burden of killing. Thord was not well liked and many must have felt he deserved his end. He simply was not a proper object for zealous reaction.[54] Getting Thorstein outlawed was enough; it provided a symbol of Bjarni's willingness to stand by his household members, but to his mind that was all the matter called for.

Then there is the way in which Bjarni handles the insult he overhears his servants Thorvald and Thorhall make. They question his courage and make, as it seems most characters do when talking to or about Bjarni, a needling reference to the battle at Bodvarsdale, gracing him with the nickname Killer-Bjarni for the role he played there. It was at Bodvarsdale that Bjarni fought against his kinsmen and killed his mother's brother (*Vapn.* 18 : 63). The story makes clear in its typically subtle fashion that the fact of having been a kin killer complicates Bjarni's position in the dispute with Thorstein. No one lets Bjarni forget about Bodvarsdale. Thorvald and Thorhall, Thorstein, Thorarin, and even his wife—"you lie still when you should act, and act when you should lie still"—all make mocking references to the misfortune. From the point of view of Bjarni's servants and thingmen there is good reason to doubt that Bjarni values properly the bonds of attachment and obligation he should value. Having been a kin killer and then having not aggressively followed up the killing of his servant Thord provokes the concern of Thorvald and Thorhall. And when Bjarni takes no action at all for the deaths of Thorvald and Thorhall his thingmen start to wonder whether he will protect them. In other words Bjarni's past makes his clients less willing to tolerate ambiguity in Bjarni's response to Thorstein and leads them to urge more direct and uncompromising actions than would otherwise have been acceptable.[55]

When Bjarni sends Thorvald and Thorhall to sever Thorstein's head, he makes it quite clear to them that he is avenging the insulting remarks they made about him—"they thought now that they had indeed said too much." Bjarni, of course, could not very well kill his own household members even if they had insulted him.[56] But that does not mean he is unwilling to have Thorstein do the job for him. Bjarni stands to gain by either possible outcome. He either avenges himself on his outlaw or avenges himself on his tale-bearing servants. The drawback with the actual outcome is that the event is capable of being misunderstood by his wife and his thingmen who see in it only more evidence of Bjarni's lethargy and undervaluation of kinship and household obligation. It seems, however, that Bjarni's servants understand quite well what has happened. They after all were present when the disparaging remarks were made. Their knowledge explains the mordant wit with which they greet Thorhall's and Thorvald's corpses. I am also reluctant to deny the servants' knowledge to Rannveig and even to the thingmen. Servants provide the key links in the gossip and information flow among farms, and it is hard to believe that the truth about what led to Thorhall's and Thorvald's unhappy end was not either known or inferable. But the truth is not much solace to the thingmen who are only too aware of Bjarni's willingness to sacrifice his own. What they want is evidence that Bjarni will stand by those to whom he has undertaken formal obligation.

Whatever the sweetness for Bjarni of achieving revenge with irony may have been, the action was not without effect on extra-household relations. It falls to Rannveig, Bjarni's wife, to give expression to the concerns of Bjarni's thingmen. Although Bjarni treats her as if her counsel was nothing more than typical saga fare from a vengeance-minded woman, his actions betray his acknowledgment of the seriousness of the position she represents. He must move against Thorstein in some way or risk substantial erosion of his position in the district.

The confrontation between Bjarni and Thorstein shows in exquisite detail just how skillfully two principals willing to settle must maneuver to be able to negotiate the peaceful resolution both of them desire in the face of hostility from their respective household members and the demands of honor which they themselves keenly feel. Their skill is matched by the author's, whose description is a model of the economies of saga writing. We do not have to wait to the end of the story to know that Bjarni respects Thorstein. Bjarni has always been able to comprehend moral, if not legal, justification for Thorstein's killings. This is manifested indirectly by his refusal to hunt Thorstein down after outlawing him and directly in the comment to his wife: "Thorstein has killed few without reason." Moreover, he is one of the few people in his household who does not refer to Thorstein by his insulting cognomen. To Bjarni he is "Thorstein of Sunnudale."

The combat isolates the two men. But even freed from the embarrassment of their hardline constituencies, the negotiation is fraught with danger. The parley, literally proceeding with point and counterpoint, takes place between sword strokes, with the blows bearing a significant portion of the semantic burden in the discussion. The author gives us more than enough information to determine when punches are being pulled and when they are augmented to provide the appropriate nuance to the remarks they accompany. Thorstein adopts a deferential attitude throughout as suits the difference in their rank.[57] He makes it clear to Bjarni that he is eager to settle, even if he does politely stipulate the terms. "I am utterly lacking in everything needed to fight you, but I shall go abroad as soon as a ship is available because I know your character is such that you will provide labor for my father if I leave." Bjarni refuses the offer and they fight.

Both sides exchange the subtlest of verbal digs. In fact, most all saga dialogue takes place on the edge of insult. Bjarni calls attention to Thorstein's impoverished condition ("I'm less used to working than you are") and Thorstein joins the chorus of those who make snide remarks about Bjarni's kin killing in order to add a little spice to his arch appraisal of Bjarni's martial prowess ("This couldn't have been the sword you had at Bodvarsdale"). Thorstein's deference is not slavish. In fact, there might be evidence here of just what the proper signs of true deference were between householders of different means. Deference was only true if there were some signs of spirit and toughness in the person offering it. The trick was to let the other know that you knew you were lower without acting as if you were. If deference were too exaggerated, and Thorstein comes close in his references to his own bad luck and Bjarni's good luck, the excessiveness of display might, depending on what exactly was motivating the excessiveness, either insult or disgust the other.

In addition to blows and words, the parties exchange other information-laden signs. What must Bjarni be telling Thorstein when he lays down his sword as he bends to drink? What Thorstein is telling Bjarni when he picks it up and then hands it back is clear and reinforced again when he allows Bjarni to tie his shoe without decapitating him. Other saga characters who took their adversaries at their word never lived to tell about it and the contemporary audience would have experienced a little frisson when Bjarni bent down to drink and tie his shoe.[58] In case Bjarni failed to notice Thorstein's willingness to forgo these opportunities, Thorstein makes the point explicitly later: "I've had the chances today to betray you if my bad luck were more powerful than your good luck."

The remarks about his own bad luck not being stronger than Bjarni's good luck bear more information than appears at first glance. The language of luck is deferential and indirect and this is the mode of discourse Thorstein must adopt when he is making a threat, for it is a threat he is making. Consider Thorstein's words to Bjarni after he gives him a better sword and supplies each of them with new shields: "I would gladly stop this game because I'm afraid that your luck might well be more effective than my bad luck.

Everyone is eager to save his life in the end, myself included if I am able to." Thorstein allows us to see that what he means by his bad luck is not his losing to Bjarni, but Bjarni's losing to him. Bad luck is the consequence he foresees if he stops pulling his punches, as indeed he is now threatening to do. Thorstein knows what the consequence of killing someone of Bjarni's stature would be. He could be certain that it would not be as benign as the consequence of killing Thord had been.[59]

Bjarni still refuses to leave off the fight. And it is here that Thorstein makes his drift unmistakably clear. " 'Now that was a powerful blow,' said Bjarni . . . 'That same sword of yours is biting better than it did earlier.'" Thorstein now makes his final offer and this time Bjarni accepts. Thorstein's final offer is much more advantageous to Bjarni than the one he made just prior to the combat. In that offer it was Thorstein who stipulated the terms, in this one the terms are Bjarni's to make. This is an offer of self-judgment (see pp. 285– 88), the surest sign of deference and of a willingness to have peace above all.

It might seem that all the moves for settlement came from Thorstein. But Thorstein's successive moves were not made in the face of categorical rejection in spite of Bjarni's words to that effect. In addition to having armed himself with an obviously blunt weapon, Bjarni had given Thorstein a nearly unambivalent sign of his willingness to settle, at least if the terms were right. He showed up alone. The author goes out of his way to tell us this and he exposes poor Rannveig to her husband's annoyance to make the point:

> "How many men are you taking with you?" she asked.
> "I'm not going to drag along a big crowd," he said,
> "I'm going alone."
> "Don't do that, don't risk your life against the weapons of that monster," she said.
> "Are you going to be like the usual women who bewail one minute what they were inciting a little while before?"

No one expected a man to give his outlaw fair odds. One of the virtues of an outlawry judgment was precisely that one generally did not suffer loss of face for taking advantage of numbers.[60] By going alone Bjarni creates a quiet forum in which the two can carry on their very complicated settlement dance.

Although Bjarni's and Thorstein's negotiations had a ritualized gamelike quality to them the combat that accompanied them was in no way a charade. The whole dance was a matter of the highest seriousness, all the more so because it could still maintain that seriousness without the participants sacrificing their wit. At every moment there existed the possibility of miscommunication, miscomprehension, and misfire.[61] The success of the game was not a necessary part of its structure. Success was earned by the intelligence and skill of the particular players. The structure provided them a common ground on which to exercise their talents but without talent the structure was not always sufficient to save them.

There is a darker side to this tale. It's not just a warm story about two men who recognize each other's merit and are able to effect a reconciliation in spite of the spiteful urgings of their household members. Reconciliation had a cost and the cost came at the independence of Thorstein's household. At the story's beginning Thorstein and Thorarin had their own independent farm; at the story's end Thorarin is maintained at Bjarni's direction and Thorstein is a member of Bjarni's household, a respected member, to be sure, but no longer independently established. This single observation provides the crucial information to explain the fundamental given of the story: Thorstein's original choice to ignore the affront of Thord's blow and the derogatory nickname. Thorstein, I assume, was fluent enough in the realities of disputing in his own society to know that when a small householder got involved in a serious dispute with a nearby powerful household the outcome was likely to mean the end of the smaller unit as an independent entity, unless for some reason the weaker party was able to enlist the support of other powerful neighbors. Even old Thorarin understands this, although his knowledge either came too late or was simply ignored because militant honor was more important to him than independence: "Anybody who lives near a powerful man and then contends with him and gives him offense can't figure on wearing out too many new shirts. And for this reason I can't feel sorry for you because I think you've done much to deserve it."

Even Bjarni was aware of this likelihood. His entire strategy prior to the duel indicates as much. He consciously wishes to maintain the independence of the farm at Sunnudale; this is why he chooses not to hunt down his outlaw. And for this reason we cannot attribute Bjarni's decision—that Thorstein serve him in the place of the three men he killed—as a disingenuous attempt to dispossess Thorstein of his farm. It does not appear to have been worth the taking, as the unnamed servant made very clear. But once he is forced to the confrontation he has to come away with something to quiet the very complaints that compelled him to seek out Thorstein in the first place. Any money compensation assessed to Thorstein appropriate for having killed three servants would probably bankrupt the farm just the same. But there has to be a change in the status quo to serve as a sign to his thingmen that he *did* something. The outward sign looks not much different than debt-slavery; the reality, however, is significantly more benign.

Bjarni is not without some doubts even with the solution he arrives at. This, I think, is why he goes in to see old Thorarin after he and Thorstein have settled. The purpose of Bjarni's misrepresentation is to elicit the old man's consent to the arrangement already agreed to by Bjarni and Thorstein, or in the absence of consent to contrive to have a claim against Thorarin that can justify taking his son away from him. But why Bjarni should resort to lies to accomplish this purpose is not easy to account for. Presumably, Bjarni is motivated by a belief that the old man would never agree to be bound by a peaceful resolution negotiated by a son, who, to the father's mind, had already lost honor by not pursuing claims to a violent conclusion. There is a wonderful energy in the irascible old Viking. And it is his anti-chieftain speech, more than anything else, that corrects any inclination to view the outcome of the affair in too rosy a light. He interjects a powerful and unpleasant note about chieftainly rapaciousness and acquisitiveness that the later sagas of the *Sturlunga* compilation suggest was a mid-thirteenth century reality.[62] Even if Bjarni was well-intentioned—and the story is clear that he was—the objective outcome is the same. Given the relative power of the disputants, the realities of the disputing process pretty much preconditioned the outcome: one less independent farm.

The dark side should also raise suspicion as to the story's surface view that the sum of the changes in Bjarni's and Thorstein's honor comes to more than zero. Are we witnessing the ideology of honor being used to compensate Thorstein for his loss of independence? Or can we say that these men's honor was funded entirely by the nonplayers in the game: women, old men, and servants, in short, by their dependents? Are we seeing here an expansion of the boundary definitions of the honor game to the greater subjection of women and servants, indeed to the impressment of independent farmers into the ranks of servants? Are we being given a brief justificatory glimpse of processes and structures that enabled a certain class of men to augment their power and gain greater control over the lives of women and other men?[63]

What I hope to have accomplished by taking the time and space to read *Thorstein the Staffstruck* with some closeness is to show how reasonable an account it gives of social and legal processes. In this case we observed a mutual confirmation between law code and saga. Both show an ambivalence about accident, the saga providing social sense and context to what would be an extremely recalcitrant set of legal provisions if we were not fortunate enough to have the so-called fictional sources to help construe them. There are times when the sagas and law codes deviate. Historians of the period, with the notable exception of Heusler, have tended to accept the legal provision in the face of hostile saga evidence. My tendency is to trust the saga as long as the account it gives is not marked by obvious indicia of incredibility and as long as the account it gives fits in fairly well with the ranges of types of dispute processing that modern sociology and anthropology have helped discover and describe.

An implied argument I have been making in this chapter is that the superlative artfulness of the account does not necessarily make it untrustworthy as a historical source. It is rather the tale's very artfulness that gives us sufficient social and normative structure to make social and moral as well as literary sense of the events it relates. Good art in the saga mode is not the art of inventiveness, it is the art of incisive description, which, with sure and brief strokes, gives so much context and standard by which to reveal the social significance of the activity being described. Not all literature lends itself to the use that I would make of the sagas and the great information density of the sagas may well be less a function of their being literature than of their being sagas. But I still suspect that most all "fiction" has more social historical value than the history profession has been willing to recognize.

The strong claim I would make is that the sagas describe a real world external to themselves, a world that we can recover fairly well in those areas where the saga description is thick enough and makes sense in the light of relevant comparative data. Those still agnostic on the matter should find a weaker claim unobjectionable: that is, we may or may not be recovering the experienced world of twelfth and thirteenth century Icelanders, but, in any event, we are at least recovering the world of the sagas *and* the laws, a world that, furthermore, has the virtue of looking very much like some worlds that we can prove to have existed and in fact have been carefully studied.

# Some Aspects of the Economy:
# The Problem of Negotiating and
# Classifying Exchanges

A few matters of method behind us, we can now attempt to reconstruct certain aspects of the social order of early Iceland that but for the sagas would elude us entirely. The sources are frustratingly porous in matters of domestic trade and the provisioning of the population. Still, we are able to construct an account that makes sense of the sources we have. The problem, as usual, is how to discount for the evidence that has been irretrievably lost or suppressed. Even if I forgo on occasion the subjunctive voice, the style of scholarly hedging, I am forever mindful of the black holes that surround my reconstructions. That one big hedge accomplished, consider the following.

Near the end of *Eyrbyggja saga* there occurs this brief vignette:

> Thorir asked Ospak and his men where they had gotten [the goods they were carrying]. Ospak said that they had gotten them at Thambardal.
> "How did you come by them?" said Thorir.
> Ospak answered, "They were not given, they were not paid to me, nor were they sold either (*Hvárki váru gefin né goldin né sǫlum seld*)." (*Eyrb.* 58:161)[1]

Earlier that evening Ospak had raided the house of a farmer called Alf and made away with enough to burden four horses. Ospak admitted as much when he wittily eliminated the more legitimate modes of transfer by which he could have acquired the goods.[2] There was no question of thievery here. An Icelandic thief had to conceal the taking, and Ospak was not so craven. His taking was open and notorious, and Thorir did not fail to conceive his meaning. This was a *rán*, an open, hostile taking.[3]

Ospak is also saying something about modes of exchange in early Iceland. He is listing, apparently in descending order of probability, just how goods were likely to be transferred between two people of roughly equal social standing: as a gift, as a payment[4] (presumably by way of compensation in the settlement of a claim), or as a purchase. Last comes *rán*, unmentioned and implied by indirection because it was unsociable. Students of the early Icelandic economy have been less willing than Thorir to understand Ospak's message.[5] Ospak had declared himself outside their bailiwick by claiming himself to be neither borrower nor lender, purchaser nor merchant, importer nor exporter. Discussions of the early Icelandic economy have tended to focus on long-distance trade, because that was where the most obvious evidence of trade as trade was to be found. Internal trade is very poorly documented, unless we are willing to look beyond mercantile transactions narrowly defined to the circulation of goods themselves. The sagas contain much evidence of goods circulating, but only rarely via straightforward buy-sell transactions. If we expand our range of relevance to include gift-exchange, compensation awards, raids, transfers in consideration of marriage, the evidence is all of a sudden, if not as full as we would like it, still much better than has been assumed. When the sagas speak of the host who sends his guests away with good gifts, or when they take care to note that two men took turns inviting each other to feasts, we are not entitled to dismiss this as mere literary commonplace (e.g., Lönnroth 1976, 54; Sveinsson 1933, 140–41). Nor need we look to Celtic sources to explain the appearance of a cattle raid in a saga (e.g., Magnússon and Pálsson 1969, 37). Goods in fact circulated, property changed hands by feast and raid.

The household farm was the basic unit of production as well as the basic unit of residence. The larger farms were mostly self-sufficient, although the demands of feasting, hospitality, and garrisoning might require the acquisition of provisions from other farms (e.g., *Ljós.* 7:120, 30:100; *Þorg. sk.* 24:148); the smaller farms often depended on loans of stock or rentals of land. Between larger and smaller farms there must have existed a fairly permanent series of exchanges regularized in creditor-debtor or landlord-tenant relationships. The amount of attention *Grágás* gives to loans, especially of livestock, and the proper procedures for their repayment and the recovery of delinquent debts, suggests the frequency of these kinds of transactions and the likelihood that they were a frequent source of conflict as well (*Grágás* Ib 140–48, II 213–28, 236–38; see Jóhannesson 1974, 334). But our direct evidence of these exchanges is thin indeed and incapable of supporting thick description (see, e.g., *Hœn.* 1–2:6–7, 4:11–12; *Gísli* 19:63; *Njála* 6:22).

The sagas, however, confirm the existence of internal trade and specialized employments, although we have little way of recovering the levels of activity or how regularized such mercantile-like exchanges were. All in all, evidence of systematic local trade involving goods of local origin is sparse. Peddlers and beggars are depicted wandering from farm to farm bearing both gossip and goods (*Drop.* 3:144; *Hœn.* 1:6; *Njála* 22:59–63, 49:125; see also Ebel 1977, 4–8); they are uniformly painted as an unsavory lot. This characterization receives some confirmation in legislation adopted at the Allthing which refers to those "moneyless men who operate dishonestly and buy goods from people" (*DI* II 6–7).' Occasional mention is made of isolated sales between people who do not hold themselves out as peddlers or merchants (e.g., *Reyk.* 7:170, 25:229), and in one instance we find evidence of a reputable man who appears to have devoted considerable efforts to selling goods: Vali, described as well-liked and popular, "sold [his] wares throughout the district" (*Band.* 4:313). One casual detail suggests that a person might buy a large quantity of goods at a ship's landing and renegotiate the goods throughout the countryside (*Reyk.* 1:154), but this is really an aspect of long-distance trade. Some farms bred horses for sale (*Reyk.* 23:221; *Þorst. stang.* 69); others supplied wood (*Reyk.* 25:229). One man loaded a ferry each summer with "fastday-food," presumably fish, and bore it about the district selling to the farmers (*G.dýri* 5:169); another person, described as a wanderer, sold casks (*Íslend.* 94:365). Grain sales are mentioned once in conjunction with a guild feast, but the source indicates that the sales were irregular (*Hafl.* 10:27). Provisioning the episcopal sees required buying and selling, as is indicated by the ban three chieftains impose on trading with Bishop Gudmund (*Íslend.* 20:245–46).

Exchange of fish for farm produce must have been fairly common between fishing stations and inland, nonriparian farms, but our evidence is indirect. We know of the existence of a fishing station on the Snæfellsnes peninsula, which one saga implies did a regular trade with the surrounding region (*Bjarn.* 18:156; also *Eyrb.* 53:147 and *Lax.* 14:29; see Jóhannesson 1974, 303–5). Buying fish was sufficiently regularized in the North Quarter (*Prest.* 29:158) so that it could provide the pretextual cover for spying expeditions and other unusual movements of men (*Íslend.* 183:507; also *Ljós.* 30:100). The same regularization is indicated by the remark of one chieftain: "We won't need to buy fish anywhere but from you" (*Hafl.* 5:16). And we know of at least one instance in which luck in fishing provided the initial funds to launch a very successful career in long-distance trading (*Band.* 1:293–97). But the structures of dominance in Iceland were constructed as if fish did not exist. The society, as we have already mentioned, was organized around animal husbandry. The marks of status were land and livestock, not fish and fishing boats (Gunnarsson 1980b).

Whatever trade there was, domestic or foreign, it was not sufficient to support the continuous and regular existence of marketplaces. The Things, however, provided annual meeting places where various types of exchanges and the settling of debts could occur, and the laws provide evidence that craftsmen—shoemakers and sword cutlers—plied their trades there (Grágás Ia 176, II 347).[7] Fairs were held in conjunction with certain feast days at the two episcopal sees. But the usual practice was for markets to spring up ad hoc whenever and wherever a trading ship might land (Gelsinger 1981, 32, 214nn36–37; Þorláksson 1978, 112–14). This tended to be at the most frequented natural harbors, but the existence of a market depended on the presence of a recently arrived ship.[8]

Under usual circumstances, when harvests were adequate and the weather bearable, the households of the classes most favored by the sagas were able to provide themselves with basic necessities. There were regular exchanges of tangibles between households of the same rank, but these exchanges were submerged in social relations rather than undertaken for purely economic reasons.[9] Friends, kin, and affines exchanged invitations to feasts and sent their guests away with gifts. The parting gift was a saga commonplace and the saga writers were not above varying it for wry effect to indicate especially unfriendly leavetakings of guests and hosts: "It was not mentioned that he was sent on his way with gifts" (Lax. 85:243; also Hafl. 10:27). These exchanges were domesticated by habit and ritual. This is not to say they were free of conflict. Feasts were the occasion for insult and slighted sensibility (e.g., Eyrb. 37:98–99; Hafl. 10:23–27; Ljós. 13:17–18, 21:58–59; Njála 35:91) no less than for conviviality and for renewing and reaffirming bonds of blood and alliance. Gift-exchange, though sociable, was hardly disinterested and could mask strategies not so amiable.[10] But the gamesmanship and tactics of sociable exchange had the virtue of familiarity and regularity. Overt conflict was euphemized or even suppressed entirely by densely hedging the transaction with safeguards of peacefulness. Shows of generosity were to be met with shows of gratitude.

When transfers of goods not already regularized by well-defined norms or habit were sought, and especially when they were not initiated by the present possessor, tensions and uncertainties surfaced. This did not mean there would be no transfer, but it put the parties to the burden of defining the transaction. If food and fodder were consumed at another's farm, if the host's horse or cloak left openly with the visitor after a meal, the transfer was unambiguously by way of gift; this was true even if the gift was a thinly disguised payment for support, or a kind of enforced hospitality (e.g., *Ljós.* 6–7:117–21). But if food and provisions were taken away uneaten, if swords and horses were removed secretly or without a meal having first been taken, the nature of the transaction was uncertain unless the parties first actively defined it. The uncertainty made for irritated sensibilities and could lead to misunderstanding and easy offense. The transfer still might be by way of gift, but alternatively it could be a purchase, or a payment in settlement of some prior wrong, or, to recall Ospak, an open expropriation.

I do not propose here to offer a model of exchange types,[11] but some general remarks are nevertheless in order. Each mode of exchange had its norms and vocabulary. The words of the parties, checked for irony and misrepresentation by reference to their deeds and to the narrator's commentary, are our best evidence as to the mode in which the transfer took place. This is not a wholly satisfactory solution, for the parties might disagree about how to define the transaction. Disputes arose, for example, as to whether a transfer was a *rán* or a sale (*Háv.* 14:337), *rán* or gift (*Háv.* 15–16:343–45), or gift or loan (*Eyrb.* 33:91). *Grágás*, in allowing gifts to servants that exceeded the maximum permissible wages, tried to distinguish between gifts and payments: "It is not counted as a gift if a verdict is given that it was a private prearrangement" (Ia 130). Moreover, all transactions of whatever type were subject to redefinition over time to accord with the present state of relations between the parties or their successors. What the original parties thought was a gift need not be thought so by their heirs.[12] The modern observer also might be hard-pressed at times to classify an exchange because the economic effect of the various modes were often indistinguishable. But the Icelanders were not subject to the same sources of confusion since they lacked the accounting methods and theory to see all classes of exchanges in purely material terms (see Finley 1973, 20–27, 110, 116, 144).

I assume that when a party sought to *fala* or *kaupa* something, he typed himself as a buyer. If the other party in response to this sold or gave for a price there was a bargain or purchase (*kaup*). *Fala*, "to ask to buy, to seek to purchase," generally described the initiatory action of the would-be purchaser. *Fala* is to be distinguished from *kaupa*, which referred to the completed action of acquiring or agreeing to acquire a thing for a price (Cleasby and Vigfússon 1957, s.vv. *fala, kaupa*).[13] In transactions where payment was in kind, or in money substances that also had a common use-value, like *vaðmál*, it may be conceptually difficult to determine exactly who was the buyer and who was the seller. Where both parties sought the exchange, and payment was in kind, each party played both roles (Chapman 1980, 35). But the natives seemed to have thought otherwise. Lexical criteria often reveal the native assessment of who played what role. A buyer will *fala* or *kaupa* and be obliged to *gjalda* (to pay) a seller who will *selja* or *gefa* for a consideration. The seller was the person who was willing to part with his goods first. He was the creditor. This is confirmed by both the sagas and the laws, which, with rare exception, show that buyers take the goods first and arrange for future payment (see *Grágás* III 600, s.v. *eindagi* and Andersson and Miller 1989, 123n7). In the buy-sell mode of transfer, the amount of return and the time and place of payment were bargained over and specified. A significant feature of this arrangement, in theory at least, was that it purported to relate only goods to each other, not people, and as such was a denial of continuing social relations between the principals (Gregory 1981, 124–25). Once the debt was discharged, there was nothing in the transaction that bound the parties to continue dealing with each other.[14]

Gift-giving, by contrast, gave rise to social relations and adjusted the status of the parties in relation to each other.[15] The giver gained prestige and power from the exchange. He exacted deference from the receiver and obliged him to reciprocate.[16] But the amount and place of return, and above all its timing, were left open and to the discretion of the recipient, although the discretion was not entirely unfettered, hedged in as it was by normative and contextual constraints. This absence of prior formal agreement regulating the amount and timing of the return is explicitly mentioned in *Grágás*, in the passage cited above (p. 81), as the defining characteristic of gift-exchange: a gift could not be the result of a private prearrangement. In gift-exchange, time was not something that burdened the debtor with exponential increases in the value of his obligation;[17] time was his to manipulate, so as to readjust and redefine the relations between himself and the giver. He could choose the insult of a refusal to accept or of a too hasty return, the sullenness of excessive delay, or he could make no return at all, which, depending on the circumstances, could signal utter contempt for the giver or permanent subordination to him (see Andersson and Miller 1989, 51–55). Social relations, their definition, and the determination of status were much of what motivated gift-exchange.

It is not always possible to consider all transactions called gifts as gifts. When, for example, *Grágás* required men to make a gift of one-fifth of their Sunday catch to poor farmers or suffer a three-mark fine

(Ia 25, 32; II 30, 41), the word *gjǫf* had become a euphemism for a forced offering, forced in a different way than the norms of gift-exchange mandated requital.[18] The law made the initial transfer obligatory and specific as to time and amount; it, furthermore, expected no return, except perhaps for the unfelt deference almsgivers expect to receive from their beneficiaries. On the other hand, some transfers called gifts, that at times were little more than a *quid pro quo* for services rendered, were "misrecognized" as gifts because the parties wished to define their relations more amicably than an open admission of pure cash-nexus would allow.[19] The modern retirement gift to an employee or, in early economies, the gifts given to servants, clients, and slaves are examples. Such transfers are still part of the world of gift-exchange, because they specifically use its idiom and desire its significances. No verb is exclusively associated with gift-exchange. *Gefa, veita,* or *launa,* to give, to grant, to repay, may all mark a transfer by gift but need not do so. It is necessary to heed the surrounding circumstances. Between equals outside a designated marketplace, gift-exchange is the expected mode of transfer unless another mode is actively substituted for it. The use of *gefa* to describe a handing-over will indicate a gift, if a value in a money substance is not then stipulated as a return. Haggling is inappropriate to the mode, although it may be difficult at times to discern a difference between this and some requests for gifts (see, e.g., *Auðun* 1:362; *Hafl.* 12:30).

*Rán,* like gift-exchange, admitted reciprocity and defined social relations. But it inverted the movement of property as against the duty to make return. It was now the prior possessor who owed a response, not the raider; and it was the raider who achieved social dominance from the transfer, not the prior possessor. Here too, the timing and quality of return were left to those who had the return to make. And timing was no less significant here than in the world of gift-exchange: "Only a slave avenges himself immediately, but a coward never does" (*Grett.* 15:44; see below p. 193). The meaning of the mode of exchange, whether *rán,* gift, sale, or payment, was dependent on a host of variables provided by the context, which I will return to in more detail later.

Some of the social complexity that attended exchanges and the uniqueness of some of the saga evidence can be discerned in the cases that follow. In them the parties were forced to deal with each other outside the regularized convivial channels and outside the boundaries of a place clearly designated as a marketplace. The context, in other words, didn't normalize the appropriate mode of exchange and it was up to the parties to define the nature of their transaction. At times the pressing need of famine and hay shortage brought them together, at times the desire for a specific prestige good, like fine horses or fine swords, and at times the demands of liability in law and feud. The cases are remarkable in their detail, and they reveal how difficult it might be, in the absence of a market economy and its accompanying mercantile assumptions, to transact without ill-feeling. In the jargon of economists, the transaction costs were high. We find that the completion of a transaction did not depend on the determination of a mutually acceptable price, but rather on the determination of the mode in which the transfer, if there was to be one, would take place. We also see that there was a resistance to transfers by sale between members of the same social rank. The cases presented do not give a total picture of exchange in Iceland, but by discussing those cases that gave rise to trouble, I hope to get a view of certain essences that, to some extent, informed all transactions. The cases that follow show members of the *bóndi* class dealing with each other explicitly about goods and my conclusions are limited by the limitations of the cases. The probabilities of possible outcomes varied with variations in the relative status of the principals and with the subject of the exchange. Different issues attended the transfer of women in marriage or of land than the transfer of movable goods. Still, despite their limitations, the cases are useful in suggesting the extraordinary amount of social and practical knowledge that was needed to negotiate the hazards imposed by the nervous competitiveness that informed so much social interaction. What appear to us as simple exchanges, as for instance a purchase of hay, were hard to keep simple. The concern with adjustments of relative social ranking, with prestige and honor, kept intruding.

## Case I: Food and Feud

The facts below are a summary of a failed transaction and the consequences of its failure, as recorded in *Njáls saga* (chapters 47–51). These events represent the initial phase of a dispute that expanded into a complex and bitter feud. It will lead to the death of Otkel and his close kin and to the death of Gunnar as well.

Gunnar Hamundarson is a *bóndi* and a great warrior; he keeps good kinship; he is a loyal friend and generous too. Although not a chieftain, he is looked to as the leader of his own formidable kin group and as a big man in the district in which he lives. Because of famine conditions and his own generosity, Gunnar runs short of hay and food. He seeks out Otkel Skarfsson, a wealthy farmer, who is apparently well stocked in spite of the famine. Gunnar offers to buy hay and food from Otkel. Following the counsel of his friend Skammkel, who is described as ill-willed, a liar, and also unpleasant to deal with, Otkel refuses to sell and also refuses Gunnar's request for a gift. Tempers start to get hot among the members of both parties but nothing comes of the encounter, except that Otkel offers to sell Gunnar a slave, which he buys. The slave falls well short of contemporary standards of merchantability, but Otkel makes no effort to inform Gunnar of the slave's defects (*Njála* 47: 120–22).

Later in the summer, while Gunnar is attending the Allthing, Hallgerd, his wife, orders the slave to steal enough butter and cheese from Otkel's farm to load two horses and to burn the storehouse so that no one will suspect a theft. Gunnar returns to discover the theft, knowledge of which Hallgerd does not try to keep from him (48: 122–24). Eventually it becomes general knowledge, and Gunnar decides to make an offer of compensation to Otkel. Otkel, again heeding Skammkel's counsel, refuses several very generous offers of settlement (49: 127), choosing instead ultimately to summon Hallgerd for theft and Gunnar for illicit use of another's property (50: 129–30). Once at the Allthing the lawsuit never gets off the ground, because Otkel's supporters abandon him. Gunnar is granted self-judgment and ends up judging himself absolved of all liability (51: 132).

We are never told why Gunnar initially sought out Otkel, but it can be assumed that the state of Otkel's stores was not unknown. The saga describes the encounter thus:

> Gunnar then summoned Kolskegg [his brother], Thrain Sigfusson [his mother's brother], and Lambi Sigurdarson [a first cousin] to go with him on a journey. They traveled to Kirkjuby and called Otkel out. He greeted them and Gunnar took the greeting well.
>
> "It so happens," said Gunnar, "that I have come to ask to buy hay and food from you, if there's some available."
>
> "There's both," said Otkel, "but I will sell you neither."
>
> "Will you give it to me then," said Gunnar, "and leave it open as to how I'll reward you?"
>
> "I don't wish to do that," said Otkel (Skammkel was contributing bad counsel).
>
> Thrain Sigfusson said, "It'd be fitting if we took it and left what it was worth in its place."
>
> "The Mosfell men will have to be dead and gone," said Skammkel, "before you Sigfussons [Gunnar's kin group] will be able to plunder them."

"I won't take part in a raid," said Gunnar.
"Do you want to buy a slave from me?" said Otkel.
"I won't refuse to," said Gunnar. He bought the slave
and then they went on their way. (47:121–22)

The passage shows the parties raising three ways of transferring
the food and fodder: (1) sale for a price; (2) gift with the prospect of
a return gift in the future; and (3) *rán* with an immediate return
dictated by the taker. All three modes are rejected. Otkel does not
want to sell or give and Gunnar does not want a *rán* even though
supporters of both principals were willing to agree on this mode.
Skammkel, in fact, by doubting the ability of Gunnar and his companions to succeed in a violent taking, is challenging them to do so
and thereby accepting Thrain's "offer" to raid.

Just why the transaction failed is complicated and requires a
rather full discussion, but several propositions can be dismissed at
the outset. Otkel did not refuse Gunnar's requests because he feared
inadequate compensation. There is absolutely no discussion about
price here. And to object that there would be no point in discussing
price because in famine times the value of food reaches infinity
in relation to noncaloric money substances[20] does not account for
Otkel's lack of concern later when he hears about the fire and loss
of food (48:123): "He took the loss well and said that it probably
happened because the storehouse was so near the kitchen." Otkel
is not worried about depleting his own supplies. Something else
is motivating him, and it is not merely a matter of Skammkel's
malice, although, at one level, this is what the author apparently
would have us believe. Otkel is also the recipient of much good
counsel from his brother Hallbjorn, but he chooses to reject it
(49–50:127–30).[21]

When Gunnar arrives at Kirkjuby, he calls Otkel out. This is the
usual procedure and it gives no occasion for insult (see *G.dýri*
12:184). Otkel's greeting and Gunnar's friendly acceptance of it
show as much. Gunnar gets to the purpose of his visit immediately
by asking to buy hay and food. The quickness with which the request is made indicates that Gunnar does not wish to stay; he is not
a seeker of hospitality. The haste could have been motivated by a
desire to signal his own sense of social superiority or by polite concern not to impose himself and his followers without having first
been invited. Either interpretation implies a sense of social distance,
one benign and one less so. Otkel's reading of Gunnar's motivation
would have depended on the accompanying manipulation of other
codes of sociability, like body language, the significance of visits at

certain times of the day or seasons of the year, the number of companions, how they are dressed, the arms they bear, and their relationship to the principal, among many other things.

Each party appears to misread the other's intentions. Gunnar's expedition is not as hostile as Otkel suspects it might be, and Otkel is not as amenable to supplying him with food as Gunnar thinks he will be. This may account for Gunnar construing Otkel's remark—"there's both, but I will sell you neither"—as a hint to ask for a gift, that is, as an indication of hostility to selling rather than hostility to him. Or it may be that the proper protocol for asking for a gift is to proceed by asking first to buy. There is evidence to suggest that was indeed the case.[22] Either way, the shift from the idiom of buying and selling to the language of gift-exchange is not a euphemistic way of discreetly haggling over price. It is an attempt to define the social significance of the transfer by negotiating the mode of exchange; at issue is the quality of relations between the parties, not price.

Otkel clarifies, or perhaps first formulates, his position when he refuses to make a gift. Relations have now been established between the groups and they are hostile. Otkel's refusal to transfer voluntarily threatens to turn Gunnar's trip to no account. Such fruitless expeditions are, everywhere in the sagas, sources of humiliation (e.g., *Gísli* 27:88; *Heið.* 27:296; *Vápn.* 17:58)[23] and humiliations create debts that demand repayment. This is why Thrain urges a forceful taking and why Hallgerd later will connive a taking of her own. By refusing to transfer food, Otkel chooses to transfer insult instead. And that will be repaid. The two groups will henceforth engage in unsociable transactions, exchanging lawsuits and killings. These are not exchanges of intangibles. Legal actions, arbitrations, and killing are invariably accompanied by property transfers, whether as compensation awards and wergeld payments,[24] confiscations pursuant to outlawry judgments, or raids. Such are the reciprocities of the bloodfeud.

Otkel does not look especially admirable in this dealing. Merely to be possessed of plenty in famine times is grounds for suspicion as to character. But elsewhere Otkel is capable of generosity; he does not deny gifts and hospitality to everyone (47:121, 52:133). Something in the transaction itself or in the identity of the would-be purchaser provokes the refusal to transfer food. Consider the events from Otkel's point of view. Otkel and Gunnar, though they reside in the same district, are not mentioned as having had any relations prior to the present incident. No ties of kinship or affinity bind them or any members of their kin groups. But Gunnar's request forces the parties to establish relations that will extend beyond this one occasion unless Otkel is willing to deal in the buy/sell mode, where obligation is specific as to amount and time, and future dealings are not intended unless explicitly agreed to. Once Gunnar initiates the dealings, Otkel cannot refuse to deal without insulting the other party. A refusal to sell or give might be taken as a challenge to take forcefully; and it was so construed by Gunnar's uncle Thrain. The three men accompanying Gunnar are at all times a potential raiding party.[25] Gunnar seems to have anticipated Otkel's anxieties. He limited his entourage well below the saga norm of six to twelve, trying to avoid the aura of intimidation that a larger party would bring with it. Gunnar's sensitivity about the size of his party suggests a general knowledge of the intimations of insult, intimidation, and violence that attached to going to another's home uninvited. People were sensitive, and not without reason, about groups of men approaching their farmhouses.[26] If Otkel were a fisherman at a fishing station, Gunnar's arrival would be regularized and insignificant, but Otkel is not a dealer in foodstuffs.

Otkel is not alone among reluctant sellers in the sagas. Accounts are uniform in showing parties who have been approached to sell goods to be defensive about what they perceive as aggressive acts.[27] And would-be buyers are only too ready to confirm their fears.[28] In *Sturlu saga* (25:98–99) a request to buy food is made specifically for the purpose of harassing the other party. The refusal is not only anticipated but wished for so as to provide the pretext for even more aggressive action (see also *Íslend.* 32:261–62). An earlier phase of the same case reveals that a completed purchase need not spell the end of tensions. A *bóndi* who sold Sturla's son some wormy meal was given the choice of being summoned or of fostering another of Sturla's sons (*Sturla* 25:98). The *bóndi* chose the latter. Forced fostering as a means of reprisal evidences a keen sense of the symbolic and ironic possibilities inherent in the transfer of food: calories could be "purchased" just as well by transporting gaping maws to the food as by bringing the food to the maw. These cases illustrate that the ominous significances of attempts to buy were available to disputants to be consciously manipulated in the strategies of the disputing process.

Gunnar's failed attempt to buy hay and food ends up, strangely, with Otkel offering to sell Gunnar an extra mouth to feed, a slave whom Gunnar buys. The slave had already been an object of exchange at the chapter's start. Melkolf the slave was originally a chattel of Otkel's brother Hallbjorn. Otkel, however, "asked to buy the slave from his brother; he said he would give him the slave, but added that the slave was not the treasure Otkel thought him to be"

(47:121). The episode is included for no other reason than to invite comparison with Otkel's sale of the slave to Gunnar. The plot only requires the sale of a slave to Gunnar, not the prior transfer of that slave to Otkel. The comparison between Hallbjorn and Otkel as sellers is easy and obvious. One volunteers the commodity's defects, the other conceals them. Hallbjorn, in fact, refuses to sell the slave, choosing to give him away instead. By giving rather than selling, he intends several things: he leaves the return entirely to the estimation that Otkel will make of the slave's value at some unspecified later date; he announces his own low estimation of the slave's value; and he attempts to absolve himself of all liability for the slave's quality. The vignette illustrates how context-specific the significance of a particular mode of exchange is. In this instance, giving rather than selling is a statement of the worthlessness of the object transferred and not much else. No reason is provided for why Gunnar is willing to purchase the slave at a time he is having trouble provisioning his own household. Presumably, his action is intended to patch over the hostility that has already surfaced; at the least he does not wish to exacerbate tensions by refusing Otkel's offer.

In a nice ironic turn it is the slave who is the means by which food gets transferred from Otkel to Gunnar; it is he who carries out Hallgerd's command to steal the food from Otkel and burn his storehouse. Theft, in Iceland and elsewhere in early Germania, was a contemptible deed, sharing with murder (the unannounced killing) the shame of secretiveness. Even the good-for-nothing Melkolf must be threatened with death before he will steal (48:123). The successful theft is not within the system of reciprocities.[29] Unlike *rán*, its secretiveness prevents reprisal and, as such, denies all social relation between the parties to the exchange. But Hallgerd is not completely secretive about the theft. She ostentatiously lets Gunnar know about it in front of visitors, proud that she has avenged her husband's humiliation.[30] Once the theft becomes general knowledge, it prompts another attempt at exchange between Gunnar and Otkel. Gunnar again rides to Kirkjuby and indicates his willingness to compensate Otkel for the losses he has suffered. This time, however, Gunnar is accompanied by eleven others, and we may presume that the significance of the increase in numbers was not lost on Otkel. As before Gunnar calls Otkel out and as before Otkel and his companions greet him. Then the following negotiations take place, and they hold the clue as to why Otkel refused Gunnar's requests in their first encounter (49:126–27):

> Otkel asked where Gunnar was traveling to. "No further than here," said Gunnar. "My purpose is to tell you

that the terrible damage that occurred here was caused by my wife and the slave I bought from you."

"That was predictable," said [Otkel's brother] Hallbjorn.

Gunnar said, "I wish to make a good offer: I propose that the men of the district decide the matter."

Skammkel said, "That sounds good, but it's not fair; you are popular with the farmers and Otkel is unpopular."

"I will propose this," said Gunnar. "I will judge the case myself and conclude the issue right here: I offer my friendship [see chapter 3, n. 47] and, in addition, I will pay you a twofold compensation and discharge it all now."

Skammkel said, "Don't take it. That would be demeaning if you were to grant him self-judgment when you should have it."

Otkel said, "I won't give you self-judgment, Gunnar."

Gunnar said, "I notice here the counsel of those who will eventually get their just deserts. Anyway, judge yourself then."

Otkel leaned toward Skammkel and asked, "How should I answer now?"

Skammkel answered, "Call it a good offer, but submit your case to Gizur and Geir; then many will say that you are like your father's father, Hallkel, who was the greatest of warriors."

Otkel said, "That's a good offer, Gunnar, but, still, I want you to give me the time to meet with Gizur and Geir."

Gunnar said, "Have it your way, but some would say that you can't see where your honor lies if you don't accept the opportunity I have offered you."

This passage offers a nutshell exposition of the procedures for reaching a settlement without going to law and for determining payment (damages) after possession has been transferred. But just like the earlier negotiations over the purchase of food, these also break down. Here too price is not at issue, although Gunnar mistakes the rejection of his offer to submit the dispute to the arbitration of the local farmers as expressing such a concern. This is why, it seems, his next offer stipulates double compensation. The rejection of this offer turns on the significance of letting Gunnar articulate the terms of the award by conferring on himself the right of self-judgment. The issue is not money, but prestige and honor. And when Otkel, following Skammkel's advice, postpones accepting Gunnar's very generous offer to let Otkel judge the dispute, it is clear that the dispute is no longer about the value of hay and food at all, but about competition for power and prestige in the district. In this context Skammkel's advice is right. Otkel gains no prestige if Gunnar freely grants the power of self-judgment. Units of prestige would only be transferred if Otkel were to force Gunnar to offer self-judgment, or if Gunnar's offer were motivated by fear that Otkel could force it from him and not by impatient irritation to be done with the matter.

In Skammkel's *sotto voce* advice we can ascertain the reasons for Otkel's earlier refusal to sell and present refusal to settle. Skammkel's reference to Otkel's paternal grandfather, Hallkel, the great warrior, notes a falling-off in Otkel's lineage from the previous generations. We learn from another source that Hallkel, in fact, acquired his reputation by being rather particular about modes of exchange (*Land.* 389 : 388). (He had thought it cowardly to accept a gift of land from his half-brother and preferred instead to challenge another settler to a duel for his claim). Skammkel's comment suggests that Otkel is moved by a concern to reestablish the status his lineage once had in the district. There would be no better way to accomplish this than to be known as the person who had bested the great warrior Gunnar. It is significant that Skammkel appends the reference to Hallkel to his counsel to turn the matter over to Gizur and Geir. Both these men are chieftains and both are Otkel's patrilateral second cousins. The message to Gunnar is unmistakable. Otkel wishes to expand the dispute beyond the two households now involved. Nothing could be more suitable to Otkel's agenda than to take political advantage of Hallgerd's disgraceful act. The theft provides a perfect opportunity to humiliate Gunnar, just as Gunnar's shortage of supplies had provided earlier. Otkel does not mean to lose this opportunity and so chooses to initiate legal action against Hallgerd and Gunnar (50 : 129–30).[31] This can be his only motive, since in terms of the dispute as narrowly conceived—that is, as a case of reparation for theft and fire—there was little more Otkel could realistically achieve once Gunnar offered him self-judgment. Gunnar's status and popularity were such that it would have been virtually impossible for the prosecutors to have obtained an outlawry judgment against either him or his wife.

Gunnar's knowledge of Otkel's purpose is revealed in the terms of his self-judged award delivered later at the Allthing in the wake of Otkel's failure to muster sufficient support for the theft case. "This is my judgment: . . . I determine that you summoned me in order to libel me and I assess that to be no less in value than the storehouse and everything that was burned within it" (51:132). The lawsuit was an insult, and the insult, significantly, ends up being valued in terms of food. As for the theft, that is judged to be a *quid pro quo* for the faithless sale of the slave: "I will not compensate you for the slave's acts since you concealed his defects; but I adjudge him to be returned to you, because ears look best where they grew" (51:132).

The impediments and difficulties that seem to attach to the transfer of food and hay contrast rather drolly with how easily property in humans is transferred. Melkolf, the slave, was the subject of a gift, a sale, a payment pursuant to an arbitration award, and even a *rán*. His Celtic name (Melkolf is cognate with Malcolm, OIr Mael-coluim), coupled with the brief notice that Hallbjorn brought him to Iceland, makes it highly probable that he was introduced into the stream of commerce as the spoil of a Viking raid.

Up to now the discussion has focused on the principals, to the exclusion of uninvolved third parties. Skammkel has told us that Otkel is unpopular with the farmers in the district, but we are not certain if this is the consequence of his hoarding in this famine or of a cumulation of past unpleasantnesses. But Otkel's refusal to sell elicits unambivalent comment and direct action by others. Thus Gunnar's friend Njal to his wife Bergthora (47:122):

> "It's reprehensible to refuse to sell to Gunnar. There is no hope for others there if people like Gunnar can't obtain anything."
>
> "Why do you need to talk so much about it?" said Bergthora. "It would be more manly to share food and hay with him since you are short on neither."
>
> Njal said, "That's absolutely right; I shall provide him with something." He went up to Thorolfsfell with his sons. There they loaded fifteen horses with hay and five with food. Njal arrived at Hlidarendi and called Gunnar out. Gunnar welcomed him well. Njal said, "Here is hay and food I want to give to you. I don't want you ever to seek out anyone other than me if you are in need."
>
> "Your gifts are good," said Gunnar, "but the friendship of you and your sons matters even more."
>
> After that Njal went home.

If Gunnar had a friend nearby with full stores, why did he choose instead to turn to a stranger? One reason can be fairly deduced from the saga. At this time the wives of Gunnar and Njal were embroiled in a bitter feud; they had been exchanging the killing of slaves, servants, and other household members over the course of the previous decade. The strong friendship between the husbands managed to keep the dispute within compensable limits, but there were still unsettled scores, and dealings between the households, even between Gunnar and Njal, needed to be handled with delicate circumspection. Gunnar did not wish to upset this balance by asking for a gift; nor was Njal ready to offer a gift, unasked for, without the consent of his wife, who had nothing but hatred for Gunnar's household. Only in an Icelandic family saga, where terseness is a way of life as well as a matter of prose style, could Njal be accused of talking too much after such a brief indulgence in sententiousness. But his wistful lament ("There is no hope for others . . . "), by design I think, gets Bergthora's consent to a gift he wishes to make by annoying her into suggesting it herself.

Both Njal and Bergthora invoke norms of proper behavior in this discussion. Njal condemns Otkel ("it is reprehensible to refuse to sell"), Bergthora exhorts Njal ("it is manly to share"). One is not merely the obverse of the other. Njal's statement refers to selling; it implies that Otkel was under no obligation to give, but that he was under some moral constraint to sell to someone to whom he was not otherwise obligated. Bergthora's statement, addressed to a friend of Gunnar, speaks of gifts, not sales. The sociable thing to do with food and hay during a famine when a friend is in need is to give, provided "you are short on neither," and when solicited by members of the general community, to honor requests to purchase.[32]

## Case II: The Politics of *rán*

The second case is from *Hœnsa-Þóris saga* (chapter 5). Blund-Ketil is a wealthy and popular farmer. One summer when the hay yield is very poor, he has his tenants pay their rent in hay and then advises them how many animals they should slaughter in order to get their remaining stock through the winter. The tenants, it turns out, do not kill as many animals as they were instructed to and by midwinter they are in desperate need. Three of them ask Blund-Ketil for hay; he shares out some and slaughters forty horses of his own to make more available (*Hœn.* 1:5, 4:11−13). When still more tenants ask for hay, Blund-Ketil refuses. He suggests instead that they see Hen-Thorir, who is rumored to have hay to sell. The tenants ask Blund-Ketil to accompany them because they anticipate that Thorir will not sell to them unless Blund-Ketil acts as their surety (5:13). The tenants, it seems, may have already been indebted to Thorir, since "he had loaned large amounts at interest to just about everyone" (1:6).

Hen-Thorir is wealthy and unpopular. He acquired his wealth by "selling in one district what he bought in another." His having peddled hens on one occasion earned him his nickname as well as a profit. He bought land near Blund-Ketil and continued to make money by lending to the farmers of the district. He also undertook to foster Helgi, the son of Arngrim the chieftain, and assigned the boy half his property in return for Arngrim's support. This meant debts owed to Thorir got paid, and "he became the richest of men" (1–2:6–7). The following takes up at the point Blund-Ketil has entered Thorir's house after Thorir would not come out in response to Blund-Ketil's request.

"We're here because we want to buy hay from you, Thorir," said Blund-Ketil.

Thorir answered, "Your money is no better than mine."

Blund-Ketil said, "That depends on your point of view."

Thorir asked, "Why are you short on hay, rich man?"

Blund-Ketil said, "Actually, I'm not short on hay, but I am asking to buy it for my tenants who need some help. I would gladly get some for them if there is any."

"You are entitled to give your things to others, but not my things."

Blund-Ketil replied, "We are not asking for gifts; let Odd and Arngrim determine the price on your behalf and I will give you gifts on top of that."

Thorir said he did not have hay to sell and "anyway, I don't want to sell."

[Blund-Ketil and his men went out and took inventory of Thorir's livestock and hay reserves and determined there was a five stack surplus.] They went back in and Blund-Ketil said, "About your hay situation: it seems to me that you will have a good amount left over though all your animals were barn fed until the Allthing, and I want to buy that amount."

Thorir said, "What shall I have next winter if there's another one like this one, or worse?"

Blund-Ketil answered, "I make these terms: to provide you with the same amount of hay in the summer no worse in quality and to transport it to your enclosure."

"If you do not have hay now," said Thorir, "what do you expect to have in the summer? But I know that there is such a difference of power between us that you will take the hay from me if you want."

Blund-Ketil said, "That is not the way to go about it.
You know that silver pays any debt in this land and I will
give you that for the hay."

"I don't want your silver," said Thorir.

"Then take such wares [i.e., *vaðmál*] as Odd and Arngrim determine on your behalf."

"There are few workmen here," said Thorir, "nor am I
inclined to travel and I don't want to be bothered with
such things. . . . "

[Blund-Ketil conceded all of Thorir's objections regarding transporting the payment, place of payment, wrap-
ping the wares, and where they would be housed, all to
no avail.]

Blund-Ketil said, "Things will get worse then; we will
have the hay all the same, though you say no, but we
will leave the price in its place and take advantage of the
fact that we outnumber you."

Then Thorir was silent and he was not in a good
mood. Blund-Ketil had rope fetched and the hay bound
up; they packed it on the horses and took it away . . .
(5 : 14–16)

The saga chooses to make this a black and white case. Thorir is
evil and mean-spirited; Ketil is nobleminded and munificent. We apparently are not supposed to be troubled by the fact that Blund-
Ketil takes his rents in hay. To give his actions their most benign
gloss, they are less a simple expropriation of his tenants than part of
a pooling arrangement, undertaken in distressing times to better
handle shortages of small producing units (see Sahlins 1972, 188–
89). But even then it does not appear that there was a complete reciprocity of benefit; Blund-Ketil benefited considerably more from the
arrangement than did his tenants. The saga has a moral to tell that
does not depend on the extraction of surpluses from small farmers,
since to the writer that is neither good nor evil, but rather on who
extracts them and whether he is good or evil. Blund-Ketil's patience,
his refusal to take offense, and Thorir's mean-spirited hostility approach the allegorical (Andersson 1967, 115–21). Yet this exemplum
of patience, in contrast to traditional hagiographic material, does
not deal with the temptation of the spirit or the suffering of the flesh
but with the painfulness of trying to conclude a bargain with a reluctant seller, who in this exemplum takes on the role of a petty
devil. Unlike Gunnar, who abandoned his attempt to purchase in
the face of a refusal to sell, Blund-Ketil perseveres, conceding any
point Thorir puts forth as an obstacle to agreement. There is no

question here of treating the refusal to sell as an invitation to ask for a gift. Instead it is Blund-Ketil who offers gifts as an inducement to Thorir to accept Blund-Ketil's generous offer to have the price determined by Thorir's patron, Arngrim, and Blund-Ketil's enemy, Odd. But Thorir wants Blund-Ketil's gifts no more than his money. In fact, Thorir, hardly a stranger to trade and haggling, does not use the famine as an occasion to exact exorbitant prices. Although a hoarder, Thorir is singularly unconcerned about price. Money is not an impersonal commodity to him; he prefers his own to Blund-Ketil's: "your money is no better than mine";[33] nor is he able to conceive that a transfer of possession by sale extinguishes his rights and person in the goods: "you are entitled to give your things to others but not my things."

These responses do not suggest the sensibility of the marketplace, nor much interest in profit either.[34] In Thorir's estimation, since what Blund-Ketil would pay him would be the value of the hay and nothing more, why not keep the hay? However mistakenly, Blund-Ketil construes Thorir's initial reticence as a disagreement over price. Price was much constrained by the force of customary equivalences or by annual price schedules determined at the Things (Gelsinger 1981, 36–44; Jóhannesson 1974, 320–22). And this helps explain the indirection of Blund-Ketil's offer to pay more: that is, to let the issue of price be submitted to the arbitration of two chieftains partial to Thorir and to add gifts on top of that. There are two things to note about this offer, both of which indicate that it is an attempt to shift the transaction to familiar and more regularized structures: (1) chieftains (goðar) claimed the power to set prices on imports—referring the matter to them would be an easy analogical extension of this chieftain prerogative to include local goods;[35] (2) for face-to-face dealing, the stuff of trade, the offer substitutes a model of dispute resolution, the stuff of law and feud—an especially attractive model because it was not only familiar, but more appropriate to station than haggle. The issue of price, as we shall see, could be dealt with directly by bargaining, but it is remarkable how quickly the issue is euphemized or mooted by shifting to the structures and idiom of gift-exchange, or how it is "legalized" by shifting to the structures and language of law or arbitration. Blund-Ketil's offer to submit the price to arbitration transforms the wished-for exchange in much the same way his rán will: both move the exchange from trade and bargain to courts and feud.

The rapidity with which Thorir rejects Blund-Ketil's offers, coming up with a new excuse each time, makes all Thorir's reasons look contrived. It would be easier to believe his concern about depleting his hay reserves in anticipation of bad yields the next year if this were his only objection, or if it were even feasible to store hay for more than a year and a half in a damp climate without silos. In this regard consider Arngrim's comment to Thorir later: "The hay which he took will have a better end than that which *rots* with you" (6:17). Yet, in spite of their bad faith, Thorir's objections are instructive. They show how difficult it could be to negotiate a sale where the means of payment and units of account had to be hashed out (that is, whether it would be in hay, silver, or ells of woolen cloth); where the quality of the means of payment had to be determined (also *Ljós.* 13:23), and where, if payment was to be made in hay or cloth, the place and time of delivery of the payment (see *Vall.* 6:248–49), and the means of transporting it and of protecting it from damp and mildew had to be stipulated (*Hœn.* 5:16). Did these stumbling blocks help push the parties to modes of transfer, like gifts and raids, in which possession passed immediately and the noisome details of requital were postponed and left to the discretion of one of the parties or to the judgment of arbitrators?

Thorir's refusal to sell is attributed by the saga writer to his character defects. Thorir's sensibilities are so calloused that it is unlikely that he took the request to buy as an insult to his newly acquired landowning status. On its surface the saga makes his malignity purely motiveless; he is a true villain. And it may be that this is all there is to it. Yet if he had a motive, it lies in this: we saw in the preceding case that offers to buy made at the home of the owner were not neutral acts. They carried with them an implied threat, which could be ignored if the parties chose to gloss over the inherent tenseness of the situation with politenesses and courtesies. But if a party wished to engender dispute he need not do much to get one going. The situation was rife with evil possibility. Thorir must have suspected that the outcome of his surly refusals might well be a *rán*, and he proceeded knowing that this was a risk his manner entailed. It was he, in fact, who first raised the possibility of a forceful taking: "But I know there is such a difference of power between us that you will take the hay from me if you want" (5:15). He wished to define a formal hostile relationship with Blund-Ketil for reasons the saga does not give us. Resentment of Blund-Ketil's prestige and wealth is a likely candidate: "Why are you short on hay, *rich man?*" (5:14). And Thorir judged that his position vis-à-vis Blund-Ketil would be improved if Blund-Ketil were provoked into leaving behind a cause of action for full outlawry (*Grágás* Ib 164), rather than just the purchase price of some hay or nothing at all (see also *Kristni saga* 8:15). The definition of relations was accomplished by simply shifting the mode of exchange from barter and trade to raid.

*Rán* does not deny reciprocity. This is openly admitted in this case and is suggested in the previous one by the willingness to leave behind a consideration. Otherwise a forceful taking invited reciprocity in the form of a reprisal or a lawsuit.[36] Blund-Ketil endured all three: he left behind a price, he was summoned for an outlawry action, and he was burned in his house (8–9:21–24). Having given value for the expropriated goods did not absolve Blund-Ketil of legal liability for the *rán*; state of mind was not an element of the formal legal action (*Grágás* Ib 164). But this did not mean that Blund-Ketil's intentions were without significance. The payment gave concrete representation to a lack of hostile intention and it thereby worked to subvert reprisal by undermining the moral basis of any future claim Thorir might make, since the lack of justice in Thorir's cause would appreciably affect his ability to recruit support for any legal action. Blund-Ketil almost succeeded. Thorir's patron Arngrim denied him support, as did Blund-Ketil's enemy Odd, who in fact said he would have done the same as Blund-Ketil. But Thorir is able to purchase the support of Odd's son, Thorvald, and it turns out that this was all he needed (6:18; 7:20–21).

The justifiability of Blund-Ketil's *rán* is somewhat more problematic than the saga's partisan account would have us believe. Even within the saga, contrary normative statements appear. Alongside Arngrim's statement cited above—"The hay which he took will have a better end than that which rots with you"—is Thorvald Oddason's "Each is entitled to control his own" (7:20). And though it might have been reprehensible to refuse to sell to such men as Gunnar and Blund-Ketil, men like them were aware that forceful taking was not any more sociable; they were reluctant raiders if they raided at all.[37] The "people" also seemed to have had conflicting sentiments about the matter. The issue of compulsory transfers of hay from those who had surpluses to those who were in need was squarely faced on a national level in 1281 with the introduction into Iceland of the Norwegian law code known as *Jónsbók*. In the new code the *Grágás* rule that protected the owner's right to dispose of his hay as he wished was replaced by a rule providing for forced sales at the customary rate. If the sale was resisted, the owner was to be fined, the hay taken without payment, and any injuries he received defending were to be uncompensable (*Jónsbók* 139–40, c.12). One source mentions that the provision was opposed by the bishop and *bœndr*, which must mean those farmers who could count on having surpluses, that is those *bœndr* who like the bishop had access to tithes.[38] The cases we are dealing with suggest that some of the hostility to mandating forced sales might have been not only because they were forced but because they were sales. People wished to control their surpluses, not only to take profits, but to control with whom they dealt and on what terms. There is no way of determining how widespread the antipathy to the new rule was. The "people" were also quite capable of expressing sympathy for those who took when necessity compelled them to. In 1243, when Thord kakali and his company were outlawed for *rán* for having helped themselves to a meal of whipped milk against the owner's will, the community was outraged by the excessiveness of the response (*Þórð.* 7:14, 15:30). But in this instance the community had to content itself with outrage since the power of the prosecutor was more than sufficient to vindicate the letter of the law without regard to the popularity of the cause.

We also learn later that Blund-Ketil, like Gunnar in the previous case, had a friend close by who was well stocked and would have been more than willing to give hay and pasturage to Blund-Ketil (10:26–27). There is no hint of any troubles between the friends' households as there was between Gunnar's and Njal's. The saga does not mention why Blund-Ketil did not seek out his friend. Blund-Ketil proposed seeing Thorir because he heard that Thorir had hay to sell. Thorir's farm was only two miles away from Blund-Ketil's, while the friend lived about fourteen miles away. But the difference in distance, by saga standards, was insufficient in itself to determine the course of conduct. Both were near enough to qualify as neighbors. Some significance should attach to the fact that Blund-Ketil was asking for his tenants rather than in his own right; for them, he might not have been as willing to exhaust the credits he had established with his friends and relations.

Blund-Ketil's reticence about turning to friends when in need adds a new wrinkle to the riskiness of requests to transfer material wealth from one household to another. There are cases which suggest that the existence of prior obligations of mutual aid did not make the situation any less touchy than it was when dealing with so many Otkels and Thorirs. One's affines could also be reluctant suppliers. For example, when Bardi Gudmundarson sought out his wife's father for supplies to maintain forces to protect himself against a vengeance expedition, his father-in-law disclaimed the duty (*Heið.* 32:311). Bardi immediately declared himself divorced; he also refused to release his wife's marital property, substituting, in effect, a *rán* of his wife for a gift from her father.[39] In a similar case with a happier ending, Steinthor went to his sister's husband to request either a gift or sale of supplies ("I had wondered whether Atli would give or sell me some provisions?" *Háv.* 15–16:343–45). The request in the alternative points up the uncertainty as to the least offensive mode to adopt. Steinthor's sister obliged the request with a gift, but her husband objected, claiming the transfer was a *rán*. The wife's sexual ministrations eventually persuaded the husband to reclassify the transaction as a gift. In these instances the shortages were created by a sudden increase in mouths rather than a decrease in yields, and the voluntariness of the shortage may have made these affines more reluctant than usual.

Some of these ambivalences about *rán* reflect nothing more than the opposing positions of takers and possessors, each having a stock of proverbs to help legitimate their claims.[40] The views of the uninvolved about the moral and social significance of *rán*, however, were subtler and they varied with, among other things, the relative status of the principals, the particular motive for the taking, and the degree of urgency motivating the taking. *Rán* arose in different settings. In the cases we have dealt with it was a direct response to a refusal to sell or give in times of shortage and was geared, initially at least, to the acquisition of specific goods. In these instances the sympathies of all but the possessor favored the forced distribution of the surplus. Forced takings motivated simply by a desire to possess another's goods were never well thought of except by the faction benefiting from the dispossession (e.g., *Íslend.* 32:261–62). In the turmoil of the last decades of the commonwealth, *rán* was also undertaken as a way of provisioning forces assembled for battle. Sometimes compensation was awarded for these expropriations pursuant to a settlement between the principals (*G.dýri* 3:165–66); but often farmers had to endure these depredations, even if not so quietly (*Hrafn Sv. St.* 12–13:213–15; *G.dýri* 19:201–2). Elsewhere, *rán* figured primarily as an act of vengeance or self-help, a tactical maneuver, in a dispute already clearly defined (e.g., *Lax.* 19:45–46; *Vápn.* 7:38–40). In many instances the goal was less the acquisition of specific goods than the infliction of damage, material or psychological, on one's adversary. These takings invariably ended up being paid for in some way, either by reprisal or an arbitrated compensation award (*Sturla* 10:75–76, 21–22:91–95; *G.dýri* 17:196, 19:201, 22:206). And as long as such raids were narrowly confined to the disputants, the reaction of the community was no different than it would be for any other move in the feud. Third parties would urge peace and compensation, favoring the side who appeared to have made its actions look more justified than its opponent's.

Our cases show that requests to bear away food were not to be lightly undertaken. Presumably the sensitive seeker of provisions avoided imposing on his friends and affines unless it was absolutely necessary. This meant undertaking expeditions to buy from people not willing to sell. Blund-Ketil and Gunnar thought there was less

to be lost by making an enemy of someone who had not previously
been a friend than to risk destroying a friendship.

## Case III: The Movement of People against Goods

The difficulties encountered in the following case from *Laxdœla
saga* (chapter 37) owe nothing to famine. At issue are four fine
horses. The pattern should by now be familiar, but the case adds
further contour to our discussion. The scene is the Allthing.

> Thorleik was sitting in his booth when a tall man
> entered alone. He greeted Thorleik, who acknowledged
> his greeting and asked him his name and where he was
> from. He said his name was Eldgrim and that he lived at
> Eldgrimsstead in Borgarfjord. . . .
> Thorleik said, "I've heard it said about you that you
> are no weakling."
> Eldgrim said, "What brings me here is that I want to
> buy those costly studhorses from you that Kotkel gave
> you last summer."
> Thorleik answered, "The horses are not up for sale."
> Eldgrim said, "I am offering you the same number of
> studhorses for them plus certain additional items; many
> will say that I'm offering twice the value."
> Thorleik said, "I'm no haggler; and furthermore, you'll
> never get these horses even though you offer three times
> their value."
> "It's no lie to say that you are proud and self-willed,"
> said Eldgrim, "and I would only wish that you get a less
> favorable price than I've just offered you and that you'll
> give up the horses nonetheless."
> Thorleik reddened deeply at these words and said,
> "You will have to get much nearer, Eldgrim, before you
> scare me out of these horses."
> "You do not think it likely that you will be defeated
> by me," said Eldgrim, "but this summer I will come to
> look at the horses and then see which of us chances to
> have them from then on."
> Thorleik said, "Do as you promise, but don't offer me
> a difference in numbers." With that they broke off their
> conversation. Those who heard them said that some-
> thing fitting would come of their dealings. (*Lax.* 37:
> 102–3)

Again, a willing buyer confronts an unwilling seller. Eldgrim's initial offer to buy is rejected by Thorleik, and firmly too: "The horses

are not up for sale." Eldgrim construes the rejection as a bargaining tactic designed to evoke an offer of a higher price. Unlike the would-be buyers in the preceding cases, he faces the issue of price directly by offering to pay double the value of the horses. Thorleik rejects this offer also and in a manner that shows he is irritated at being typed as a "habitual" seller: "I'm no haggler and furthermore you'll never get these horses even though you offer three times their value." This response cuts off Eldgrim's next move in the mercantile mode of exchange by anticipating and rejecting it beforehand. Eldgrim gets the point, but instead of breaking off negotiations completely, he shifts to another mode of exchange. With only slight indirection he offers to take the horses forcefully. In this mode the minds of the parties meet. Thorleik may have been a reluctant seller, but an offer to be raided is a challenge to his manhood that would be dishonorable to refuse. He dares Eldgrim to follow up on his threats, and Eldgrim greets Thorleik's counterchallenge by promising to raid: "This summer I will come to look at the horses and then see which of us chances to have them from then on."

The bargaining and haggling Thorleik found offensive when a sale was being negotiated are acceptable enough when the ground rules of a raid are being hashed out. The issues to be settled are the timing of the raid and the size of the raiding party. Thorleik and Eldgrim reach an agreement on both matters: the raid will be that same summer and Eldgrim will not come in force. We learn about the agreement later from Eldgrim when he comes to take the horses and is held to account by Thorleik's uncle Hrut, who intercepts him in the process of taking Thorleik's horses: "I have fulfilled the promise I made [Thorleik] at the Thing to come for the horses without reinforcements" (37:104). Any dealings between Thorleik and Eldgrim will either be purely mercantile or purely violent. These most unsociable of men are at home in modes of exchange of low sociability. The author, however, takes care to record a notice that the eagerness with which these two agreed to raid was opposed to the community norm. Hence the judgment of the bystanders: "Those who heard them said that something fitting would come of their dealings."

It should not be hard to guess the results the bystanders had in mind. Raiding was dangerous business. Consider the conclusion of Eldgrim's bargain. Hrut questions whether indeed Eldgrim has lived up to his end of the bargain as he claimed. "It's no act of courage to take the horses when Thorleik is lying asleep in his bed. You'll fulfill your agreement better if you visit him before you ride out of the district with the horses" (37:104). Hrut is needling Eldgrim a bit. He is suggesting that Eldgrim looks more like a thief than a *ráns-maðr* ("raider"). Thievery, as noted earlier, is a concealed taking.

Generally it was a nocturnal crime, not of necessity but of convenience. Lack of light assisted its secretiveness and anonymity. Eldgrim is cutting a pretty fine line. He shows up when it is light, which may be more to the credit of the summer sun in northern latitudes than to Eldgrim; but it is so early that people of consequence, namely Thorleik, are asleep. There is something else that casts doubt on the classification of Eldgrim's taking. He is alone. Solitariness was always ground for suspicion. Being alone gave one the option of holding one's counsel and thus the option to be a thief or a murderer, a secret killer. Solitariness was the state to which the outlaw, as well as the kinless and impoverished, was condemned. Only in the rarest of circumstances in the sagas does a man of good character and intention go somewhere alone.[41]

Eldgrim wishes to erase all doubts as to his character and the taking; he tells Hrut to warn Thorleik, accompanying the statement with some martial puffing. Hrut, however, tries to settle matters himself by initiating another exchange. He offers Eldgrim a gift of some of his studhorses, "though not quite as good" (37:104), if Eldgrim will give up the others. Yet this founders also. The offer of the gift is too late. The fact that it is conditioned upon release of the horses Eldgrim already has in hand makes it impossible for Eldgrim to accept without losing face by losing an advantage already realized. Although Hrut couches the offer in the language of gift-exchange, the classification of the transfer is in Eldgrim's view suspect. If it is a gift, it is a gift to the absent Thorleik, not to him.[42] Moreover, the offer was prefaced with a declaration of purpose unambivalently confrontational: "I will not let Thorleik be raided" (37:104). To Eldgrim, the offer is no more than a "threat" and a *mútugjǫf*, a word whose semantic range extends from bribe to barter (Cleasby and Vigfússon 1957, s.v. *mútugjǫf*). Eldgrim's refusal to accept the substitute horses has the unfortunate consequence of attracting Hrut's battle-axe to his back.[43]

There is one last matter about these studhorses. The preceding chapter of *Laxdœla saga* provides a detailed description of their prior transfer to Thorleik. They were originally owned by Kotkel, a troublemaker and recent Hebridean immigrant who came to Thorleik in urgent need of protection (36:101). When Thorleik saw the horses he asked to buy them. Kotkel conditioned their transfer on Thorleik's providing him patronage and a dwelling in the neighborhood as Thorleik's tenant. Thorleik thought this dear, but some flattering words and skillful argumentation by Kotkel, not to mention Thorleik's desire for the animals, ended up with a bargain being struck.

The transfer was accomplished without offense or threat. There are some significant contrasts with the previous cases which suggest why this was the case. For one, Kotkel was a foreigner, someone with whom nonsociable modes of exchange, like buying and selling, were usual and to be expected. For another, Thorleik did not seek out Kotkel in order to buy the horses; Kotkel sought him out. The change of locus changed the meaning of Thorleik's request to buy. Because the meeting was not forced on the owner of the goods it was no great threat to him. Moreover, Thorleik getting in his offer to buy before Kotkel made his request for protection does not alter the identity of the "reluctant seller"; it was not going to be Kotkel, but Thorleik. Because Kotkel came to Thorleik, the transaction would only incidentally be about the price of horses; the negotiations were first and foremost about the creation of bonds of dependence, the procurement of patronage. And it may have been that Thorleik's initial attempt to define the transaction as a purchase of horses was undertaken with the hope of frustrating what he anticipated was Kotkel's purpose in coming. Thorleik had no special desire to become associated with the ill-famed Kotkel. But the return Kotkel demanded for his horses—protection and a lease of land—made it impossible to keep the transaction in the mercantile mode that Thorleik tried to put it in.

It is not very helpful to see this exchange as a bartering of a non-money good against a service, with each party playing the dual roles of buyer and seller. The economic aspect of the transaction is subordinated to the social one. The dealings do not fit the model of idealized market exchange where people transfer goods and services and go their separate ways (Gregory 1980, 641–44). Here two people come together and stay together. The possession of the horses is transferred, but with them comes the prior possessor and his family. The horses are never quite dissociated from Kotkel; they were the first prestation in a bargained-for relation of continuing exchanges. A year later Eldgrim still identified them as "the horses that Kotkel gave you." This need not mean that the horses were a gift; "give" would apply equally well if Kotkel had paid the horses to Thorleik. But it does show that in the opinion of a stranger the horses were not bought or sold.

## Conclusion

Our cases show no offer to buy goods leading to a transfer of them by sale. Apparently everyone knew there was more likelihood of transfer in another mode of exchange, and they negotiated with this in mind. There was thus little time spent bargaining over price, the hasty abandonment of which marked the rejection of the mercantile mode. Resistance to selling led to requests for gifts, offers of gifts from second and third parties, and to open as well as secretive expropriations.

The cases give a strong sense that buying and selling was hostile; it was something one did with those from a distance, either spatial distance, as with Norwegians, or social distance, as with peddlers and hawkers of marginal social status like Hen-Thorir.[44] In any event, it was not something a *bóndi* went to another *bóndi's* house to do without running the risk of misunderstanding and slighted sensibility. Attempts to trade with equals within the community could produce the disturbing results of the preceding cases. This is not to deny that *bœndr* never bought and sold from each other without incident. A brief episode in one saga indicates that a request to purchase seal meat need not occasion any special tensions (*Bjarn.* 19:164). But seals, like fish, raised different issues than hay. Hay was something all were supposed, at least theoretically, to be able provide for themselves. Seals and fish were necessarily unavailable to inland farms unless traded by farms with easy access to sealing areas. Another case recording a successful barter of oxen for horses between two householders is preserved (*Reyk.* 11:177), but the negotiations take place at a neutral site, in the convivial circumstances of a wedding feast to which both parties had been invited. The sources are more likely to record sales that proved to be sources of conflict; yet this should not be pushed too far since frictionless transfers by gift are regularly mentioned, whereas frictionless sales of hay, food, or prestige items between *bœndr* are only rarely noted. It is hard to argue confidently from silence and I do not pretend to confidence here. It may be, of course, that domestic sales were sufficiently unnoteworthy because they were common occurrences, but it's difficult to believe, if they were so common, that they would have failed almost completely to penetrate the saga record at all. The bonds of friendship and neighborhood, it seems, could tolerate an occasional purchase, but the sagas do not show *bœndr* involved in continuous trading activities at home.[45] Such arrangements were regular for trading expeditions abroad,[46] but that is a different issue entirely. Gift-exchange and the structured hostility of the feud, with transfers of compensation and lawsuits, were the preferred means of exchange. It was bad form to seek openly to bear away goods without some attendant mystification. The course of these cases makes this point vividly.

These general statements pertain to only a narrow range of transactions because our case evidence represents a very specific type of transaction: the request to purchase nonmaritime provisions or prestige goods. What the party who initiated the transaction was seeking was crucial to the level of tension and the likelihood of a conflict-free conclusion to the meeting. The sagas, for instance, are filled with descriptions of people coming to another's farm or booth at the Thing seeking marriages or fostering arrangements, support for lawsuits, arbitrations, and vengeance expeditions. To be sure, these transactions could also lead to insult and bitterness, but the impression is that they were distinctly less troublesome, less anxiety-provoking, because they were more familiar and regular than requests for goods.

The comfort of the familiar was obtained when goods moved as an incident to the establishment and maintenance of social relations. Kotkel's horses moved into Thorleik's possession because Thorleik promised Kotkel protection (Case III). Hen-Thorir undertook the fostering of Arngrim's son and transferred property to him in exchange for Arngrim's support (Hœn. 2:7). Njal gave Gunnar gifts of food and hay because that is what friendship meant (Case I). The familiar meant dealing directly in humans and about social ties, and only secondarily in the products of human labor. Social relations meant that human bodies moved between groups for various lengths of time. Marriage and fostering sent live bodies for relatively long periods to other households. Friendship meant bodies went back and forth regularly between households. Even outright purchases of support, a frequent saga practice, represented the transfer of human capital, albeit briefly, from one household to another. And in this regard it is significant that the relationship established by purchases of support were often socialized positively by being formalized as "friendships" (e.g., Hœn. 2:7; Njála 138:367–68: "I wish to give you this ring, Eyjolf, for your friendship and support").[47]

All these relations were characterized by positive or at least neutral sociability. Bodies also moved between households in modes of low sociability, but they were maimed or lifeless. In feud the exchange was in injuries and corpses. But all movements of bodies, living or dead, between households were accompanied by exchanges of goods: by gift and hospitality at the sociable end, by wergeld, compensation, and rán at the other end.

The mercantile mode inverted the relation between goods and bodies. Bodies moved as an incident to the transfer of goods. Buyers and sellers came together only to exchange, preferably at a neutral place designated as a market, after which each returned to his producing unit. The goods, not the buyer and seller, were to be related

to each other, and the relationship was openly expressed as price
(Gregory 1980, 641–44 and 1981, 126–28). This is, of course, an
idealized representation. The mercantile exchanges of two *bœndr*
could never be those of the faceless market. People already knew
about each other, as Thorleik had already heard tell of Eldgrim (Case
III), and they were likely to see each other again. Still, to seek to
exchange by purchase and sale carried with it a message of low sociability that sought to deny accountability by refusing to establish
the social relations that held people to account. Perhaps nothing
confirms the strangeness of mercantile exchange with its inversion
of the relation of goods to bodies more than the fact that the one
good which flowed smoothly in the stream of commerce did so because it mimicked the "right" order by sending bodies to other
households. It was thus much easier to sell Melkolf the slave than
the food needed to feed him. There is even evidence in the laws that
slaves could serve as a means of payment.[48]

A different set of values accompanied the transfer of land, at least
during the period of colonization, although other evidence suggests
these values reflected the attitudes of the twelfth and thirteenth
century, the time in which the sources were written. Whereas gifts
of food and hospitality could be requited with return invitations,
and prestige goods like cloaks, weapons, and fine animals could requite hospitality and each other, a gift of land, it was feared by some,
might indicate a long-term subordination of the recipient and his
successors to the giver and his heirs because nothing but a return
gift of the same land could extinguish the obligation (see, e.g., *Egil*
82:287–88; see also Charles-Edwards 1976, 183). Instead of disfa-
voring the mercantile mode, prospective recipients might try to
shift the classification of the transfer to purchase and sale, or to
expropriatory modes in which the act of taking clearly indicated the
taker's dominance.[49] The social distance of purchase was just what
Steinud the Old wanted:

> Steinud the Old, a kinswoman of Ingolf, went to Iceland
> and stayed with Ingolf the first year. He offered to give
> her Rosmhvalaness . . . , but she gave a spotted cloak for
> it and wished to call it a purchase; it seemed to her there
> would then be less chance of undoing the transfer.
> (*Land.* 394:392)

Others preferred dueling for land as did Otkel's grandfather in Case
I, while some thought it better to be beholden to no one: "Hallstein

Thorolfsson thought it cowardly to accept land from his father and he went west over Breidafjord and took land there" (*Eyrb.* 6:11). But with land as with moveables, what the sources show is concern not about price or discussions of it, but about the classification of the transfer, the mode of exchange.

There is a lesson in Hallstein Thorolfsson's sensitivity in the preceding paragraph. It reveals that no exchange was just a two-party affair. The community passed moral and social judgment on a transaction, allocating in the process honor and prestige between the parties. And if no third parties were there to pass judgment, the principals would hypothesize the judgment anyway. A person risked some part of his reputation in every social interaction, even in exchanges, as we gather from Hallstein, between father and son. All knew that in the process of defining social relations between the parties there would necessarily be an adjustment in the standing of the two relative to each other. And because this adjustment was figured in units of prestige and honor, its effects would also determine the quality of one's relations with others. People cared how the property transfers they were party to were denominated. It was there, not in monetary profit, that honor resided. Consider, for example, these negotiations that take place in a case we will have occasion to discuss in another context. The scene is at the Allthing, and Haflidi is proposing an offer of settlement in his case against Thorgils.

> Haflidi said, "I will give Thorgils the value of eight cows for the sake of his honor and reputation; but I call it a gift and not at all a payment."
> And they could not agree on that because to one it seemed as if there was nothing to pay for and to the other it seemed better to have a small payment for the cause of action than to have to repay a gift. Each thought his honor depended on how it was to be designated and that issue stood in the way so that no settlement was made. With that they parted, each thinking worse of the other than before. (*Hafl.* 15:32)

The skillful participant in exchange was the one who knew how to manipulate the multitude of signs that attended the classification of a transaction to the increase of his honor, not his net worth. The adept players in this game, that is, the honorable men and women, were those who knew whether and when to pay and to pay back, to give and to receive, or to take a thing and leave behind what they thought it was worth. Our cases suggest that they were more likely to exchange goods and services in the forums of dispute processing or in the festive hall, by compensation payment or gift, than in a marketplace or the countryside, by sale and purchase. And whether the exchange was to be by feud or feast was what they bargained over.

CHAPTER FOUR

# Householding Patterns

## Debates and Definitions

In *The Story of Thorstein the Staff-struck* (chapter 2) we were able to observe the intimate connection between alignments of power and influence within the household and the negotiation of power and status between different households. In the preceding chapter we described some of the links connecting householding units into systems of exchange with other householding units. Of all the overlapping solidarities to which a twelfth- and thirteenth-century Icelandic man or woman belonged—kin group, household, neighborhood, Thing-attendance grouping—for the great majority the household had the most immediate significance. Kinship was not far behind and is intimately connected to householding patterns, since co-residents and the class of potential co-residents, as one might expect, were often related by blood or marriage. I have nevertheless decided to treat household and kinship organization serially rather than together, although the kin will necessarily make their share of appearances in any discussion of householding patterns.

The last twenty years have seen a vast amount of literature from historical demographers, social historians, and anthropologists devoted to the "household question," that is, to the demographic features of household organization. Efforts have been made to determine the average number of inhabitants, their generational and age distribution, the number of married or cohabiting couples constituting the household, the effect of inheritance practices, of class, occupation, wealth, etc., on household structure. As is to be expected with a trendy area of academic interest, many points of definition, method, proper scope of subject, and correctness of conclusion are hotly contested. What has emerged as the central point of contention in the field, what has indeed become *the* household question, is the extent, through time and space, of the so-called simple household, that is, the nuclear or conjugal family household. Research associated with the Cambridge Group for the History of Population and Social Structure takes the view that the orthodox assumption that preindustrial families were large and extended was simply wrong for early modern England especially and northwest Europe generally.[1] This work has been very influential and has led some to extend the claim further into the medieval period (see, e.g., Smith 1979).

The extended kin group and large extended households have now been claimed to have given way to the simple household and the nuclear family in every century from the ninth (Hammer 1983, 243–46; but cf. Herlihy 1985, 70–72) to the nineteenth (Degler 1980, 8–9; cf. Kertzer 1989). One marvels at the incredible perseverance of a household form that it took a millennium to kill. I am reminded of the role long played by the "rising middle class" in accounts of historical change from the twelfth to the twentieth century, where at last, according to some, that remarkably tenacious feudal aristocracy bit the dust. What was it about that old aristocracy and that old extended kin group in their crowded and dimly lit extended households that took the middle class and the simple household nearly a thousand years to replace?[2] Whatever the merits of the opposing arguments, one suspects that much of the fuel for the household question, and indeed much of the fuel that kept that middle class rising so long, is ideological (Goody 1983, 24–26). Classical liberals wish to and do discover ever-earlier declines of collectivities and risings of utility-maximizing individuals nurtured in simple households (see, e.g., MacFarlane 1978). Communitarians, usually but not always slightly left of the individualists, wish to find cooperating collectivities the dominant form in early times and, in post-industrial times, to find them heroically reviving, reforming, or remaining in spite of brutal efforts to extirpate them.

Inevitably the attempt was made to add early Iceland to the number of regions that socialized people in nuclear families within simple households (see Jochens 1985, 106). As we shall see, what the sources tell us about the shape of Icelandic householding must compel a different conclusion. The sources, both sagas and laws, are not without their own special problems in this particular topic. For one thing, the laws take an explicit interest in households and even define what constitutes a household unit. But this "juridical" household does not seem to correspond with what archaeological evidence there is, nor with saga descriptions of how the main economic unit, the farm, was populated and managed. Outside the passages in the laws directly dealing with the legal household, information on householding must be culled from passing comments in the laws and sagas and inferred from contexts devoted explicitly to other matters. The fact that most of our information is acquired incidentally is in its way quite reassuring. Even the most committed member of the Icelandic school of saga scholarship would have a hard time giving any reason as to why a thirteenth-century saga writer would want to situate his characters in households that had no basis in reality. But sometimes plot might well interfere with the representations of households, and these instances will be duly noted when they occur. It is also reassuring to note that there is no discernible difference in the picture of householding that emerges from the two main classes of narrative sources. The households of the family sagas look strangely like the households of the *Sturlunga* compilation. Some small consolation might also be obtained from the strong likelihood that there was little, if any, regional variation in householding practices.

Neither laws nor sagas lend themselves to statistical analysis. Because of the smallness of sample size and the nonrandomness of selection, attempts to acquire meaningful statistics on early Icelandic household types would be futile. The sagas, for instance, tend to give relatively dense descriptions of only the wealthier households of chieftains and comfortable farmers. Middling farmers get less attention. But the most serious deficiency of the narrative sources is that they make only the barest mention, with little or no description, of the impoverished households of poor farmers, tenants, and *búðsetumenn* (cottagers).[3] *Thorstein the Staffstruck* (chapter 2) is exceptional in devoting so much attention to a poor farmer, but that farm is presumably considerably more secure than the households of cottagers and tenants. We only see these latter after their households have disintegrated and they have undergone a status change, either being integrated into the households of others as servants or left to wander the countryside as day workers and beggars. The lives of cottagers and tenants are lost to us.

There has been much discussion—most of it inconclusive—as to how to define the household in a manner suitable for comparative purposes (see Berkner 1975; Yanagisako 1979; also Verdon 1980; Netting et al. 1984; Wall 1983a; Hajnal 1983; and Laslett 1983). Certain conventional criteria are not very useful in the Icelandic context, where it appears that a person could be attached to more than one household (cf. Hajnal 1983, 99–100; Laslett 1983, 514), where the laws suggest it was possible for more than one household to be located in the same uncompartmentalized farmhouse, and where household headship might often be shared (cf. Hajnal 1983, 99–100). Definitions, for example, based solely on co-residence or on commensalism (Verdon 1980; Laslett 1983, 515; Hajnal 1983, 99) do not fit very well with the pastoral transhumance practiced by the Icelanders. It would seem that a serviceable definition would have to take account of common production as well as common consumption and residence.

A certain definitional roughness and subjectivity is needed in order to accommodate native categories and conceptions (see Wall 1983a, 35 and 1983b, 423–26), particularly keeping in mind that the precise sense of household might change depending on the context in which it is invoked. A household unit as identified for recruitment to the feud is not the same as the household unit used to determine whether someone qualifies for service on a jury or is required to attach himself to a chieftain for the purposes of Thing attendance. I thus consider a person's household to be where he or she eats, works, and sleeps most of the time and where, even when not sleeping or eating there, he or she is perceived to have some right or duty to do so. This kind of looseness will cause trouble in marginal cases, but it is fairly serviceable nevertheless. It allows for the possibility of multiple household membership, something the ethnographic evidence suggests exists as a matter of fact, but which has often been defined out of existence by categories adopted without much refinement from the census taker (Berkner 1975); it also takes better account of the demands of the native style of pastoralism.

For convenience and in order to address some of the issues raised by the "household question" I use, with some modification, the terminology of household types settled on by the Cambridge Group (see Laslett 1972, 28–31; Wall 1983a, 19).[4] They classify households initially as either simple or complex. A *simple* household has as its base the conjugal family unit, that is, a married couple and their unmarried children, but a household is still considered simple if it is headed by a single parent with children or by married couples without children. Simple households become complex by additions of relatives who are not members of the nuclear unit. *Complex* households are said to be *extended* if they include other relatives who do not form conjugal units of their own. They are *joint* or *multiple*[5] if they are comprised of two or more related married couples, although to make sense in the Icelandic context, the class of married couples must include those living in loose marriages, namely, open and regularized concubinage. Also, native classifications of multiple householding did not depend on a kinship connection between the married couples.[6] I thus consider, contrary to the Cambridge typology, that a farmstead run as a unified economic enterprise can constitute a single complex household even if some of its members are not related or do not recite kinship or service as the reason they are housed together.[7]

The philology of residence generally designated the farm and its buildings as a *bœr*. The farm buildings were also called *hús* (sg. and pl.), although *hús* could also indicate rooms within the farmhouse and were not necessarily detached structures (see, e.g., *Grágás* II 260–61). Partially congruent with the notion of *bœr* was that of the *bú*, deriving from the same root (de Vries 1961, 63). The *bú* was the household, it included the livestock, the place, the enterprise, and the juridical unit. When two people had a *bú* at the same *bœr*, they were said to have a *bú* together (*eiga bú saman*). To set up a household or to start farming was to *gøra bú*, *reisa bú*, but also *gøra bœ* (acc. of *bœr*). The complex of buildings and the juridical unit was also known as a *híbýli*, the first element of which was related to *hjú*, *hjún*, which designated the conjugal unit, husband and wife. Both of these forms—*hjú*, *hjún*—were extended in meaning to include the entire population of the *híbýli* or *bú*—especially the servants, and even the family. The laws explicitly defined a *skuldahjún* (literally, obligatory *hjún*) as "all those a [householder] has to maintain and those workmen he needs to provide the labor to enable him to do so" (*Grágás* Ia 159, II 320). The definitional criteria of membership in the *skuldahjún*, it should be noted, are common production and common consumption. It might be convenient to summarize the above in tabular form:

| | |
|---|---|
| *bœr* | farmstead |
| *hús* | building; house; room |
| *bú* | household; the productive enterprise |
| *híbýli* | household; farm |
| *hjú(n)* | man and wife; servants, the entire household membership |
| *skuldahjún* | a householder's legal dependents and those workers needed to provision them |

Complex householding arrangements are indicated by the terms *tvíbýli*, *félagsbú*, *búlag*, and the phrase *eiga bú saman*. The sources, however, are not circumstantial enough to determine the precise arrangement indicated by each term. A *félagsbú* and a *búlag* seem to indicate a unified economic enterprise with property held in a kind of partnership.[8] *Eiga bú saman* was used to indicate all of these arrangements. Modern Icelandic usage and etymological inference suggest that a *tvíbýli* involved the separation of some economic functions. Much of the farm's management was still unified, with headship (probably) being shared, but the livestock and tools of each *bóndi* were separately owned and accounted for. It is a matter of definition whether a *tvíbýli* should be counted as two independent households sharing the same farmhouse or as a type of complex householding arrangement. Since there is no evidence whatsoever that the members of a *tvíbýli* did not eat together, share sleeping quarters, and, for that matter, engage in many joint productive activities, it seems better to treat the *tvíbýli* as a complex household. This is the sense given by a brief passage in *Eyrbyggja saga* (14:24): "I am not willing to divide Helgafell [the farmstead]; but I can see we are not suited to have a *tvíbýli* together so I wish to buy you out." The speaker is unwilling to partition the farmstead into two completely independent economic and residential units; he is also unwilling to have a *tvíbýli*, which is contrasted with the physical division of the farm and which the speaker finds unattractive because it requires too much intimacy with his interlocutor.

None of these terms fits precisely the definitions of the Cambridge group, but then nothing is to be gained by rejecting native categories in favor of imposing categories generated from other types of sources in other historical settings. The exact sense of household is bound to be strongly dependent on the culture the researcher is describing. The *bú* is something more than the co-residential unit, including as it does the economic enterprise. The *hjún* too was defined in reference to the economic enterprise. Its semantic range integrated household head and his wife with the servants and dependents who made up what was perceived as a social solidarity. The various terms for complex householding are also economically based. But given the nature of the economic enterprise, a sense of household deriving from economic arrangements will necessarily also indicate a co-residential and common consuming unit.

## The Household in the Laws:
## The Problem of the Juridical Household

Icelandic legal process placed an extraordinary significance on the formal attachment of everyone to an identifiable household and on the status of the people therein as to whether they were householders (*bóndi*, pl. *bœndr*)[9] or servants.[10] We are thus given a fair amount of information about households in the sections of the laws dealing with summoning procedure, with the calling of neighbors as witnesses and as members of jury-like panels, and with Thing attendance (see, e. g., *Grágás* Ia 128–39, also Ia 51–52, 63; II 320–25). One section provides that anyone who starts a household (*bú*) in the spring must declare himself to be "in Thing" with a chieftain (see chapter 1). The text then defines household so as to clarify exactly who must make the declaration:

> a household exists when a man has milk animals, but if he is a landowner he must also declare himself in Thing even if he does not have milk animals. If he is not a landowner and has no milk animals, he then belongs to the Thing of the householder into whose care he puts himself. (*Grágás* Ia 136)

As a property-based definition, this provision has little in common with structurally based definitions and only marginal connection to economic-functional definitions. Still it is suggestive. The provision allows tenants, even the lowly *kotkarl* and *búðsetumaðr* (cottager), to qualify as independent householders. It suggests, too, the possibility of several "juridical households" existing concurrently at the same farmstead whenever someone other than the true household head can claim ownership of a few cows. (By "juridical household" I mean to indicate the theoretical household defined by the minimal property requirements that give rise to the obligation to declare one's Thing-attachment as provided in the *Grágás* provision just cited). The provision also allows brothers, or a father and his adult sons, to farm together without some having to be deemed dependents of another of them, in effect recognizing the possibility of householder status of several adult males at the same farmstead[11] and thus suggesting also the possibility of shared headship among such kinsmen. The sagas, however, offer little evidence of the merely juridical household whose "householdness" is solely a function of the rules of Thing-attachment. In other words, servants who have acquired sufficient property to make them *bœndr* are perceived neither as householders nor as occupying a *tvíbýli* at the farmstead where they are in service. We might need to be a bit less categorical to account for the situation of certain farm managers. One Mar Hallvardsson, for example, moved to his brother's son Snorri's farm with a lot of livestock (*mart búfé*) and took over the management of Snorri's household. Mar surely must have qualified as a *bóndi* yet the saga is clear that there was but one household and it was Snorri's (*Eyrb.* 15:26).

There are other laws that point to the existence of complex households, although here too it is not altogether clear whether the provisions refer to more than one discrete simple household at the same location or to complex households. We find clauses, for instance, in a section dealing with the eligibility of neighbors to serve on a panel that tell how to proceed when people have a *bú* together and one is a landowner and one is a tenant, when both are landowners, or when both are tenants (*Grágás* Ia 160).[12] We are unable to recover the actual arrangements behind these regulations, but it seems fairly clear that they refer to different types of property pooling that might be undertaken at a particular farm site.[13]

An earlier clause in the same section states that "if two men live together in one house, it is right to call them both if needed, but only the one who is nearer if both are not needed" (*Grágás* Ia 160).[14] The other main legal codex defines, in a different context, what it means to live nearer: "He lives nearer to the place of action if he lives in that part of the house which faces in that direction" (*Grágás* II 376). This is obscure. Archaeological evidence shows that by the twelfth century the hall-house of the settlement period had developed the amenity of a living area in addition to the hall and several other specialized rooms, and literary evidence confirms the existence of separate rooms and even outlying buildings as guest quarters (*Ísland.* 173:492; cf. *Njála* 109:277); there is, however, little that indicates separate living quarters for different households at the same farmhouse, although the women may have had a separate room detached at some farmsteads in which they weaved (*Gísli* 9:30).[15] The reference to living in a part of a house may be to the location of a bed-closet, chest, or seat on the long benches running the length of the hall or perhaps to more than one detached living space at the same farm. Or the reference may be one of a number of places in the law texts where juristic hypercategorization was more a function of the aesthetics of legal thinking and writing than of social reality. Still, it is not possible to show conclusively that the "juridical household" had no function outside of the narrow administrative purpose of regulating matters of Thing-attachment, although for the most part it seems that the juridical unit was functionally unimportant when compared to the farmstead itself.

The sagas do not give us much detail about the day-to-day management of farms whose residents included more than one person who qualified as a juridical householder. But the glimpses we get suggest they were run as unified enterprises with divisions of labor along agreed upon lines and not as discrete entities with each qualifying *bóndi* hiring his own servants and arranging to pasture his animals separately (see, e.g., *Eyrb.* 15:26; *Gísli* 9:29–30, 10:34–35; *G.dýri* 11:181–82; *Njála* 14:45–47). Even the instances of *tvíbýli* do not show separate management. What we know for certain is that in the context of the feud the other side made no such fine distinctions between multiple discrete juridical households and true complex households. Most males attached to the farmstead of an opponent, as well as kin and affines established independently elsewhere, were fair game; this was the case despite a law that purported to limit the class of possible expiators when men householded together by providing for a means of giving notice to the opposing group of one's refusal to be identified with the actions of the other householder.[16] The same lack of concern with the category of the juridical household is also reflected in the attribution of names to groups. Group names were frequently taken from farm names or occasionally larger geographic units in which the chief residence was located (e.g., *Haukdœlir*). The names usually reflect a grouping that might include people unattached to the central household, but bound by kinship, affinity, or political ties to it (e.g., *Ljósvetningar, Oddaverjar*, etc.). Kinship also figured just as prominently in pan-household group names. A group of brothers could be collectively identified by their patronym (*Sigfússynir, Sturlusynir*), while the name of wider kin groupings is formed by suffixing the *ing, ung* patronymic to a first element taken from the name of a prominent ancestor (*Sturlungar, Ásbirningar*). One interesting hybrid—*Veisusynir*, 'the sons of Veisa' (*Ljós.* 22:64)—combines a farm name and a kinship term to describe second cousins who were fostered together by a common kinsman at a farm named Veisa. As the name *Veisusynir* would seem to indicate, common residence was what in people's mind constituted the primary bond linking the foster-brothers, so much so that the farmstead bringing them together becomes, symbolically, their mother. Evidence like this suggests that, to outsiders at least, the farmstead was the crucial entity and whether some residents had sufficient property to make them juridical householders was only important if such a resident actually shared headship of the economic unit.

Shared headship was in fact not uncommon. It appears to have been the norm when brothers shared a joint household. When the extension was vertical, that is when father and son shared a farm, headship normally was the father's until he retired and formally handed the management over to his son (*Egil* 56:151; *Lax.* 20:49). Still, there are subtle indications of shared headship even between fathers and sons. In *Njáls saga* (36:95), for instance, a man who was looking for a position intended to "meet with Njal and Skarphedin to find out if they [would] take [him] in." The outsider evidently considered the son (Skarphedin) to have equal say with the father (Njal) in matters of offering lodging to strangers. The answer he received from Bergthora, Njal's wife, should further indicate some of the difficulty of speaking of sole headship in Iceland: "I am Njal's wife . . . and I have no less power to hire servants than he does." Women too, both Bergthora and the laws[17] remind us, could head households. In some cases it appears that a man who married a woman householder might find himself sharing headship with her. The evidence is thin but such an arrangement might be indicated by a brief notice where a person is said to be a *landseti* (tenant) of Snorri *and* Hallveig (*Íslend.* 69:324).

A farmhouse, then, generally had at least one householder, either male or female, but it could have more than one. Households also had, of course, dependents—children, of which more later, and destitute kin or other people judged incapable of maintaining themselves (*ómagi, ómagar*). Households with sufficient means could have occasional winter lodgers, usually Norwegian seamen, but also other transients who might be visiting by formal invitation, or claiming shelter by right as part of a general obligation of householders to house people traveling to the Things and bearing bodies to burial (see *Eyrb.* 51:143–44) and to lodge traders and wedding guests unable to complete their travels in accordance with rules regulating Sabbath observance (*Grágás* Ia 8, 24, 27; II 9, 29).

## Servants

Everyone not him or herself a householder had to be attached formally to a household. Men over sixteen and single women over twenty were allowed to make their own lodging arrangements; others had theirs made by the person responsible for them.[18] The arrangement was a matter of contract, with uniform year-long terms beginning and ending during the Moving Days (*fardagar*) in late May, during which new arrangements were made for the coming year (*Grágás* Ia 128–29; see Jóhannesson 1974, 355–58). Most households mentioned in the sagas had some servants. As we saw in *Thorstein the Staffstruck* (chapter 2), even the poorest of them had a serving woman or two who did the milking (see also *Ljós.* 13:16, 18:51; *Hrafn Sv. St.* 17:221). The laws, however, in several places indicate the possibility of servantless households. The situation is sufficiently noteworthy that the head of such a household merits a descriptive term of his own and is granted special attention in matters of being called to serve on a panel of neighbors. He was called an *einvirki*, "sole-worker," and is eligible for panel service only if he has twice the value of a cow for each member of his household (*Grágás* Ia 128, 159, II 320–21). An *einvirki* lost that designation as soon as he had a male servant at least twelve years old. Apparently an *einvirki* could have female servants and still be an *einvirki*. This provision adds to the plausibility of the saga evidence in which the poorest households have only women servants. Presumably many tenant householders were *einvirki*, but the sources give us virtually no information regarding their householding arrangements.

Of special significance is the fact that the laws assume that servants could be married, with spouses located on the same farm or on another; this is confirmed by scattered saga evidence as well.[19] Marriage, in other words, needn't always depend on coming into an independent estate. Married servants with their dependents could be lodged together in their master's household (see *Grágás* Ia 131–32). A certain Thorstein, for example, lived with his children and his mother in the household of Hneitir for whom he worked and "and was repaid well for his labor" (*Hafl.* 1:12–13, 5:17). But the laws give the impression that servant families were often split up, with members parceled out among a variety of households.[20] Servants were not absolved of responsibility for their dependent kin, but, in fact, their limited circumstances must have absolved them nevertheless. One brief notice in the laws intimates that the prospect of a servant's dependents showing up was of more than passing concern to the householder (*Grágás* II 147). If dependents of his servants or his tenants appear and these servants or tenants have not the means to sustain the dependents, the householder was to call a meeting of the *hreppr*.[21]

The ranks of servants were comprised of people of greatly different expectations. *Sturlunga saga* on occasion shows the sons of householders as homemen in other *bœndr*'s households, that is as life-cycle servants, biding time until their fathers died or decided to share or cede authority in the management of the family farm. Women, too, apparently could be life-cycle servants, although the evidence is thin indeed.[22] We are given a glimpse of the degree of independence such people had in the households to which they were attached in a brief account where Solvi Thoroddsson, described as a housecarl of the Thordarsons, refused to join his masters in an attack on their enemy (*G.dýri.* 10:179).[23] Some housecarls were able to acquire enough to buy farms and establish themselves independently (*Gunn. þ.* 1:196–97; *Sturla* 2:64, 15:81), but the lot of a large number must have been permanent household service.

Occasional evidence in the sagas (e.g., *Hrafnk.* 8:126) and reasonable inferences in the laws (*Grágás* Ib 3–28, II 103–51, especially Ib 3–4, 11, 26–27) suggest that a good portion of the permanent servants were poor relatives whose position in the household was a function both of the requirement of finding household attachment and of the obligation of kinsmen of sufficient means to maintain their poor kin (see chapter 5). Such people must have had dim prospects of marrying. In any event, the laws tried to discourage them by stipulating a minimum property requirement for marriage or cohabitation unless the woman was incapable of bearing children (*Grágás* Ib 38–39, II 167). Violations were punished with lesser outlawry. The provision is difficult to assess. Although it evidences a clear interest in controlling the fertility of the poor, there is no way of determining its effect on nuptiality or fertility. The provision goes on to cast an especially wide net, suggesting that violations were frequent and that enforcement was problematic. Thus, the man who acted as the woman's *fastnandi*, that is, the one who gave her in betrothal, was also subject to lesser outlawry unless he had sufficient means to support the children. And he was to take them in himself; they were not to be foisted off on his kin. In some cases even the person who housed the wedding feast was subject to the same liability. A provision like this could not hope to achieve its goal unless there were also effective ways of discouraging illegitimacy. The general legal strictures against fornication and seduction provided for a declining scale of punishment for the male depending on the status of the woman involved. If we assume for the sake of argument that the laws could channel behavior, then these strictures would have the effect of insulating men of the householding class in their depredations on servant women while protecting their wives and daughters from poorer men (*Grágás* Ib 48, II 177–78), but it would not do much to discourage illegitimacy. The sagas show no prosecutions for violating the ban on inadequately funded marriages; they also show, as mentioned above, servants married or in fertile concubinage, but not with sufficient frequency to give any secure sense of the prevalence of marriage among servants of small expectations.

## The Fostering of Children

The sagas devote relatively little attention to children, and, not unexpectedly, less time is devoted to little girls than to little boys. What evidence there is suggests that the children of *bœndr* were so frequently sent out for fostering that some saga writers thought it noteworthy to record that a boy or a girl "was raised at home" (e.g., *Lax.* 28:76, 74:215; *Glúma* 10:36).[24] There were several types of fostering arrangements. In one type, supported by a number of well-known saga examples, foster-parents were of lower status than the child-givers (*Drop.* 5:150; *Hœn.* 2:7; *Lax.* 16:37) and there is some suggestion that the foisting of children on lesser households was a mulct the big made upon the little (*Sturla* 25:98). In a second type, the parents and foster-parents were of fairly equal rank, at times kinsmen by blood or marriage. The motivating force of this kind of arrangement was to heal breaches in relations or to confirm and buttress settlements (e.g., *Lax.* 27:75; *Njála* 94:237; *Sturla* 34:113; *Glúma* 12:40–41). Kin figure prominently as fosterers in yet a third type of relation. The obligation, mentioned above, of kin to maintain their poorer relations meant that a significant number of children grew up in the households of their better established kin or were shunted among the households of kin equally obliged to care for them (see *Grágás* II 107–8 and chapter 5). Such arrangements in effect were the inverse of those fosterings in which the child-givers were superior to the fosterers. In either case the children may have been perceived as burdens, but in the first type they cemented an ongoing patronage relationship between the fosterer and the parents of the child, whereas in the other type the wealthy fosterer gained little but a drain on his household stores and a small hand to assist in chores as soon as the child was old enough to produce as much as he or she consumed. In the first and second type of fosterage the exchange of the child was, ostensibly, a voluntary arrangement, while in the third type the child was forced upon the fosterer by the law.[25]

Fostering was the social construct within which the circulation of children was comprehended, just as household service was the construct within which the circulation of adolescents or young adults was subsumed. Most people did not stop circulating among households even when they finally became *sui juris*. It was just that, with the passage from childhood to adulthood, the bond that attached them to their new household changed from fosterage to service. Relative permanence of household attachment was the privilege of the well-established. Among the poorer classes the sagas confirm what the laws suggest: the realities of poverty meant that many young children of both sexes did not grow up in their parental homes. The evidence is patchy indeed, but what there is is consistent in suggesting a remarkable amount of circulation of children, either by virtue of formally concluded fosterage or by virtue of the consequences of impoverishment.

The fostering of impoverished kin (and abandonment to whatever extent it was engaged in)[26] and even the more formally negotiated fosterings of the first two types had the effect of equalizing the distribution of children among households. We do not see the sagas explicitly explaining fostering in terms of making up for short-term demographic dislocations, but factors of this kind might well have influenced the type of bond that was used to establish cross-cutting ties between groups wishing to forge links between themselves. Whether such bonds would be created by marriage, say, or fosterage had to be sensitive to the availability on one side, respectively, of marriageable women or children, and on the other side, of a need for wives or of space for children. Some groups bound themselves together both with bonds of marriage and fostering. When, for example, Njal married his son to Asgrim Ellida-Grimsson's daughter, he also took home Asgrim's son to foster. Later events suggest that this fostering was undertaken to provide Asgrim's precocious young son with legal training (Njála 27:74). Not surprisingly, there might be a number of reasons motivating any particular fostering. Considerations of support and property were supplemented by concerns for education and training (Prest. 4:123). Some fosterings were arranged to preserve peace in the parental household as in those instances where fathers sent away young unruly sons.[27] We also see pubescent girls removed from the parental home to keep them safe from the attentions of young males (Ljós. 1:4–5, 5:110).

The Icelanders also used the terminology of fosterage to describe an intrahousehold relation. Children who were raised at home had foster-parents selected from among the household servants. The roles of these fosterers were clearly different from those of interhousehold fosterers. Foster-mothers were wet nurses (e.g., Egil 40:101); foster-fathers appear to have been male servants to whom some special responsibility for the child was assigned. Inferences from the sagas suggest that they might have been bodyguards to young girls, or instructors of young boys in martial skills (Njála 9:29; 39:103; see Miller 1988c). The affective ties within the Icelandic farmhouse must have been quite complex, a tangled web, and one can imagine that there must have been an active political life of faction and alliance within households as well as between them.

## Household Size

The sources are especially recalcitrant about household size. To credit the numbers given in the sagas, the size of the larger and wealthier households was substantial. Njal's household had nearly thirty able-bodied men, to say nothing of women and children (Njála 128:325). Thorodd, a wealthy farmer in Eyrbyggja saga (54: 150; see also 11:18) had thirty servants (hjún) and Gudmund the Powerful, it is said, had one hundred servants and one hundred cows (Ljós. 5:109).[28] This is comparable to the size of the bishop's household at Skálholt, which had "seventy or eighty servants" (*Pál* 5:131–32). Njal's household is the most well-known joint household of the sagas. In addition to Njal and his wife, three sons and a daughter with their spouses live in and share in the administration of the household.[29] Thorodd's household type is complicated by the fact that he has taken in and maintains an old neighboring couple who have retired from their farm (*Eyrb.* 50:139). In these large units, servants, some of whom were married, ate and slept in the main hall on benches that ran its length on both sides, while the head of household might enjoy the security and privacy of a locked bed-closet. It would seem that the Cambridge classification scheme is simply inadequate to the task of comprehending set-ups like these.

It is the larger and wealthier households of the chieftains and big farmers that generally capture the saga writers' interest. But there is enough light in the sources to see that tenants, some widows, and middling householders must have had very small set-ups. Thorkel Hake, a chieftain's son no less and by some accounts himself a chieftain, had a household peopled by his wife, a four-year-old daughter, a few women servants, one housecarl, and one lodger (*Ljós.* 13:16, 18:51). His poor household was cause for insults directed his way in another saga (*Njála* 120:305). There was also a poor *bóndi* named Amundi "loaded with children," who was killed as he was mowing hay, while his wife raked behind him with a child she was still nursing strapped to her back. There seems to have also been one woman servant in the household who evidently was not a wet nurse (*Hrafn Sv. St.* 17:221). Other modestly populated households elicit complaints from teenage sons and daughters about how boring they are (*Ljós.* 8:125).[30] The evidence is such that any guess as to average household size would have no claim even to being "educated." The only thing we can feel fairly certain about, and which both reasonable deduction and the sources confirm, is that household size varied directly with wealth.

## Residence at Marriage

One of the key variables in determining household type is whether newly married couples set up a new household at marriage, continue in one of the parental households, or establish joint householding in another preexisting household. The sagas often show new simple households being established at marriage, mostly among the wealthier families, but neolocality was hardly a rule in a prescriptive sense, and the tendency admits so much exception as barely to be a rule in the descriptive sense.[31] This is necessarily so when we recall the possibility of servant marriage. I have only been able to discover two normative statements regarding preferability of household type. Not surprisingly these proverbs cut in quite different directions. One appears to favor neolocality: *hús skal hjóna fá*—"a house shall have a married couple" (*Hungr.* 1:60)[32]—although the sentiment is also consistent with complex households, for example, by having a room or building at the parental farm. The other, whose context we will discuss later, favors complex households: "It's best for the property of brothers to be seen together" (*Gísli* 10:34).

The degree to which neolocality was realized would depend, among other things, on the strength of the preference; it would also be sensitive to the demographic characteristics of the population. Assuming a roughly constant stock of working farms, a declining population in the twelfth and thirteenth centuries would facilitate neolocality; a rising one, if we also assume no change in the age at marriage, would mean that a number of conjugal units would not have farms available to them at the outset of their marriages and that some units might never be able to establish themselves in simple households, either in a new location or on the parental farm. Our knowledge of marriage ages for men and women is too spare to discern trends or even to determine a fixed point. What information there is suggests that marriage age for those women who did marry was low.[33] But even in a stable and stationary population, where a pool of farms might well be available to newly married couples, the realization of neolocality would still depend on the existence of an active land market.[34] Although there is plenty of evidence that farms were bought and sold during this period, the evidence also suggests that these transfers provoked disputes; bargaining was never quite free of duress and intimidation. The market, in other words, if market there was, was subject to the inefficiencies imposed by the pre-market mentalities of the people operating in it (see chapter 3).[35] But the near-perfect darkness engulfing Icelandic demography gives us no basis for preferring one trend to another (see, e.g., Hastrup 1985, 165–77). Hypotheses and assumptions remain just that. We know that the number of householders wealthy enough to pay the *þingfararkaup* was declining,[36] but this tells us nothing about the population as a whole, nor does it allow us to make any special assumptions about household type. Tenants and poor farmers, after all, formed households too, and their ranks might have been growing (Hastrup 1985, 172–77).

There is another factor which suggests that even if neolocality was aspired to, it would not always be easy to achieve. There is reason to believe that the amount of land available for exploitation was shrinking in this period (McGovern et al. 1988; Jóhannesson 1974, 29–34, 345–50; Hastrup 1985, 189–96). Farms established at altitudes too high for economic exploitation in the settlement period were abandoned and acreage was wasted by volcanic eruption. The mayhem the settlers and their sheep committed on the environment took its toll (Thorarinsson 1970, 320–25). Soil erosion was assisted by the destruction of woodland and the cutting of turf for housing and fuel. As noted in chapter 1, what productive land there was was already being exploited by the early eleventh century. New farms were not to be had by occupation of unexploited lands and there is no overwhelming evidence that heirs divided working farms into smaller parcels when dividing inheritances (see pp. 128, 133). Neolocality would thus appear to be a prerogative of the wealthy who could acquire extant farms by purchase, or, all too often, by extortion.[37] We thus find a certain Eyjolf buying up the expectations of parties to an inheritance dispute because "he had two sons and wanted to get them an estate" (G.dýri 1:162).[38] A prevailing neolocal rule among the wealthy would reinforce the movement, already initiated by the church, toward the assimilation of smaller independent farmers into the households of chieftains and big farmers, either as servants or as tenants maintaining households on smaller holdings.

The sagas are explicit in revealing a multiplicity of possibility with regard to residence at marriage, which should make us wary of talking in terms of residence rules at all. Sons could take over their parents' households upon marriage by a kind of premortem inheritance, with the parents staying on in retirement (Sturla 7:69; G.dýri 1:161; cf. Egil 79:275) or sons, whether married or not, could stay on and farm jointly with their parents (Egil 56:151; Lax. 20:49). Married daughters might remain home with their husbands coming to join them (Lax. 35:96–97, 43:130; Njála 61:154; Sturla 25:97; Vatn. 29:78; see chapter 4, n. 12). Sons could also be established independently prior to marriage, at least among the chieftains' families, often with a concubine or kinswoman to assist running the household (Lax. 20:49; Íslend. 39:284, 86–87:358–60; see also Jochens 1985, 97, 101). Those neolocal simple households once established tended to extend laterally quite quickly as brothers went to live or sought refuge with their married sisters or brothers (Gísli 10:34; Íslend. 4:232, 81:344, 83:346–47; Sturla 9:72).[39]

## The Prevalence of Complex Households

Several factors promoted the formation of complex households. Inheritance rules provided that legitimate sons took equally (*Grágás* Ia 218, II 63), and at the parent's death brothers might continue running the parental farm together rather than dividing the property (*Gísli* 4:16; *Ljós.* 22:62; *Sturla* 3:65).[40] Brothers could also formally divide the inheritance. Still, as far as I know, there is mentioned in the sources only one partition in kind of a family farm at the death of a parent when the decedent's sons were the heirs (*Vall.* 3:241). Among the wealthier families, which might control more than one farm, property divisions among brothers at the death of a parent tended to keep farms intact (e.g., *Hrafnk.* 10:133; *Njála* 78:192). A practice noted in the family sagas has one brother take his share in livestock, the other his share in land, with the ancestral farmstead thus passing on undivided (*Lax.* 26:73; *Gísli* 10:35). Partitions of lands were more likely when the land devolved to people unrelated to each other (*Glúma* 5:15; see also *Eyrb.* 14:24–25). There are many instances in the sources of brothers living together, presumably householding jointly.[41] And households might be shared by father and married sons (*Egil* 56:151), brothers and sister's husband (*Íslend.* 86:358; *Lax.* 32:86–87) or wife's brothers (*Íslend.* 33:262), and father and daughter's husband (*Njála* 61:154; *Sturla* 25:97).

The whole politics of marriage arrangements assumed that a man stayed close (affectively if not always geographically) to his married kinswomen just as it was expected that his wife was to stay close to her kinsmen. The husbands of daughters and sisters, and the brothers and father of one's wife, figured prominently in providing support in feud and lawsuits. When times were rough they were usually looked to for shelter and lodging. It was not at all unusual to find affines as household members, or stated from another perspective, kin of either spouse were eligible for household membership.

The demands of feud could lead households to merge formally for reasons of defense and protection. Thus, at Sturla's suggestion the household at Budardale combined with his in a *félagsbú*—a joint household (*Sturla* 19:87; see also 15:82). Household mergers motivated by defense or protection were, it seems, seldom an affair of equals. It is hard to imagine that these arrangements ever led to shared headship. Protégés were often constrained to purchase protection either by assigning their property to the protector (*Sturla* 28:103) or, as we observed in *Thorstein the Staffstruck* (chapter 2), by entering into service in the protector's household. Even though the laws stipulated the assignment was to be for fair value and gave a cause of action to the heirs or ward to set aside any wrongful transfer, the sagas show very few successful reclamations by the heirs.[42] But the assignor's farm would continue as a productive unit. It could become the endowment of a new household for the protector's kin, be managed by overseers, let to tenants, or be run by the assignor himself or his wife with aid from his patron (*Lax.* 16:37, 22:62; *Íslend.* 16:241; *Eyrb.* 31:84; *Sturla* 28:103).

One nearly obvious observation requires brief comment: households broke up and were assimilated into wealthier ones because of poverty. Much of the substance of the Icelandic poor law, which will be discussed more fully in the context of obligations based on kinship in the next chapter, was devoted to assigning the liability for maintaining people whose households were of insufficient means to provide for their members. For now it will suffice to note that the law sundered marriages, parceled out children, and even forced people into debt-slavery in order to solve the problem of maintaining the poor. What the law did not do was enable the continuance of the impoverished household. The nuclear family, it seems, was a luxury of those who could afford it, but it was precisely those who could afford it who were obliged to take in their poorer kin, thereby moving their households toward complexity: wealth and the complexity of household type also varied directly.

Evidence like this should make us wary of looking for and finding simple households inhabited by nuclear families in early Iceland. The evidence, such as it is, shows how varied householding arrangements could be, how unconstrained by rule, how open to formulation by agreement of the parties. The sources could also be culled for a multitude of instances showing simple households and neolocal marriage. But many of these simple households are captured by the source at a particular phase, a phase prior to household breakup if the family was impoverished or a phase prior to complex householding if the unit was wealthy.[43] Although our evidence does not allow any way of determining how many joint and other complex householding arrangements there were as a percentage of how many there could have been—given the constraints imposed or the possibilities enabled by mortality, nuptiality, fertility, the strength of cultural preferences, land markets, and carrying capacity—the number of complex households was most assuredly significant. In the absence of more scientific measure, the best proof for this assertion is the utter ease with which examples can be found in the sagas. The sources—both laws and sagas—simply give no sense at all that complex households were unusual. The large number of examples is especially noteworthy given that presumably high mortality rates must have both severely reduced the number of families where shared householding might even have been demographically possible and also substantially reduced the amount of time a household could have had a complex phase for those families where complex householding was demographically possible.

The significant presence of complex householding is all the more remarkable considering that these households existed in the face of laws facilitating their dissolution. The laws do not speak directly about partition of joint households, but they have much to say about concurrently owned property. Although nowhere explicitly stated as a general rule, there was a right to partition most all property jointly held. Sections of *Grágás* detail the procedures for partition of jointly owned land along with the buildings and water supply, of jointly owned woods, of concurrent fishing rights in a stream, and for regulating the limits of use of jointly owned pasture (e.g., Ib 86–90; 108–12; 122–23; 113–16). As long as the petitioner owned a share of the property there was no defense to a partition action. There was thus no legal way to keep jointly owned property from passing into single ownership at one person's will, while nothing, except the coincident circumstances of death and a class of heirs greater than one, could force individually owned property into joint property. The legal deck was stacked in favor of individual ownership.[44]

The sagas, so rich in detail about feud between households, and about strife and feud between kin residing in different households, are rather impoverished in accounts of fission of joint and complex households. We have some cases, which I will turn to shortly, but they are not graced with the dense web of circumstance typical of saga accounts. There are several possible reasons, not entirely consistent, for the relative silence. The simplest, and most unsatisfying, is that saga subject matter tends to be tales of feud, that is, of inter-household disputes. The literary form focused on extrahousehold affairs and only in the fuller accounts do we get more than an occasional detail of internal household politics. There are also indications that breakups were relatively peaceful and hence unlikely to merit a detailed account. Certain factors stifled internal strife before it was actualized. If the joint arrangement were of the kind suggested by the laws, such as where one householder is the landowner, another the tenant, or where one is the protector and the other the protégé, that is, when we have several juridical households at the same farmstead, one party was usually so much the weaker that his opportunities for articulating grievance beyond a mumble here and grumble there might be limited. Joint or extended households of the type where father and son shared authority were more likely to be divided by death than dispute even though the sagas do not hesitate to show. sons at odds with their fathers or fathers jealous of their sons (e.g., *Band.* 1:294; *Egil* 40:102, 58:173; *Eyrb.* 30:81ff.). Mortality rates would also be responsible for ending many joint fraternal households before friction did the same.

We know from the sagas that shared ownership of property interests by people of different households was fertile ground for dispute, leading to some of the best-known feuds in the sagas (*Eyrb.* 30: 82–83; *Njála* 36:92). The paucity of similar descriptions regarding disputes between joint householders may indicate the effectiveness of certain countervailing forces that kept these arrangements from causing serious dispute. The norms against kinstrife might not prevent kin from having and articulating antithetical interests once independently established, but these norms appeared to have been honored when kin lived together, at least to the extent that disputes within the household did not end in violence but in avoidance.[45] It may be that many of the brief notices that so-and-so went abroad are, in fact, recording a resolution of intrahousehold discord. If brothers didn't get along they often knew this before their father died and did not embark on joint householding to begin with. In such cases the separation of brothers would take place at predictable times that were already liminal periods where transition and transformation surprised no one. A situation that could have led to a breakup of a joint household was prevented by an uncontentious succession. Or even if the succession were contentious it was perceived and processed as an inheritance dispute and not as one having its origins in household type (e.g., *Ljós.* 22:61–62; *Hrafn Sv.* 8:652).

Although the sources are at best indirect about this, the structure of both internal and external household politics, as much as norms of peacefulness, gave rise to forces that promoted cooperation between joint heads. The demands of defense in the feud, the identity of interest imposed by opponents and competitors, served to unite the farmstead membership against the outside world. But these same forces could lead to the articulation of competing positions within the household. Cooperation between joint heads was assisted by a fairly predictable resistance they endured at the hands of their charges. The more disenfranchised household members had their own district and neighborhood agendas. As we saw in chapter 2, their status depended on how the wives, sons, aging parents, and servants at other households perceived them and their household and how opinion and gossip determined their relative standing. The way they went about acquiring and maintaining status often opposed them to their own household head whose dealings with other household heads required different strategies (see *Njála*, chapters 35–45). Numerous cases in the sagas show wives, mothers, old fathers, and even servants urging and sometimes compelling the household head to a more violent course of action than he appears to have desired.[46] These internal stresses are well documented, but we lack detailed accounts of their effect on joint households; conjecture must unfortunately suffice. There was never, however, a very clear demarcation in Iceland between inter and intra, external and internal, although as a rough division it still reflected a real difference between the directedness of the roles assumed by household heads as opposed to their charges. Internal household politics were greatly complicated by competing loyalties occasioned by kinship, affinity, fosterage, and friendship of individual household members with people resident in different households. Whatever forces of adhesion household politics might engender between joint heads could be quickly offset by the consequences of bonds each might have to different outsiders. And when that occurred, as we shall see in the second case below, any consequent household fission, because more "public," would have a better chance of becoming the subject of a saga account.

## Thicker Descriptions and Summation

Some sense of the factors leading to the formation and dissolution of complex households can be acquired by considering more closely two of the relevant saga cases. This brief account is from *Ljósvetninga saga*.

> Gudmund's property passed to his sons Eyjolf and Kodran. Eyjolf wanted to have the inheritance all to himself and had no wish to deal evenhandedly with his brother. . . . When Kodran came of age, he asked Eyjolf for a division of the property, to which Eyjolf answered, "I don't want a joint household (*tvíbýli*) at Modruvellir and I don't want to move on your account."
>
> Then Kodran met with his foster-father, Hlenni, and told him how things stood: "Is there no valid defense if I'm going to be robbed of my inheritance?"
>
> "Eyjolf's arrogance comes as no surprise to me," replied Hlenni, "and I do not advise you to forfeit your inheritance. You should rather build a house outside the enclosure at Modruvellir."

He took that advice and it was agreed later that Kodran should live at Modruvellir. (22:61–62)

We do not know the marital status of the brothers; we do know
that Eyjolf was not always the most fairminded of men. But guard-
ians often come to see their wards' property as their own and there
is something rather predictable, if not altogether admirable, in
Eyjolf's highhandedness.[47] His reluctance to have a *tvíbýli* is doubt-
less attributable to having grown accustomed to the "simple" household in which he was the head (see also *Eyrb.* 14:24–26). The
conclusion of the dispute, apparently establishing the *tvíbýli* that
Eyjolf had resisted, suggests that the dispute would not have arisen
had Kodran been of majority when Gudmund died. The indication
is that the brothers would simply have lived together—"it was
agreed later that Kodran should live at Modruvellir." There is no
evidence here of strong norms against brothers staying on together
on the paternal farm. On the contrary, Hlenni's advice involves a
symbolic statement of Kodran's right to be part of the household at
Modruvellir in equal standing with Eyjolf. Kodran is to build a *hús*,
not establish a *bú*, right under his brother's nose, a building which,
though an outbuilding, is still a part of Modruvellir, which Kodran
still claims is at least half his *bú*. The plan is designed to annoy
Eyjolf and to embarrass him in the eyes of the community by providing a vivid emblem of his lack of good kinship. At the same time,
Kodran avoids the unseemliness and dim prospect of suing his
brother or engaging in violent self-help. To be noted also is Eyjolf's
precise response to his brother's request for a property division.
Eyjolf does not take this to mean that Kodran wishes to move out,
but construes it as a request to set up a joint household, although
with individual ownership of personal property (i.e, a *tvíbýli*). This
is a small but significant indication that property division upon inheritance did not necessarily mean physical partition of a working
farm. The household remained thus constituted until Kodran was
killed years later.

The second case likewise deals with the joint household of two
brothers. After the death of Thorbjorn, his two sons, Thorkel and
Gisli, marry and continue to farm together. Their sister Thordis
marries a short time later, receiving the entire farmstead as her
dowry (*Gísli* 5:19). Her husband Thorgrim relocates there, while
the brothers obtain a farm and set up household on neighboring
land. Thorkel comes to suspect his wife of having an affair with
Gisli's best friend, who is also the brother of Gisli's wife, Aud, and

at the next Moving Days Thorkel approaches Gisli to request a division of their property.

> "I want us to divide our property. I want to move and join householding with Thorgrim, my brother-in-law."
> Gisli responded, "It's best for the property of brothers to be seen together. I would surely prefer there to be no disruption and no division."
> "We can't continue to have a household together (*eiga búlag saman*)," said Thorkel, "because it's a great wrong that you always do all the work by yourself and have all the care of the household and I do nothing useful."
> "Don't make anything of it," said Gisli, "as long as I haven't mentioned it; we've managed when we've gotten along and when we haven't."
> "It doesn't matter what is said about it," said Thorkel, "the property has to be divided; and because I'm the one requesting the division, you shall have our residence and land and I shall have the moveable property (*lausafé*)."
> "If there's no other way than for us to separate, then do either one or the other, divide or choose, because I don't care which of the two I do."
> It was concluded that Gisli make the division; Thorkel chose the moveable property and Gisli had the land. They also divided the dependents, two children; the boy was named Geirmund and the girl, Gudrid; she stayed with Gisli, Geirmund went with Thorkel. (10:34–35)[48]

At the time of their parents' deaths the brothers were of age. And unlike the preceding case, there being no conflicting interest between guardian and fraternal ward, the brothers established a joint household on the parental farm. The arrangement was resilient enough to survive the transfer of the farm to their sister and the establishment of a new farmstead nearby. The timing of joint household fission in this case had nothing to do with the major transitions in a household's life cycle. Death, marriage, birth, or retirement were not at issue. We know the brothers did not get along all that well. One would expect the difference in the amount of labor contributed by each to have been a source of contention. But neither that, nor other difficulties in the past, if we credit Gisli—"we've managed when we've gotten along and when we haven't"—had been sufficient to sunder the household before.[49] It seems that up until now Thorkel had neither felt enterprising enough to set up independently, nor had had a convenient opportunity to set up common householding with someone else. But the establishment of his sister next door provides such an opportunity and the new knowledge that his wife was involved with the brother of Gisli's wife provides the occasion for taking advantage of it.

If we abstract from Thorkel's actions a general principle about household fission it would involve the impingement of extrahousehold attachments and bonds on intrahousehold politics. Each brother has an extrahousehold attachment to a person that the other brother is hostile to and, in this case, each brother favors his nonresident friend. As long as the household was only one of several noncongruent solidarities claiming effort and commitment from a person, householding arrangements would be subject to the state of affairs in the other groupings. It is clear that Thorkel's wish to break off householding with Gisli had nothing to do with his feelings toward joint householding per se. He just prefers sharing a residence with his sister and her husband to sharing with his brother and his brother's wife. The property division causes no net loss of joint households to the society. Thorkel's new arrangement, however, is shortlived, not because of conflict within his new household, but because of mortality rates, this time objectified in the person of Gisli, who kills his sister's husband a year later (16:53).

The lot of the two dependents calls for comment. In accounting terms and according to *Grágás* they are liabilities and subject therefore to division (see, e.g., Ib 5, II 106–7). They are brother and sister and very possibly kin to Gisli, although the saga is unclear about this (Þórólfsson and Jónsson 1943, xiv). The history of their household attachments reveals much about the fluidity and instability of residence in early Iceland for all but those who headed households. They were born in one place, raised together in another, presumably because of the poverty of their parents, and then separated from each other when the joint household broke up. The sources, both legal and narrative, are consistent in giving the impression of constant circulation of children and servants from household to household, either by way of fostering, poor relief, employment, or other lodging agreements. Discussions of household types and the family relations accompanying them, unless set forth with life-course diagrams, tend commonly to give a misleading sense of stasis and of order. In Iceland people moved a lot. They circulated to make up for localized demographic dislocations, to ameliorate localized shortfalls in production occasioned either by production failures or fertility successes. It was much more likely for people to move to food than it was for food to move to people, as we saw in the previous chapter.

And in this case, people moved because of discord, something the nature of the saga sources would have us believe was, next to marriage, the most prevalent cause of relocation.

What must Geirmund and Gudrid have thought about all this? The saga tells us that Geirmund remained loyal to Gisli and Thorkel both. Elsewhere in the sagas, household attachments of even brief duration gave rise to future claims of support, mostly in matters of feud and dispute (see, e.g., *Ljós.* 9:130–31). For the nonhouseholding class, the possibility of changes in residence needed to be faced annually during Moving Days. For those who were the sons of householders, the residential life course was likely to have been only a little less volatile: reared for a time in the parental household and for a time in a fostering household, a homeman in another's household, a juridical joint householder still largely subject to the power of his better propertied fellow householder, or perhaps a householder independently established by his father. He might share household authority with his father, or set up joint householding with brothers at the time of the father's death or divide the inheritance and set up a simple household. A daughter of the householding class would probably be reared at home, but could be sent out at an early age for fosterage or service; she could then remove to a husband's or lover's residence, unless she was an heiress or widow, in which case the man could relocate to her lands.[50] In marriage her residence would be that of her husband unless they divorced; or in concubinage that of her consort until they separated. If widowed she might return to her kin (*G.dýri* 1:162; *Glúma* 11:40), or if propertied, remarry and relocate.[51] For the daughters of the wealthiest, the cycle was similar except they were unlikely to be sent out for service and somewhat less likely to be involved in concubinage.

Few could escape obligation toward or claims by several different households. Although one was legally a resident at only one place per year, there are suggestions that this was, at best, a juridical ideal not confirmed by a reluctant reality. Some people were in fact attached to more than one householding unit. Take, for instance, Hoskuld, Njal's illegitimate son, who is part of his father's household but who frequently stays at his mother's farm nearby. Simultaneous or shifting membership in two households must have been fairly common for illegitimates, of which, according to genealogy and saga, there were a multitude,[52] and for those destitute people shunted among the households of their wealthier kin who were obliged to care for them. On the other hand the numerous brutal provisions in the laws regarding the *gangamenn* and *lausamenn*,[53] those unattached to any household, serve as a reminder of the economic limitations that made householders unable to absorb all those who were available for service. Thus the words of one Helgi Sealball: "I never have a home; I never have the fortune to have a full year's lodging. But I'm always hired on for wages in the summer" (*Fóst.* 14:195).

The nature of the sources does not allow for much more precision than we have been able to muster. Given the woefully unsatisfactory demographic information that is available, there is not much hope of doing better, at least until the archaeologists can give us more information about district settlement patterns. What the sources make very clear is that, whatever the nature of Icelandic householding, the norm was not the simple household of the Cambridge typology. Given the organization of the farmstead, the concepts of nuclear family and simple household severely misrepresent the household's variety of shapes throughout the course of the life cycles of its residents. The evidence reveals no unambivalent systemic pressure toward the formation of simple households. Complex householding, we saw, was discussed in the laws and confirmed by the sagas with such frequency that attempts to push the northwest European household pattern as far north and as far west as Iceland and as far back as its twelfth and thirteenth centuries cannot be supported by the evidence. The shrinking availability of land, the pastoral transhumance directed from large lowland farms, the demands of defense in the bloodfeud, and limited evidence of partible inheritance of working farms were all factors that presumably were relatively constant throughout the twelfth and thirteenth centuries. None of these factors was especially conducive to the formation and maintenance of simple households. The orthodox terminology—simple, multiple, joint, complex—while useful for comparative purposes, ultimately misrepresents the richness of possibility in the constitution and interrelations of the population of an Icelandic farmstead.

# CHAPTER FIVE

# The Bonds of Kinship

The last chapter described the movements of people among households. Few had the luxury of being attached to the same household for their entire lives. And those who did saw the membership of that household constantly shifting, so that those people who did not relocate among others found others relocating around them. Even the most sedentary of souls moved among households to some extent, as visitor, as guest, as seeker and giver of aid and advice. If we could abstract a person's movements and graph them into a network, we would find that the greatest predictor of the identity of the various households in which he or she gained entry, either as visitor or lodger, would be the presence of kin within that household. Kin, of course, lived together in households, and a wider network of kinship and affinity linked households together. Among the free-farming class the bond between thingman and *goði* bore a heavy burden in the prosecution and defense of lawsuits, but the more frequent extrahousehold exchanges and reciprocities involved kin. The networks established and maintained by blood and marriage were mobilized in matters of sustenance and support, law and feud, conviviality and mourning. This chapter will try to flesh out the picture of group formation begun in the previous chapter by adding to the obligations created and imposed by co-residence the burdens imposed and the benefits conferred by kinship.

The study of early Icelandic kinship has never quite recovered from Bertha Phillpotts' elegantly presented argument that the "constitution of the country was based on the bond between thingman and *goði*, and not in any sense on federated kindreds" (1913, 46). In her view, kindred solidarity could never have survived the migration to Iceland. The evidence of Skallagrim Kveldulfsson's migration, she says, shows that colonizing expeditions were recruited in Norway on the basis of household and neighborhood. Even had whole kindreds migrated together, they would have been shattered in Iceland given what is known about settlement patterns (1913, 35, 260).

And although three centuries would have been more than enough time to reconstitute kindreds, she felt that the rampant kinstrife of *Sturlunga saga* more than demonstrated that this had not occurred.

There are some fundamental problems with Phillpotts' views.[1] For one, she had rather demanding ideas as to what it meant for kin to act in groups or action sets. She assumed that because kinstrife was a fairly common theme in the sagas and because kin did not always act together, there was no meaningful sense in which kinship could be a fundamental principle for group recruitment (also Sawyer 1987). This is simply wrong, as I would assume anyone who has grown up in a family knows. Most actively functioning groups, in fact, provide the raw material for strife as well as for concord among their memberships. Only people who do not deal with each other do not fight. To be sure, when the discord within a group reaches certain levels the group may split or disintegrate and reform. But fission leads to new groupings whose members will still recite the same bases for mutual identification as the previously constituted group. Phillpotts, however, was looking for "the *corporate* aspect of the kindred" (1913, 3; emphasis in the original), in spite of the fact that she knew that the "Teutonic kindred was not a corporation in the strict sense of the term." This corporate aspect, she felt, was to be found in wide participation of kin in wergeld payment and receipt, in organized bloodfeud, in oath helping, and in formal rituals for repudiating offending members of the kindred. Although she found ample evidence of wergeld payment and bloodfeud in Iceland, she found no evidence to suggest that the whole body of eligible kin participated in these matters. But Phillpotts' notions of what constituted kindred solidarity were too formal and too narrow. By her criteria she was able to show that the kindred did not behave as a corporate body in matters of wergeld and bloodfeud because kin participation was selective, including only a small number of those kin formally eligible for participation. Phillpotts' argument asks too much of kindreds, which by definition are not corporate bodies of fixed and certain membership.[2] Ego-focused kin groupings of shifting composition, as we shall see, were quite important in Iceland in a multitude of social and legal settings, even if these groupings were variously constituted depending on a number of personal, social, and other contextual factors and did not include all eligible members. Kinship mattered, even if not all people related to a person felt obliged to assist him or her. Phillpotts imperceptibly extended her argument against the existence of extensive kindreds of "corporate aspect," an argument for which there is firm basis, to suggest that kin connection was not important, a view for which this chapter will show there was no basis.

The direction of Phillpotts' argument is largely a function of the scholarly context in which it took place. The nature of Germanic kinship was being hotly disputed in the decades bracketing the turn of the century and she was concerned to show that the historical record did not support those who argued for patrilineally recruited corporate groups. The chief issue in dispute was the existence of unilineal descent groups, and then along which line, male or female, they were recruited if they did exist.[3] The entire discussion had a distinctly anachronistic legal cast to it, with people expecting medieval and primitive groupings to behave as Roman legal persons or English corporations.[4] The legal historians, lawyers, and lawyerly anthropologists who debated these issues confused two separate things: the question of legal personality and the question of group behavior. It was the first question that interested them and they felt that, once it was answered, it concluded the second. If a group was "corporate" it was expected to act that way, that is, as an undifferentiated "person."[5] Phillpotts was able to make a compelling case against patrilineal descent groups, but like those she argued against, the quest for corporateness was still in her veins. In her view, for kinship to be a key principle of social organization, kin had to act together in ways that are different from "the solidarity frequently exhibited among kinsmen of today" (1913, 3). Mutual aid, gift-exchange, hospitality, therefore, because a common marker of kinship now, she felt, had no different significance for social organization then. Her view ignores, among other things, the significance that context imparts to what appear in isolation to be similar activities. Kin were not just a source of comfort, a safety net when individual effort failed; there was much more at stake. Most social action was not just inconvenient, but was simply inconceivable without the consultation and active assistance of one's kin. Asking favors and granting favors on the ground of kinship and affinity was not small change; it was what made the Icelandic social world go round.

It is important to distinguish between how people thought about kinship and the practical uses people made of kinship. Not all meditations on kinship structure or kinship obligation were abstracted from practice. Some of these meditations sought to shape practice and were codified as laws. In this chapter we divide our discussion into two broad headings: theoretical or formal kinship and practical kinship. In the first part we seek the implicit structures of kinship as these are reflected in genealogy, inheritance and wergeld laws,

rules governing appropriate marriage partners, and in the complicated system of poor law. In this section we see how kinship provided a structure for organizing systems of rights and duties. We will
see that there was not a single unified theory, but several variants
that appear in different substantive areas of the law. It is thus the
case that the outer limits of recognized common blood will vary
from second-cousin level to fourth-cousin level to (under the influence of church theories of kinship) sixth-cousin range. In the
second part we will see how kinship and affinity provided people
with an idiom for making claims, for requesting favors, loans, gifts,
and support. We will detail the way in which claims were advanced
and avoided, how groups alleging kinship or affinity as their basis
were organized. By postponing the discussion of practical kinship
until after the discussion of theoretical kinship I do not mean to
imply that theory is privileged or that practice represents a falling
off from or a series of exceptions to the formal structures of the
laws. My own predilections are to privilege practice, but that too
is not wise. Both theory and practice affected each other in some
ways. Practice was undoubtedly the starting point of much theory, but some theory was, in all probability, the consequence of
formal exercises of legal experts interested in categorizing and system building. And the world of practical kinship was not closed
off from theory, even when theory was an airy construct of legal
experts, for when theory manifests itself in law it can impinge in
many ways on practice. One final caveat: discussions of kinship
structure are not always immediately accessible to readers. The
jargon is part of it, but the fact density necessary to describe adequately the complexity of the structures of rights and duties in
the poor law is not an easy read even without jargon. Bear with it.
The chapter will show how important kinship in both its formal
and practical aspects was in the constitution of Icelandic society,
Phillpotts notwithstanding.

## Theoretical Kinship: The Formal Structures of Genealogy and Law

### The Evidence for Cognation

Icelandic kinship was reckoned bilaterally, meaning that kinship
was traced through both male and female links (Meulengracht Sørensen 1977, 32–33; Hastrup 1985, 70; Vestergaard 1988). But as a
practical matter, in some settings, male links might be preferred to
female links or vice versa. For example, although daughters and sons
were both possible heirs to their parents, certain objects might tend

to pass unilineally: weapons from father to son, or, in the absence
of sons, to the nearest agnate; bedclothes and jewels from mother
to daughter. A unilineal "look" might even arise as an accident
from something like a tendency toward patrilocal residence on
marriage. That is, if daughters tended to move to husbands' people
while sons brought their wives to the parental farm, residential
groupings might look as if they were recruited patrilineally. But
as we saw in the last chapter, there was no clearly dominant residence rule.

The evidence for bilateral, ego-focused kinship comes from a variety of places. Of a randomly selected sample of sixty-two genealogies from *Landnámabók* that are more than five generations deep,
descending from the settlement (870–930), forty-seven are cognatic,
that is, they have one or more female links, while fifteen have only
male links.[6] A smaller sample of six genealogies, ascending from the
original settler back in time, shows five with male links only and
one with female links. In the cognatic genealogies male links outnumber female by slightly more than two to one. The numbers
would suggest a preference for male links if they were to be had.[7]
The genealogies ascending from the original settler back in time
were mostly invented and they indicate that clearly fictional links
were likely to be males.[8] What mattered most, however, was not the
sex of the link, but the existence of a link of any kind. The most
important thing was to be able to get where you wanted to go. No
one spurned a distinguished ancestor because of the sex of the links
connecting them. Jon Loftsson and his issue were proud to be able
to claim connection to King Magnus Barelegs through his illegitimate daughter Thora (*Ættartǫlur* 1:51). And it was hardly to the
discredit of Snorri Hunbogason the Lawspeaker that his pedigree included two and three female links before reaching Thorbjorg and her
father Olaf Hoskuldsson of saga fame (*Sturla* 2:64; see, e.g., *Lax.*,
*Grett.*, *Fóst.*).

I know of no statement in the sagas in which someone's status is
impugned for claiming kinship through female links rather than
through male links, although, as we shall soon discover, the laws
show a bias in one place in favor of male links. Nor is there anything
in the presence of intervening female links that prevents the transmission of masculine virtues through females to a male descendent.
Thus Gudmund the Powerful is flattered by the prospect that his
daughter's son will inherit his capacity for leadership (*Ljós.* 5:112)
and in another instance a family's luck was passed from a mother's father to his grandson (*Glúma* 9:31). If there were anything like descent
groups, they were cognatic; but it would be wrong to see descent as

the chief organizing principle even where it arguably might have been at play. It was the farmstead or locality of a central household that supplied the sign identifying most fairly permanent groupings (e.g., *Oddaverjar, Mýramenn*). And though a fair portion of the membership of these could recite some connection by blood to a prominent ancestor of the group, membership need not be based on common descent, but could be based on fosterage, vicinage, or alliance.

The inheritance law adds to the evidence opposing unilineality. The sex of the links connecting the taker and the decedent did not matter at all from the first-cousin level and beyond, although within the first-cousin level there was some preference shown to males and male links. Thus, daughters could inherit only if the decedent was not also survived by legitimate sons, while brothers with the same father took ahead of brothers of the same mother.[9] But the legal disinheritance of women with legitimate brothers did not prevent their participation in parental property. Saga evidence shows that daughters with brothers were provided dowries, the distribution of which could be made either before or after the death of the parent. A certain Gudny Brandsdottir, who had living legitimate brothers, was provided with a dowry of land in her father's lifetime (*Sturla* 11:76). In another instance, Thordis was given the parental farmstead as a marriage portion by her brothers after their parents' deaths (*Gísli* 5:19; see also *Íslend.* 86:359). The laws confirm the right of daughters to participate in parental property by way of dowry, but an undated "new law" (see p. 231) requires the consent of the sons if the dowry is to be more than any one son's share of the inheritance (*Grágás* II 64).

There is, however, a small intimation of unilineality in the wergeld law. The wergeld law, or *Baugatal*, details an incredibly complex scheme in which the killer's kin, out to fourth cousins, are to pay blood money to their counterparts of the victim's kin (that is, the killer's second cousin pays the victim's second cousin, etc.). Elaborate rules stipulate what occurs should a class of payers or takers not exist. The law has been assumed to be older than most of the sections in *Grágás* (Hastrup 1985, 87; cf. Sawyer 1987, 34) and it is highly problematic. Phillpotts considered it "quite unthinkable that *Baugatal* was ever actually followed in Iceland" (1913, 37). And Sawyer, following her, considers its details to be purest "fantasy, a good example of the artificiality and unreal systematization much loved by medieval lawyers" (1982a, 44; also 1987, 33–35). The entire corpus of saga literature shows more than one hundred examples of compensation payments for killings, but no examples of *Baugatal* determining the form and manner of payment. And as to its presumed great antiquity, Phillpotts notes that, given the circumstances of migration, the existence of fourth cousins wasn't even a biological possibility for nearly a century (1913, 37). The case against *Baugatal*'s currency, either in settlement times or in the twelfth and thirteenth centuries, is strong indeed and almost certainly conclusive. But its inclusion in *Grágás* does show that distinctions based on unilineal constructs were conceivable to some people in the culture, even if only as an exercise in systematization under the influence of Norwegian models (see Phillpotts 1913, 46n1; also Vestergaard 1988). *Baugatal*, for instance, provides that lines established solely through males are to pay and receive three-fifths while cognates in the same degree from the killer or the corpse are responsible for or entitled to two-fifths. The difference between the lines is reflected in explicit terminological distinctions: "And the payment men take whose kinship is traced through men is called ring payment, while the payment men take whose kinship is traced through a woman is called cognate payment (*nefgildi*)" (*Grágás* Ia 196). Except for this instance, filiation through males alone does not figure in the laws at all. Distinctions are made between paternal and maternal sides—*fǫðurætt, móðurætt*—but not between the patriline and other lines.[10] Rights and duties in matters of guardianship, in determining to whom a cause of action for killing or fornication falls, are ordered with only minor variation cognatically as they are in the inheritance provisions (*Grágás* II 77–78; Ia 168, II 145; Ib 48, II 177; see chapter 5, n. 9).

## The Limits of Kinship

The extent of the kindred, that is, how genealogically distant two people can be and still count each other kin, is formally set in some provisions in the laws at fourth cousins. A fourth cousin of a killer who happened to be lodged in a household with a fourth cousin of the victim was required to leave (*Grágás* Ia 136). One could be held in some circumstances to sustain an impoverished fourth cousin, and *Baugatal*, as we saw, purported to oblige fourth cousins to participate in wergeld transactions (*Grágás* Ib 25–26, II 140, cf. Ia 37; Ia 194). Kin were no doubt reluctant to be burdened with such thin blood. Elsewhere, the laws take the view that shared interests because of shared blood will be presumed through the second-cousin level, but no further. Second cousins, for example, could not sit as judges or jury for their kinsmen, whereas second cousins once removed could (*Grágás* Ia 47, 62, II 318).[11] The sagas do show people as distant as second cousin once removed calling each other or being referred to as a *frændi* ("kinsman") ( *Vall.* 1 : 236–37; *Eyrb.* 10 : 16; 26 : 67). And third cousins find themselves frequently taking concerted action in lawsuits (e.g., *Eyrb.* 17 : 31), though it is clear that shared political goals rather than shared blood provide the inducement. Thus Vigfus Viga-Glumsson is willing to aid his third cousin Gudmund by challenging his third cousin Einar to a duel ( *Ljós.* 17 : 41). I have been unable to find kinship being explicitly invoked between people more distant than that. It appears that somewhere between the second- and third-cousin range most people found themselves, on a practical level, at the limits of perceived kinship in spite of the law.[12]

Native thought on kinship structure also drew on ecclesiastical constructs in matters of marriage. Following the theories of the eleventh- and twelfth-century church, Icelandic law purported to require kinship reckoning as distant as the seventh canonical degree, that is to the sixth-cousin level (Goody 1983, 134–46). Punishment for violation of the marriage prohibitions was graded according to proximity of kinship. Marriage with a second cousin or nearer was to be punished with full outlawry, and ignorance of the relationship was no defense ( *Grágás* Ib 59–60, II 181–82). For third cousins and fourth cousins, the punishment was lesser outlawry and a defense of ignorance was accepted (Ib 31, II 157). This would seem to suggest that many people stopped keeping accurate track after the second-cousin level. It is also an admission of the likelihood of mistaken computation in more distant degrees of kinship. Beyond fourth-cousin range, violations were punished by a series of fines ranging from a tenth of one's property to ten ounces for marriage with a sixth cousin once removed.[13]

The extent to which these provisions were enforced is another matter and one has the distinct impression that when the elaboration of a particular rule leads to fourth, fifth, and sixth cousins we are dealing with a "theoretical reflection on a principle, not an accompaniment to practice" (Dumont 1970, 82). The genealogies of the chieftain families of the twelfth and thirteenth centuries suggest that the rules on marriage were ignored or excused. Bishop Thorlak (d. 1193), who was rather zealous about enforcement of all rules regulating sexual matters, earned the enmity of one couple whose marriage he invalidated on the grounds that the husband and a former lover of the wife, by whom she bore a child, were third cousins ( *Oddav.* 3 : 140; *Prest.* 9 : 131–32). The forbidden degrees, however, did not succeed in preventing Bishop Klæng from fathering a daughter, Jora, with his first cousin, although they were sufficient to invalidate the union of Jora and a certain Thorvald a generation later ( *Íslend.* 3 : 230; also *Haukdæla þ.* 1 : 61–62).[14] Thorvald, who loved

Jora dearly, went to Norway and managed to get the archbishop's dispensation for ten more years with her "after which they had to separate whether they liked it or not."

One case gives some insight into the use the laity might make of these prohibitions and what others thought of those who invoked them:

> Thorfinn Onundarson asked for the hand of Ingibjorg the daughter of Gudmund dyri. She was illegitimate; Valdis was the name of her mother. Gudmund considered it would be an appropriate match for Thorfinn only on the condition that it was allowed by church law. They were related and Gudmund claimed that he would not agree to her marriage with Thorfinn when both secular and ecclesiastical law prohibited it.[15]
>
> Thorfinn and his father [Onund] took this response as an insult and they considered Gudmund's reasons to be worthless. (G.dýri 9:175)

Gudmund and Onund didn't get along especially well and the suitors clearly suspected that Gudmund was raising the matter of prohibited degrees not out of respect for the law but out of disrespect for them. In the suitors' view, the reasons alleged for refusing the proposal, even if justified by law, were not sufficient when one's good faith was already in doubt. Thorfinn, however, did not lose his interest in Ingibjorg. He and Onund went to ask for her again, accompanied by thirteen others at a time when Gudmund was home with only a few men. The narrator reports the results wryly: "I don't know what they said to each other, but there is this to say about the end result: Ingibjorg was betrothed to Thorfinn" (9:178). The next summer the bishop declared that their children would be illegitimate, but no one seemed to pay any heed.

## The Structures of Kinship and the Burden of Poor Relief

The laws, with great specificity, imposed the maintenance of the poor on their kin. And because this topic will close some gaps left open in the preceding chapter, and is not without some interest in its own right, I will allow myself more detail and circumstance than is conducive to smooth exposition, but still considerably less than is merited by the complicated legal regulatory scheme occupying some fifty densely printed pages in one of the *Grágás* recensions. The broad outlines will suffice and I dispense with rehearsing the numerous internal inconsistencies among the strictures. The open-

ing lines of Ómagabálkr, the section of Grágás devoted to the maintenance of dependent persons (ómagi, pl. ómagar), begins with a
general principle followed by an ordering of responsibilities.

> It is prescribed that every person in this land has to
> maintain his dependents. A person shall first maintain
> his mother. If he is able to do better, then he shall main-
> tain his father. And if he can do better still, then he shall
> maintain his children; if better still, then his siblings. If
> he can yet do better, then he shall maintain those people
> from whom he stands to inherit and those people from
> whom he has already acquired the right to inherit in ex-
> change for furtherance. And if he can still do more, then
> he shall maintain his freedman whom he manumitted.
> (Grágás Ib 3, II 103)

Lack of means did not excuse a person from maintaining his father
and mother. He was to become a debt-slave in order to sustain
them.[16] The laws show greater solicitude for mother than for father.
Thus if a person had gone into debt-slavery on behalf of his father
and subsequently his mother needed maintenance, the liability for
father then passed to the father's kin and the child's slavery was to
accrue to mother's benefit (Ib 4, II 104). Such a provision, it is to be
noted, assumes the possibility of the physical separation of the parents and of the separation or separability of their property.

Scholars have assumed that slavery of all kinds was either dead or
dying out by middle of the twelfth century (Karras 1988, 135–36;
cf. Foote 1977a; Jóhannesson 1974, 352–54; Hastrup 1985, 108),
having disappeared partly because of its inefficiencies, partly from
Christian influence, partly from the failure of new supplies of cap-
tives once the Viking era wound down. But debt-slavery was so un-
equivocally part of the legal administration of poor relief that I am
not willing to assume that debt-slavery's demise coincided precisely
with the decline of common slavery, even in the face of thin saga
evidence.[17] Even if actual incidents of debt-slavery were infrequent
(which is not all that certain), the mere fact that debt-slavery was
legitimated by the law must have had some social and psychological
effects, if only because the legal possibility of debt-slavery, positively expressed, would have put people to some trouble to avoid it.
Debt-slavery remained a possibility that had to be worked around.
Still, Ómagabálkr, in its way, lends support to the notion that
people might not have been all that pleased to fund outlays to the
aging by enslaving the old person's children. The law thus gave the
person (A) who had to support his parents by becoming a debt-slave

the right to *compel* his nearest kinsman with means (B) to accept him as a debt-slave for the parents' benefit. This right presumes B's reluctance to be burdened with a debt-slave the value of whose labor was quite unlikely to fund two parents and himself as well.[18] The provisions create, in effect, a series of dependencies: parents on children[19] and then children on nearest kin with the child's body securing the debt.[20]

Once outside the conjugal family, the ordering of obligation generally followed propinquity of kinship as set forth in the inheritance law (see chapter 5, n. 9), but even within the nuclear unit the teeth of the obligation grew duller as the obligation moved beyond parents. Whereas a person without means had to offer himself up to debt-slavery to support his parents, he had a choice with his children: he could either go into slavery on their behalf or sell them into debt-slavery instead (*Grágás* Ib 4–5, II 105). No saga case is quite on point, although we do see a father with *ómegð mikla* (a large number of dependents) order one son to take lodging elsewhere because the farm was inadequate to feed them all (*Hrafnk.* 2:101). But it would seem that the father did not need this particular legal stricture to empower him to make such a decision. The law texts consistently recognize the difference between debt-slavery and service, although in some respects the lived experience of one or the other might not have been all that different.

The general rule was that two-thirds of the cost of the children's maintenance was to be undertaken by the father, one-third by the mother, in the absence of some other agreement. This rule adjusted property divisions on the dissolution of the marital unit by death, divorce, or separation caused by poverty. Subsidiary regulations allowed for deviation from the general rule to reflect the differing means of the parties. So, for example, if there was a divorce, the children were to be maintained according to the means of the parties, but the mother was to keep any child who was still sucking "even though they might wish to divide them up differently later" (Ib 5).[21] But if both parents were utterly without means the children were to be divided between the father's side (*ætt*) (two-thirds) and the mother's side (one-third).

The significance of the unequal distribution of responsibility is not all that easy to interpret, but seems to be justified partly by analogy to other preferences expressed in the inheritance and dependency laws. Throughout the law of *ómagar* greater responsibilities are assigned to those who stood to inherit from the dependent than to those who did not (e.g., *Grágás* II 142), and since fathers were called to inherit ahead of mothers, the father's side was "favored" with the children. This, coupled with a general cultural tendency as evidenced in the inheritance law to favor males over females, provides some, but too much explanation, since it gives reason for assigning all the children to the paternal kin. There is also an argument based on legal symmetry that may explain the unequal ratio. The responsibility for unacknowledged illegitimates belonged to the maternal kin, to the paternal kin for acknowledged illegitimates (von Amira 1895, 910), and somewhere in between for legitimates, set at 2:1 to accommodate a fairly systematic bias in favor of males. None of these views is very satisfying but no less so than chalking it up to a custom to do things that way because that's the way they were done. We would still be put to explain that custom.

The support spouses owed each other was considerably less than what they owed to parents or children. They were obliged to maintain each other but only so long as the propertied spouse had one year's means for each dependent whose heir he or she was (Grágás II 141). And the obligation to care for a sick spouse was contingent on the care not being a drain on household reserves. Sick spouses were thus to be returned to their kin unless they could be cared for without having to add members to the household.[22] In other respects, additions to the household attributable to one spouse could give grounds for divorce. In fact, the prospect of a spouse's dependent kin showing up provided such strong grounds for divorce that the bishop's consent for the dissolution of the marriage was not required:

> In a case where one spouse has property and another
> none and the propertyless one has dependent kin there,
> or who have been there and used up the property, then
> the one who still has property is to announce to five
> neighbors and name witnesses that "I will divorce my
> spouse for the reason that I do not want my spouse's de-
> pendents to use up my property." (Grágás Ib 39–40,
> II 168)

The inferior position of the spouse to parent shows that prime responsibility of married men and women might be directed outside their own household units in those cases in which the parents were not co-resident. Women and men, in other words, were obligated more by law to their natal kin grouping than to the grouping established by their own marriage.[23] This provides rather strong evidence that, in native theory at least, kindred and kinship were still matters of great importance.

A person was obliged to care for impoverished kin from whom he would not inherit only if he had sufficient means. Sufficiency was judged to be "four half-years" worth for all his present dependents plus those who were now seeking to be sustained (*Grágás* Ib 23, cf. II 139–40). But if the *ómagar* seeking sustenance were more distant than second cousins, the minimum wealth requirement was increased to six half-years per person and to eight half-years per person for third cousins once removed and fourth cousins (Ib 25–26). For the last most distant class of kin the support obligation could be discharged by a one-time payment of sixty ells.[24] There is no way of judging how consistently behavior accorded with these laws since saga evidence in this area is very thin. My suspicion is that dependent kin are rather fully represented in the sagas but not as *ómagar* so much as servants.

This morass of regulation is supplemented by lengthy rules governing the procedure by which dependents were assigned to those responsible for maintaining them and by which the division of dependents was made among those equally obliged to care for them. Lots were the usual mode of decision in the latter case if the parties were incapable of coming to an agreement on their own. When there were fewer dependents than eligible households, lots were used to determine the order of rotation of dependents among the households (Ib 16, II 108). The initial determination of liability was made by procedures ranging from those as informal as *ex parte* oaths, to full-fledged lawsuits in which the dependent was forced on the obligated kin under pain of lesser outlawry (Ib 7–12, II 112–24).

The laws suggest that people might forcibly resist the arrival of the dependent, or that dependents might be forcibly imposed on someone who was not properly obligated (*Grágás* Ib 8, II 113). And on this score the sagas offer some confirmation. In one case Sæmund, using the oath procedure, imposed a dependent on a tenant of Ogmund. Ogmund objected, claiming that the tenant had insufficient means, and he had his men return the dependent. Sæmund felt aggrieved and brought suit against Ogmund. That is all we are told about this particular dispute. It was quickly submerged into more expansive general hostilities between the parties, leading ultimately to the death of Sæmund (*Svín.* 4:89). A similar incident is described in *Hrafns saga Sveinbjarnarsonar* (St. 14:216–17) when Thorvald, a chieftain, imposed a dependent on a thingman of Hrafn, a rival chieftain, who in turn assembled eighty men to bear the poor soul to a man who appears to have been a thingman of Thorvald. These *ómagar* seem to have been district or Quarter dependents not at all related to the men they were imposed upon. In this regard it should be noted that not all poor relief was assumed by the kin. The responsibility for maintaining the dependents of outlaws, for example, fell to the the local Thing or the Quarter of the defendant (*Grágás* Ia 86–87, 115–16). One saga describes the unenviable lot of a certain Olaf Hildisson, an outlaw's son, who was adjudged a dependent of the Quarter (*fjórðungsómagi*) and was shunted among various households in the Breidafjord district (*Hafl.* 4:14). And it will be recalled that it was precisely the burden of maintaining an outlaw's dependents that Bjarni, as one of the district leaders, sought to avoid when he refused to execute his outlawry judgment against Thorstein (see chapter 2). In other cases, where no kin were able or available to maintain an *ómagi*, the burden was assumed by the local administrative unit, the *hreppr*.

Our two saga cases suggest some of the difficulties that might accompany a determination of liability for the maintenance of *ómagar*. The assignment of a dependent to a household was not divorced from the disputing and feuding structures in which district politics was mediated. The determination of liability itself was susceptible to some manipulable ambiguities. It required an assessment of property and in most cases a determination of kinship. Both were easily subject to misrepresentation, or in the case of kinship enumeration, to a lack of knowledge of the actual connection linking the dependent to the party sought to be held liable.[25]

One tidbit of saga evidence suggests that kin often shirked their support obligations. Bishop Gudmund found himself frequently at odds with the followers of Kolbein Tumason on various grounds, one of which was "the maintenance of their impoverished kin" (*Íslend.* 20:246). The law was not blind to the possibility of people seeking to escape the burdens of blood. It imposed sanction after sanction. If a person abandoned his dependents and fled to another *hreppr*, he was liable for lesser outlawry at the suit of the men of *hreppr* stuck with the abandoned dependents (*Grágás* Ib 15, II 124). Nor was a man permitted to leave the country unless he had made suitable provision for his dependents. A formal ban on his travel could be announced at the Law Rock or at the ship and if the ship's captain knowingly violated the ban he made himself liable for lesser outlawry also. Some sense of the expansiveness of Icelandic notions of liability can be had from the knowledge that the crew did not escape scot-free either; they were each subject to a three-mark fine (Ib 15, II 125).

The viability of these provisions is confirmed in saga accounts. In one instance, some men threatened to ban Mar's voyage unless he made provision for his leprous kinsman (*Ljós.* 28:94). Mar disposed of the matter by disposing of his kinsman; he murdered him. A happier account in *Auðunar þáttr* (1:361) describes how Audun funded his mother's food and shelter for three years, the exact amount *Grágás* says was needed to prevent the prohibition of his voyage abroad (Ib 15, II 125). The laws also suggest that shirkers who preferred to stay in Iceland might deliver their dependents overseas instead (Ib 21, II 133). The prohibition against such action was not general: one could not send abroad his parents, wife, or children, nor any other kin "*unless* [somewhat obscurely] their flaws are such that their value is lower if they were bound to servitude for their faults."[26] Still, the lingering sense of Bishop Gudmund's difficulties with Kolbein's followers suggests widespread and perhaps defiant evasion of the duty to maintain impoverished kin. This sense is reinforced indirectly by the fact that one of the sagaworthy signs of Gudmund's exemplary character was that, while a priest, he supported seven *ómagar* on his annual stipend (*Prest.* 11:135).

*Ómagabálkr* envisages kin sending kin abroad, presumably into some kind of bound service. It contemplates kin enslaving or being forced to enslave kin for the benefit of kin. If this, in fact, was a regular practice, we may have to revise our sense of what the more degrading forms of dependency involved. Was slavery less slavery for being a way of recouping the costs of sustaining impoverished kin? Or were kin nothing more than burdensome liabilities whom one would like to discourage from making too many claims on one's resources? In other words, were kin less kin for being slaves, or were slaves less slaves for being kin? It may only be that these rules are a lawman's attempt to legalize the types of behavior that the norms of kinship obligation and reciprocity had "moralized" positively already. Rich kin should help poor kin and poor kin should pay back the favor with work, if that was all they had to give, or with property, if they should ever acquire the means.

The trouble with this last observation is that it is too sanguine. *Ómagabálkr* is distinctly not in the business of encouraging gifts between kin. It knows of them and gives them rather short shrift. A maintainer, for example, only has a claim for reimbursement against subsequently acquired property of the dependent if the care was *not* provided by way of gift (Ib 27, II 138); he is also denied reimbursement if he was not actually obligated to sustain the dependent (II 137). In the latter case, an appreciative return gift from any subsequently acquired property of the one-time dependent might also be set aside by the dependent's heirs if it is judged to disinherit them (Ia 249; cf. II 127). *Ómagabálkr* even empowers a kinsman to castrate his more remote kin who are in the habit of fathering bastards: "No one is obligated to accept more than two illegitimate children of third cousins unless the father of the children is gelded" (Ib 26, II 150). Still, one might observe a certain optimism permeating *Ómagabálkr*, the optimism of the lottery ticket purchaser. The effect of the ordering of obligation almost always worked to impose a dependent on those who stood to take from him as his heir. There is in such ordering a sense or hope that there would eventually be a *quid pro quo*, that fortunes would change, that dependency was transitory and that, consequently, the maintainer would see some return for his outlay. But it is equally possible to reorder the reciprocities of what was requiting what in a bleaker way, the idea being that the duty to maintain the person from whom one might inherit was itself the *quid pro quo* for the right. The maintainer "owed" the dependent for the fortuity of being his heir. Never mind that all of *Ómagabálkr* assumes that the value of the bare right is on average substantially less than the cost of the duty.

Formal kinship, we see, played an important role in determining the distribution of legal rights and obligations. Kinship provided a structure, or at least an organizing metaphor, that the culture used to administer intergenerational property transfer, the care of dependent and incapable people, the guardianship of property, and the determination of who bore the burden of suing or being sued for the wrongs of others. The concern, even the obsession, with genealogy that is evidenced in *Landnámabók* and the sagas shows that people either had the necessary information or were willing to invent it to be able to compute connections that depended on finding a common ancestor as many as five generations back. Nor were they aided in the bookkeeping process by a unilineal system which, by eliminating one gender entirely from formal kinship computation, might bring with it certain economies of memory. As we will soon discover, kin did in fact actively look to each other for support. What we have just learned is that they were often compelled by law to suffer being looked to. The poor law imposed a definition of the kin group on a person, and he was held to it by sanctions ranging from fines to lesser outlawry, whether or not he included some of the people imposed on him in his own definition of his kin group. A theory of the kindred out to fourth cousins informed the poor law. But only a very small part of the significance of kinship in medieval Iceland is to be found in the forms of genealogy and in the legal structures of rights and duties imposed by virtue of kinship. The more interesting story lies in the active world of practical kinship.

## Practical Kinship

Bilateralism, the tracing of relationship through links of both sexes, meant that not all a person's relatives were related to each other. An example from our own bilateral system is sufficiently illustrative: your mother's brother and father's sister are both kin to you but they are not kin to each other unless there has been some intra-kin marriage in prior generations of your family. An important feature of bilateral kinship reckoning is that your kin will not entirely coincide with your cousin's kin; or, from another perspective, you are by virtue of kinship eligible for membership in several different kin groups with different overlap. One consequence of this is the possibility and likelihood of greatly divided loyalties; another is the need to assemble actively one's nonresident kin for those functions that required some type of concerted action. The kin group, in other words, was not a closed corporation of determinate membership; it did not constitute itself automatically. It always fell to someone to recruit his or her kin for the particular enterprise at hand, whether it was vengeance, legal action, or consultation regarding the suitability of prospective marriage partners.

But it would be a gross misrepresentation to consider each adult male or female, or even each group of siblings, as an ego, each the center of a kindred computed in relation to him or her. Some people could never realistically figure as egos, and even on the level of theoretical modeling, nothing would be gained by so doing. Kinship groupings were not quite as relativistic as a pure model of ego-centered bilateral kinship computation assumed. Generally speaking, the poorer a man was, the more likely he was to occupy a position within a more powerful kinsman's ego-centered construct, as tenant, ward, servant, perhaps even as debt-slave; the same held true for women and children. The poor, especially, must have seldom indulged in figuring their kindreds with themselves at the center of the construct. Too much reality would have intervened and intercepted the fantasy. Cutting against the model of a world of promiscuous overlapping ego-centered kindreds was the more limited world of kindreds whose ego was a head of household, and an even more limited world of kindreds where the egos were big farmers, neighborhood leaders, and chieftains. The shape of lesser peoples' kindreds was distorted by the gravitational fields of bilateral groupings centered in more powerful people. The sagas frequently identify certain people as the head (*fyrirmaðr*) of their kin groups (e.g., *Lax.*

16:37; *Ljós.* 22:62). Any kin group in which there was a chieftain would invariably be defined in relation to the chieftain. The same held true for the heads of substantial farms (*Njála* 88:220). Such people were very conscious of their position, as is more than evident in the words of Thorvard Thorgeirsson to his nephew Gudmund, the future bishop:

> You know, kinsman (*frændi*), that I have been the head (*hǫfðingi*) of our kin group (*ætt*) as my father was before me. Your father and my other kin deferred to my views. I advise you to do the same. And you will be destined for the leadership after me. (*Prest.* 25:151)

We can thus imagine that certain bilateral kin groupings had some stability of membership and focus, if not quite anything approaching structural permanence. It was still up to the people involved to keep their kinship connections in good working order and to participate in the exchanges of gifts, support, and favors that were the stuff of practical kinship. The discussion that follows will tend, like the evidence, to be skewed toward the better-heeled segments of society.

While the laws formally imposed kinship out to fourth cousins, kinship in the practical world depended on more than just biological or affinal connections. Just who would be counted kin was clearly subject to much situational variation and was quite context-specific. A second, even a third cousin with whom one shared common interests and with whom one consequently acted or consulted would be counted kin, while a first cousin with whom one was less involved might cease, for practical purposes, to be counted kin at all. Nor might the people with whom one claimed kinship for the purpose of invitations to feasts and weddings be the same people one counted as kin when it came time to assist in a lawsuit or help pay compensation for their wrongdoings. The class of a person's avengers might be differently constituted than the class of his heirs, and neither of these groupings need be identical to the class of people for whom one was obliged to take vengeance. The precise makeup of an actively assembled grouping of kin depended on numerous variables: the popularity, wealth, and persuasive skills of the organizer; how well he had kept up relations before; the competing goals and designs of those sought out for assistance; the extent to which competition within the class of recruitable kin could be suppressed in the pursuit of common interests or in the interest of maintaining relations of exchange and indebtedness; the substantive issue at hand, etc. The strength of kinship bonds tended also to vary inversely with geographic distance. It was easier to keep in touch with people nearby. But this tendency was offset somewhat by Allthing attendance and the interhousehold mobility discussed in the previous chapter.

## The Idioms and Norms of Kinship

What practical kinship meant above all else was making claims on others using the idiom of kinship obligation. There is a sociolinguistics of medieval Icelandic kinship that yet needs to be written. For our purposes, it will suffice to trace a few key features: the forms of address kin used to each other and the kind of normative statements about kinship, either implicit or explicit, they recited. When Thorvard Thorgeirsson in the passage above (p. 156) admonishes Gudmund to acknowledge his leadership, he addresses him, appositively, by the general relational term "kinsman" (frændi). This is a frequent marker of saga dialogue between blood kinsmen, just as the word mágr is between affines. Brothers, fathers, and sons address each other as frændi (e.g., Njála 33:86; Ljós. 20:57), and so also do more distant relatives. Precise descriptive terminology is rarely used in dyadic conversation unless a single primary term—such as father, mother, brother, sister—will suffice.[27] One can address a brother as "brother," but not a first cousin as "mother's sister's son," although it is not unusual to find descriptive terms applied to third parties (Íslend. 34:267). The recitation of a kinship term was a usual part of the diction of request and admonishment, both of which are nicely exampled above in Thorvard's speech. It was also used as a marker of solidarity once the obligation was admitted and the request accepted, a constantly recited sign of connectedness (e.g., Eyrb. 27:70).

The appositive use of mágr and frændi implicitly invoked the entire constellation of values of good kinship.[28] It meant mutual aid, common concern; it meant duty and, above all, moral obligation (Bloch 1971). Practical moral discourse and practical morals in medieval Icelandic society were intimately bound up with kinship and its idiom. The moral component of kinship terms is clear in such exhortations as when Pal asked his father "whether he intended to sit still, even though Magnus, his sister's son, would be killed outside" (Íslend. 34:267); or in requests like "I do not wish to conceal this, Bard frændi; there was something behind our invitation: we'd like to have your support and accompaniment" (Lax. 54:163); or in a woman's refusal to abandon her kinswoman to flames her husband intends to set: "I will not take leave of Alfdis, my kinswoman (frændkona)" (Ljós. 20:57).

The fact that kinship terms could provide the proper linguistic setting for making moral claims also suggests that the same terms could be used ironically or deviously. One saga example shows a person "cousining" another, that is, falsely claiming kinship, in order to elicit a certain desired action.[29] The possibility of cozening in this manner ironically confirms the moral component of kinship; it also shows that not all asserted kinship connection need be based on demonstrable genealogical linkages.[30] Ironic uses of kinship and affinal appellation in direct discourse are fairly common in the sagas (e.g., *Þórð.* 22:44; *Glúma* 8:27). Take the case of Sturla's altercation with Pal and Pal's wife Thorbjorg in an inheritance dispute in which Sturla was assisting his father-in-law, Bodvar (*Sturla* 31–32:109–11). The sides were assembled to negotiate a settlement when Thorbjorg grew impatient and attempted to stab Sturla in the eye. She missed, but succeeded in giving him a nasty cut on his cheek. As was his wont, Sturla was able to turn the incident to his advantage, using his new-found cause of action as a lever to induce the other side to accept a settlement favorable to his party in the inheritance dispute. Sturla is about to address Pal, Thorbjorg's husband:

> He held his hand to his face and as the blood flowed
> down his cheek he said, "It is greatly to be expected that
> Pal and I will settle our dispute [i.e., the case of Sturla's
> fresh wound] and no one else needs to get involved. Now
> Pal, *mágr*, let's sit down."
> Pal responded, "I will certainly discuss an accord with
> Bodvar, but, nonetheless, it seems worth mentioning
> that as it happens things are taking a turn for the
> better."
> Sturla answered, "We'll first discuss a settlement be-
> tween you and Bodvar. Our affair is of no great concern,
> and Pal, *mágr*, we will discuss it later."

Even in such short space Sturla's manifest cool and ruthless intelligence comes through. It so happens that Pal is Sturla's affine by virtue of Pal and Sturla's wife being first cousins once removed. This is a kinship connection of such remoteness that its invocation can only operate in an ironic or vexing register. Besides the clearly threatening aspect the repetition of *mágr* bears, Sturla uses the term to make Pal's wife's behavior appear even more inappropriate than it would otherwise have been and to provide the discursive environment for making a very vexing request of Pal, his "dear in-law." Pal is convinced to grant Sturla self-judgment and he shamelessly judges himself nearly all of Pal's substantial property. Sturla was thus able to conjure up the notion of kinship obligation solely as a way of denying its obligatory force.

The kinship terms of daily discourse were themselves so charged with a normative aspect that the express invocation of the norms of keeping good kinship was not all that frequent. The norms were mostly implicit in the requests made and the burdens undertaken pursuant to an invocation of the mere relation. Even when people were moved to give expression to the norms, a terse "for kinship's sake" (fyrir frændsemi sakir) usually sufficed. On occasion people wistfully wished that their kinship relations were better and expressed regret that they were not. Says one second cousin to another, "We think it's a shame that our kinship has been not been kept up better, and we fervently wish that it would be" (Glúma 8:27; see also Ljós. 14:26). The kinstrife that is the substance of the greater part of Laxdœla saga gives rise to several normative utterances, among which are, "It is not proper that you kinsmen should fight" (37:108) and, "It is the greatest of misfortunes that you kinsmen should continue to kill each other" (54:164). What is striking about these few examples, and they are representative, is how unpreachy they are, how unproverbial.[31] This, however, is not an indication of the weakness of the norms, but rather of the strong normativity implicit in the recitation of the relationship itself. The words frændi and mágr were moral concepts and were perceived as such. The economy of expression achieved by the semantic surcharge born by these terms helped create the terseness that characterizes the saga style; it might well be supposed that a corresponding reticence characterized native discourse as well.

That the positive expression of norms of good kinship was mostly implied, or incidental, did not mean that breaches of the norms were accepted with the same taciturnity. Violations of good kinship made for gossip and mocking verses. Thus Olaf advises his son Kjartan not to give others "a cause for laughing that we friends and kinsmen should quarrel" (Lax. 46:142). And when Sæmund is slow to render aid to his brother's son, Loft, he is made the subject of verses and "very heavy words because he had not supported his kinsman" (Íslend. 39:284).[32] Recall too the constant needling that attended Bjarni for having killed his mother's brother in the fight at Bodvarsdale in Thorstein the Staffstruck (chapter 2). Serious breaches of good kinship often prompted third-party intervention, as when father and sons threatened to battle each other in Ljósvetninga saga (3–4:10–15). The norms were clearly not strong enough to prevent frequent kinstrife (Phillpotts 1913, 15–18; cf. Heusler 1912, 24–25), but they were still capable of giving rise to some anxiety and regret for egregious breaches (e.g., *Íslend.* 61:316, 62:318).

There was no way the norms could have been strong enough to effect an end to kinstrife. Kinstrife was to some extent inevitable because of competing claims deriving from the bonds of *goði*-thing-man or of marriage, and even of competing claims among different branches of one's own kin group. It was also structurally mandated by the internal dynamics of power relations and competition among kin. This is readily observable in Thorvard's claims to deference from Gudmund (above p. 156) and his admission that the leadership of their kin group would eventually pass from one collateral branch to another. Tension between collateral branches was not uncommon in families that owned chieftaincies since the holder of the office was often then recognized as the group's leader.[33] A good portion of *Íslendinga saga* and *Laxdœla saga* bears witness to this (see also Andersson and Miller 1989, 35). Tensions were also structurally inevitable between fathers and sons; examples are easy to come by and strongly inform the plots of several sagas (e.g., *Njála*, *Ljós.*). Competition over familial resources took on an added urgency in a culture where the opportunities to create new wealth were so limited. The father-son bond might have borne an even greater burden in Iceland than on the continent because the new church was still too young, too poorly funded to offer an opportunity for impatient youth. Mortality rates were usually quite obliging to the generation of sons by disposing of their fathers with some dispatch, but when mortality was tardy, sons could grow restless.[34] Not all the tension, however, need originate with sons. One saga in a passing comment thinks it noteworthy to observe that a father did *not* feel envy at his son's popularity (*Lax.* 24:66). In spite of the stresses that the culture imposed on the father-son bond they rarely led one to oppose the other in such a way as to endanger each other's lives.

It is of some note that in the entire saga corpus there is no patricide, nor for that matter is there matricide or fratricide, exactly the kind of enormities that would have been preserved had they occurred.[35] A few wives have their husbands killed (*Njála* 11:34; *G.dýri* 5–6:169–71), and *Landnámabók* (152:194) records one case in the settlement period of a husband killing his wife. We might muster up one filicide, if we include the cruel omission of one father: A certain Valgard had done Thorgils a small offense and was led out to be killed by Thorgils. Valgard's wife offered all her property to spare her husband's life but Thorgils refused the offer, saying he would only accept payment from Valgard's father, a priest named Thorkel. Thorkel, however, was unwilling to pay anything for such petty grievances and his response was abrupt:

"They'll have to show greater reason for money than
that."

"Then he shall be killed," said Thorgils.

Valgard requested that his father hear his last confession and that was immediately permitted him. People
thought they heard Valgard ask his father to pay compensation and redeem him, but it was to no avail. Thorgils
appointed Eyjolf the smith to strike at him and Valgard
was led out and killed (*Þorg. sk.* 30.158)

The saga only notes that the community view of the incident was
unfavorable to Thorgils. There was no mention of what others
thought about Thorkel's lack of action.

Others express a willingness to sacrifice kin if those kin happen
to be in the wrong place at the wrong time. Gudmund the Powerful
says he will burn his wife if she does not leave the building in which
the killer of his servant is being harbored (*Ljós.* 20:57); one and
one-half centuries later, his namesake Gudmund dyri evidences
the same cold heart with regard to his daughter, whose husband,
Thorfinn, and father-in-law, Onund, Gudmund is in the process of
burning inside their home (*G.dýri* 14:190): "Thorfinn spoke to his
father-in-law, Gudmund, 'It's too bad your daughter Ingibjorg is not
in here.' Gudmund replied, 'It's a good thing she isn't, but that still
wouldn't deter me now.'" The setting is the same for a colloquy
between a son and his father in an example often cited to show the
decay of kinship bonds in the turmoil of the mid-thirteenth century.
Three times a son asked his father to exit a burning farmhouse.
Three times the father refused unless the target of the attack were
also given quarter. The son at last gave his exasperated response:
"Then burn in there, you old devil" (*Þorg. sk.* 32:160). Fortunately,
the attackers lost heart before the old man died. Only in this last
example does there appear to be a nonhypothetical expression of a
willingness to kill a very close kinsman and even that one is ambiguous; after all the attack is broken off. What these cases do show
is that there is perhaps no greater way to give expression to the ve-
hemence of present purpose than to give a verbal disavowal of close
blood ties. Rather than showing the weakening of kin ties, the rhetorical and tactical goals of such expressions perversely affirm the
normative component of the relationship they deny.

Normativity in kinship obligation also finds expression in cases
in which the problem is a conflict between conflicting obligations.
These cases are especially interesting because they occasionally allow us to acquire an abstract ranking of obligation, or, more accurately, they allow us to observe how certain people argue for the

priority of some bonds to others. Skarphedin felt that his having avenged Grani's father should rank ahead of his having killed Grani's first cousin once removed (*Njála* 129:328): "You repay me for avenging your father according to your character; you value your lesser obligation more." We see people claiming others are overvaluing their affinal connections at the expense of their blood (*Njála* 91:226). The classic case from Germanic epic involves the woman torn between husband and brother. And when in less epic Iceland Thordis chose husband over brother, her brother Gisli expressed his disapproval in verse by citing the precedent of the legendary Gudrun who, he felt, had chosen better (*Gísli* 19:62).

One case merits lengthier comment. In various places in the laws a sister's husband (SiHu) is considered an especially close relation. He is disqualified for interest from sitting on juries and from judging his affine's cases just as if he were a blood relative (e.g., *Grágás* Ia 47, 62, II 318). *Baugatal* even makes him one of the payers and receivers of wergeld (Ia 201). A wife's brother (WiBr), however, is not included in *Baugatal*, nor is he disqualified from hearing legal actions. Yet, from SiHu's viewpoint it is with his WiBr that the law assumes he shares common interests and presumably he would expect mutuality of obligation even if the laws do not assume it. The relative ranking of the relations is explicitly at issue in one saga (*Drop.* 4:148). The problem involves the obligations of Holmstein in a dispute involving his SiHu and his WiBr. The cast of characters are connected as follows:

Helgi A = Holmstein's si    Holmstein = Aslaug    Hrafnkel

Hrafnkel is Helgi A's nephew.[36] Hrafnkel asked Helgi for a half share in the chieftaincy that had once belonged to their common ancestor. Helgi refused, so Hrafnkel went to Holmstein, his SiHu, for aid. Holmstein, reciting his obligation to Helgi, said he could not help him personally: "I will not oppose Helgi A because he is married to my sister." He sent Hrafnkel to another Helgi, named Helgi D, for aid and also promised him the support of his own thingmen. Hrafnkel then went to Helgi D, who remarked that "Holmstein should value more greatly the fact that he is married to your sister," than the bond to his SiHu. Holmstein, we see, denied neither claim. He would not oppose his SiHu, nor did he leave his WiBr out in the cold. He offered him the support of his thingmen and provided him with counsel. The end of the matter was that Holmstein broke up a fight at the Thing between the two factions and was instrumental in bringing about a settlement.

The case is remarkable, however, in that one character, Helgi D, claims to have seen no real conflict of duty in Holmstein's position at all. Helgi D followed the sense of the laws and assumed that Holmstein must first fulfill his role as a SiHu, that is, he should support his WiBr, Hrafnkel. But was Helgi D right to think that the dilemma was easily solved by a simple application of rules? Most people in the sagas never drew the line as precisely as Helgi D did here. People did not conceive of kinship duties, or conflicts among these duties, as matters to be governed by rules. Duties conflicted not because there was a conflict in rules but because people were tied to many different people who had competing interests. People felt their way through these dilemmas, some with more skill than others, by practical knowledge, by give and take, by a feel for what the ranges and limits were, and not just by applying rules. There is good reason to believe that Helgi D was invoking rules solely for practical strategic purposes. He was at odds with Helgi A. He was not about to spurn any culturally endorsed normative language that could help legitimate his position and delegitimate Helgi A's or that of any of Helgi A's people. And it is important to note in all these cases that the issue of prioritizing conflicting obligations only occurs because two people differ as to what the preeminent bond should be. Reasonable people differed about these things. The ranking was not writ in stone. It was subject to the vagaries of context, to negotiation and argumentation. The language of normativity in these situations, then, is as much evidence of the relativity and disputability of the norm asserted as of its force and currency.

Conflicts of loyalty were often resolved as Holmstein resolved his. Those caught in the middle frequently attempted to resolve their dilemma by trying to resolve the conflict that gave rise to it. These are the people who are structurally positioned to want peace and to have the necessary connections to both sides to be able to get a hearing from the principal antagonists. We will take up peacemaking, and the way in which cross-cutting ties facilitated or exacerbated it, more fully in chapter 8. For present purposes we need only note how kinship connection affected actions even when kin found themselves on opposite sides of a dispute. It was, in fact, not unusual for kin and friends to be opposed, not so much as principals to a dispute, but as part of the musters of the contending principals. To be unsparing to kinsmen in such a situation could be cause for notoriety. In *Ljósvetninga saga* (31:105) there is the tale of Oddi Grimsson, who, when in Denmark, was asked by the king if he were "the Oddi who fought against his kinsmen in Iceland." Oddi replied that there were men present related to him but that he had spared them.[37] Kin and friends gave each other quarter (grið) both before and after major affrays (e.g., Íslend. 39:281; Þórð. 42:79). The expectation was that if they perchance should meet in battle, they would not fight (Bjarn. 32:202).[38] In one case in which a man was opposed to his wife's nephews, the respect both parties held for her affected the course of action to the extent that they avoided lethal violence during her lifetime (Svín. 6:92–93, 9:96–97). When kin, affines, or friends did oppose each other, their connection would be a significant factor in determining the level of hostility and the suitability of tactics, even if at times the expectation might be disappointed.

## Assembling the Kin

The kin group, we have noted, was not self-constituting. Keeping good kinship did not come naturally. It required work and foresight to maintain the bonds in working order. This task was aided by norms of mutual aid and reciprocity. And it was also aided negatively by anticipated threats from others. A person could not go it alone. Moreover, even when he did act individually, those whom he wronged invariably assumed that he had the support of a group whose membership they in effect defined and in which the particular wrongdoer need not figure as the focal ego. This is the so-called passive solidarity, the group as constituted by outsiders opposed to it. The cultural fact that others assumed a person was acting as part of group meant that there were strong inducements for those who were linked to him by others to take an active interest in his affairs. Active group formation was thus doubly motivated. It was in part an actualization of the passive grouping imposed by others and in part a positive undertaking necessary for reproduction and production and general well-being. Passive and active groupings seldom precisely coincided, but they usually deviated from each other only around the edges.

One of the chief activities kin undertook with each other was mutual consultation. Since the target of a vengeance killing might not be the wrongdoer himself, but one of his kin, there was every reason why kin would want to have some say in actions for which others might hold them to account. Taking counsel gave the moving person the chance to get broad-based support among his kin for his proposed course of action, thereby increasing its chances of success; it also gave his kin the opportunity to dissuade, modify, or ratify his proposal. Uncounseled deeds were considered reckless deeds. Those who acted repeatedly without taking counsel, either with kin or chieftain, were judged harshly by the sagas (e.g., Hrolf, Vall.;

Vemund, *Reyk.*). Mutual consultation was perceived as a duty and breaches of it were enforced with informal sanctions, mostly by a cooling in relations, but at times by actual repudiation.

Consultation with kin was especially important in matters of prospective marriage proposals. Einar, who did not get along with his brother Gudmund, still felt obliged to consult with him before agreeing to accept a marriage offer for his daughter from a suitor who was at the time embroiled with Gudmund in a serious lawsuit (*Ljós.* 11.136). In another instance the aggressive party seeking the hand of Gunnar's daughter had to bully him into abandoning his desire to get his wife's brother's approval for the marriage (*Hœn.* 10:29–30). Another saga writer thought it necessary to explain why the girl's mother's brother was not involved in her marriage negotiations (*Íslend.* 6:235; cf. *Glúma* 10:37). And after Hoskuld had arranged his daughter's marriage without consulting his brother Hrut, he adopted an apologetic tone when inviting Hrut to the wedding: "I hope, kinsman, that you won't take it amiss that I did not send for you when the deal was being negotiated" (*Njála* 10:32).[39] Prospective grooms had more control over their own marriages than brides, but consultation with their fathers, brothers, or key supporters was standard practice (e.g., *Lax.* 58:174; *Njála* 2:7, 13:41–42). These examples show that the group of people consulted usually did not extend much beyond the sibs of the groom or the sibs of the bride's parents but more distantly related important males could also be included. Uncounseled marriages are invariably described as having evil consequences. The marriage Unn arranged on her own behalf "without consulting any of her kinsmen" produced the villain of *Njáls saga* (25:70), while Gunnar's redeless marriage to Hallgerd enabled its central feud.

The process of taking counsel about risky matters like vengeance and lawsuits was integrated into the process of seeking out kin for support in carrying out the intended action. A litigant needed bodies in court to ensure that his opponent would not overcome him by force. His kin network would be called on to provide some of the bodies, though the bond primarily relied on in routine lawsuits was the *goði*-thingman bond. Musters for violent purposes, like vengeance and raids, tended to be recruited primarily from the household and kin networks, although chieftains would make use of their thingmen in these affairs also. Recruitment for vengeance is something that merits a fuller discussion and will be dealt with in the next chapter. For now, I note only a few general issues. Kin living in the same household formed a group already organized at the household level, but kin living in other households had to be sought out and convinced to join in. Those doing the recruiting were not without a number of conventional rhetorical devices to elicit consent. They recited obligations of kinship, the duties of vengeance; they enumerated prior wrongs, they goaded, insulted, cajoled, and threatened. Consider Thord kakali's exchange with Asgrim, his first cousin once removed, whom he sought to enlist for violent confrontation against the powerful Kolbein (*Þórð.* 5:12). Some aspects of it will by now be quite familiar to the reader:

> He said that the least honorable thing to do would be not joining up with him, "Above all for kinship's sake; second, because Sturla, my brother, improved your position; and third because of the torment you endured at Orlygsstead[40] witnessing the fall of your kinsmen and their men, people who will always be present in your mind."

Honor, kinship, favors accepted and still needing recompense, wrongs inflicted on him and his kinsmen by the person Thord wishes to move against, and the duty to take vengeance are all invoked. But it is necessary to recall that this is all a mode of argumentation, a rhetoric of persuasion that did not automatically achieve its end in spite of the litany of obligation and duty. Asgrim is not without his own rhetoric of excuse and exception:

> Asgrim parried this skillfully in numerous ways. And because he was quite smart he raised fine points of law on his behalf. First there were the oaths he had sworn Kolbein.[41] Then he said, which was true, that he lived too close to the Northerners [Kolbein] to be in a state of enmity with them. In the end he simply said he would not go.

The fact that kin might not always be willing to undertake dangerous missions did not stop the organizer from turning to them first. Thord, for instance, prior to meeting with Asgrim, had had success in recruiting other first cousins once removed (*Þórð.* 4:9) who were only too eager for vengeance. But Asgrim's prevarications represent something as real in this culture as the ethics of blood and honor, and that was the art of being able to back down, to back off, to excuse, and equivocate, and still not lose face. The source is not sufficiently concerned with Asgrim to bother relating how he came off in this particular case. He was not especially cowardly. He had earlier in his life been involved in much combat, and he later did Thord the service of spying on his behalf. Apparently both his honor and his relationship to Thord survived this refusal.

Kin clearly did not have to say yes to every claim made upon them. Keeping bonds in good working order did not always require people to forgo prudence and critical intelligence. Geography made Asgrim's position considerably riskier for reprisal than it made the itinerant Thord's, and even the beseecher at some level would credit such excuses. But eventually there had to be exchanges. Continued refusal, or from the beseecher's perspective, the refusal to continue making claims, meant in the end a denial of kinship. The living link rusted away, though it would continue to exist at the theoretical level where it would still provide the basis for computing relationship to others and for making legal claims to property via inheritance. Phillpotts and others have used the evidence of abandoned links to argue against kinship as a principle of group recruitment. This simply cannot be entertained plausibly in the face of the ubiquity of support-gathering expeditions in the sagas that show people seeking out kinsmen and affines, beseeching them for bodies for offense or for shelter for defense. Even when the link had been seldom activated, the very fact of a blood connection could always provide the basis for reactivating it: "Thorgils skarði [harelip] and Thorvard Thorarinsson were related in the third degree [second cousins] and *because of this it entered Thorvard's mind to seek him out* for reinforcements or other support" (Þorg. sk. 39:165).

## Affinity

Affines, relatives by marriage, were counted kin and the general word *frændsemi* ("kinship") was used to describe affinal relations as well as relations by blood. When Grim sought out the husband of his great aunt (MoFaSiHu), he hoped for some assistance "for the sake of kinship (*frændsemi*)" (*Hafl.* 11:28).[42] Kin were thus not only recruited by consanguinity, nor was a small family necessarily condemned to being bullied by more powerful neighbors. Much of what we would call political activity involved ways of extending the claims one could make on others. And this extension was mainly accomplished by exchanging people with other groups: children via fosterage and women via marriage. The bonds created by marriage were every bit as important as blood itself. Affines (*mágr, mágar,* pl.), that is, people with whom kinship was claimed by virtue of a person's marriage or the marriages of his blood kin, figure prominently in support groups, whether for taking vengeance, providing shelter in times of distress, or helping prosecute and defend lawsuits. A few of the examples in the discussion up to now have already indicated this. But the evidence is rich and merits its own attention.

The laws in several places distinguish a set of "three *námágar*," "three close affines"; they are, in addition to the husband of a sister, as we have already noted, the husbands of a person's daughter and mother (e.g., *Grágás* Ia 47).[43] The term *mágr* is used generally in the sagas as a way of addressing and describing both the *námágar* and affines more remote. The term is applied variously to an aunt's husband (FaSiHu, *Íslend*. 58:311; *Njála* 99:253), to a niece's husband (BrDaHu, *Njála* 116:293), to a first cousin's husband (FaSiDaHu, *Þórð*. 3:8; MoBrDaHu, *Hafl*. 31:49), to a wife's first cousin (WiFaBrSo, *Njála* 148:423); and to a wife's first cousin once removed (WiFaFaSiSo, *Hafl*. 31:49; WiMoFaBrSo, *Sturla* 31:110); and even to the father of a husband of a niece (BrDaHuFa, *Íslend*. 39:283). These examples indicate that affinity could be claimed to the second-cousin level with the kin of one's spouse or the spouses of one's kin without great ado. Presumably it could be claimed beyond this level in those cases where the blood links in the chain were in good working order, but I sufficiently distrust the thoroughness of my search to say this confidently. In any event, as the last example in the list above reveals, affinity could be claimed with the kin of the spouse of one's kin; we also find instances of people connected through two married links calling each other *mágr* (e.g., WiSiHu, *Íslend*. 32:260) and when Kari Solmundarson spared the husband of his wife's sister he alleged their affinity as the reason: "I have no wish to kill the man riding last, Ketil of Mork, because we are married to two sisters" (*Njála* 146:418).[44]

Two cases suggest that concubinage and perhaps even looser arrangements could form the basis of affinal obligation or at least provide the basis for making a claim alleging affinity. Thorgrim alikarl (fat man) claimed support from Sæmund to help avenge the death of his wife's father "because two of [Sæmund's] children, Pal and Margret, were Thorgrim's sister's children" (*G.dýri* 15:192). Here it seems the important thing was that the union was not casual but sufficiently regularized that it produced children who were kin to both Thorgrim and Sæmund. In another case the kinsmen of Asgrim Gilsson begged Kolbein for quarter on Asgrim's behalf so "that [Asgrim] would have the benefit of affinity (*mágsemd*), because Kolbein had previously been with his sister, Hallbera" (*Þórð*. 34:66). It is not known that Hallbera bore Kolbein any children; in any event, Kolbein was utterly unmoved by the claimed relationship. He refused to see Asgrim and "ordered him decapitated."[45] These cases would appear to indicate that it was actual relations between a man and a woman that formed the basis of the claim, not the juridical condition of marriage, although, as Kolbein demonstrated rather

forcefully to Asgrim, the ability of the obligation to overcome competing claims might vary directly with the regularity and legality of
the conjugal link.

As was evident from the discussion of householding patterns, relations with close affines tended to be remarkably strong. There was
perhaps a very slight tendency to favor links through women of one's
own blood as against links through one's wife. It was given legal
recognition in the class of *námágar*, the husbands of ego's sister,
daughter, and mother, the laws evidently assuming that in practice
these were likely to be links kept in working order. The tendency
is an indication that, once married or remarried, men perceived
their daughters, sisters, and mothers still as members of their own
kin groups and they expected the women to feel the same way.
Young unmarried men tended to look to their independently established married sisters for aid (e.g., *Gísli* 10:36; *Prest.* 4:123). The
only reason I take this as an example of affinal connection and not
simply another example of mutual aid among blood kin is that the
sagas describe it affinally, as a relation to a sister's husband, not as a
relation to a sister. When Thorkel leaves his brother to move in with
his sister and her husband, the saga says that he "moved in with
Thorgrim, his *mágr*, and lived with him" (*Gísli* 10:36). And when
Thorvard visits his sister in Hvamm, it is said that he was staying
with "Sturla, his *mágr*" (*Sturla* 9:72). Only the redoubtable Stein-
vor gets nearly equal billing with her husband when her brother
Thord kakali shows up empty-handed looking for support (*Þórð.*
2:6). The male bias is instructive and underlines that what made
affinity so important was the extra males it added to one's support
group. Still, both types of affine—the spouses of one's kin and the
kin of one's spouse—were available at a fairly distant degree for recruitment to ego's support group. We thus find affines as distant as
the husband of ego's first cousin and ego's wife's first cousin once
removed standing surety to guarantee performance of an arbitrated
settlement (*Hafl.* 31:49).

No less than blood kin, affines were under strong normative constraints to aid and avenge each other. The obligation of a daughter's
husband to avenge his father-in-law is the accepted norm underlying
Gudrun's goading of her husband Otrygg to avenge her father Thorkel: "'It is true enough that Thorkel Hake was related to me, not to
you,' Gudrun said, 'so I will go.' Otrygg answered, 'It's up to me to
go and I will'" (*Ljós.* 24:77). The obligation of the man who gives
his kinswoman in marriage to assume the feuds of the man he betrothed her to occupies a central position in the plot of *Hœnsa-Þóris
saga*. The fact that the marriage was forced upon the bride's kin and

the betrother's participation was obtained by trickery gives no cause for embarrassment on the part of the deceivers, only an occasion to invoke the norms of affinal obligation: "you are now obliged to support your in-law, and we are obliged to help you, because many people heard you give the woman in marriage" (11:33). Moreover, anyone who happened to be married to a woman who had vengeance on her mind, whether it be for a father or a prior husband, could expect to be goaded into taking up her claim. Thus Thorkel Eyjolfsson expresses concern about marrying Gudrun before her former husband is avenged (*Lax.* 58:174; also *Glúma* 22:74). The fact was that women were frequently active organizers of vengeance taking (see Miller 1983b and below pp. 211–14). To the extent that revenge was being sought for a dead husband, the widow's kin, who were affines with respect to the corpse, were often actively involved in taking vengeance. And when the tables were turned and it was the woman's kinsman who was the corpse, her husband was a likely avenger of her kin.[46]

Among the chieftain and *bóndi* classes marriage was, before anything else, a way of adding bodies to one's support group, either immediately, by acquiring *mágar*, or prospectively, by reproduction. Marriage extended support networks. A typical marriage proposal might run: "My purpose in coming is that we are proposing a marriage and the contracting of bonds of affinity (*mælum til mægða*) with you, Flosi, by seeking the hand of Hildigunn, your brother's daughter" (*Njála* 97:241). Or a father would argue the advantages of a certain match to his son by referring to the increase in his strength that would come from alliance with the prospective wife's kinsmen (*Lax.* 22:62). The art of marrying well was much of what politics was about and this fact was openly admitted:

> One evening when Snorri was sitting in the bath the conversation turned to the subject of chieftains. Men said that there was no chieftain like Snorri and no other chieftain might now contend with him on account of his affines. Snorri confirmed that his *mágar* were not insubstantial men. (*Íslend.* 64:319)[47]

There were some affairs of the heart ending in marriage, but most of these also made social, political, or economic sense (e.g., *Ljós.* 5:109–13; *Njála* 33:86–87). There were, of course, other inducements to marry. Land-hungry men swept down on heiresses and widows. One widow, in fact, staged a successful hunger strike to prevent her remarriage (*Íslend.* 57:309–10). She gave as her reason a desire to retain her property for the benefit of her daughter. The reason did not impress her kinsmen very much and they were greatly displeased with her behavior since the rejected suitor was a very well connected man. In the middling range of the social scale, marriage was still undertaken for political reasons, but here politics was the politics familiar to peasant communities: marriage offered opportunities to increase flocks, pasture, and prestige. By creating connections to other households it provided insurance against the vagaries in productive and reproductive cycles. At the bottom end of the social register, the bonds established by marriage, if marriage was even possible (see pp. 121–22), gave way in importance to bonds indicating some kind of clientage: fosterage, tenancy, and household affiliation.

## Fictive Kinship

Kinship also provided the ideology and metaphor for fictive kinship bonds based on fosterage, blood brotherhood, and sponsorial relations. We have dealt with some aspects of fosterage in our treatment of householding, but we need to discuss briefly the practical nature of the bonds it created. Foster-father or foster-mother (fóstri, fóstra),[48] as mentioned, designated two types of arrangement. In one the children were sent to another farm and raised by the householder at that farm; in the other, the children remained in the parental household but some special relationship was established between them and a household servant of either sex. With both types of fostering, the sagas consistently portray the bond running as deep as, if not deeper than, that between parent and child. The laws also recognize the strength of the bond. A man has the privilege to kill for sexual assaults on his foster-daughter and foster-mother, who are thus members of a class that includes his wife, daughter, mother, and sister (Grágás Ia 164, II 331). Foster-children figure as the avengers of their foster-parents. The Njalssons make a clean sweep of all those who participated in the killing of their foster-father (Njála 92:232); Egil Skallagrimsson kills his father's esteemed steward in retaliation for his father's psychopathic killing of Egil's foster-mother, a slave in Skallagrim's household (Egil 40: 101–2); and Vigfus Viga-Glumsson finds an eventual way to kill the slayer of his foster-father without technically violating a settlement his father bound him to honor (Glúma 18:61). It is perhaps instructive that these three cases all have to do with foster-parents who were members of the parental household. We can thus discern that this relationship was an indulgent one, a notion that receives additional support from the fact that *fóstri* is also a term of endearment and a way of addressing favorite pets (e.g., *Hrafnk.* 3:104; *Hafl.* 25:44; *Njála* 77:186; Maurer 1893, 104).

Interhousehold fostering was considerably more complex. As mentioned briefly earlier, one type of fostering arrangement involved a confirmation of status differentiation between the two households. As the proverb would have it, "he who fosters another's child is always considered the lesser man" (*Lax.* 27:75). This sentiment was manipulated in a variety of ways. It could be accepted literally to justify exploitive appropriations of the fosterer's property by the father of the child. Thus Sturla forced his young son on a man who had sold him wormy meal, and in another source, one man desperate for protection agreed to foster Hoskuld's son and make the boy his heir, if Hoskuld would grant him protection (*Sturla* 25:98; *Lax.* 16:37).[49] Alternately, the sentiment could provide the basis for a mild ritualized humiliation, a formalized act of deference, by the more powerful to the less powerful. It was this meaning that Njal intended in expressing a willingness to foster the son of a man his sons had killed and that Jon Loftsson had in mind when he offered to foster Snorri at the conclusion of a settlement he had arbitrated to the disadvantage of Sturla, the boy's father (*Njála* 94:236; *Sturla* 34:113). In each of these instances the offer was an act of kindness, of reconciliation; but at another level, the child also looked a little like a hostage to secure the maintenance of a nervous peace. And what of the poor child in the example above who was foisted by his father on the seller of bad meal solely to annoy the fosterer?[50] In fact, no evidence in the sagas indicates that such children were perceived as hostages. There are no examples of a foster-parent threatening harm to the child, nor any instances of natural parents acting out of fear of what a foster-parent might do to the child. The children, it seems, were treated no differently than any other child would have been. Certainly they do not appear to have been treated with any special indulgence.[51] It is, for instance, considered quite unusual and noteworthy that Gudmund the Powerful does not make the well-born boys he fosters do any other work "other than to be always in his company" even though "when they were home . . . it was their custom to work" (*Ljós.* 5:109).

The bonds created by fostering did not give rise to the web of claims that marriage did. A fosterer's first cousins did not make claims on the fosterling or his parents, nor did the fosterer ever look beyond the child-giving household for support. The bond linked only the child to his new household and that household to the parents' household. Interhousehold fostering tended to create conflicts of loyalty that intrahousehold fostering could not. The likelihood of

such a conflict was one of the main attractions that fosterage had
when it was undertaken between two already contending households. But the fosterling's conflict did not always work for peace.
Sometime he simply chose one side over the other. Bjarni's foster-
father had killed Bjarni's father and even though Bjarni greatly preferred his foster-father, he responded to a formal charge to take blood
vengeance and killed his foster-father. People deplored the deed and
he himself suffered great remorse (Vápn. 14:52–53) Snorri Sturluson, on the other hand, remained strongly attached to the Oddaverjar among whom he was fostered even when the attachment brought
him into conflict with his own blood (Íslend. generally).

Blood-brotherhood was a formalized relation undertaken between
two or more men in which each vowed to avenge the death of the
other "just as if he were his own brother." The ritual involved passing under a raised strip of turf and mingling blood in the dirt (Gísli
6:22–23; Fóst. 2:125).[52] The ritual does not appear to have survived
the Saga Age. No performances of it are mentioned in the Sturlunga
compilation and the institution itself is not mentioned in the laws.
The author of the account in Fóstbrœðra saga feels obliged to defend his characters on account of participating in the ceremony,
thereby suggesting that if there were twelfth- and thirteenth-century
performances they would have been performed secretly for fear of
leading to accusations of carrying on pagan practices: "even though
people were called Christian at that time [the first decade of the
eleventh century], the faith was still young and very undeveloped."
One family saga shows how Christianity might be used to justify a
downward revision in the terms of the compact. When Bjorn proposed a mutual vengeance pact with Thorstein, the latter, quite
aware that he was likely to outlive Bjorn, found it convenient to
invoke the new dispensation:

> but I would like to amend what you say about vengeance
> because we now know more fully than before [the con-
> version] what should be done. I propose that each of us
> obtain either self-judgment or outlawry and compensa-
> tion on behalf of the other and not blood; that is better
> suited to Christian men. (Bjarn. 29:191)

The same term—fóstbróðir—was employed to designate a blood-
brother and a foster-brother. Foster-brothers acquired their connection by virtue of having been raised together, usually one or both
being fostered by the head of household. Whatever the reason for
collapsing the two relationships under one heading might have
been, one effect was to cause the duty to avenge to inhere in both

relationships (cf. Maurer 1893, 104–5). One of our few reasonably circumstantial accounts of blood-brotherhood shows four men, already bound by various ties of kinship and affinity, agreeing to undertake the ceremony in the hopes of forestalling the effects of a bad prophecy concerning their future relations (*Gísli* 6:22). The sense is that the implicit obligations of kinship, friendship, and affinity needed occasionally to be supplemented by obligations explicitly undertaken with great formality: "we should bind our friendship with greater fastness than before."

The fictive kinship achieved by sponsoring someone's primesigning,[53] baptism, or confirmation, brought the marriage prohibitions into play (*Grágás* Ib 31, II 158). They also disqualified that man from judging or serving on a panel of neighbors in a legal action involving the person sponsored (Ia 47, 62, II 318). The sagas take little interest in this relationship. But one account set prior to the conversion of Iceland tells of two men meeting in battle, one of whom (Ozur) had sprinkled the other (Helgi) with water when he was newly born. The heathen ceremony, like baptism, signaled the acceptance of the newborn child into the family and indicated that the child would not be exposed (Steffensen 1967–68, 109–12). Helgi told Ozur he would not attack him "because you sprinkled me with water." Ozur, too, was reluctant to attack Helgi and had not been actively involved in the fighting. But when Ozur had to choose between defending his chieftain and attacking Helgi, it took him no more than a few seconds to make up his mind: he preferred spearing his "godchild" to sparing him (*Drop.* 10:164). If the account reflects twelfth- and thirteenth-century attitudes about sponsorial kin, we can make the unsurprising observation that such bonds could indeed influence behavior, or at least provoke some anxiety when they were disavowed.

## *Repudiation*

Some social ties were relatively unambiguously created and unambiguously dissolved. A man had to announce formally his attachment to a chieftain's Thing unit and he could change his attachment by a witnessed public announcement. Annual service contracts had their clearly demarcated commencements and terminations. Less clear-cut was the initiation of procreative units. Casual sexual union was on one end of a continuum with a formally concluded marriage on the other. And likewise, the dissolution of ménages might be clearly marked by death or divorce,[54] or they might simply dissolve unclearly by degrees upon separation. The entry of a child into his father's kin group (*ætt*) was indicated by any of four clearly demarcated actions and these four were exclusive. They are enumerated in

*Grágás* II 192: (1) if the child is born of a man's wife with whom he lives; (2) if he formally guarantees paternity and accepts the child; (3) if a woman proves him the father of the child by ordeal; or (4) if he is adjudged the father by verdict. "By these means just listed shall a person be filiated legally to a kin group and by no other means. Neither gossip nor evil tongues shall make the attribution." In the absence of all of these the child was fatherless and, if free, could only be a member of his mother's kin group. If entry into a mother's kin group was marked by birth[55] and into a father's by the criteria just noted, exit from the kin group was considerably less clearly demarcated.

There were no ritual or formal repudiations, nothing at all approaching the Flemish *fourjurements* (Phillpotts 1913, 179). The lack of formality is a direct consequence of the lack of corporateness of the kin group (see Moore 1978, 122–26). The group's boundaries were not well enough defined to allow for formal expulsion. The collectivity with well-defined boundaries, from which formal expulsion was the ultimate sanction, was the society itself. Thus it is that the only sanction the law knew for all but the most trivial breaches was either temporary exile of three years – lesser outlawry – or permanent loss of juridical being—full outlawry.[56] Nevertheless, kinsmen would deal with their unwanted members in a variety of ways that in effect removed them from the kin group for various periods of time. Unruly men were often encouraged to go abroad to take out their excesses on people too far away to contemplate reprisal (e.g., *Lax.* 38:111). One saga case actually shows a man counseling and agreeing to the killing of his brutal and unruly nephew (*Vatn.* 19:53). There is also the *Grágás* provision noted earlier (p. 153), which allowed a person to send burdensome kin abroad.

An example in *Njáls saga* gives us a glimpse of how a group might deal with a troublesome member. The case involves the foster-father to one of the group's women. Thjostolf was ill-tempered and fast with his axe. His primary function seems to have been providing protection for his foster-daughter, the beautiful young Hallgerd. He accompanied her to the home of her first husband whom, acceding to her desires, Thjostolf killed for having slapped her. When it came time to negotiate Hallgerd's second marriage, Hrut, Hallgerd's father's brother, suggested the following to the suitor:

If the marriage should take place, Thjostolf should not be allowed to go south with her [to her new household], and under no condition should he stay there more than three nights without Glum's [the new husband] permission. If he stays longer he can be killed by Glum with

impunity, although Glum shall have the right to allow
him to stay, but I advise against it. (13:43)

Imagine how Thjostolf would feel knowing that two people were
contracting over the right to kill him, a right which purported to
bind the world. If Thjostolf had violated the condition, Glum could
have killed him without being sanctioned. Can this really be what
is happening? Although the saga is somewhat ambiguous on this
score, it does not appear that Thjostolf was a slave. He was a free
man who had been a member of Hallgerd's father's household for
some time. Was a free man's right to immunity from bodily harm so
evanescent as to allow two people to contract the right away in his
absence in such a fashion that they would be immune to public
sanction? It seems that we are seeing something a little less absolute. Hrut's proposal is more accurately conceived of as a condi-
tional repudiation of Thjostolf by his own group. With only a brief
ellipsis, Hrut is telling Glum that if he kills Thjostolf in accordance
with the stipulated conditions, then Hrut and his party will take no
action, neither lawsuit, vengeance, nor request for compensation.
This acquiescence coupled with the fact that Thjostolf, a Hebridean,
was without kin in Iceland immunized Thjostolf's killer, for all
practical purposes, from reprisal.[57] Thjostolf was, in fact, treated to
the ultimate repudiation. Hrut killed him after Thjostolf had justified Hrut's initial uneasiness by killing Hallgerd's second husband
as well. And Hrut's action was effective in absolving his kin group
from liability for compensating Glum's kin:

> [Glum's brother]: "Will you pay me some compen-
> sation for my brother, because that was a great loss
> to me?"
> [Hallgerd's father]: "I did not kill your brother, nor did
> my daughter encompass his death, and as soon as Hrut
> heard about it he killed Thjostolf."
> [Glum's brother] was silent, for it seemed his claim
> was in trouble. (17:51)

Most repudiations of kinsmen took place posthumously in the
fashion suggested by Hrut. When unpopular troublesome kin finally
got their deserts, their surviving kin were singularly unaggressive
about taking redressive action. If they sued, they pleaded faintly, if
compensation was requested the amount would be modest, and no
one had much interest in taking blood vengeance. When Sigmund
was killed for having composed scurrilous verses about Njal and his
sons, Sigmund's kinsman Gunnar took no action whatsoever (*Njála*

45 : 117—18). And in *Eyrbyggja*, only one of the several kinsmen of the unpopular Vigfus was willing to give even so much as advice to the widow who wanted some action taken (27 : 68—69).

What is remarkable is how many pretty awful people were tolerated and not disowned by their kin during their lifetimes. Take the case of Mar Bergthorsson. Among his several dubious achievements were the brutal beating of his amiable foster-father, the unprovoked killings of two decent men, and an attempted rape. Yet after each of these deeds he was taken in by his prominent and respected father's brother, Haflidi Masson, the same Haflidi who headed the commission in 1117 charged with drafting a written law code (see p. 224). Haflidi registered strong disapproval, saying one time that Mar was "a shame to his kin" (*frændaskǫmm*) and claiming another that *hann mjǫk segjast ór sinni ætt* (*Hafl* 5—6 : 18—19). The Icelandic literally means that Mar by his actions had "emphatically declared himself to be outside his kin group," but in context has a softer extended meaning more on the order of "in his actions he showed himself to be unlike his kin." The idiom suggests literally a formal renunciation or repudiation ritual, but this sense, if original, had long since become a figure of speech by the time it occurs in the saga. Similarly, the term *frændaskǫmm* is linked with repudiation. Consider a source describing events c. 996:

> That summer a law was enacted at the Allthing that the
> kin of Christians who were further than second cousins
> and nearer than fourth cousins should prosecute them
> for blasphemy. That summer Stefnir was prosecuted for
> being a Christian. His kinsmen brought the action
> against him because Christianity was then considered a
> shame to one's kin (*frændaskǫmm*). (*Kristni saga*
> 6 : 10—11)

In pre-Christian Iceland, at least if we can trust the source, we have kin outlawing a kinsman on the grounds that he had disgraced his family by being Christian. The law obviously did not survive the conversion and what little evidence we have suggests that the formal legal means of repudiation of kin, like the legal exposure of infants, did not survive it by much either (see p. 35).[58] Haflidi shows us that the memory lives on as metaphor available to curse an obnoxious kinsmen in the same breath that one decides to stand by him, for in the next sentence after Haflidi says Mar had in effect renounced his kin it is reported: "But for kinship's sake [Haflidi] felt that he could not disassociate himself from Mar's case."

## Conclusion

Practical kinship, whether based on shared blood, marriage, or even fictive kinship relationships, provided one of the chief bases for group recruitment in saga Iceland. People looked to kin and affines for aid in law and life. They avenged each other's wrongs; they invited each other to weddings and funerals; they gave each other gifts. They stood surety for each other and hired on their poorer cousins as servants. Kinship terminology had practical application. It provided a language of implicit obligation and subtle admonition, a diction of request and reciprocity, the very tools with which support networks were constructed. On a darker side, practical kinship meant competition, jealousy, and strife. Kin competed for preeminence among their own blood; they resented the demands enabled and legitimated by ties of blood and marriage. And the sense of the law codes, confirmed to some extent by the sagas, is that they acted on their resentment by disowning their poorer members. The rosy picture of kin reciprocity usually applied only to kin of roughly the same social standing, unless we are willing to define reciprocity sufficiently downward so that it would include the room and board poor kin received for their labor, or even the outlay that the debt-slave had dedicated his or her body to discharging.

On the formal level kinship was clearly figured bilaterally and in keeping with this style affinity was claimed both with a spouse's blood kin and with spouses of one's own blood kin. But the theory of ego-focused bilateral kindreds was, in practice, sharply contained. Kin groups realistically did not form around every possible ego. Kin groupings tended to center around leading men and lesser people had to content themselves with being satellites in someone else's gravitational field. In theory, kinship was claimed up to the fourth-cousin level and even further in matters of marriage prohibition. In practice, links that distant were unlikely to have been kept up or to have prevented any marriages, but they still, theoretically at least, could provide the basis for imposing burdens of poor relief. Active kinship pretty much petered out before the third-cousin level. The chapters that follow will take up again many of the issues raised here in slightly different settings. There is simply no way to keep the kin out of discussions of revenge, law, and peacemaking.

# Feud, Vengeance, and the Disputing Process

## Definitions and Models

The surviving sources, as we have seen, had much to tell us about householding, kinship, and marriage. But they said it indirectly and incidentally. The information had to be teased from casual details, constructed from inferences in sources interested in other things. But now we shift our focus to the disputing process and our task is utterly transformed. Once desperately hungering for fact, we now desperately hunger for principles of selection among myriads of facts. Only the most passing experience with Old Icelandic literature is needed to know that the sagas are about feud and dispute, about the incidents that give rise to them, the means of pursuing them, and the attempts to conclude them. The bloodfeud informs every aspect of Icelandic political and legal life. It variously appears as a structure within which political activity takes place, as a means by which that activity is pursued, as the ultimate sanction behind arbitrated settlements and legal judgments, and more.

There has been much recent interest shown in the bloodfeud by medieval and early modern historians,[1] who for the most part have drawn their inspiration from anthropological studies of primitive dispute processing.[2] No universally accepted definition of feud has emerged from this literature. Several anthropologists have tried to develop one, but invariably the definition does much better describing the particular culture with which the anthropologist is most familiar than describing a cross-cultural phenomenon. The most recent systematic attempt at definition tries to avoid ethnocentricity by abandoning conventions of terseness traditionally associated with the definitional style and choosing instead to list more than a dozen distinctive features (Boehm 1984, 218–19). Historians have for the most part avoided definition, some without discussion, some explicitly doubting the wisdom of confining such varied and complex activity under one rubric (White 1986, 196), some recognizing that feud can have various forms in various times and places (Brown 1986, 2–3). Historians who bothered to define feud have been content to give roughly serviceable definitions so as to get on with the real business at hand. Wallace-Hadrill (1962, 122) is an example:

> It is not difficult to arrive at a working definition of feud. We may call it, first, the threat of hostility between kins; then, the state of hostility between them; and finally, the satisfaction of their differences and a settlement on terms acceptable to both. The threat, the state and the settlement of that hostility constitute feud but do not necessarily mean bloodshed.

This definition is similar to the implicit one of Andreas Heusler, who considered feud, at least in the Icelandic context, to be characterized as much by lawsuits and arbitration as by vengeance (1911, 38).

I share with other historians the reluctance of starting with a definition, which inevitably proves inadequate once the richness of the experience is described. I prefer to let a sense of what the feud is emerge slowly with nuance from the discussion that follows. Nevertheless, I will list certain features and impressionistic observations that, to me, seem to characterize feud in a way that distinguishes it from other types of violence like war, duels, or simple revenge killings that involve no one beyond the killer and his victim. The list is intended to serve as an orientation to the reader, nothing more. Some of its items are borrowed with modification from Boehm (1984, 218–19), Black-Michaud (1975, 27–31), and Nadel (1947, 151); some are my own, but in the end Heusler's loose definition is more than adequate for the purpose of initiating discussion.

1. Feud is a relationship (hostile) between two groups.
2. Unlike ad hoc revenge killing that can be an individual matter, feuding involves groups that can be recruited by any number of principles, among which kinship, vicinage, household, or clientage are most usual.
3. Unlike war, feud does not involve relatively large mobilizations, but only occasional musterings for limited purposes. Violence is controlled; casualties rarely reach double digits in any single encounter.
4. Feud involves collective liability. The target need not be the actual wrongdoer, nor, for that matter, need the vengeance-taker be the person most wronged.

5. A notion of exchange governs the process, a kind of my-turn/your-turn rhythm, with offensive and defensive positions alternating after each confrontation.[3]

6. As a corollary to the preceding item, people keep score.

7. People who feud tend to believe that honor and affronts to it are the prime motivators of hostilities. Cross-culturally, there appears to be a correlation between the existence of feud and a culture of honor.

8. Feud is governed by norms that limit the class of possible expiators and the appropriatenesses of responses. For instance, most feuding cultures recognize a rough rule of equivalence in riposte, the *lex talionis* being but one example.

9. There are culturally acceptable means for making temporary or permanent settlements of hostility.

The bloodfeud is frequently moral, often juridical, and always political. It is moral in its retributive aspect when it is the means for punishing violations of social norms. It is juridical when, as in Iceland, it provides the sanction behind arbitrated settlements and legal judgments, in effect serving as the executive power of a polity that has no other formally instituted state executive apparatus.[4] And it is political because it is one of the key structures in which the competition for power, the struggle for dominance, is played out.

One further caveat. It is often the case that people use the term feud as shorthand for its most violent manifestation: vengeance killing.[5] I do the same on occasion, but in such a way that I hope will not introduce analytical confusion. The feud was more than the series of overt actions that made it up. It was the relationship between the groups, the state of the participants' minds, the postures of defiance, antagonism, and coldness filling the intervals of time between hostile confrontations. These things were every bit as much a part of the feud as vengeance killing. Nevertheless, the overarching image, the nonreducible core of what it meant to be in a state of feud or to have feuding relations, was ultimately the obligation to have to kill and in turn to suffer the possibility of being killed. As the feud's most chilling aspect, vengeance killing is occasionally suitable as a metonymical figure for the thing itself.

What of the native conception of feud? Can we even speak of one when the Icelanders had no name for it? Old Norse had no reflex of PrmGerm *faihiþa* meaning feud. Feuds were designated loosely, in roughly descending order of frequency, as disputes, suits, transactions (*mál*), dealings (*deild*), or coldness (*fæð*) and enmity (*heipt*). The lack of a term for the institution evidently led Maurer (1910,

51–102) to avoid talking about feud, preferring instead to discuss vengeance, a concept admitted in the native vocabulary (*hefnd*). At least one recent writer has done the same (Gottzmann 1982, 172; see also Sawyer 1987, 28).[6] The sense from the terminology, however, is not that there was no native consciousness of the disputing process as process (the remainder of the chapter will dispel the mere suggestion); on the contrary, what the natives perceived was process itself, not a reified institution. They saw that there was coldness between parties, that parties mustered support, sued, attacked, settled, broke settlements, requited wrongs, made claims, shifted allegiances, etc. What they observed and experienced was capable of being adequately captured in such generalized polysemous concepts as "dealings," "transactions," and "coldness." The predictability of the disputing process, its inevitability, made it a part of the given of social experience; feud was in the air, it was part of the natural order of things. The very lack of a specific term also coincided nicely with a native propensity toward understatement, irony, and a tendency to achieve these styles by an indirection that often manifested itself in naming things by denying their antitheses. Thus "unpeace" (*ófrið*) is war, "unfriend" (*óvinr*) is enemy and so on.

The Icelanders did have a model of feud and of the disputing process. It was a model of balance and reciprocity. The central notion was one of requital, of repayment, captured variously in the verbs *launa* (to repay, requite), *gjalda* (to repay, return, to pay), and *gefa* (to give). The model takes over the entire vocabulary of gift-exchange and inverts it (see chapter 3). Spears thrown at someone are "gifts" that demand requital (*Vall.* 8:257), as are broken bones (*Grett.* 78:249) and insults (*Njála* 44:114). Wrongs done to someone, like gifts given to him, unilaterally make the recipient a debtor, someone who owes requital. But in the world of feud, unlike the world of gift-exchange, the debts are debts of blood. The complete congruence between the worlds of gifts and feud supplies the basis for a natural irony in both worlds. The dark side of giving and paying back is never quite suppressed and it is available for rhetorical effect when needed. Bergthora is not very subtle when she tries to goad her sons to avenge insults leveled at them and their father: "Gifts have been given to you, to father as well as sons, and your manhood will suffer unless you repay them" (*Njála* 44:114).

The model involves careful scorekeeping, an alternating rhythm of giving and taking, inflicting and being afflicted. It receives its most systematic representation in the stylized dispute between two women in *Njáls saga* (35–45:90–118), in which the sides annually alternate offense and defense. I will set forth the events briefly.

Njal's wife Bergthora and Gunnar's wife Hallgerd exchanged insults at a feast. The next summer, when Njal and his sons and Gunnar were at the Allthing, Hallgerd sent a slave named Kol to kill a slave of Njal and Bergthora named Svart. After some prompting, Kol sank his axe in Svart's head. Hallgerd then sent a messenger to the Allthing to inform Gunnar, who in turn went to Njal offering him self-judgment. Njal accepted the offer and immediately awarded himself twelve ounces of silver. Bergthora registered displeasure with the settlement and indicated that blood vengeance would also follow. To this end she engaged a man named Atli as a servant. The following summer at Allthing time, Bergthora sent Atli to kill Kol and sent a messenger to Njal to inform him of the killing. In a mirror image of the prior year's events, Gunnar accepted Njal's offer of self-judgment and awarded himself the same sum of twelve ounces. Njal paid over the same purse and silver that Gunnar gave him the year before. Gunnar, the saga tells us, recognized the money. The killings of and by household members would continue back and forth for several years, with each killer being killed in his turn one year later in the sequence outlined in the table*:

|  | Bergthora | Hallgerd |
|---|---|---|
| 12 oz. men | 1. Svart (slave) ← | → 2. Kol (slave) |
| 100 oz. men | 3. Atli (freedman) ← | 4. Brynjolf (free kin of Hallgerd and of ill repute) |
| 200 oz. men | 5. Thord (freedman's son) ← | 6. Sigmund (free and ill-mannered kin of Gunnar) |
|  | 7. Skarphedin (Bergthora's son)[7] |  |

*each man kills the person with the next lower number

This feud is rich in significant details of great interest, but I confine myself here to a few brief observations. The account is meant to establish an ideal type of feud and is consciously stylized to indicate that that is what is intended. Nowhere else in the sagas does the process of a dispute ever look this elegant and symmetrical. Here corpses are matched with each other in an ascending scale of value based mostly on juridical rank. Killers get their just deserts; the interval between each killing is the same, not indecorously hasty, nor excessively dilatory. The symbolism of equipoise is reinforced by giving the slaves synonymous names (both mean black). Even the apparent asymmetries are ordered systematically. Two of the people on the right side are balanced against two people of lower status on the left side. The disparity is intentional. The author indicates in this way which side had greater right and where the reader's sympathies are to lie. Men of low juridical status on one side are of such moral quality that they appropriately merit the same compensation as people of higher juridical status on the other side. The model thus indicates that the native "rule" of equivalence was not the formal equivalence of the talion. The eye of a free scoundrel, the tooth of a free rascal, were not the eye and tooth of a free man of good will. More than just the juridical quality of the corpse was properly considered.[8]

The model also has some disconcerting aspects to it. First, it makes escalation or its possibility a structural feature. The victims are thus of ever increasing status, moving from slave to freedman to freedman's son on one side, and from slave to scoundrel free man of low status to ill-mannered free man of fairly substantial status on the other. Second, it implies that settlements providing for compensation need not bring closure to the disputing process. In one respect, compensation can be seen as actually facilitating the breach of the settlement it was meant to conclude, for the compensation received is available to finance the return blow.[9] Njal himself takes care to make this point when he pays for Kol's death with the very same money he received for Svart's death. The reality is not quite so bleak. It was not easy financing that fueled this feud. The failure of Gunnar's and Njal's settlements to conclude the strife between their household memberships had less to do with structural contradictions in the model than the simple fact that they didn't bother to control their household members or involve the real parties of interest in the settlement process: the women.[10] When the male heads of household finally cared to keep their wives and servants in line, a more enduring settlement was reached. The settlement over Sigmund's death (no. 6 in the table), was in fact technically never breached.[11]

The balanced-exchange model, to give it a name, served as a kind of constitutive metaphor adopted by the saga characters to explain the courses of their disputes. People articulated actions in its framework, even when a recalcitrant reality was not quite so obliging. The metaphor of symmetry and balanced exchange informed many arbitrated settlements in which corpse was set against corpse, injury balanced against insult, and what was left over was weighed against compensation in property (see chapter 8). Most hostile action could be integrated into the model, either by exploiting the ambiguities in group boundaries and membership and the relative worth of victims, or by the manufacture of new claims provoked to justify what might often be naked aggression. But, as we shall see, the model had little predictive power. It could explain things only after the fact and then only if the persuasive powers of those seeking to officialize their actions in terms of the model were sufficient to convince others of the explanation (see Bourdieu 1977, 21). The model simply could not account for two crucial things in the feud as practiced: the iden tity of the vengeance target and the timing of the return blow. Nevertheless, the model had a firm hold on the imaginations of most actors; in its terms saga people understood their conflicts. Lacking a theory of politics or even the conception of an autonomous universe of political action, they understood politics largely in the terms of the balanced-exchange model of feud. The social structures produced and enabled by the systems of reciprocity, that is, by feud and gift-exchange, produced, in Foucault's terms, a regime of truth (Foucault 1980, 131).

There is an aspect implicit in the model that is confirmed by the ethnographic literature and anthropological typologies of violence. Feud is something that takes place between people of relatively equal status and resources. Chieftains feud with each other or with farmers of means; *bœndr* feud with each other. Feud generally did not exist across social strata. This does not mean, however, that interclass conflict did not exist. It's just that such conflict was perceived differently. A slave did not feud with his master. A slave could revolt and kill a master in revenge for having castrated him (*Draumr Þorsteins* 323–26), but the immediate torture and execution of the slave terminated the affair once and for all.[12] A farmer might be raided by a chieftain interested in provisioning his forces for combat, but this did not give rise to feud between the chieftain and the farmer. The differences in power left the farmer to lump his losses unless he could enlist another chieftain to take up his case. Then there might be feud, but it was the chieftain's, not the farmer's. For the continuing hostile exchanges that constitute feud, each party had to consider the other worthy of giving offense and worthy of retaliation. In other words, feuding relations were congruent with the boundaries of the field of honor (see pp. 29–34). One contended for honor with those who had honor to lose and of the kind that one could acquire.

In strata below the middling farmer there was no feud; the means and the bodies for continued hostile exchange were lacking. The slaves and servants killed in the hostilities between Bergthora's and

Hallgerd's households were attracted to the feuds of their masters and mistresses. The trouble that these people might get into on their own either becomes the trouble of their masters or it is ignored as unworthy of attention.[13] But, unfortunately, the fact that members of the lower strata lacked the means to engage in a proper feud on their own account did not mean that they did not suffer some of the consequences of feud. The course of a feud between chieftains might lead one of them on occasion to vex, harry, or even kill the other's thingmen (e.g., *Hrafn Sv. St.* 17:221; see White 1986, 202). And of course, one's household servants and slaves were just as capable of stopping spears of the opposition in a general affray as were the householder and his sons.

Anthropologists writing on feud have noted a high correlation between societies characterized by an egalitarian ethos and those that feud (Boehm 1984, 232–40; Black-Michaud 1975, 150–51). Historians, however, have discovered that social stratification need not be inconsistent with feud. But within stratified feuding societies, the anthropological model tends to hold true within each stratum (Brown 1986; Wallace-Hadrill 1962; White 1986; J. Wormald 1980). In any event, such was the case in early Iceland.

Two of the more influential scholars of feud have argued, primarily on the basis of North African materials, that the feud is by nature interminable (Peters 1967; Black-Michaud 1975). Their view is disputed by Boehm who, drawing from a more diverse sample, concludes that feud functions to limit the extent of possible conflict and that it necessarily involves the possibility of resolution (1984, 199–207, 218). The Icelandic model combines elements of both views, but the feud as practiced in Iceland is distinctly closer to Boehm's formulation than to Black-Michaud's. The model of balanced exchange, at least as it is presented in *Njáls saga*, contemplated both escalation and settlements that initiated periods of peace of varying duration. Money as well as blood were elements in it. Favoring interminability was the fact that few return blows ever precisely balanced the wrong they were matched against. The notion of balance itself was innately ambiguous since it was not mathematical, but socially contingent on a host of shifting variables, some of which were subject to conscious manipulation by the parties. There were always new debts to pay or old ones that had not been completely discharged. There was also the problem that each new killing wronged a class of people constituted slightly differently than the one which originally gave offense, thereby creating the possibility of new conflicts with different groupings and providing a structural impetus for expansion of the dispute. Moreover, vengeance attacks were usually group affairs mustered not only from kin but from neighbors, thingmen, and household servants, meeting an opposing group similarly constituted. These affrays usually involved no more than twenty to a side, but sometimes quite a few more; in any event, more than just the vengeance target was likely to suffer injury or death.

But the theoretical possibility of geometric expansion envisaged by the model was in reality limited if not utterly inhibited. The death of neighbors, thingmen, or household men recruited to the principal's cause did not usually give rise to a new feud between that victim's kin and his killer on the other side. The feud remained the feud of the principals or the big men they recruited to assist them. The corpses of the supporters who died in these affrays were balanced off against each other in settlements or paid for with compensation, but rarely, if ever, were their deaths pursued with blood by groups formed specifically for that purpose. In the absence of settlement it was the principal himself who bore the burden of compensating the kin of his own followers (e.g., *Reyk.* 13:189; *Vápn.* 18:62–63; also *Bjarn.* 20:171) and there the matter ended.

Feud also did not arise between people of roughly equal standing in every situation in which there were wrongs that could justify it. More than a wrong was needed to activate the feud. The social setting had to conspire with the wrong. When the parties' relations were good, or when there was no present impetus to compete for status and dominance, the incident would usually be quickly settled, at least in those cases where the reserve of good will exceeded the animosities arising from the incident. But it is a little too glib to attribute such generative power to something as nebulous as a personified State of Relations without recalling the darker side of good relations. Settlement was not automatic even when relations were good. In every incident there lurked the possibility of escalation, the possibility that the most trivial offense could transform good relations into feud. Feud was never too far away. It was, adopting Holmes' metaphor, a brooding omnipresence in the Icelandic sky. The continuance of good relations was assisted greatly by the fear of feud. Still, very little was ever buried and forgotten, for the fact of a prior wrong could be resurrected at a later date to justify a newly conceived desire to establish hostile relations.[14]

The practical process of feud, however, was less a matter of models than of the marshaling of practical knowledge and skills in strategy and tactics, the cultivation of public opinion, and the activation of support networks. Much of the actual work of feud came down to getting help or to preventing the adversary from getting help. Seldom was vengeance undertaken alone. It was not easy to get at most vengeance targets. The landscape, providing no trees for cover, the settlement pattern, with each farm situated independently of others, made hostile approaches self-evidently visible. Moreover, farms wealthy enough to be involved in feuding relations usually had a fair complement of servants. Ambushes were, of course, possible. And it is not unusual to see vengeance attacks made when people are traveling between farms or returning from the Thing. Consequently, few people who felt themselves subject to reprisal were likely to travel alone. Even if an avenger was able to succeed alone, he would eventually need to recruit support to defend against the inevitable reprisal.

Bodies were also needed in the less glamorous phases of feud, for lawsuits and arbitration. Although an occasional vengeance killing might be stealthily accomplished by a hired assassin, the successful prosecution or defense of a legal claim could never be accomplished alone. The litigant needed bodies to make sure his adversary did not disrupt the court, railroad the judgment, or simply use his advantage in numbers to forgo law in favor of battle or to do these things himself if his adversary were undermanned. Special people were also recruited because of their pleading skills. The same was true for arbitration. In fact one of the chief inducements eliciting agreement to arbitrate was seeing the size of the adversary's assembled support group.

The work of assembling bodies was an ongoing enterprise. The groundwork coincided with all those activities by which bonds of kinship and affinity, clientage, and neighborhood were maintained; it was the ongoing process of creating obligation. But during times of active conflict this labor altered its quality; it intensified, it meant actively seeking out others, asking them to undertake real risks. This labor was self-conscious; it knew its object; it was not completely coincidental with the normal activities of social connection. It was motivated by more than the hypothesis of danger that ultimately motivated all social interaction, it was motivated by immediate fear for life and limb.

The success of feud and dispute at the practical level meant influencing others, both the members of one's own support groups and the great class of the uninvolved. The uninvolved were a force to be reckoned with. They were, of course, a potential pool of bodies for oneself as well as for one's adversaries. But most importantly, they were the audience, they were the judges of the success of most social interaction. It was their judgment that determined the key issue of who gained and who lost honor. The true merits of one's cause were theirs to determine. And their favors were not just posthumously granted. There were tangible consequences to their opinions, for they often backed them up with active commitment.

Group boundaries were never so clear, however, that it was always unambiguous whether a person was a member of one's social network or a member of the class of uninvolved. The support seeker's work was to convince the other that he was bound to the seeker or that justice and right behavior demanded his commitment to the seeker. The advantage and safety of the person being sought out often meant denying the group definition argued by the seeker. One was greatly aided in the recruiting process at the margins by having succeeded in legitimating one's cause. It deprived those people who might prefer to remain aloof of some of their most fertile grounds for justifying aloofness. Legitimacy was acquired in various ways. It was the presumption accorded the popular man, or it could be the consequence of having a popular cause; and the latter was something over which the skilled disputant exercised an extraordinary amount of control. Or legitimacy could be, as it often was, the real issue in dispute. It is best to let these topics develop in the course of the next two chapters. The issues touched on briefly in these few pages will reappear often in the ensuing discussion.

## Vengeance: Norms and Expiators

The general outline of the following discussion is organized loosely around certain "rules." This arrangement is not intended to confer analytical priority on rules or norms. The discussion constantly adverts to practice and shows that practice was too rich, too infinitely suggestive, too complex to be governed by rule. Still, the range of possible action was not infinite. Disputants had to "sell" their choices of action to others. To do so the choices had to accord with people's sense of right and propriety. The importance of currying favorable opinion, or preventing unfavorable opinion, was inseparable from the process of legitimation, a process in Iceland that every disputant engaged in at some level or another. This social fact did not elevate the norms of disputing into rules that governed outcomes or predicted results, but it made them into something more than mere ways of speaking. They had practical consequences.

The feud was hedged in by norms of varying strength, generality, and applicability. And if articulated acontextually, some could be contradictory. The culture had contempt for the man too eager to give up on vengeance and too willing to settle for compensation at the same time that it honored men of peace and admitted infinite negotiability: "everything is compensable" (*Þórð.* 14:28). Even with context supplied the contradiction might not fade. There were easy cases. A small claim over a money debt should be settled with compensation, the burning of one's kin called for blood. But even at the extremes it was usual and proper in cases demanding blood for third parties to counsel peace and urge settlement and in cases over small property claims for the wronged person to desire blood. If context, in every case, could not resolve the ambivalences of competing cultural norms, it could at least clarify who amongst the range of participants in a dispute should be governed more by one norm than a competing one: who, for example should play the hothead and who the peacemaker. In any event, killers expected their victims to be avenged and some people took preemptive measures, on occasion extraordinarily cold-blooded, to prevent it. For example, after a certain Asbjorn killed Atli, he set off to do the same to Atli's brother, Thormod, with whom he had no prior quarrel. Thormod's offers of settlement were given short shrift because, as Asbjorn noted, Thormod "could never be trusted because of the death of his brother" (*Þórð.* 14:28).

Vengeance need not always take the form of killing. Many a disputant considered the wrong sufficiently avenged if he won an outlawry judgment. Even some arbitration awards might satisfy the blood urge, especially if the wronged party was able to extract a grant of self-judgment from his adversary. People recruited to the cause of another often preferred the more peaceful alternatives— law or arbitration—as Flosi indicated to his niece Hildigunn when she asked what kind of action she could expect from him to avenge her husband: "I shall prosecute the case to the full extent of the law or assist in a settlement that right thinking people will perceive as honorable to us in every respect" (*Njála* 116:291). But there was a distinct sense that in those situations in which blood was considered appropriate, taking payment was never as satisfactory as taking lives. The sentiment was nicely captured in a figure of speech showing people's dislike for "carrying their kin in their purse" (e.g., *Grett.* 24:84) and in Hildigunn's response to her uncle Flosi: "[My husband] would have taken blood revenge for you if he had to act on your behalf."[15]

The influence of Christianity had an effect in convincing some to substitute arbitrated settlement for blood revenge, but vengeance in a just cause was something that God and his faithful were not quite willing to relinquish (see Foote 1984, 53–56; Wallace-Hadrill 1975). *Njáls saga* contains a brief account of a small miracle in which Amundi, a blind illegitimate son, was led to the booth of his father's killer at the district Thing to ask compensation. The killer, Lyting, denied the claim, giving as his reason that he had already paid compensation to Amundi's father's father and father's brothers. In frustration, Amundi put his claim to God: "I do not understand how that is right before God considering how near my heart you have struck; and I can tell you that if my eyes were healed, I would either get compensation for my father or else blood vengeance. May God decide between us!" God was not deaf to Amundi's request. The account continues thus:

> After that [Amundi] began to leave, but when he reached the entrance he turned back toward the inside of the booth. At that moment his eyes opened.
> Then he said, "Praise be to God, my Lord. His will is revealed."
> He rushed inside the booth to Lyting and plunged his axe in his head right up to the hammer. He jerked the axe out and Lyting fell forward, instantly dead. Amundi went toward the door and as soon as he reached the spot where his eyes had opened they closed again; he remained blind the rest of his life. (Njála 106:273)

The chronology of Njáls saga has these events take place a mere three years after the conversion. Perhaps it was the saga's way of showing that God was still making accommodations with the old ways, as he did with regard to the exposure of infants and private pagan worship (see p. 35). But the difficulty of repressing the blood urge and the uneasy tension with which it was integrated into the new dispensation is powerfully conveyed in an account describing events that took place almost two centuries later in 1198. Two brothers, Snorri and Thorstein, had been hunted down by the avengers of some people they had helped kill. They prepared themselves for execution by confessing to a priest, washing their hands, and combing their hair "as if they were to go on a social visit."

> Then Snorri said, "I would appreciate it if I were killed before Thorstein, because I trust him better to be able to forgive you, even though he should see me executed." (G.dýri 18:198)

The genius of this speech is self-evident, as are the tensions within it. Besides showing remarkable courage, it reveals the cool rage of Snorri, who knows that he would be incapable of forgiving his brother's executioners and hence would risk undoing his final absolution with new sin. The milder mannered Thorstein, he supposes, will better be able to keep his soul safe. The ambivalences of the sentiment are striking. There is Snorri's refusal to give up his wish for revenge balanced against his fear of damnation; there is brother love and some small brother contempt. He cannot forgo the competitive urge to die more heroically than his brother, and his heroism comes at the expense of devaluing Christian values against the old heroic ones (Heusler 1912, 31). Even his fear of undoing his absolution is not so great that he forgoes completely a refusal of forgiveness. His concession to maintaining the purity of his absolution is simply to express his present refusal to forgive as a hypothetical future failure to forgive, a nicely casuistic resolution.

It is not unusual to find punctilious observance of Christian form and respect for holy artifacts coupled with pragmatic brutality (Foote 1984, 53). Before being led to his execution, Kalf takes communion and receives confession; he sets the cross he is holding against the church fence and lays down next to it to receive his death blow. One member of the executioner's party feels obliged to comment: "Kalf, you're not paying attention to what you're doing. Don't place yourself so near the cross that blood will splatter over it" (*Íslend.* 96:370). Kalf made a small protest but moved over nonetheless.

The laws purported to introduce real rule into matters of vengeance. They conferred a right to kill (*vígt*) and then limited the right with restrictions on time, place, and person.[16] Thus blows that left no bruises had to be avenged at the time and place they occurred, but a blow that left a bruise or caused bleeding could be avenged up until the next Allthing. The right to avenge belonged to the injured party and to those who accompanied him; it was also lawful for anyone else to take vengeance legitimately on the wrongdoer within a day of the incident (*Grágás* Ia 147, 149, II 302, 303–4). Should vengeance not have been taken before the Allthing, the right terminated; after that the claimant was relegated to an outlawry action. An explicit right to kill was, as previously mentioned (p. 171), given for sexual assaults on a man's wife, daughter, mother, sister, foster-daughter and foster-mother, but it had to be carried out at the time and place of the assault. Likewise, a slave's death could be avenged at the time and place of the killing (*Grágás* Ia 164, 190, II 396). And only those persons who had incurred liability for the wrongdoing were legitimate targets of revenge. The time and place limitations of these particular laws, however, figure explicitly in the sagas in only one case (*Eyrb.* 31:86, see below p. 289; Heusler 1911, 54–55) and except for that case no saga character acts as if they existed. Otherwise the sagas confirm the existence of formal legal limits on vengeance taking, especially in those cases in which the vengeance target was not complicit in the action being avenged. It is in fact one of the costs of a vengeance killing that the avenger generally subjects himself thereby to liability for an outlawry action, which he can then defend by raising substantive defenses of justification if they are available to him.

Whatever the laws might have claimed, the timing of revenge was in the control of those who had to take it. The fact that the next move belonged to the members of the avenging party conferred a power on them. It was the power to terrorize, the power to instill fear and anxiety, the power to impose the very real costs of being on the defensive. Whereas offensive forays needed only to assemble men for short periods of time and did not impose great burdens of provisioning, the demands of defense required constant and continued vigilance and considerable expense. Groups expecting reprisal might fortify their farms with turf and stone walls and increase their household size (e.g., *Eyrb.* 57:158; *G.dýri* 19:201–2; *Heið.* 32:311). Others had to abandon their homes and relocate (e.g., *Drop.* 12:166; *G.dýri* 11:182). Those who stayed home took the precaution of sleeping in locked bed-closets (*Ljós.* 18:51; also *Drop.* 12:166). To suspend reprisal, to be able to hold it over the heads of one's adversaries, was to have the ability to alter and in some way to disrupt the routines of their lives. The great number of cases show that outside the peace of holidays there was no taboo about taking vengeance at key times in the annual work cycle and only one case goes so far as to suggest that vengeance killing might have not been appropriate during livestock roundups.[17] The ability to disrupt routine was not the kind of advantage that should be too hastily relinquished. Saga characters speak of the deliciousness of the slow hand: "And the longer vengeance is drawn out the more satisfying it will be" (*Ljós.* 13:20). Hasty vengeance was vulgar. "Only a slave avenges himself immediately, but a coward never does" (*Grett.* 15:44). This proverb, however, intimates that there was a risk in delaying too long. Balanced against the power achieved by putting the other side on the defensive was the loss of honor one suffered for not having taken action. At some point delay looked like pusillanimity. The power to put someone on the defensive depreciated rather rapidly and being too slow made delay shade ever closer to "never."

Loss of honor, however, might befall not only the person slow to avenge, but the person on defense who continued to take precaution too long. One of the many ways in which *Ljósvetninga saga* ridicules Gudmund the Powerful is to make him excessively anxious about reprisal. And another saga character, who has been awaiting the return blow of an avenger for some time, is well aware that his reputation is suffering on account of his continuing precautions: "I have frequently been the subject of reproach because I have been too cautious" (*Drop.* 13:169). Few begrudged reasonable prudence, but there was a thin line between that and cowardice. There were always enough jealous observers to make sure that borderline cases would be judged against the reticent avenger or the overly careful suspected target.

There were two normative restraints on the location of killings. Church sanctuary was the most significant. Of Ogmund Helgason we are told that "he lived so near a church that he would quickly reach it before anyone seeking to take vengeance on him could get near him" (*Þorg. sk.* 12:119). People were not just content to save themselves in church; they herded their animals in as well to prevent them from being raided (*Þórð.* 31:63; *Þorg. sk.* 61:203). But sanctuary was not honored by everyone and we see people gauging whether it was worth the bother to head for the church or if flight might not be a more salutary measure. Thord kakali advised his wounded followers to take refuge in a church but told those who "would probably not be granted sanctuary" to leave before the attackers arrived (*Þórð.* 31:63). People could be dragged out and killed (*Íslend.* 35:271) or attacked within (29:259), and threats to ignore the church were not infrequent (e.g., 23:252, 138:437). But the enduring impression is of the remarkableness that sanctuary was respected as often as it was. We even see one scrupulous soul refusing to avail himself of it because he was under ecclesiastical interdict, despite the urgings of a priest to save himself and worry later (*G.dýri* 18:197–98).

One well-known saga scene illustrates the effects of church peace, Thing peace, and holiday peace. In it Bodvar Asbjarnarson attempts to dissuade Thorgils Oddason from attacking Haflidi after these two had failed to settle a lawsuit out of court. The scene takes place during the Allthing at mass on St. Peter's day in 1120. Thorgils had just proposed that he and Bodvar assault Haflidi right there:

> "You must be crazy," said Bodvar, grabbing him and addressing him firmly.
> "I'm not crazy," he said.
> "That's true," said Bodvar.
> "Then why did you say that?" asked Thorgils.
> "You are not looking at things right. Consider where we are, having come here to make peace with God,

whose holy church we have sought out in order to pray
for grace. Your action would violate the peace of the
church and would for that reason be an appalling deed.
And, secondly, there is the peace of the Holy Day from
which our salvation shall proceed, and God Almighty
himself has let his mercy and grace shine greatly to
brighten this day. Consider too that a formal truce and
peace (grið ok frið) is in force at the Thing and the peace
of the Thing established. For these reasons your action
would be the greatest of offenses."

Bodvar's words succeeded in restraining Thorgils. They resumed
their conversation back in their booth:

Thorgils said to Bodvar, "People say that you are not a
believer, mágr, and only of middling good will—but you
did not display those traits just now."
Bodvar said, "What you say is true, but it was not faith
that moved me when I prevented your attacking Haflidi.
I was thinking rather of something more than what we
were discussing. I saw that their forces had us sur-
rounded; we were penned in. And I discerned that if your
plan had been acted on there would have been a melee
and each of us would have been killed one right after the
other. But I didn't tell you that, because I understand
your temperament well enough to know that you would
have paid no attention if I raised those reasons against it.
However, if it weren't for that, I could have cared less
whether you killed him either in violation of the peace
of the church or the peace of the Thing. (Hafl. 16:32–33)

Besides offering a much needed reminder that belief was not automatic in the so-called Christian middle ages, at least not in Iceland,
the scene suggests that some people did indeed pay heed to formally
inaugurated peaces, not because of expediency, but because they felt
it was proper to do so. Yet outside these few constraints virtually
any place or anytime one could get his man was acceptable.[18]

There was some sense of limits on the methods of taking revenge,
but for the most part success was more important than glorious failure, although the more risk the avenger undertook to accomplish
his deed, the more honor he achieved. Parties showed little hesita-
tion to take advantage of uneven odds. When Sturla Sighvatsson intercepted the men who had raided his farm, killed his servants, and
threatened his wife, he took no special offense at their insinuating
observation about the unfairness of the odds he was now offering

them. He simply responded while smiling, "I will make full use of the fact that I have greater forces than you" (Íslend. 85:352; also Vatn. 35:94). Bjarni, it may be recalled, was considered foolhardy by his wife for giving equal odds to Thorstein (see chapter 2). Another saga figure overrides the urgings of his more aggressive companions when he declines to engage his adversary, who outnumbers him by a scant sixteen to fourteen. "This is not the difference in forces I would choose" (G.dýri 12:186). The same man preferred instead to kill his adversary by burning him in his house, a mode of attack the sagas uniformly portray as inappropriate.[19] In one place, however, it is noted that taking advantage of twelve to two odds is ignoble (Bjarn. 18:157–58). In yet another saga, a man sends his companion to get aid as three men with hostile intent approach, refusing to flee himself because the leader of the attackers "is a better man than someone who would attack me with three men. But if there were two of us and three of them, then they would take advantage of the difference in strength" (Glúma 19:64). There evidently were limits beyond which one was deemed to have offended rough norms of fairness, but they were generous limits.

Parties also employed hired assassins without great opprobrium.[20] Nor does it seem especially reprehensible for the principal to delegate the actual killing or maiming of captured enemies to one of his followers as is the frequent practice in Sturlunga saga.[21] The sagas have more than their share of axings in the back, killings encompassed by treachery and trickery, narrated without accompanying moralizations. Some people perversely adhere to certain rules of propriety by honoring the letter but not the spirit of the rule. It was, for instance, considered a skammarvíg ("shameful killing") to kill a sleeping man (Njála 146:417), but this did not prevent one avenger from prodding his victim awake and killing him before he could arm himself (Fóst. 15:200). Again the saga makes no moral judgment.

The extent to which torture and maiming was expected or legitimate is hard to determine. The family sagas show only about three instances (Gunnl. 13:105; Hrafnk. 5:120; Háv. 21:352; see also Vatn. 40:104), but Sturlunga saga is graced with numerous accounts of handhewing and leghewing and occasional geldings (Íslend. 44: 292, 115:395, 177:502). The uneven distribution of these incidents between the two types of saga seems to suggest the existence of a norm against it,[22] but clearly not strong enough to prevent its frequent breach. Explicit statements of the norm do not deal with mutilation per se, but with the appropriateness of mutilating particular classes of people. It was thus níðingsverk ("reprehensible and shameless action") to handhew a sick man (Þorg. sk. 29:156)[23] or leghew an old man (Þórð. 15:32). One scene reveals that the victims were meant to live mutilated and shamed, not die lingering deaths:

> They found out that Thorstein was in the sheiling. Bjorn Dufgusson rode there with four men. They held Thorstein; Bjorn asked who wanted to chop off his hand. Sigurd ..., a Norwegian ... who had come to Iceland with Snorri and was at Reykjaholt[24] when Snorri was killed, asked for an axe and said that he had it in his mind when they killed [Snorri], his master, that he should harm every one of those people who were present if the opportunity ever was given to him. Thorstein put out his left hand. Bjorn told him to put out his right; he said that was the one with which he would have struck Snorri, his kinsman, "and therefore it's the one that's coming off." Sigurd then chopped off Thorstein's hand. They did not do more because Thorstein was weakened by the bleeding. (Þórð. 16:33–34)

It is not surprising to find that some of these amputees live to be rather uncompromisingly hostile to their mutilators.[25]

The chief way in which the laws governing the right to kill and actual feuding custom differed was in the size of the class of people upon whom the avenger's axe could justifiably fall. The laws limited expiation to those who had actually engaged in liability-producing conduct. The sagas, however, tell a different tale. The object of revenge did not have to be the wrongdoer; he simply had to be, in the avenger's estimation, someone associated with the wrongdoer. The determination, however, was not left to the unbridled whim of the avenger. A person could not go out and kill just any random person and claim himself avenged. His opponents would hardly be aggrieved and a sane man should hardly be satisfied. Normally, the range of permissible expiators was confined within rather narrow limits to the wrongdoer himself or to his brothers (e.g., Íslend. 43:289, 90:363; Ljós. 30:99–100; Vatn. 45:123, 47:129). But the sources give no indication of deviance when the victims were as distant as first cousins (Gunnl. 13:105–6; Íslend. 21:249). Feuding parties might assassinate each other's servants on occasion without people registering great concern (Hafl. 13–14:30–31). No one, however, felt Hjalti behaved properly by avenging the killing of his follower on two old infirm men who merely happened to be from the same valley as the killer (Þórð. 15:32).

The fact that the avenger's victim need not be the actual wrongdoer had several consequences. From a functional point of view, it had the effect of inducing people who might be held accountable for each other's actions to involve themselves in each other's affairs. As we had occasion to note in the previous chapter, if a man could die for the actions of his brother or first cousin, he would take more than a passing interest in their affairs. He would, in effect, become his brother's keeper just as the other side assumed he had been all along. Group liability, it could be argued, thus rendered the feud or fear of feud much more effective as an instrument of social control than it would otherwise have been if only the actual wrongdoer suffered the consequences of his actions (see generally Moore 1978).

Group liability gave avengers the power to make choices about whom to kill in addition to the power they had by being able to control the timing of requital. The power to choose the expiator introduced a political aspect to vengeance taking that the balanced-exchange model could not account for. That model was a model of retribution, not a model of politics and domination. The power to chose a victim, and the power to determine when to make him one, could get the avenger much more than retributive justice when he finally made his move. The retributive act could be used to confer legitimacy on what might appear to be fortuitous secondary gains that attended the act. These gains usually came in the form of increases in honor and power, not only relative to the adversary but to every one else as well.

Some of the considerations that motivated the choice of expiator, and the understanding the actors had of the events in which they participated, can be illustrated by the main events from *Hrafnkels saga*.[26] Sam,[27] with the aid of the Thjostarssons, outlawed the chieftain Hrafnkel for having killed a kinsman of Sam named Einar. With the help of his patrons, Sam was able to take Hrafnkel by surprise and hold a court of confiscation at Hrafnkel's farm. There he tortured Hrafnkel and his men but granted Hrafnkel his life in exchange for a grant of self-judgment. Sam awarded himself Hrafnkel's farm and chieftaincy, but Sam's patrons doubted the wisdom of having spared Hrafnkel. Hrafnkel moved further east and within a few years had acquired a new chieftaincy. He and Sam met often at local meetings and never made mention of their past dealings. Matters continued like this for six years until Sam's brother Eyvind, who had been abroad for seven years, returned to Iceland. Eyvind had had immense success as a merchant and had acquired a fine reputation. Sam rode to the ship to meet Eyvind and informed him of his dealings with Hrafnkel. Sam then returned home and sent pack horses to the ship. Eyvind's route to his brother's farm took him right past Hrafnkel's place. A woman servant washing clothes in a stream saw Eyvind and rushed in to inform Hrafnkel:

The old proverb is very true, "a man gets more cowardly as he ages." The esteem a man acquires early is of little value if he afterwards loses it with dishonor and hasn't the means to avenge his rights again. Such is a great marvel for a man who used to be brave. Things are quite different for those who grew up with their father, whom you considered beneath you, for when they grew up they traveled abroad and were thought to be of great importance wherever they went, and when they come back home they are considered even greater than chieftains. Eyvind Bjarnason crossed the ford with such a fine shield that it glistened. He's a fine enough man to be a worthy object of revenge. (8:126–27)

The woman servant's goading recalls Hrafnkel's prior glory and the debt he still owes. It alludes to Hrafnkel's enterprising youth, when he set up an independent household at age sixteen, and to the contempt he had for people like Eyvind, who lived with his father until he went abroad. But if those who set up early on their own had cause for self-congratulation, those who traveled abroad had even more cause. For now Eyvind is "greater than chieftains" and a "worthy object of revenge." The message is not lost on Hrafnkel, who immediately arms himself and summons reinforcements. The long and the short of it is that Hrafnkel kills Eyvind, takes Sam by surprise, extracts self-judgment from him, and reclaims his former chieftaincy and farm. Hrafnkel reveals some of his thoughts on the matter when he announces the terms of the settlement he imposes on Sam:

You shall leave Adalbol [Hrafnkel's farm] and return to [your old residence]. You can have the goods that Eyvind had. But you shall not remove anything from here that you didn't bring with you. That's all you may take. I will reclaim my chieftaincy as well as my farm and estate. I see that there has been a great increase in my property, but you will not have the benefit of it. There shall be no compensation for your brother Eyvind, because of the brutal way you prosecuted the case over your kinsman. You've had enough compensation for your kinsman Einar by having had the use of my chieftaincy and property these six years. I don't consider the killing of Eyvind and his men to be worse than the torture of me and my men . . . (9:131)

Sam goes west to enlist again the support of his patrons, the Thjostarssons, for, as a matter of law, Hrafnkel is subject to prosecution for the killing of Eyvind. They refuse this time but not before Thorgeir Thjostarsson supplies some reasons:

> Things have gone just as I suspected they would when
> you let Hrafnkel have his life. I knew you would have
> great cause to regret it. We urged you to kill him, but
> you wanted to call the shots. It's now clear how much
> smarter he is than you when he let you sit in peace
> and didn't make a move until he was first able to kill
> the person whom he knew to be the greater man . . .
> (10:132–33)

These three speeches give us three variant explanations for why the killing of Eyvind made sense: one based on honor, another on balanced requital, and a third on a shrewd understanding of strategy. The servant woman's argument depends on the vengeance worthiness of the target. Eyvind is the perfect expiator because he is "greater than chieftains." True, the native model of the feud depended on balance, but the determination of equivalence in human beings as has been noted was not without its ambiguities. Human worth was negotiable and could be subject to much posthumous change. As we saw in the model feud in *Njáls saga* (above p. 183) a freedman, like Atli, who is compensated for as a free man and balanced off against his juridical superior, has his status raised posthumously to the same degree that the status of the man he is balanced against must have suffered. For Hrafnkel to avenge himself on Sam he would have had to admit Sam as his equal, something he was clearly not willing to do. Hrafnkel had always held himself above all others; he flouted the law and no other chieftain had ever managed to get him to pay compensation for the wrongs he had done others. Who then could be a better expiator to balance against the humiliation and torture Hrafnkel received at Sam's hands, than Sam's brother who was "greater than chieftains?" Paradoxically, to kill Eyvind is to honor him because his death honors his avenger. Sam is not vengeance worthy, because in Hrafnkel's eyes he is contemptible. There is thus a built-in bias for avengers to overvalue their own losses and to undervalue the worth of their adversaries, for the status of one's own group was raised if it could somehow convince the world that its cadavers were worth more than they might first appear to be, as indeed Njal's household was able to succeed in doing against Gunnar's (see above p. 184). By reminding Hrafnkel of both his dishonor and his relative value vis-à-vis his opponents, the servant woman masterfully laces overt insult with subtle flattery, playing beautifully on all the careful and particular knowledge of those who are jealous of their standing and ever vigilant about their own status relative to others.

Hrafnkel's own viewpoint is colored by the context in which it is given. He is formally articulating the terms of the award that he has been empowered to give. The diction of settlement always adopts the style of balance and equivalence. But the crucial thing to note is how closely his views accord with the servant woman's. He cannot, under the circumstances, openly admit that he killed Eyvind because he was a more noteworthy target than Sam. Nevertheless, he confirms Eyvind's special value by balancing Eyvind's death against the most grievous injury Sam had done him: the torturing. Hrafnkel suggests that such ignoble behavior justified his choice of expiator. He displays his contempt for Sam by leaving him in exactly the same condition he was in prior to his dealings with Hrafnkel. He has his old farm with his old animals and as before his brother is "abroad." Even the intervening six-years' usufruct is entered into the accounting and redefined to accord with the balance being struck. Part of Hrafnkel's feel for symmetry of repaying humiliation with humiliation and contempt with contempt is manifested in his willingness to give Sam life, as Sam had given him life.

But the most interesting interpretation of the events comes from the Thjostarssons. These astute and practical men knew better than to torture someone and then let him live. They also saw that Hrafnkel's choice of expiator had been politically motivated, a decision of grand strategy. The most powerful argument in choosing the other side's best man as the expiator is that the avenger's side is going to have to deal with him eventually anyway. Had Hrafnkel killed Sam, Eyvind would have been his avenger. And it would be his turn to be on the offensive. How much wiser to take one's turn on the defensive with the other side's best man out of the picture. How much better to use this feud as a vehicle for ridding the district of someone who promises to be a serious competitor for preeminence.

To what extent was Hrafnkel aware of the strategic motivations as distinct from those motivations socially constituted by the balanced-exchange model of feud and the idiom of honor? The Thjostarssons believe that he was well aware of the politics of his position. The presence of this awareness in Hrafnkel and its absence in Sam is the proof they allege for Hrafnkel's superior intelligence. The language of the arbitration award and the servant woman's goad are rhetorical styles that are the stuff of "officializing" discourse (Bourdieu 1977, 21, 38–43). The presence of these styles, however, does not mean an absence of practical knowledge. But the presence of practical knowledge need not indicate a purely cynical manipulation of the model either. People accepted the model's view of the universe and their views of politics were shaped accordingly. It was unlikely, in fact, that they could ever think completely outside the model's terms. Nothing in Thorgeir Thjostarsson's statement, for instance, denied the metaphor of balanced-exchange, the structure of give and take. Quite the contrary. Practicality does not mean alienation from one's own culture. Practical knowledge in the feud meant recognizing and choosing the best moves from the range of all the possible moves countenanced by the model. People, to be sure, could manipulate the ambivalences and ambiguities of particular norms to their strategic advantage, but most norms and the normative order itself had a powerful hold on their minds. If they didn't, what great strategic advantage could there have been in manipulating rules and values that no one held very deeply (see Elster 1989a, 125–40)?

The saga does not tell us what people thought of Eyvind's demise, but the saga writer clearly wants the reader to experience Eyvind's death as a genuine misfortune.[28] Killing an adversary's brother who had been abroad for the entire duration of the dispute was probably brushing against the limits of the acceptable. In other sources we find statements of regret on the part of avengers that an "innocent man," who had also been abroad, should be the object of revenge (e.g., *Vall.* 6:251), or that a well-intentioned peacemaker should have been killed merely for his structural position in a competing kin group (*Njála* 115:289; Miller 1983a). Much vengeance was not undertaken without some misgiving. People were aware of the moral and legal ambiguities the feud often entailed. But in those close cases, when the merits of action or inaction were in equipoise, the cultural disposition favored erring on the side of action.

If, however, there were reasons for singling out the opponent's most prominent man to expiate the wrongs of his kin, there were also countervailing factors that functioned to insulate prominent men from attack. As a matter of logistics, the big man was harder to get at. He was unlikely to travel unattended, his household would be well populated and hence well defended, and his position was often a consequence of his own demonstrated courage and disputing skills. When vengeance was more than an immediate hotheaded response, the avenging group had time for reflection. The more popular the target, the more likely his death would elicit aggressive response, and the more likely the uninvolved would become involved on the side of the popular victim's kin. Such concerns were openly admitted. Thus, Thord's men did not want to attack Thorstein Jonsson "because of his popularity" (*Þórð.* 18:35–36).

From the avenger's perspective, the popularity of the corpse to be avenged should affect his choice of response no less than the popularity of his intended victim. The likelihood of commuting blood into money varied inversely with the popularity of the corpse. But the avenger also had to weigh the costs of making himself liable for outlawry rather than making the killer his outlaw. For a vengeance killing, no different from any killing, provided the grounds for an outlawry action, the success of which would be intimately connected to the availability of valid substantive defenses of justification or to people's sense of justice.[29] This view is expressly articulated in two cases in which the expiators chosen by the avengers were only guilty of being kin to the people having given offense. When Flosi heard that "a more than innocent" Hoskuld had been killed and that his death was treated by everyone as a great loss, he noted the killers "will then have a hard time getting support" (*Njála* 115:289). And in the other instance one man tries to soothe a plaintiff's anxieties about the strength of the forces mustered by the avenger he is prosecuting: "people's perception of justice can be relied on in this matter" (*Ljós.* 30:101).

The idea of balance, the rule of equivalence, as has been noted, assumed that responses would be of roughly equal gravity to the offense. Although expansive notions of group liability could justify killing someone who had given no offense, at some point not all people who had given offense could be justifiably killed in a vengeance killing. Take the case where ten people attack one person and kill him. An avenger who hunted down and killed all ten would be considered as having acted without a sense of measure. Thus we have King Olaf resorting to an extended metaphor to make the same point to a certain Thormod who had taken an overly energetic revenge for his foster-brother (*Fóst.* 24:259):

> With regard to your killings in Greenland, you have done more than what the fisherman calls 'purchasing the release' from his fishing: if he catches one fish he considers himself discharged, a second discharges his ship, a third his hook, and fourth his line. Now you have gone very far; just why did you kill so many men?

It would not, however, have been inappropriate to kill one and proceed against the others at law. There is thus somewhat of a paradox. The rule of equivalence insulated certain wrongdoers from being the targets of blood revenge at the same time that it made certain innocent people eligible for attack.

We should not underestimate the extent to which convenience, expedience, or chance affected the choice of victim. One took who one could get. Surely some of the reason Eyvind was such an ideal vengeance target was that he happened to be riding by Hrafnkel's farm; the same was true for several other unfortunate travelers in the sagas (e.g., *Njála* 98:249–50; *Vall.* 6:249–52). Convenience was openly admitted as a basis of selection. The terms of one deal between a principal and his hired assassin were that the latter should hew an arm or leg off the wrongdoer, if possible, but if he couldn't get at him, then he should kill his innocent brother (*Vatn.* 39:101, 40:104).

One of the special virtues of the sagas as sources is that we get explicit statements of motive and reason. A remarkable scene in *Laxdœla saga* (59:176–78) shows two characters discussing who among a group of eligible targets should be the target of blood revenge. The question here does not involve vicarious liability, since all the people being discussed participated in the attack in which Gudrun's husband Bolli was killed. The scene is set twelve years later and Gudrun is consulting with her friend and adviser Snorri:

> "I want to talk about vengeance for Bolli. That should hardly catch you unawares, because I have reminded you of it on occasion. I also note that you have promised to assist me if I waited patiently. But now it seems a fond hope to think that you will give any attention to our case. I have waited as long as I have a mind to, but I still would appreciate your good counsel as to where vengeance should fall."
>
> Snorri asked what her ideas were.
>
> Gudrun said, "My wish is that the Olafssons do not get off scot-free."
>
> Snorri said he would veto an attack on those men who are the most prominent in the district, "and their near kin would pursue vengeance aggressively; it's time that these kin killings ceased."
>
> "Then Lambi should be attacked and killed," said Gudrun. "That would eliminate the most evil one."
>
> "There is good cause to kill Lambi," replied Snorri, "but I don't think that that would quite avenge Bolli. If their deaths were to be balanced against each other in a settlement, the difference in their worths would not be fully realized."
>
> "It might be," said Gudrun, "that we shall not be able to come up with any one his equal in Laxdale. But someone shall have to pay the bill, in any dale he might happen to be. Let's turn now to Thorstein Black, because no one has played a worse role in this affair than he has."

> Snorri said, "Thorstein's liability is no different from
> any of those who participated in the expedition against
> Bolli, but who did not actually strike him. But you
> are letting off those[30] who seem to me to be the best
> suited for vengeance: the man who killed him, Helgi
> Hardbeinsson."
> "That's true," said Gudrun, "but I don't want to think
> that those men, against whom I have for a long time had
> such antipathy, are going to sit in peace."[31]

Gudrun's choices reflect, as she says, her antipathies. She produces
people in the order of her hatred. For each person she proposes,
Snorri voices an objection. They are reasons that are already familiar. The targets suggested first are of too high a status and the consequences of killing them would elicit too energetic a retaliation.
Snorri even gives lip service to keeping good kinship (Bolli was
killed by his first cousins and Gudrun is a fourth cousin to the Olafs-
sons, whom she wishes to kill). The next suggested victim is not of
sufficient standing to reflect adequately Bolli's worth. Although arbitrators were capable of taking account of the differences in quality
of the victims, they did not cut it very fine (see Heusler 1911,
91–93). They would account for the differences between a servant
and a *bóndi*, but the corpses of two *bœndr*, in the absence of egregious circumstances, were not going to be distinguished. It was up
to the avenger to make the fine distinctions about relative worth by
picking an appropriate target. None of Gudrun's proposals satisfies
Snorri, who finally appropriates the selection to himself. To convince Gudrun to accede to his suggestion, he reminds her that his
preferred target is, after all, the actual killer. Gudrun accepts the
reason, but with resignation, a sign that she recognizes that the
price of Snorri's support is that he will make the decisions. The passage reveals with clarity how Snorri is motivated by more than
avenging a corpse and how even Gudrun's wishes reflect more than
just issues of culpability. We again note something we will return to
in more detail below, that what we would view as aggressive political and personal action can be legitimated when articulated in the
idiom of vengeance taking.

Avengers were able to distinguish individuals in their opposition.
They did not see the opposing group as an undifferentiated Them.
Nor did singling people out always work to that person's disadvantage, as it did when they were identified as "worthy objects of
revenge." People were able to discern the varying levels of commitment that members of the opposition had to the cause they were
often compelled to take up. "I will not kill the man riding last," says

Kari, "we are married to sisters and besides that he has always behaved well in these dealings" (Njála 146:418). Such ability to distinguish, however, did not always prevent unfortunate killings of
well-intentioned people as the case of Hrafnkel and Eyvind demonstrates with cold clarity. But when a well-liked and respected man
fell who was not the chief focus of hostility, the pleasure of vengeance, the satisfaction of a duty fulfilled was leavened with a sense
of guilt and shame. The ambivalence of sentiment is succinctly captured in a brief comment in Ljósvetninga saga after Hall had killed
the enemy's best man, a peacemaker whose virtue was admitted by
everyone. Says the leader of the avenging party: "[Hall] has *suffered*
and *purged* shame on our account" (25:82; see Andersson and Miller 1989, 222n173).

It was thus not always wise for a man, not himself the wrongdoer,
to trust in the ability of his adversary to make discriminations to
his benefit based on his own mental state or on his actual level of
commitment to the cause of his kin. Some people went to greater
lengths to secure themselves. After Bard insulted Vigfus in such a
way that demanded vengeance, Halli, Bard's father, advised him to
leave the country and then paid a vagrant to spread the story that
Bard fled the country because he feared Vigfus and Vigfus' father.
"This stratagem," says the saga, was devised so "Bard's kin could sit
in peace" in spite of the insult (Glúma 18:62–63). The stratagem's
presumed effectiveness depended on Vigfus being sufficiently assuaged by gossip specially contrived to flatter him and humble Bard
to feel no urgent necessity to take immediate vengeful action. Concrete and unambivalent action was often required to distance oneself from the wrongs of one's kin.[32] Gunnar not only disapproved of
his kinsman Sigmund's slanderous verses about Njal and his sons,
he proved that he disapproved by taking absolutely no action over
Sigmund's death. Years later, Gunnar's behavior in this regard was
explicitly invoked to explain why one of Njal's sons was willing to
avenge Gunnar (Njála 45:117–18, 78:194; see Miller 1983a, 331).
All in all there was a very strong presumption that having been with
the wrongdoer at any time proximate to the wrong meant complicity or conspiracy. This rather generous willingness to impose liability was not just a matter of feuding custom, but of the formal
law also. The father of two of the burners of Flugumyr, who did not
himself participate in the expedition, was outlawed for "plotting to
kill and having known of the burning": "The jury found against him
because Asgrim his son [one of the burners] had been with him a
little before" (Íslend. 180:506).

We can start to see that a mere recitation of norms is not very helpful for predicting the choice of expiator among a group of men without a precise knowledge of the goals and personalities of the avengers, the relative standing of the proposed targets, the community's views of the relative right between the factions, etc. But certain people were clearly exempt from reprisal, and only the deviant would quibble. Small children, women, and old men were not appropriate vengeance targets. Thorgrim alikarl gives some idea of the strength of the norm regarding children when he rushes forward to prevent his men from killing the young son of a man they have just killed: "No one here shall strike either children or women, even though this boy may become the death of us all" (G.dýri 18:199). To Thorgrim, the inappropriateness of killing the child outweighs his safety and the safety of his men, who are by their leniency sparing their victim's avenger. But in another setting a boy (sveinn) of unknown age is coldly denied quarter and delivered to execution, although the conflict in which this action takes place looks more like war than feud (Íslend. 138:437–38). It would seem that at roughly twelve years of age a boy might have to start being wary. This inference is deducible from the fact that some boys of twelve pleaded lawsuits (Íslend. 39:283) and were considered eligible to be avengers (Lax. 59:176, 60:179).

The norms governing appropriateness of vengeance target were frequently articulated in terms of male honor. The underlying idea was that people not socially privileged to bear arms were excused from having arms brought to bear on them. Thus Thorgils skarði refused to plunder a farm from which the men had fled: "There is no renown when only women are at home" (Þorg. sk. 69:213). But this statement cuts two ways. The farm happened to belong to Thorgils' kinswoman with whose husband Thorgils had been at odds. It may have been that it was not so much that only women were at the farm that forestalled the raid, but that one of them happened to have been Thorgils' second cousin. Thorgils, it should be noted, also invoked, in addition to sex, the kinship connection to justify his decision. Thorgils' statement suggests too that had men been present there would have been no great aversion to putting a few women at risk. Women, in fact, did get hurt when men went at it. Some were simply in the wrong place at the wrong time, as when old Ysja lost her breasts and her life to the indiscriminating hacking of the men from Vatnsfjord (Íslend. 71:328). And although attackers who set fire to the farms of their enemies usually gave women and children passage from the flames, there were times when they did not (e.g., Hœn. 9:24; Íslend. 173:491). Some women were injured in the course of trying to separate the combatants. Aud lost her hand attempting this risky sort of peacemaking (*Eyrb.* 18:36). There is more than enough evidence in the response to these actions to suggest they violated a norm. Thus Aud's hand is avenged with immediate ferocity; old Ysja's death is the subject of verses shaming the attackers; and it would seem that the ferocity of the vengeances taken for the burning of Njal and of the men and women at Flugumyr (*Íslend.* 175–77:494–502) owe some of their uncompromising thoroughness to the fact that women, and in *Njáls saga* (129:330–331), a child and an old man, perished in the flames.

One haunting scene tells us with typical saga restraint that it was the men, not the women, who were meant to die on raids, even the very warlike expeditions that pitted Kolbein the Young against Thord kakali.[33] Kolbein was in the midst of a brutal advance into the Westfjords, in which he cringed at neither killing nor maiming. At Reykjaholar, the people stood outside in the dense fog and quarreled over whether the faint noise in the distance was the sound of livestock approaching or men: "To those who were fated to die it seemed that it was livestock, but the women said it was a troop of men coming" (*Þórð.* 24:47). The women were right; it was Kolbein and his men. The men were butchered and the women left to live. It is the figure, "fated to die," which in this context signifies men, balanced against those astute enough to recognize the approaching danger, namely the women, who are not figured as fated to die, that suggests that women could expect to survive Kolbein's raid. This is also confirmed by the fact that women never appear in the comprehensive casualty lists at several points in *Sturlunga saga* (e.g., *Íslend.* 138:438). These lists are unlikely to have been skewed by the underreporting of women casualties since, as we have seen by the verses prompted by the death of old Ysja, the killing of women was not unnewsworthy.

But does that mean they weren't raped? The sagas are extremely reticent about rape (see Heusler 1912, 40–41). Rapists, according to the sagas, lived mostly in Norway and Sweden and were berserks besides. Still there are some clues. The chieftain Gudmund dyri threatened to put a woman named Thorunn "in bed with every Yahoo," apparently for having aided Gudmund's enemy (*G.dýri* 19:201). Only the intervention of another chieftain saved her from gang rape. In another source, Hallfred forces his ex-mistress to sleep with him after she had married the man with whom Hallfred has been feuding. He also tells the eleven men accompanying him that they can do as they please, to which the saga adds: "There were several milking pens there and it is said that each of them had a woman for the night" (*Hallfr.* 9:181). And one person intended that he and his companion should rape the wife and daughter of a *bóndi* he was contending with (*Hafl.* 6:18). One of the reasons Thorgils skarði (above p. 207) might have been so unwilling to find renown in raiding a farm defended only by women was that the action would make him complicit in the rape of his kinswoman. There is certainly an ominous inference to be drawn in Thord kakali's instructions to his men to spare women and churches as they set out to raid in the west (*Þórð.* 18:39). Sanctuary was violated and we should probably assume, unfortunately, that women were too. But arguments from silence are fraught with danger. The evidence is not sufficient to know whether rape was so common as to merit little comment or so infrequent that there was nothing to comment on.

The norms governing the appropriateness of attacking old men are considerably vaguer (see Miller 1988c). Some normative statements about treatment of the elderly follow directly upon a breach of the norm. After Flosi calls Njal "Old Beardless" before the assembled multitude at the Allthing, Skarphedin admonishes him: "It is wrong to taunt an old man, and no worthy man has ever done that before" (*Njála* 123:314). A certain Glum must remind his men intent on ridiculing an old beggar that it is cowardly to taunt old men (*Reyk.* 24:225). And when an old ill-tempered troublemaker receives a minor wound in a scuffle at a horsefight, he adopts a tone of outrage: "I don't know how things would have gone had I been younger, but to strike a sixty-year-old man in the head and to have the other ride away without his head in bandages!" (*G.dýri* 12:183). But the saga world displays an ambivalence toward old age reminiscent of our own. Being old was also cause for scorn. When old Egil stumbles and falls, the serving women laugh and mock him (*Egil* 85:294). A marriage of an old man and a young woman provokes the abduction of the beautiful young wife. Even the saga writer makes light of the situation by turning it into farce: "Hall said that an old man should not befoul such a good-looking woman any longer, so he took her and the man's horse too. The horse was named Mani and was the best of all horses" (*Sturla* 12:78). The laws, in fact, legislate against this kind of marriage to the extent of disinheriting the issue of a man of eighty years unless he had the consent of his kinsmen to marry (*Grágás* Ia 224, 246, II 68). Perhaps the figure is not meant to be taken precisely, but rather to indicate any age at which a man was deemed old, either admitting it himself by handing over the management of the farm or having the admission thrust upon him, presumably by his sons. Some men maintained active political and martial lives well into their sixties. There was thus no special opprobrium that attached to the killers of Sighvat Sturluson, who died in battle at age sixty-seven, or even of his brother Snorri, who died cowering in his cellar at age sixty-two (*Íslend.* 138:434, 151:454). These men were still legitimate targets of violence because they claimed no status as a function of old age and hence were not old.

## Vengeance: Process, Ritual, and Legitimation

The exact makeup of the vengeance-taking group depended on a number of variables. In local conflicts, the group tended to be recruited from the household and among close kin and affines independently established, but residing within the same region. The muster for vengeance expeditions to be carried out in other districts and involving problems of provisioning was recruited more widely. The selection criteria for these expeditions are set forth in a passage in *Heiðarvíga saga* (16:266):

> For this reason you shall choose these men to travel with
> you rather than other men of the district: they are con-
> nected by affinity to each other, all are prosperous as are
> their kin . . . and they are the bravest of all of those
> here in Vididale and our districts. They are our best
> friends and will be predisposed to you. . . . Your servants
> and neighbors are prepared to go with you as are your kin
> and affines.

To reprise some observations made in passing in chapter 5, vengeance-taking groups tend to be more narrowly recruited than support groups for lawsuits and arbitration, in which arenas the chieftains assumed a greater role. Feuding chieftains, however, did call on their thingmen, as well as their kin, for aid in vengeance-taking expeditions. Except for the household, which existed as a functioning group on a daily basis and whose members had little option but to follow their master's orders, none of these constituencies were already organized and ready to go. The group had to be actively assembled. Consider the case of Thorgerd whose husband, Vigfus, was killed by Snorri. The same day that Vigfus was buried, Thorgerd sought out Arnkel, her uncle, and asked him to take up the prosecution of the killers. Arnkel refused, saying it was the duty of Vigfus' kin to take up the action. Thorgerd sought out her husband's relatives, but she found the three men she approached no more interested than her own kinsman, Arnkel, had been. They all had excuses. One second cousin excused himself on the ground that he had promised the killer not to sue him as long as there were others available to take up the claim; another second cousin and a

second cousin once removed saw no reason why they should be involved when there were others equally or more closely related to
Vigfus than they were. There are several reasons why they were
reluctant to act. For one thing, Vigfus was not well liked; in the
saga's words he was "a difficult man." The events leading up to his
death confirm that view. Troubles started when Vigfus' nephew was
wounded by Snorri's steward in an argument over sheep. Vigfus sued
Snorri for the injury to his nephew and lost. The outcome rankled
Vigfus considerably, and so he offered one of his slaves his freedom
if he would kill Snorri. The attempt failed; the slave talked, and on
the same day Snorri and six others killed Vigfus (*Eyrb.* 26–27:65–70).

Vigfus' actions were foolhardy and ill-advised. More accurately,
they were not advised at all, and the unwillingness of his own kin
to take action for his death may have been owing in part to his not
having taken counsel with them before acting. The sense of the saga
is that Vigfus got what he deserved. Even his widow admitted as
much by scaling her demands to less drastic action. She asked for
legal action, not for blood vengeance. It was not that the victim's
wrong excused vengeance taking, but it made it easier for fairly distant kin to justify refusing to act.[34] There was also another factor at
work. Vigfus had directed his assault against a man, Snorri, who was
not only a chieftain but also a rather difficult man himself. No one
was all that eager to prosecute a case against Snorri.

This case provides a much-needed reminder that most people
weren't all that eager to be avengers. It was dangerous business and
they would excuse themselves on any number of grounds if they
could. Some of these grounds reflect the culture's view of rightness
and justice, some reflect good-faith prudence, and others are simply
available to give inertia a reasoned aspect. A man's honor was not
going to suffer much for failing to avenge a kinsman whom everyone
felt got his just reward. In fact, those who followed up the killing of
their unpopular group members with too much energy were themselves risking reputation (e.g., *Ljós.* 20:55–57). These were the kinds
of cases that were appropriately settled quickly by compensation
(e.g., *Glúma* 18:61), if compensation were obtainable.

Thorgerd, however, was given a bit of strange advice by one of
Vigfus' kinsmen. He told her to have Vigfus' body dug up, the head
severed, and to return to her uncle Arnkel with the head in hand,
display its grisly aspect, and tell him that "this head would not have
left it to others to take up the case" if their roles were reversed.
Thorgerd returned to Arnkel and asked him again for his help. He
was no more willing than before to aid her until she pulled the head
from under her cloak. Arnkel was taken aback, as was only to be ex-

pected, but the end result was that he agreed to prosecute the killing case. In a lengthy article some years ago, I described in detail the elements of this bloody-token ritual and why it was so compelling (see Miller 1983b). I will not repeat that here except to note a few relevant matters regarding the vengeance-taking process.

This episode gives us some indication of the stylized modes of discourse a woman adopted when she in fact was playing a central role in organizing the actions which she was socially disabled from undertaking herself.[35] The conventional woman of the sagas is strong-willed and uncompromising. She is the self-appointed guardian of the honor of her men and as such she generally sees honor as unnuanced heroism. She repaid the men for caricaturing her as vengeful and cold of counsel by caricaturing them as mindless axe-wielding automatons to be manipulated by her goading. Such seem to have been the social roles the culture forced on the sexes in certain highly charged settings. The saga woman provoked her reluctant men to action by impugning their manhood. They were no better than women, they would better have been their father's daughters, they have the memories of pigs, or they are merely contemptible (see, e.g., *Eyrb.* 18:36; *Íslend.* 168:481; *Lax.* 48:150, 53:162; *Þórð.* 2:6).

Some would say the vengeance-minded woman was nothing but literary commonplace (e.g., Heller 1958; Jochens 1986). But if she was a commonplace, it is indeed remarkable how much social and psychological sense her role made. Her fury had more motive than that imputed to her by the clerical antifeminism the saga writers might have drawn upon. Not having had an especially active juridical existence of her own, she depended on her men for her status, her property, and safety. She had to act through them and she wanted them tough-minded, honorable, and punctiliously mindful of their rights and reputations. Women were not the only people who played this role. Old men goaded their sons (*Þorst. stang.*, above chapter 2), servants both male and female goaded their masters (*Heið.* 18:270; *Reyk.* 13:184; see also above p. 199), and thingmen goaded their chieftains (*Ljós.* 14:33; 22:67). What was common to all inciters was not their sex but their dependence on the men they incited. The verbal style they adopted, to which we can add the bloody-token ritual, is clearly a type of shaming ritual well evidenced in the ethnographic literature as a vehicle for exercising upward social control (Baumgartner 1984, 318). Icelanders in the subservient position did not sit dharna or don sackcloth and tear their hair, but other verbal and ritual clues served the same purpose.[36] They had to shame and importune to get a hearing, since relative differences in power prevented them from being included as equals in deliberative sessions.

The social significance of goading was complex. Besides validating power and status differences, goading actually did allow the relatively disenfranchised to participate in group decision making, even if the range of views they could express was severely narrowed by the conventions governing the terms of their participation. We should not, however, assume that they were incapable of giving a more nuanced message within the structure imposed by the conventions of this kind of discourse, by, for example, varying the timing, the tone, and the type of insult that accompanied the performance. In fact, inciters rarely advocated aggressive action when such action was not at least arguably a rational way of proceeding, and there are examples of women counseling peace when that was the honorable course of action (*Hafl.* 16:33, 18:34–35; *Lax.* 19:47–48; see below chapter 8, n. 2). Theirs was a view that had to be considered. For this reason we should not think of men as dumb tools of feminine fury. The men gained in several ways by having things constituted this way. They acquired the benefits of counsel from their women and servants, they integrated them in a limited way into the decision-making process, they were able to confirm dominant male stereotypes of female vengefulness and irrationality and they had a scapegoat whom they could blame should the action fail. The social constitution of goading also served to integrate and confine the structurally generated hostility that the socially disempowered—the women, the servants, the elderly—must have felt toward their own dominant males into a form that confirmed the cultural values of manliness.[37]

People expected a woman to play the role of the inciter and when she did not there was a minor upset in the order of things that merited comment. Consider this passage in which Alf and Brand discuss killing a certain Thoralf:

> Alf . . . reminded Brand that Thoralf had been actively involved in the killing of Kalf and his son Guttorm. But Brand's wife Jorunn would not join in [the discussion]. She was the daughter of Kalf. *And the general view was that she had not goaded Brand.* (*Íslend.* 142:443)

There are some interesting details in this passage, and in the account in which it figures, that hold a key to a more subtle view of what goading was about and how it was integrated into the broad strategies of disputing. The passage does not say that Jorunn did not goad, but rather that it was the general view that she had not goaded.[38] This notice indicates that goading was intended for more than private hearing; it was meant to get beyond household walls; it was something people had opinions about as to whether or not it had taken place. Some of the incitement's force to motivate and manipulate should probably be attributed to its "public" nature. There is good reason to suspect that Jorunn's failure to goad her husband was not inadvertent, but was purposefully intended to be noticed. To show why, we need to introduce more detail and place the events in their political context.

Jorunn's refusal to goad did not prevent the death of Thoralf. After Alf had spoken with Brand, Brand and he assembled a dozen men, captured Thoralf in his home, allowed him confession, and then killed him. They then took care of their souls by getting absolution from the bishop and sent peace feelers to Kolbein, Thoralf's powerful patron whom Brand also supported. The problem for Thoralf's killers was how to establish and justify the significance of their own action so that it did not provoke Kolbein to move against them violently. Thoralf, it so happened, had only participated in the killing of Kalf, Brand's father-in-law, as a follower of Kolbein.[39] It was Kolbein who had had Kalf killed. But Thoralf was also a general troublemaker, very unpopular with his neighbors. Moreover, he had contended with Brand when the two had been staying together at Kolbein's, giving Brand insulting nicknames. What Brand wished to do was to convince Kolbein that Thoralf had been killed because he was a nuisance. The action would then be no more than an aggressive manifestation of normal neighborhood administration; it could be proven to be such because the people who assisted Brand in killing Thoralf were other respected big men in the district. To have killed Thoralf for the purpose of avenging Kalf would have been an open act of feud with Kolbein, something none of the killers wanted to get involved in. Thus when Kolbein asked Brand why he had had Thoralf killed, Brand said "that there were a number of reasons, that Thoralf had long shown himself hostile to him, *'but I did not do it to avenge Kalf,* though that has been what has been whispered to you'" (*Íslend.* 142:443–44). Either Jorunn already had been informed or she had been able to discern that the killing was going to take place and it was important to lay the groundwork for the desired explanation of the action. Had she goaded, it would have been very difficult for Brand to disclaim avenging his wife's father and wife's brother as the motive for killing Thoralf. Such social sophistication shows the authors of these texts were considerably more astute about and alert to how "topoi" like goading might have been integrated into a social and cultural universe than the literary scholars who have claimed this topic as their own.[40]

As this case reveals, the intelligent disputant did not undertake killing without taking care to provide himself with justifications and explanations of his actions. This creation of right, the official-izing of one's actions, was the intellectual side of support gathering. Having right on one's side, as we have previously noted, disposed the uninvolved in one's favor and made it difficult for those upon whom one made claims for support to excuse themselves from as-sisting. There were various ways disputants had of dressing them-selves and their actions in the forms and styles of legitimacy. They could play by the rules when the facts, law, and societal norms fa-vored them rather than their opponent. And when the facts weren't with them, they could invent new ones. Some of the methods were rather crude. For example, disputants planted goods in order to make theft accusations (*Hrafn Sv.* 6:646; *Reyk.* 2:156, 18:207); they rigged ordeals (*Lax.* 18:42–43; see Miller 1988a); and they swore equivocal oaths (*Glúma* 25:86).

More sophisticated were the attempts people made to provoke an adversary into supplying the justification for reprisal. People might test the waters before taking drastic aggressive action by floating out possible justifications and then abandoning them when their suffi-ciency seemed doubtful. One particularly good example describes how the Njalssons went about finding a way to kill Thrain, a rival claimant for local preeminence. The Njalssons had received some cuts and humiliation in Norway at the hands of Jarl Hakon as a con-sequence of their refusal to betray Thrain to the jarl after Thrain had harbored Hakon's outlaw. Polite practice probably should have re-sulted in Thrain compensating the Njalssons for their trouble by way of gift. But the Njalssons pressed the matter by sending some-one to ask for compensation on their behalf. The request was re-fused rather rudely and they wished to retaliate. Their father told them that "if [Thrain] were killed for that, it would be consid-ered groundless" (*Njála* 91:226); he instead advised them how to manufacture the necessary grounds: in this case, to provoke in-sults that would merit lethal reprisal. The plan was followed and Thrain's death occasioned no community uproar (see Miller 1983a, 320–26).

Cases like these show how difficult it could be to find a specific wrong that was being avenged in any vengeance killing. Depending on the circumstances, any number of justifications could be put for-ward. Moreover, justifications changed over time. When Skarphedin killed Sigmund, the reason given at the time was that Sigmund had composed libelous verses about him and his father and brothers (see chapter 6, n. 7). Years later, however, Skarphedin revealed that it was because Sigmund had killed his foster-father (*Njála* 92:232). The

latter reason was not asserted earlier because Skarphedin had promised to honor a settlement reached over the killing of his foster-
father, of which Sigmund was the beneficiary. And Skarphedin was
only now asserting it to his sister's husband and then only because
Gunnar, the person with whom the settlement had been concluded
on Sigmund's behalf, was dead. Justifications, of course, also varied
among participants at the same time. The same action might have
recruited people with different claims against the target and some
with no claims at all except the obligation to assist those who had
the claim to make.

In any event, some specific justification was always needed. It was
clear that killing on the basis of mere feelings of generalized ani-
mosity was not appropriate. Such action, to be legitimate, had to be
integrated to the model of balanced-exchange. General bad feelings
needed to be reified into a "gift," a wrong of some specificity that
the relevant community would recognize as demanding repayment.
And if on the social level the motives for vengeance were complex,
at times ambiguous, and not always what they appeared to be,
the same seems to have been true on the psychological level. Some
people, for instance, transformed the avengeable offense from the
offensive act itself into the humiliation suffered for having had an
excessive emotional reaction at hearing of the offense. When Thorhall Asgrimsson was told that his foster-father Njal had been burned
to death, he swelled up, bled from his ears, and fainted. Upon reviving, he vowed to avenge his somatic reaction on the people who had
burned Njal (*Njála* 132:344–45). Similarly, but more as a figure of
speech, one person was said to have avenged his tears (*Gísls þ.*
5:340).

People also tested the waters before taking aggressive action in
more indirect ways. The interpretation of dreams was a favorite pas-
time (see, e.g., *Þorláks saga* 16:109); people produced dreams for
consumption.[41] They would dream dreams that suggested that so-
and-so had stolen some sheep, or committed a murder, or that a
killing was going to take place. They read people's reactions to their
dreams and could in turn orchestrate those reactions by the choice
of dream. Likewise, people consulted diviners about thefts and possible culprits, thereby testing the community reaction as to who
most people felt was an appropriate target. Above all, people talked
and talked; they withdrew information from the gossip networks
and they put information in, hoping to manipulate the flow of information to their advantage (Miller 1986b).

The law, of course, figured into the legitimation process also, by
liberally enabling outlawry prosecutions and by, if not quite as lib-

erally, justifying blood revenge anterior to the lawsuit. But I post-
pone discussion of the law until the next chapter except to note that
it assisted in the process of legitimating aggressive action in some
insidious ways. *Grágás* provided that the right to prosecute the
breach of a substantial number of prohibitions belonged to "anyone
who wanted it" (*sá á sǫk er vill*, e.g., *Grágás* Ia 15, 129, 174). The
family sagas show no instances of any such cases (Heusler 1911,
102), but one is noted in *Sturlu saga* (25;99) where we see a disputant summons another for using false measures solely as one tactic
in a general strategy of intimidation (see *Grágás* Ib 169, II 290). One
could also arrange for the transfer of the right to prosecute from
those who conveniently happened to have had an outstanding claim
against the intended target (see, e.g., *Ljós.* 13:23; *Njála* 64:160–61).
As we shall have cause to discuss in the next chapter, some people
banked claims, keeping a stock of them available to transfer to
people who needed them (*Njála* 64:160–61). If the particular opponent was clean, with no current liabilities, action could be taken
against his clients, servants, or kin who were not so clean. Gudmund the Powerful thus indirectly pursued his feud against Thorir
Helgason by prosecuting Thorir's thingmen for "fornication, illicit
riding of another's horse, or whatever he could hit on" (*Ljós.* 5:20).

The balanced-exchange model also had no way of fixing any particular action as either a wrong or a nonevent. Over the course of
time something dismissed originally as of no account could be recalled at a later date as being an unrequited wrong. This reinterpretation of the significance of past actions figured prominently in the
legitimation process. If the party one wished to oppose gave no present basis for a claim, and if the means of manufacturing one was not
available, the past was a rich reservoir of inherently ambiguous
events rife for being reunderstood. Such instances are hard to get at
in the sources because the story is always told with the benefit of
hindsight. The saga teller, of course, knows when an earlier event
will be used to justify later action, and consequently some of the
later importance the event will have is attracted to its original presentation. Merely to put the insignificant prior event in the tale is
to confer on it more significance than it would have been perceived
to have had at the time it occurred. Still, there are some saga accounts that allow us to recover the insignificance of the prior action
and its subsequent reinterpretation. I offer one example.

According to Lyting, Hoskuld Njalsson had been riding by Lyting's farm frequently for some fifteen years (*Njála* 98:248–49). On
the last of these occasions, when a number of his kin and affines happened to be present, Lyting conceived the notion, with some prompt-

ing from a goading servant, to avenge his wife's brother, Thrain, by killing Hoskuld. He claimed he had never received compensation for the death of Thrain and that he had always found Hoskuld's journeys annoying. But why does the present time vex him sufficiently to act? Why does his failure to receive compensation justify a vengeance-taking now, fifteen years later, when it had not been used to justify a claim when the slight was fresher? The short answer, without going into the complex politics of the saga (see Miller 1983a), is that the constitution of his kin group was now such that it could consider competing again with the killers of his brother-in-law, whereas his group had been without the means to do so following his brother-in-law's death. Hoskuld's previously unremarkable journeys past Lyting's farm can now be claimed as provocations not to be endured.

The model of retribution and requital continued to inform even the large-scale nonfeud-like conflict between the great chieftains in the last thirty-five years of the commonwealth, but with ever greater division between the model of balanced-exchange and actual practice. The style of combat changed. Larger forces were mustered for more sustained campaigns, which began to look more like small wars than feud. The my-turn/your-turn structure was pretty much abandoned as forces recruited largely on the basis of territoriality confronted each other. In these conflicts, as we noted in the introduction, the real costs were rarely borne by the principals. The real losers were small farmers whose farms were raided to provision the large musters and whose wounds and lives often went uncompensated. Yet for all that, the understanding of events is quite the same as in feud. The sources understand battles with several hundred on each side in the same way as if there had been fifteen on each side. Both were called *bardagi* and both were conceived of as moves in a game of debt and repayment. The principals still articulated politics in terms of vengeance, if not always in terms of feud. The same psychology of honor held sway. Conflict was still deemed arbitrable, with one side's wrongs balanced against the others. But the leaders, who still conceived of themselves in the traditional heroic terms, were out of touch with the views of the smaller people who bore the brunt of these "wars" and who started to resent these leaders as an exploitive class (see Karlsson 1972, 37–48).

The account we have constructed in this chapter mostly describes a more limited style of conflict management than the style of big-time political conflict that plagued the last decades of the commonwealth. This limited style characterized the disputes of the family sagas, of those *Sturlunga* sagas set in the twelfth and early thirteenth centuries, and even of a substantial number of conflicts that surface briefly in *Íslendinga saga*'s chronicling of the machinations of the four or five families fighting to control whole regions of the country. Our story is the story of local and district politics in a still largely stateless society. *Íslendinga saga*, *Þórðar saga kakala*, and *Þorgils saga skarða* are telling the story of the chaotic and painful beginnings of state formation. Still, the style of conflict and the manner in which conflict was culturally constituted in these sagas remains more like than unlike the world that preceded it and still continued to co-exist with it on the local level.

In early Iceland, no particular institution, such as the law, which it had, or the state, which it didn't have, had a monopoly on legitimate violence. Legitimacy was not irrebuttably attached to certain state and corporate institutions no matter what the substance of the particular actions attributed to the institution. Legitimacy was something people had to struggle to acquire. Certain people clearly had a presumption of legitimacy in their favor. This presumption was one of the benefits of popularity, honor, past successes, and a reputation for acting legitimately. The presumption for others was weaker and for some it was utterly inverted. In any event, legitimacy was something that no one could take for granted for too long and something that the skillful disputant took care to cultivate. The adept player in the feud was a person who was able to legitimate his aggression as justified retribution by making his actions look as if they were only sensible retributive reactions. Much of taking revenge was the legitimation of taking pure and simple, vengeance being one of the key constitutive ideas of power and truth in this culture. All political action, the quest for power and dominance, was cased in the idiom of honor and the avenging of perceived wrongs.

Not seeing politics as an autonomous sphere of knowledge did not mean people were incapable of astute strategy involving the skillful application of the signs and discourses of honor, feud, and other exchange cycles. The conceptual structures that formed their social universe were able to accommodate considerable complexity, surely no less complexity than a view of politics that sees it as a function of tabulating preferences or counting votes in elections and legislative bodies. Is there any reason to believe that a foundational metaphor of reciprocity and retribution, such as informed early Icelandic society, organized knowledge and truth less rationally than a metaphor based on counting? If I am claiming a certain sophistication for the politics of vengeance, that sophistication may well be mostly a function of the practical knowledge that the members of any culture must have to function sociably in their own society. In other words, claiming sophistication for Icelandic culture in the way it subsumed complicated political behavior into feud may be to claim little more than that sophistication is a feature of the central social arrangements in any culture, simply because human socialization is itself sophisticated. But if it might be that sophistication is not a very useful concept for comparing human behavior across time and space, there is a sense that it is a concept that is applicable to institutions, often as a proxy for degrees of social differentiation and division of labor. It might not be meaningless to propose, for instance, that the Icelandic feud was more complex than Nuer feud. And if we were to propose the hypothesis, the first thing we would turn to to prove it is the extraordinary richness of early Icelandic legal culture. The Icelandic feud was inseparable from Icelandic law and to solve its mazes one needed special, almost proto-professional, sophistication. We turn now to the law.

# Law and Legal Process

The division of law, feud, and peacemaking into three chapters is somewhat artificial, but justifiable nevertheless by the conventions of chapter length and a rough folk sense that a category called "law" is somehow distinguishable in a meaningful way from the broader categories of social norms and disputes.[1] The focus here will be on the social integration of formally articulated rules, the breach of which gave rise to claims recognized by courts, and on the formal legal process by which these claims were heard. But the nuance, the shading, and the fuller picture of law's role in the disputing process require the simultaneous consideration of the issues already discussed in the preceding chapter and the issues to be discussed in the succeeding one on peacemaking and arbitration.

## The Legal Culture

Law played a role in more than the definition and processing of disputes. The chapters on kinship and householding showed the inseparable interpenetration of law and society. Norms of good kinship provided the basis for imposing legal obligation, which in turn buttressed the norms and so on in continual feedback of mutual influence. Similarly, household makeup and the forms of production and reproduction were intimately connected to laws requiring everyone to be attached to a functional household. Law was part of life in Iceland and was perceived as such. *Vár lǫg* ("our law") was our community as opposed to others (von See 1964, 187–93). But *lǫg* was not just undifferentiated custom either. Law was in a narrower sense the positive law, the formal legal process and the rules applied and enforced in the courts. When, for instance, the word *lǫg* figures as a prefix, as it frequently does, to such words as fence, summons, divorce, ounce, man, (*-garðr*, *-stefna*, *-skilnaðr*, *-eyrir*, *-maðr*), it means law in the positive sense, as a particular body of rules.[2]

The existence of rules and the forms they take are not without their interest. The explicit articulation of prescriptive rules, whether as laws or something less, is not common to all cultures (Roberts 1979, 32, 170; cf. Edgerton 1985). Some go in for it more than others.[3] Iceland is a case on point. People argued their claims sophisticatedly, in law and arbitration, by explicit and implicit reference to rules (see, e.g., *Eyrb.* 32:87). And if we were to construct our view of the role of law in Icelandic society from the law codes alone, we would see a society dominated by formal rules articulated in the form of laws. *Grágás* contrasts, for instance, in every way with the patchy and interstitial quality of the Anglo-Saxon and continental barbarian codes. It is distinguished both by the range of its coverage and its detail within each area covered. Consider, as an example, the rules governing the relocation of a cemetery:

> If a church is moved a month before winter or is so damaged that it cannot be used, the bodies and bones are to be moved from it before the next [October]. The bodies and bones are to be taken to a church at which the bishop permits burial. If a man wishes to move bones, the landowner is to call nine neighbors and their serving men to move the bones as if he were calling them for ship hauling [see Ib 69–70]. They are to have spades and shovels with them; he himself is to provide hides in which to carry the bones and draught animals to move them. He is to call the neighbors who live nearest the place where the bones are to be dug up and is to have called them seven nights or more before they need to come. They are to be there at midmorning. A householder is to go with his serving men who are in good health, all except the shepherd. They are to begin digging in the outer part of the churchyard and search for bones as they would for money if that was what they expected to find there. The priest who is asked to do so is required to go there to consecrate water and sing over the bones. The bones are to be taken to a church at which the bishop permits burials; there it is lawful to do whichever one wishes, make one grave for the bones or several graves. . . . If a landowner does not have bones moved as is prescribed, or if those men who are called do not go, each of them is fined three marks, and the case against him lies with anyone who wishes to prosecute. The summons in these cases is to be made locally[4] and five neighbors of the man prosecuted are to be called at the Thing, and the court is to enjoin them by judgment to move the bones, and to bring them to church within the

fortnight following the end of the Thing. (*Grágás* Ia
12–13, II 14–15)

This gravedigging scene is rich in suggestive detail, from the colorful
metaphor to look for bones as carefully as if one expected to find
money to the exclusion of shepherds from the general enterprise.
Were shepherds excepted because of the nondeferrable nature of
their tasks or because their lowly position disqualified them from
touching hallowed bones? Most probably it was the former, though
both laws and sagas testify to the low status of shepherding (*Grágás*
Ia 129; *Hrafnk.* 3 : 101). But, detail aside, there are several general
things to note about this provision. For one, it shows that matters
which elsewhere would have been handled in ecclesiastical jurisdiction were, in Iceland, secular matters. For another, consistent with
*Grágás'* style throughout, the law has the look of having been abstracted from specific cases rather than deduced from disembodied
principle. But having that "look" need not require actual cases. The
casuistical style of thinking was more than capable of generating
cases as hypotheticals, as creatures of juristic imaginings, which
sometimes might, and sometimes might not, have corresponded to
actual cases. Another point worth noting is that in legislating about
the removal of bones, the shadow of legal liability fell on a fairly
wide class of people, not only on the landowner where the defunct
church had been, but also on his neighbors and their servants. Expansive notions of liability were no less foreign to Icelandic positive
law than they were to feuding custom.

Few, I would bet, have ever sat down with *Grágás* for a casual read,
but if one were to do so, the unavoidable impression would be of a
distinctly oversanctioned society.[5] *Grágás* attempted to regulate virtually every facet of farm management from employment contracts
to the separation of and accounting for hay blown into a neighbor's
field (Ia 129–30; Ib 106–7, II 460).[6] Some provisions even established liability for the failure to exploit hay production at maximum
levels. A landowner was constrained to rent his farm if he would not
farm it himself (Ib 92, II 461–62, 466) and a tenant was liable for a
three-mark fine if he left any meadow unmowed (Ib 136, II 499). The
poor law intruded, as we have seen, into matters of kin obligation.
*Grágás* regulated marriage contracts, sales of goods, repayment of
loans, pledging of land and livestock, rights in driftage and more, all
in ways every bit as detailed as the provision governing removal of
bones. And, of course, there were sanctions. In addition to restitution,[7] the penalties for breach ranged from three-mark fines and the
enjoining of certain actions in cases of minor property damage and

violations of simple regulations, to lesser and full outlawry for other offenses. *Grágás* was remarkably free with lesser outlawry, a fairly stiff punishment, which involved confiscation of property and a three-year banishment from Iceland. As a rule of thumb any negligent damage in excess of a mere five ounces was punishable by lesser outlawry (*Grágás* II 429) and many religious matters were sanctioned in the same way. The person who did not bring a child for baptism (Ia 3, II 2), the priest who withheld baptism (Ia 4, II 2) or who forgot to bring the holy water (Ia 4, II 3), the person who refused to lend a horse or boat to one taking a child to be baptized (Ia 5, II 3–4), the person who having sufficient mental capacity did not know the *Pater noster* and the *Credo* (Ia 7, II 6) were all subject to lesser outlawry. And not only was the man who had a berserk fit punished with lesser outlawry irrespective of the harm he might have committed, but those who were present were also liable to the same punishment if they did not succeed in restraining him (Ia 23, II 28).[8]

*Grágás'* style and its bulk evidence a cultural predisposition for law and lawmaking. Some of the rules themselves display a rococo complexity that suggests sheer pleasure in the formulation of law almost as if it were for law's sake alone.[9] The propensity for lawmaking, however, was not just the theoretical musings of juristically inclined people. The society backed its laws with courts to hear claims arising from their breach. And what is especially remarkable is that Iceland developed a legal system—courts, experts in law, rules clearly articulated as laws—in the absence of any coercive state institutions.

What was the source of this predisposition for law? In England and on the continent lawmaking was inseparable from kingship (Wormald 1977a); that was obviously not the case in kingless Iceland. And although the new literate Christian culture provided the means and even some of the models for writing the laws, there were already extensive laws available to be transcribed well before the advent of Christianity (Foote 1977b and 1984, 155–64; see Líndal 1984, 132–38). Consider the words of a source nearly contemporaneous with one of the first big steps in Iceland's transition from oral to written legal culture:

> The first summer of Bergthor's lawspeakership [*anno*
> 1117] a new law was made that our laws should be written in a book at Haflidi Masson's during the winter according to the dictation and advice of Haflidi, Bergthor, and other learned men who were appointed to the task.
> (*Íslb.* 10:23–24)

Formal transcription did not stint the propensity for lawmaking.[10] If anything it seems to have encouraged it. Within a short time, we don't know precisely how long but probably not later than the end of the twelfth century (Foote 1984, 158n8; Líndal 1984, 129–34), there was need for a citation law:

> It is also prescribed that in this country what is found in books is to be law. And if books differ, then what is found in the books which the bishops own is to be accepted. If their books also differ, then that one is to prevail which says it at greater length in words that affect the case at issue. But if they say it at the same length but each in its own version, then the one which is in Skálholt is to prevail. Everything in the book which Haflidi had made is to be accepted unless it has since been modified, but only those things from the sayings of other men learned in law which do not contradict it, although everything in them which restores things left out or makes things clearer is to be accepted. If people dispute a point of law and the books do not decide it then the Lǫgrétta is to be cleared to take up the matter. (*Grágás* Ia 213)

Peter Foote has made several thoughtful observations about this remarkable text. He notes that the provision must have been preceded by an active period of legal learning and recording. The need for the rule was clearly more than a matter of settling matters of scribal variation in the reproduction of an "official" manuscript. As this rule indicates, there never was an official manuscript. Even Haflidi's version had been amended and was considered amendable by recourse to the sayings of men learned in law. And presumably many of these "sayings" had also been written down (Foote 1984, 156–58). Sources of jurogenesis were everywhere, it seems, not just in the Lǫgrétta, as the rule of law would have it. The will to Law was too strong to be contained by mere laws. The proliferation of law and competing legal texts would be just the sort of phenomenon one might expect when a rich repository of oral rules met parchment and pen without an official body sufficiently powerful to rein in the energy of many legal experts living on farms scattered throughout the country, experts who in their own way were independently engaged in the very process of officializing and legitimating rules as law.

The Icelanders were aware that writing and literacy could assist in the reproduction of legal culture.[11] The author of the mid-twelfth-century text known as *The First Grammatical Treatise* explains the utility of his work by saying it would make it more convenient to read and write law (Haugen 1972, 12; see also *Hungr.* 1:59). But if literacy supplied some of the motive for writing laws, proliferating texts, and even inventing law, it did not create the initial proclivity for law, legalism, and litigiousness. The explanation for this must be forever lost in the silent obscurity of pre-tenth-century Scandinavia. Ari, in his *Íslendingabók*, tells us that when Iceland was fully settled (c. 930), a Norwegian by the name of Ulfljot brought the first laws out to Iceland, which were "then known as Ulfljot's Law." "But they were for the most part taken from the laws of the Gulathing[12] as they then stood. And Thorleif the Wise, the son of Horda-Kari, advised where additions, rejections, or reformulations should be made" (2:7). Thorleif, according to one source, was Ulfljot's maternal uncle (*Land.* 11:49) and according to another he had also helped establish the Gulathing law (see *Íslb.* 2:7n5). The early tenth century too had its legal experts and they came from Norway (see also von See 1964, 82).

Legal expertise soon flourished in saga Iceland. Numerous people counted as *lǫgmenn* or *lagamenn*, men skilled in law,[13] and were recognized as such by themselves and by others. The lawmen, however, did not appear to have been professionalized in the manner of the Roman jurists (Frier 1985) or even of the medieval Welsh ynads (see R. R. Davies 1986, 263). They had no colleague control, no special ethics, and no specialized literature apart from the variant manuscripts of the laws themselves. They, however, might have been able to communicate on a regular basis, a criterion of some importance in the establishment of a self-conscious profession (Frier 1985, xiii, 272). The commission that met at Haflidi's farm in 1117 to write the laws involved an intense consultation of legal experts, and the constitution of the Lǫgrétta would have offered structure within which legal experts could have met at least at regular yearly intervals.[14] From the ranks of these experts was selected the man who filled the post of the Lawspeaker, *lǫgsǫgumaðr*. They also trained young men and boys, who were sent or went to lodge with them (e.g., *Drop.* 4:147; *Gunnl.* 4:60), or were fostered by them (*Njála* 27:74). Most chieftains would have had to have some training in law and pleading since so much of their activity revolved around prosecuting and defending claims on behalf of their thingmen, but this training need not qualify them for the epithet of *lǫgmaðr* (expert in law), which appears to have been reserved only for men of special talent (cf. von See 1964, 80).[15] Nevertheless, when a chieftain had no skill in law it was considered worthy of mention (*Sturla* 6:68). The epithet *lǫgmaðr* does not appear to have been formally bestowed by those people who were already recognized as experts, but surely recognition by those already recognized must have done much to make a man's reputation in law—that and winning lawsuits. A reputation in law was a reputation that induced respect, even if that respect was at time tinged with the fear and loathing one feels for the wily practicer. The sagas take great care to note when people were known for their legal expertise, even when the talent did not figure into the plot (see, e.g., *Eyrb.* 12:20; *Hafl.* 3:14; *Hungr.* 18:82; *Njála* 1:5; *Þorg. sk.* 1:104). A man's legal skills in themselves were almost always oagaworthy.

Law loomed large in imagination and life for more than just the chieftain class (Grønbech 1932, 79). Even pauper children found in lawsuits the subject matter for plays they performed to varying levels of approval among the adults observing them (*Njála* 8:29), and servants from neighboring farms would get together to hold mock courts (*Ljós.* 9:129). The brief description of these games suggests that they were a way of training the population in the basic procedure of the Things as well as of affording a euphemized context for sublimated sexual interaction between male and female servants who appear to have opposed each other in the mock court.[16] Law and legal process even figured in life after death. The laying of the ghosts of some dead men unwilling to give up their places to the living was accomplished by summoning them to a "door-court" for housebreaking and causing sickness and death (*Eyrb.* 55:151–52). The saga genre itself attests to the cultural obsession with law. Saga plots generally deal with legal issues. In a significant number of family sagas and those *Sturlunga sagas* set in the twelfth century, the Things and the courts held there serve as the setting for much of the critical action. And surely the *Lǫgberg*, the Law Rock, the place at the Allthing where the formal publication of suits was made, was more than anything a symbol of the centrality and irreducible durability of the law in the people's imagination. It was there that the Lawspeaker sat and recited the laws and to which a formal procession was led before the convening of the courts:

> We shall go to the Law Rock on [Saturday] and move the courts out for challenging [of the judges for interest] at the latest when the sun is on the western ravine crag, seen from the Lawspeaker's seat at the Law Rock. The Lawspeaker is to go first if he is in good enough health; then the chieftains with their judges . . . (*Grágás* Ia 45)

Like the Law Rock next to which he sat, the Lawspeaker was himself an emblem. He signified the unity of law that bound Icelanders together. He was the symbol of continuity with the past, the living embodiment of the tradition of legal learning. Time and Lawspeakers were bound together in another sense. The list of Lawspeakers (*DI* I 500–501), much in the manner of regnal lists, served to order past events in time (Hastrup 1985, 47; Einarsdóttir 1964, 45–48).[17]

But the impression of excessive law needs to be qualified. First, this mass of rules was mercifully unaccompanied by any state enforcement mechanism. There was no bureaucracy to oversee their administration, no permanent presence, other than the inscrutable Law Rock, that had a vested interest in their being honored. Law enforcement, like self-help, was the responsibility of the wronged party or his successor.[18] Second, most rules, such as those governing land, livestock, marriage, driftage, were not intended to be absolute. Their purpose, to borrow an image from the world of computers, was to provide a default setting that would govern unless the parties to the transaction preferred to bargain out of the ambit of the rule. In this respect Icelandic law was no different from most modern American commercial law. Presumably many of these rules were intended to codify standard practice and hence to relieve the parties of the burden of hashing out a multitude of particular terms for each transaction. Not all rules, however, were optional. *Grágás* rather emphatically denied the right to settle cases involving killings or serious wounds unless permission had been granted by the Lǫgrétta (Ia 174, II 341). But, as we shall see in the next chapter, the will to settle appears to have been much stronger than the legal stricture purporting to limit it. Even those rules purporting to be non-negotiable were in effect negotiable if no one outside the interested parties cared to prosecute the case, or if it was to no one's advantage to be officious enough to make use of a provision, when available, allowing anyone who wanted to to prosecute the breach.

We can only guess at how the Icelanders understood their will to make law. Different laws seem to have had different types of motivation. Some seem to have been more in the nature of meditations on rules without certain relation to practice. There is reason to believe that the more elaborately structured systems of rules were juristic exercises, some of which may have actually constrained the vagaries of practice, as seems to have been the case with the poor law of *Ómagabálkr* (above pp. 147–54), some having, as far as we can discern, no effect at all on practice and the main purpose of which seems to have been nothing more than the satisfaction of a juristic and aesthetic urge toward systematization and conceptual order.[19] This, it has been proposed, was the purpose behind *Baugatal* (above p. 144). But numerous laws were undoubtedly the consequence of the blandest of functional assumptions. They were meant either to constrain practice or settle disputes arising from unconstrainable practices. On a more general level, it seems that people felt that law promoted order, not just the systemic order derived from the assignment of things to a place in a legal and social structure, but actual peace. The sentiment is captured in the Norse proverb invoked by Njal: "With laws shall our land be built, but with disorder [ólǫg, unlaw] laid waste" (Njála 70:172).[20] To what extent these feelings were justified is another matter. If a law was respected simply because it was law, then elevating a hypothetical practice or one practice of many actual competing practices to the status of legal rule could confer on the desired behavior a certain legitimacy and positive value in relation to competing behaviors, thus making the rule in some small way self-enforcing, even those rules whose original motivation may have been jural elegance rather than the regulation of practice.

We have no competent way of measuring respect for law or of knowing to what extent the law actually succeeded in channeling behavior to accord with its wishes. We occasionally find evidence of a punctiliousness with regard to obeying rules of little substantive import. Thus a group of men mustered to hold a court of confiscation left without convening it because, according to the source, "the day was advanced and it was prescribed in the laws that evidence in a court of confiscation should be presented when the sun is in the south" (see Grágás Ia 84). But the same source also suggests that the force of law was given some assistance by the presence of a powerful intervenor who threatened to oppose the party wishing to hold the court if he persisted in his desire to hold it (G.dýri 3:164–65).[21] And how are we to read the strange episode mentioned above in which ghosts obey without fuss the judgments of a "door-court" to which they had been summoned (Eyrb. 55:151–52)? Surely lethal sanction could not have been especially compelling to them. In the ghosts' willingness to comply we must be seeing a model for the behavior of the living.

In those instances in which the law codified well-established patterns of behavior, adherence to the rule would tell us less about respect for the law than about the law's respect for customary behavior. Such appears to have been the case in an instance in which a man asked his enemies to assist him in burying his father. Those requested said they had no wish to help him with his difficulties, but their father convinced them to go in this manner: "It is necessary that you carry out those things which people are legally obliged to do; and you are now asked to do something which you can't refuse" (Eyrb. 34:94).[22] But in those cases where the law tried to alter and restrict established patterns of behavior, and even in those cases where the law was lending its force to well-established behavioral patterns, it would seem that people thought sanction was more likely to induce compliance or prevent deviance than an abstract respect for laws as Law. All *Grágás* bears witness; it was nothing if not liberal in its use of the various grades of outlawry and the ubiquitous three-mark fine.

The ideal of obeying the law was, however, part of the repertoire of legitimating discourse. Respect for law was thus invoked by a disingenuous Haflidi who expressed horror that his outlawed opponent should attend the Thing and "thus violate the law of the land" (*Hafl.* 22:39). The bishop, his interlocutor, who was seeking to reconcile the disputants, understood Haflidi's rhetorical strategy; he correctly interpreted Haflidi's concern for obedience to law to be little more than an attempt to coat his prideful resistance to a peaceful settlement with a veneer of respectable justification. Haflidi's disingenuousness does nothing to disconfirm the positive value associated with respect for law. His invocation of law shows that people struggling to officialize their behavior, to validate their actions, preferred to have law on their side rather than against them, even if the specific rules at issue were not always able to determine outcomes in the situations to which they applied (see Comaroff and Roberts 1981).

Saga characters seldom speak about law as law, but they do, in subtle ways, indicate the law's synonymity with legitimacy, as when, for instance, Skarphedin says his mother has egged him on with a "legal-egging" (*lǫgeggjan*). The term suggests the legitimacy of the extralegal violence counseled by the mother. The lawfulness of that egging can only spring from the fact that the person he is setting out to kill has forfeited his immunity vis-à-vis Skarphedin. On the other hand, there are numerous rules in *Grágás* which the sagas show to have been systematically violated with impunity. Such was the case with the rule prohibiting extralegal settlement of actions involving killings and serious wounds, as was just mentioned, and the laws prohibiting Thing attendance for those men who have had wounds or mortal wounds lawfully published against them (*Grágás* Ia 174–75, II 351; see Heusler 1911, 109–11, 215–21). In the latter case, either the desire of defendants to defend full outlawry actions in person rather than by proxy was stronger than a law backed only by lesser outlawry prohibiting them from defending in person, or the provision was obsolete and preserved for antiquarian reasons, or it was a wishful innovation of some expert in law to whom we owe the present rescensions of *Grágás*.

In those instances in which saga practice deviated significantly from *Grágás*, Heusler was inclined to believe that the law did not reflect viable regulation, but rather the schoolish theory of legal experts engaged in the first hesitant steps of state formation (1911, 223ff.). The citation law (see p. 225), however, suggests that if legal theory had the look of legislation and was cast in its form and enscrolled in writing, then it would have been available to validate claims and to determine or constrain the outcome of disputes arising from those claims. We should not too readily underestimate the practical effects of law or rules that masquerade as law even when those rules are not explicitly invoked in situations to which they would apply. The mere fact that a rule is in a legal manuscript means that the possibility existed that that "law" could help legitimate claims or suggest to someone the need for its enforcement. Nevertheless, it is certain that some provisions in *Grágás* were obsolete at the time the existing manuscripts were written since they appear alongside succeeding provisions marked as "new laws" (*nýmæli*).[23] It is also likely that some *Grágás* provisions remained unenforced or, perhaps, unenacted. The sagas, in most instances, are to be preferred to *Grágás* when they show people's behavior consistently violating a law with no evidence that such behavior supplied the basis for legal action or merited special comment. The sagas deserve this deference because the picture they paint in contrast to *Grágás*, when there is a contrast to be painted, so plausibly accords with what we know about dispute processing in other preindustrial societies. The indelible image that remains from the sagas, however, is that the Law mattered, even if certain laws did not. Ultimately, any serious dispute, and nearly all feud, would eventually wend its way to the Thing and its courts, or work its way back there if that was where it had its origins.

There is another side to the multitude of laws and regulation. Putting aside proverbial sentiments about the relation of law to order, there is nothing necessarily order-effecting about law. In fact, the opposite claim could be made. Take an easy example. Before the institution of the tithe laws in 1096, there could obviously have been no disputes over tithes. But once instituted, they provided a fertile ground for strife (see, e.g., *Sturla* 25 : 99; *Íslend.* 20 : 246). The maze of regulation that Christianity brought with it increased the rule density of the culture and gave more ground for dispute than had existed beforehand. Breaches of Sabbath and holiday observance were now available as superficial justifications of disputes the deep motivations of which were purely political (e.g., *Vall.* 3 : 241). Other laws tended to focus hostility rather than to diffuse it. Inheritance rules that distinguished between classes of half-brothers could only breed hostility between those classes (see chapter 5, n. 9). And rules allowing for the free transferability of lawsuits made sure that fewer matters went unprosecuted than otherwise would have been the case.

To the disorder and strife that rules themselves may generate there must be added the violence that accompanies the processing of breaches of those rules. Only the most complacent assume that rule application is not violent. Law never eschews violence either in early Iceland or in modern industrial society (Cover 1986). Heusler was perhaps too aware of this. In his view, the legal process was only a slightly formalized version of unadorned revenge. Both were feud and both were dangerous: "Legal process is a stylized feud" (1911, 103; see also 1912, 61; von See 1964, 239–40). The law, as we saw in the preceding chapter, attempted to limit the permissible range of self-help, but it did not try to prohibit it altogether. It sought to limit the class of expiators and the time and place where self-help could be legitimately taken. If vengeance were not taken before the next Allthing, the law interposed the formal procedure of a lawsuit between the avenger's axe and the wrongdoer. The interposition was not permanent. The successful prosecution of the suit effected a semantic shift: what was once an execution was now the execution of a judgment. In either mode of resolution, legal or self-help, a corpse was anticipated. In Iceland, the violence of the law was not something removed from the general populace. There were no state apparatus to pretend to monopolize the legitimate use of force. Violence did not take place behind prison walls, there was no sheriff to issue a summons to a hostile party, to keep the peace in the court, or to execute judgment. It was up to free adult males to do the work of law.

The law then did not disown revenge and although pure blood revenge was always the most satisfying for the aggrieved avenger, no one felt themselves totally dissatisfied if they succeeded in outlawing and then killing key people in their adversary's group. But Heusler's view of law as feud was not solely a function of the law's vengefulness; it also depended on the combativeness of the legal process itself. A significant number of legal actions required summoning the defendant at his domicile (*Grágás* III 676–78).[24] Issuing the summons could provide the occasion for violent confrontation, if the defendant chose to disrupt the proceedings (*Eyrb.* 44:120–21; *Ljós.* 1:5; *Reyk.* 18:209; *Vápn.* 7:40–41). The prospect of violent response on the part of defendants led plaintiffs to muster forces for the summoning. And a defendant's vulnerability might suggest to the summoning party the advantage of avoiding the law's delays by killing the person to be summoned: "Bard took up the action against Hallvard and set out to summon him. When he met Hallvard he was able to reach a quick conclusion to the case by chopping off his head" (Glúma 18:61). The size of the summoning party was actually made the subject of negotiation in one case where a householder agreed to let his homeman be summoned only if the plaintiffs could accomplish it with a small party (Gunn. þ. 1:198). Practical considerations might call for the defendants to counter the summons with something short of violence. In the face of the superior forces of the summoning party, Sturla, contrary to the wishes of the more hotheaded members of his following, ordered his men to come up with as many cases as they could think of to provide the bases for countersummons to hurl back at their opponents (Sturla 30:108; see also Eyrb. 22:56, 44:120; Lax. 84:240–41). Sturla's tactic shows quite graphically one of the effects of the hyperlegalization of Icelandic society: there always seemed to have been claims available to bring against someone. In this instance, the availability of such claims actually worked to defer violence, although, apparently, only because countersummoning was still sufficiently belligerent to assuage the hostile desires of Sturla's most aggressive followers. If stones and axes were transformable into formal words of summons, it was also understood that the transformation could work equally well in the reverse direction.

Fueling the tenseness of the situation was the fact that initiating a lawsuit was not a neutral act, a mere ministerial requisite devoid of other social significances. The arrival of the principal and his witness-followers looked no different than an armed attack, which in fact it could turn out to be if the person being summoned looked incapable of offering resistance. The summons or publishing of a case could also be perceived as a public insult, to be avenged as such. This was especially true where the acts charged to the defendant were opprobrious, like theft or sexual deviance, or when a lesser man presumed to sue someone who thought himself a social superior (Hallfr. 3:143; Njála 50:130). This significance of going to law was not lost on certain claimants whose decision to sue was motivated primarily by a present desire to insult and humiliate (see, e.g., Lax. 84:240; Hœn. 8:22–23; Njála 8:27, 50:130). One bóndi was so concerned about offending a chieftain by summoning his son that he first asked the chieftain's leave before suing (Vatn. 37:99). The chieftain's brother was not appeased: "We may not be experts in law, but we will still be able to quash the case with our axes."

Violent confrontation was also possible at the Thing, although distinctly less likely than at the summoning stage. The numerous presence of third parties made sure of that. Still, if a lawsuit were to be processed to conclusion it was the responsibility of the litigants to provide the forces necessary to ensure the orderly presentation of the case. Most of the time spent preparing for lawsuits was devoted to recruiting supporters to accompany the principals to the Thing and then to attend the court proceeding. When Thorkel Geitisson arrived at the Thing to defend a case on behalf of one of his household members with a mere four followers, his adversary Gudmund remarked on the unlikelihood of Thorkel nullifying the case, even though Gudmund had committed a fatal procedural error. Gudmund in fact was sufficiently dismayed by Thorkel's small force to suspect a trick (*Ljós.* 10:133). Major outbreaks of violence at the Things were rare, but the prospect of being forcibly overborne was still the controlling anxiety of every litigant (see Heusler 1911, 101–7). If by the time of trial one of the parties had not managed to gather sufficient support, the judgment was usually assured, even without actual violence, although violent disruption of a case by a defendant or the railroading of a judgment by a plaintiff was not unknown (e.g., *Gísli* 21:67; *Grett.* 46:147).[25]

In cases of any seriousness the law provided for only one penalty—full outlawry (*skóggangr*)—which meant a loss of all juridical status and property,[26] privileging anyone to kill the outlaw and indeed obliging the prosecutor to do so (*Grágás* Ia 189). The judgment holder was himself subject to full outlawry at the suit of those who had captured the outlaw if he thereafter released him (*Grágás* II 398). The currency or validity of this last provision is problematic; the sagas attest to ceremonies of release and show no prosecutions by those capturing outlaws against prosecutors for releasing them (e.g., *Hrafn Sv. St.* 14:218; *Prest.* 3:122; *Þorst. hv.* 7:17; see Heusler 1911, 176–80). On the other hand, there was strong social pressure for the judgment holder to kill his outlaw. As we have seen in the preceding chapter, *Hrafnkels saga* ultimately judges Sam's decision not to kill his outlaw when he had the chance as imprudent (10:132–33). Elsewhere public scorn was the lot of those who failed to get their man (Bork in *Gísli* 27:88; Thorir in *Grett.* 63:209). The problem was especially poignant for the priest and future bishop Gudmund Arason who, after the untimely death of his patron, wished to avoid not only the humiliation of not being able to see his outlaw killed, but also the "loss of his ordination and clerical status" should he himself carry out the killing (*Prest.* 8:131).[27] (Such were the moral paradoxes occasioned by the mixing of heroic and Christian ethics). Gudmund hit upon the happy solution of offering God the wealth he stood to gain from the outlawry action if God could resolve the case without jeopardizing Gudmund's soul. In Iceland, God's ways did not have to be mysterious. In a rather unmiraculous general brawl a short time later, not only the outlaw, but also the outlaw's protector, was seriously wounded and, as a special sign of Gudmund's favor, the protector's son was also killed: "But God so took care of Gudmund that he had no involvement in the affray either by word or deed" (9:132).

The thirty-six judges selected by the goðar had no discretion in imposing the penalty in an action before them; it followed automatically as a consequence of the successful prosecution of the claim. Two weeks after the judgment in a case carrying either full or lesser outlawry, the laws required that a court of confiscation—*féránsdómr*—be held at the defendant's domicile (*Grágás* Ia 83–84). The *féránsdómr* was the procedure in which the outlaw's property was confiscated and his estate settled. After the wife's separate property was set aside, creditors' claims were satisfied, with half of what remained going to the man who got the defendant outlawed, the other half to the men of either the Quarter or the district. This latter share was to be used for the maintenance of the outlaw's dependents, if there were any, or of the district's needy if he had none. As might be expected the *féránsdómr* provided a third opportunity for dangerous confrontation (*Glúma* 27:92–93; *G.dýri* 3:164). The outlawed chieftain Thorgils Oddason gathered nearly four hundred men to thwart the confiscation court scheduled to dispose of his estate. He succeeded since the man who got him outlawed, Haflidi, had a force of a little more than a hundred (*Hafl.* 18–19:35–37). In order for Sam to conduct the *féránsdómr* against Hrafnkel (6:119), he had to take Hrafnkel by surprise in the early morning before Hrafnkel and his men had awakened. To these rather vexatious procedures we might add that killing one's outlaw was not always the easiest of tasks. Some were able to find protection among powerful men (e.g., *Hafl.* 14:31; *Sturla* 23:95), others, by sheer strength of will, were able to resist and wreak considerable havoc (see generally *Aron, Gísli, Grett., Sturla* 26:101).

Icelandic law, as we have thus described it, is only slightly distinguishable from the violence and spirit of unmediated vengeance-taking. But as it stands the picture is only a partial one, overly sensational and very much oversimplified. Legal process was indeed part of the feuding process; it could not help but be so. The law, after all, provided a theater for the continuing competition and contention of the feuding groups. And there was no state making the claim that law and feud were antithetical. No one understood law and feud to be necessarily opposed. But these facts do not so blur the lines between legal process and self-help that we are entitled to dismiss the law as little more than an obfuscatory style of vengeance-taking. Legal process was not the feud itself. If the picture of law were as bleak as its occasional misfiring and the continual possibility of misfire make it seem, we would have a hard time accounting for why people made as much use of the law as they did, or why the law occupied such a prominent position in the constitution of Icelandic society. After all, there must have been more to getting an outlawry judgment than simply being put back to the same problem one had before going to law: killing the enemy. The story yet to be told in this chapter and the next is how the law fit into the disputing process.

There is the rather recalcitrant problem of how to evaluate the saga evidence. At first view, one would expect the sagas to overvalue accounts of vengeance as against smoothly functioning legal process if only because it is easier to make a good story of the former. The sagas indeed show a marked preference for processing disputes by blood rather than by law or arbitration. Out of some 520 cases in the family sagas counted by Heusler (1911, 40–41), 297 led to blood vengeance, 104 to arbitration without prior recourse to law, and 119 to lawsuits. Of the 119 legal actions, however, fifty led to a judicial decision; sixty ended up being arbitrated out of court and nine others reached no conclusion, usually because the court was scattered by violent disruption.[28] *Sturlunga saga* confirms these ratios (Heusler 1912, 20). The numbers are admittedly inexact because of the difficulty of circumscribing discrete cases. Discreteness, the narrow definition of the subject of a dispute and the certain and continued identity of the contending parties, was greatly vitiated by the tendency of disputes to expand and suffer fundamental transformation as they wended their way from forum to forum and as the people recruited as supporters redefined the subject in dispute or replaced the original principals as the central figures in the case.[29] But the bare numbers make out rather coldly the importance of violence as ideology, and, even discounting heavily for bias in what is deemed sagaworthy, they proclaim the importance of violence as a dispute-processing mode, providing a reminder that outcomes reached by talk, although not rare, took place within the shadow of violence.

The obvious bias of the sagas for tales of feud and blood should, however, not lead us to dismiss these numbers too quickly. In fact, it is precisely because the sagas are devoted to feud that the numbers have a certain plausibility, as long as we recognize what they might and might not signify. The numbers are not meant to suggest that a random offense had a sixty-percent chance of being resolved violently. The sagas do not present a random selection of wrongs. Minor trespasses to property between small farmers are distinctly underrepresented when compared to killings and insult. Law is also overrepresented in its dispute-creating aspect and underrepresented in its dispute-preventing aspect. Nor is the distribution of wrongs among social strata in any way representative. The nonrandom sample of cases the sagas give us are the stuff of feud, that is, the way substantial disputes between substantial parties were processed. The numbers then may in fact express the upper limit of plausible probabilities when parties of the upper strata were involved in a pattern of hostile dealings, that is, when they were feuding.

But when we try to discern to what extent recourse to formal lawsuits was made in nonfeud situations, the sagas are not very helpful (von See 1964, 79–80). Although *Grágás* might take care to give causes of action for failure to put up travelers on the way to a wedding or for refusing to assist in the building of a "legal fence" between one's property and that of one's neighbor (Ib 90, II 451), we have no way of knowing whether disputes ever arose on these matters, or how they were likely to be processed if they did. We simply have lost the small suits between small farmers who did not enlist their chieftains to their cause, as well as most of those in which they did enlist them but which were processed routinely. The myriad of legal provisions governing sales, lending, repayment, and pledges of livestock rarely gave rise to disputes that penetrate the sagas. Heusler, in fact, doubts whether such disputes ever were processed at law (1912, 69). Probably most such cases were settled expeditiously and routinely by arbitration or negotiation, but, Heusler's doubts notwithstanding, many must have been commenced as formal legal action. Indirect evidence of a more general use of the courts than is suggested by Heusler's numbers occasionally emerges in the sagas. One case shows that the local courts could be used by an unscrupulous chieftain as a way of mulcting or dispossessing his inferiors (*Ljós.* 5:20). That case suggests that the routinization of small claims tended to benefit the powerful or those likely to be structurally situated so as to be frequent plaintiffs, like the local lender (see, e.g., *Hœn.* 2:7). There are also brief notices referring generally to "cases" scheduled to be heard at a Thing (e.g., *Eyrb.* 56:154; *Njála* 97:242). And scattered throughout the sagas are references to outlaws seeking service in households far removed from their enemies, although the circumstances that led to their punishment are lost.

The real problem with the numbers is that they underestimate the

importance of the law in the feuding context even as it is depicted
in the sagas and even if, as a matter of fact, resolutions by blood and
arbitration were preferred to legal judgments. For if bloody self-help
cast its shadow over the law, the law shaded self-help no less. The
mere fact that the legal alternative existed meant that it influenced
choices and decisions regarding the other two chief modes of dispute
resolution. As we saw in the preceding chapter, people took care to
find adequate legal justification for their acts of revenge. They also
planned with the knowledge that legally unjustified vengeance was
liable to legal reprisal. The raw numbers also lack context. Any dispute that continued through more than one cycle of wrong and repayment, that is any feud, was likely at some time to find itself in a
phase which employed legal process. The legal phase may well have
been preceded by some eight discrete acts of blood revenge as in the
central feud in *Njáls saga*, but eventually the dispute got to law.[30]

Law had much to offer disputants, even if what it had to offer did
not come risk-free. Cloaking reprisal in formal legitimacy had its
advantages. For all the dangers there might have been in suing, getting a judgment, and then killing an outlaw, they were distinctly less
risky than taking blood revenge. An outlawry judgment isolated the
vengeance target and eroded his support. Any assistance granted an
outlaw was itself actionable, and although incurring liability for assisting him might not especially intimidate some of the stronger
chieftains (unless the outlaw were the outlaw of another strong
chieftain) the behavior of less powerful people seemed to have been
affected. The sagas of the outlaws Grettir, Gisli, and Aron Hjorleifs-
son vividly portray their difficulties getting help from people fearful of the consequences of aiding outlaws. The *Grágás* provisions
penalizing giving assistance to outlaws were not a dead letter. Legal
reprisal for aiding outlaws was common fare in the sagas (*Finnb.*
41:331–35; *Íslend.* 3:231, 55:305–7, 129:415; *Sturla* 5:67, 23:95).
Even God, we observed (p. 235), saw fit to visit reprisal on the protector of Gudmund Arason's outlaw.

Outlawry had a subtler effect on the members of the outlaw's kin
group and support network. There was more than just the fear of
incurring reprisal for aiding an outlaw; there were more positive inducements to abandon his cause. We might imagine a small sigh of
relief among the class of people eligible to have served as expiators
in blood revenge, once the opposition chose to single out one of the
wrongdoer's group and outlaw him. The class of people subject to an
outlawry action was made up only of those who had actually engaged in liability-producing conduct. The class was thus significantly narrower than the class liable for blood vengeance. Being let

off the hook, so to speak, gave those people who had not been selected for revenge, as well as those who had not been outlawed despite having engaged in liability-producing conduct, an interest in
maintaining their disassociation from the outlaw by refusing to sustain him and even perhaps an inducement to distance themselves
from the likely defendant before he was outlawed. The avenger
united his opposition when he kept them all on edge by preferring
blood to law, but once he became a prosecutor and selected his defendant, those whom he had decided not to move against had every
reason not to give the prosecutor a reason to change his mind. These
factors are no small virtue for the usefulness of the legal option
when processing serious claims.

Going to law did not mean forgoing revenge, as we have already
noted. It was often a sensible way of going about it. The legitimacy
acquired by the judgment made it easier to gather support to hunt
down the outlaw. It may even have led someone else to kill the outlaw. Outlaws, for example, were encouraged to kill each other by a
provision in the laws granting full reprieve for killing three outlaws
(*Grágás* Ia 187–88, II 399–400; *Grett.* 55–56:179–82).[31] And ob-
taining an outlawry judgment also conferred the considerable advantage of eliminating any legal liability for the vengeance killing when
it came. To this we might add that if the outlaw were blessed with
assets, half of the unencumbered property belonged to the judgment
holder. Blood revenge conferred no such financial advantage. On the
contrary, at the very least it meant having to pay compensation for
the corpse.

In the sagas, the decision to go to law is either made following the
failure of efforts to resolve the dispute informally by arbitration, or
is made immediately following the wrong as a sufficiently aggressive response somewhat short of blood revenge. Like vengeance,
going to law required mustering support, although the process proceeded in a somewhat different fashion depending on several variables. One of these was whether the action was prosecuted by the
person to whom it actually belonged, known as the *aðili*, or by
someone to whom the *aðili* had transferred it.[32] Both the prosecution and defense of cases were freely transferable. The transfer ritual
(*handsal*) was straightforward: the *aðili* took the transferee by the
hand and recited formal words of transfer in the presence of witnesses (*Njála* 135:356–58). The transferee did not succeed to all the
rights and duties of the *aðili*; the process was less an assignment as
we would understand it, than the engagement of an attorney or the
hiring of an agent.[33] The transferee could not himself transfer the
action except back to the original transferor, unless he fell ill or was

wounded while on the way to the Allthing. An exception was made for those causes of action that might arise from the original suit but occurred after the transfer. Such, for instance, were cases involving liability for improper pleading and procedure, for delay and disruption. These causes of action were treated as belonging to the transferee and he could do with them what he wanted. If the transferee died, the transferred case reverted to the transferor. The transferee was liable for lesser outlawry at the suit of the transferor if he willfully failed to pursue the action. Judges and members of the panel of neighbors (*búakviðr*) were stricken for kinship to the transferor and not the transferee. And the benefits and liabilities of the suit accrued to the transferor (*Grágás* Ia 62, 123, 125–26; II 344–45).

Such were the rules; the reality, reflecting the social context of the transfers, was often different. The free transferability of the prosecution and defense of claims was, in its most important respect, the procedural enablement of the powerless. It allowed their claims to be processed at law if they were able to convince a more powerful kinsman or their chieftain to take them up, for under no circumstances did an unassisted person of middling or low rank have meaningful access to law as a plaintiff. But this fact also made transferability one of the key ways in which big men exercised their power over lesser people. Big people controlled lesser people's access to justice. With no administrative apparatus for taxation, the big were still able to mulct the little by acquiring their legal claims at a discount, or, for that matter, simply by prosecuting them as defendants. Still, the absence of lordship meant the weak Icelander was spared the systematic exactions that vexed the villeins of the continent.

Not surprisingly then, since transferees were almost always chieftains or other big men, the concessions made to them to elicit their commitment reflected their superior bargaining position. Transferees were often reluctant to take up cases—lawsuits, after all, involved considerable risk—and they frequently exacted a healthy consideration from the transferor either by a big cut of the anticipated take or by way of gifts up front, sometimes taken in the form of being made the heir of the transferee.[34] The beseecher was aided in his effort to enlist his chieftain to his cause by the strong norms of mutual support that attended the *goði*-thingman relation. These norms provided the spice in the eggings that an occasional thingman was forced to use to shame his chieftain into fulfilling the obligation (e.g., *Ljós.* 22:66–67). Power differences also conferred *de facto* immunity on the transferee for willfully failing to pursue the action. It was highly unlikely that the average householder would ever be able

to muster the support to sue his chieftain-agent. If he had such resources, presumably he wouldn't have transferred the case in the
first place.

But the strong were by no means always reluctant to take up
claims. Lawsuits could be very valuable commodities, and if there
was not quite a market in them, they could still be banked and saved
to be transferred when needed to provide counterclaims against zealous prosecutors on behalf of beleaguered defendants (*Njála* 64 · 161)
or when needed as offsets in an arbitration proceeding to reduce the
financial liability of one of the parties. As we noted briefly in the
previous chapter, some big men were only too anxious to take up
claims when they had interests of their own that could be advanced
by the litigation (see, e.g., *Drop.* 4:147, 5:150). Lawsuits could be
quite lucrative to the transferee. Consider the case of Bjorg, whose
husband had been killed by the nephew of Haflidi, her husband's
*goði*. She felt that Haflidi's conflict of interest would prevent him
from properly following up her claim, so she sought out a rival chieftain, Thorgils:

> Thorgils said he was not obligated to take up a case that
> concerned Haflidi's thingmen.
>   She pressed him very hard, and when Thorgils saw
> that, he said that she was in a hard predicament—
> "because it's not an easy matter to go against Haflidi in
> a lawsuit. I will pay you twelve hundreds in *vaðmál* for
> the killing of your [husband], but I will take whatever
> comes from the case against Haflidi and his nephew.
> (*Hafl.* 7:19–20)

As it turned out Thorgils did rather well for himself, making more
than nine hundreds above his outlay (8:21).[35]

It was clearly more lucrative to prosecute rather than defend and
presumably chieftains had to play each role roughly the same number of times over the long run. But as a class, chieftains benefited
more than they were burdened by their role in legal process, and it
was the little people who funded the net gain. From the perspective
of the chieftain-agents litigation was not zero-sum. When enlisted
on the defendant's side, the chieftain's property was not legally at
risk should he lose, although he was under normative pressure to
pay the damages assessed his followers in an arbitrated settlement if
they were incapable of paying. His generosity was either already anticipated by payment or gift, or would be reciprocated in some way
later by the defendant or his kin, as part of the continuing exchange

relationships that bound *goði* and thingman, big man and little. And in the same way the gains from prosecuting were not one-time gains but were just one exchange in an ongoing cycle of exchanges that tended materially to benefit the patron more than the client.

Transfer of the action was thus often the first step in the support-mustering process, unless the *aðili* felt himself sufficiently powerful to sue in his own person. In suits to be tried at the local Thing, the support-mustering process was usually completed with the enlistment of a chieftain to one's cause, for with the chieftain came his thingmen. Venue[36] was a variable that greatly influenced the support-gathering process and, needless to say, the plaintiff would choose the forum, whether the local Thing or the Allthing, that promised him the greatest likelihood of success. If the suit was to be prepared for presentation at the Allthing, recruitment of supporters was a two- or three-tiered affair. First, one sought aid locally among one's own *goði*, kinsmen, friends, and neighbors.[37] Then one might attempt to recruit chieftains from other Quarters, perhaps offering payment for their services (e.g., *Ljós.* 25:83–84; *Njála* 134:351; *Vápn.* 10:44). And once at the Allthing, the two sides would engage in a pretrial competition to see how many powerful men in attendance at the Thing they could recruit to their cause, or at least convince not to oppose them. The saga writers were especially interested in the support-mustering process and devoted some of their better performances to descriptions of it (e.g., *Hrafnk.* 3–4:109–16; *Hœn.* 10–12:26–35; *Njála* 119–20:297–306, 134: 349–53; Byock 1982, 163–67).

Follow, for instance, the progress of old Thorbjorn, who had just lost his son Einar to Hrafnkel's axe. The case provides a slightly stylized but very instructive account of the support-mustering process and the main procedural steps in the preparation of a lawsuit. Hrafnkel, it appears, was Thorbjorn's chieftain; in any event, he was immeasurably more powerful. Thorbjorn first went to ask compensation from Hrafnkel. Hrafnkel denied the request, but nevertheless made a generous offer to care for Thorbjorn and his dependents, which Thorbjorn refused. The reason for the refusal clearly was not that Thorbjorn and Hrafnkel were disagreeing as to whether some property should be paid over; they were not even disagreeing as to amounts. What they were disputing was how to classify any property transfer that would take place: whether it was an award of *sonarbœtr*, compensation for a son, which Thorbjorn considered honorable, or a gift so valuable that it could not be repaid, which he considered dishonorable. Thorbjorn proposed instead that arbitrators be appointed. Hrafnkel immediately rejected this proposal: "Then you are considering yourself my equal and for that reason we will not reach any settlement" (*Hrafnk*. 3 : 106). The failure to settle outside the law meant Thorbjorn had to resort to a lawsuit. The realities of power precluded any consideration of blood revenge, and as the saga makes clear, but for the fortuitous series of events that followed, power differences should have precluded any consideration of a lawsuit too (see von See 1964, 237).

Then began the recruitment process. Thorbjorn next went to his brother, Bjarni. Bjarni was utterly dismayed that Thorbjorn had rejected Hrafnkel's offer and told his brother that he would not get involved when Thorbjorn had proceeded so foolishly. Thorbjorn rained vituperations on his brother and then sought out Bjarni's son Sam. Sam was knowledgeable in law and a skilled pleader. He too could not believe that Thorbjorn had rejected Hrafnkel's offer. He interposed a host of sensible objections to proceeding legally, but resigned himself to helping Thorbjorn's after having succumbed to a barrage of saga-style goading:

> "What are you closer to achieving now rather than before, if I should take up this claim and both of us end up disgraced?"
> "It is a great consolation that you accept the case, come what may," said Thorbjorn.[38]
> "I am not at all eager to undertake this. I do it for the sake of our kinship, but you should know that I think a fool like you will not be of much help." Then Sam extended his hand and and formally took up Thorbjorn's case. (3 : 108)

Sam began the preparations by formally publishing the claim and by calling the nine neighbors living nearest to the place of the killing to attend the Thing (*Grágás* Ia 150, 157, II 308). (The saga also records that Sam summoned Hrafnkel, something that was not required since a killing case could be properly commenced by publication alone [see chapter 7, n. 24]). In any event, Hrafnkel thought the whole matter risible when he learned of the preparations (*Hrafnk*. 3 : 108). When time came for the Allthing, Hrafnkel set out with seventy of his thingmen; Sam, anxious to avoid confrontation, waited until Hrafnkel had left and gathered his men, a distinctly smaller and less imposing crew. These were the nine neighbors he had called to serve as the jury and some poor men with no household attachment.

At the Allthing Sam and Thorbjorn sought out every chieftain there to ask for aid. None was willing to go against Hrafnkel, until a chance meeting with the brother of a Westfjord chieftain led to the agreement of that chieftain to take up their cause. The chieftain would provide the bodies, Sam the pleading skills. With the force thus assembled Sam was able to present his case without interruption: "He went boldly into the court. He immediately named witnesses and prosecuted the case against Hrafnkel in accordance with the laws of the land, pleading firmly and without misspeaking" (4:116). Sam's supporters prevented Hrafnkel from disrupting the proceedings and an outlawry judgment was entered against him.

Sam was overjoyed at the results but his newly recruited patrons reminded him that more remained to be done: "A man is not fully outlawed until the court of confiscation is held, and that needs to be done at his home fourteen days after the Thing is dissolved" (4:118). They rehearsed the realities of outlawing a powerful man: "I assume that Hrafnkel will go home and intend to stay there. I expect he will continue to maintain his authority despite you. . . . I guess you have gotten from your lawsuit the right to call Hrafnkel an outlaw in name" (4:118). Support was needed to enforce the judgment and hold the court of confiscation. In this case his patrons accompanied him to hold the court with the results we have touched upon in the previous chapter (pp. 198–202).

The support-mustering process tended to move in an ever expanding spiral: first near kin, then remoter kin, then neighbors and other local people, then chieftains from different parts of the county. The context of different cases led to variations in this process, but only variation, not a different process. One's chieftain might have been sought out before one's kin and friends, or after. Or the structure of the dispute might have prevented the recruitment of one's chieftain because, as here, he was the adversary.

Another matter to note is the effect of differences in power between the parties on the availability of legal process. The fact that Hrafnkel thought Sam's pursuing legal action against him was "laughable" is instructive. Access to the courts was not something the weak were expected to have except as defendants, or unless they had been able to recruit powerful supporters to help prosecute their claim. Sam had a very hard time finding a powerful patron willing to take up his cause. That fact is probably the saga at its most "historical." The fiction is that Sam found support at the stroke of midnight. One gets the sense that a lot of the claims of the weak—those farmers of insufficient means to pay the Thing-attendance tax, those without substantial kin connections—were resolved by what scholars of dispute processing have termed avoidance and lumping it, old Thorbjorn's example notwithstanding (Felstiner 1974, 70, 81; Nader and Todd 1978, 9).

Avoidance means acting on the grievance by severing all relations with the wrongdoer. People who found it too unpleasant to live around someone making their lives miserable might choose to relocate or be forced to relocate (see, e.g., *Sturla* 23:96).[39] Lumping it describes the type of resolution when the aggrieved party chose or was forced to ignore his grievance and nevertheless continued to maintain contact with the offending party. Hrafnkel assumed that old Thorbjorn and Sam would have resigned themselves to this alternative. His amusement displays the contempt a superior visits upon the impudence of an inferior. Hrafnkel, as we have had occasion to observe earlier (pp. 199–201), was very sensitive to indicia of status. This sensitivity is expressed in his appreciation of the significance of an arbitrated settlement between Thorbjorn and himself: "Then you are considering yourself my equal." It is also expressed in his amusement. To have been enraged at Sam's lawsuit would have been to admit that Sam was of sufficient merit to have been capable of giving insult. But there is also a cold malevolence in his amusement that is derived from Hrafnkel's belief that Sam will suffer for his failure to defer to a man of rank.

Power is a difficult concept, at least since Foucault made it one; it can mean many things and take many forms, but in Iceland in the context of lawsuit, much of it meant having others think one had the ability to muster bodies to assist in the various procedures that made up a legal action. Power in this sense was an assessment of the probability that one had the ability to win a lawsuit, or the ability to absorb a legal loss without suffering great material damage. Power thus considered might not always be sufficient to dictate outcomes, as the case we are discussing makes clear. The convergence of a series of unlikely circumstances made Sam for one crucial period more powerful than Hrafnkel. In that period he was able to effect a transfer of much of Hrafnkel's power to himself. But it usually took more than one defeat at law for major power transfers to take place, at least in those cases where the litigant was appearing as the transferee of another's claim. And *Sturlu saga, Þorgils saga ok Hafliða*, and the remainder of *Hrafnkels saga* rather clearly demonstrate that even the outlawry of a chieftain himself need not disrupt his mode of operation for too long. Outlawry judgments like the initial lawsuit itself were negotiable; they could be released, the law notwithstanding, as part of a post-judgment arbitrated settlement of the dispute. Short-term swings in the ability to muster support were expected and were functions of the popularity of the particular cause (*Glúma* 19:65–66) or of attentiveness to preparation (*Drop.* 5:150–51; *Ljós.* 10:133–44). Because power was so intimately linked with reputation and specifically with the reputation for having power (that is, power did indeed have a strong discursive component), its loss was often gradual, requiring both a slow cumulation of discomfitures and a consequent community reassessment of one's standing relative to others. Power was hard to sever from the reputation for having it, because by conferring the reputation people assumed a deferential posture toward those they invested with the reputation.

For the powerful, that is, for those whose position in certain social networks gave them the ability to muster support more efficiently than others, the courts did indeed provide a forum that they were willing and able to make use of. Thorgils' and Haflidi's feud takes place solely in the form of lawsuits, with confrontations at Things and courts of execution (see *Hafl.*). The hostile interactions between Arnkel and Snorri in *Eyrbyggja saga* and Brodd-Helgi and Geitir in *Vápnfirðinga saga* are first played out with them acting as proxies for their thingmen before they abandon the legal theater for blood. Likewise, Einar Thorgilsson and Hvamm-Sturla meet in court numerous times both on their own behalf and as representatives of others, even outlawing each other twice before they finally meet in battle (see *Sturla*).

The fact that chieftains frequently opposed each other in court as representatives of their clients meant that interchieftain rivalry, at least among chieftains sharing the same local Thing, could not be avoided. Some of this legal combat must have been such frequent fare as to have appeared routine. And as long as the dispute being processed was clearly defined as small potatoes, losses could be shrugged off or balanced by equally innocuous victories. Competition between chieftains was thus played out in a restricted and relatively low-key context. But people kept score and at some point the chieftain who lost more than he won also lost esteem (see *Eyrb.* 32:90, 37:99). Once competition between big men began to be perceived as a defined state of hostility, the very process of transferring a claim to one of them redefined the claim. The disputes of little people could be thus transformed beyond recognition into points of honor between their more powerful agents. A simple paternity claim of a thingman's daughter could undergo successive transformations as it moved from daughter to her father to her father's chieftain, leading to battle between rival chieftains, and then to support mustering among other chieftains, and finally to the intervention of third parties to impose a settlement (*Ljós.* 22–27:65–92).

The aggressive pursuit of their thingmen's lawsuits against the thingmen of rival chieftains and the clients of big men was a common disputing strategy (*Drop.* 4:147; *G.dýri* 4:167–68; *Ísland.* 20:245–46; *Vápn.* 7–8:38–43). This disputing style occupied a position somewhere between the freer formed hostility of raid and blood and the unformed hostility of suppressed irritation and jealous watchfulness. It allowed the chieftains to articulate clearly and publicly their opposition to each other, but in a stylized manner that need not put everything on the line. The stakes in each individual case did not require the intensive attention that causes of action they held in their own right would have had and did not incur anywhere near the risks that raid and blood did. Lesser people also benefited from this to the extent that their ability to enforce their own rights was greatly enhanced when the claim they had to offer was a winner and would oppose their chieftain to another with whom he was locked in competition. This prospect would not be much solace to the thingman who was contending with a fellow thingman of the same chieftain. In such cases, the chieftain, caught in a conflict of obligation, might try to arbitrate a settlement between the disputants (*Ísland.* 33:263; *Reyk.* 1:153). But the thingmen might prefer to seek out other chieftains to take up the claim (*Hafl.* 7:19–20) or even formally transfer their Thing attachment to a rival chieftain (*Sturla* 27:102).

The legal process did much to channel, confine, and define the struggles of the powerful. Litigation reinforced the image of balanced exchange in the feud because it so neatly lent itself to scorekeeping and because it was in fact an acceptable play within the context of feud. Honor could be won and lost, and a debt of blood be repaid at law as well as in blood. In the process, the rights of the weaker were sometimes vindicated, often inadvertently. On the whole it seems that the legal process of the sagas benefited those whom feud benefited. Like feud, it was a game played by the better-established members of the society, often at the expense of lesser people. Yet there is no reason to believe that societies further along the road in the process of state formation did any better by their weaker members.

## Some Aspects of Legal Procedure and Legal Argument

There is much very useful scholarship on the formal legal process in early Iceland, on the constitution of the courts, on the pleading of actions and the substantive law (see, e.g., Maurer 1910, von Amira 1895; also Ingvarsson 1970). I do not intend to retread those paths and will touch on no more than a few salient aspects of court procedure. The section of *Grágás* devoted to procedure, from publication and summons to the court of confiscation and the execution of the judgment, occupies more than one hundred pages (*Grágás* Ia 38–143), to which should be added the extensive procedural segments contained in the homicide law. Icelandic procedure is remarkable for its extraordinary complexity and its formalism. But the formalism is not of the sort that traditional legal history has attributed to prerational prebureaucratic law (e.g., Brunner 1906, 252–60; Milsom 1981, 38–39; von See 1964, 236; Weber 1968, 761–65).[40] In most matters *Grágás* largely adopts a system of substantial compliance; he who failed in a syllable did not fail in his action, although he might still be liable for fines of three marks for his inadvertences.

Minor errors in procedure were seldom fatal to a cause of action and when *Hrafnkels saga* mentions that Sam pleaded his case "without misspeaking" (*miskviðalaust*), it does not mean to imply his case would have been lost had he misspoken. It does suggest, however, that pleaders who could proceed with great fluency were considered worthy of note (cf. Lönnroth 1976, 247). The sanction for merely misspeaking was rather informal. When Helgi Droplaugarson misspoke while reciting the rules of procedure at a fall Thing, people laughed (*Drop.* 8:156), although this was still too much sanction for him and he eventually avenged his humiliation. The testimony of a witness called to testify to what he had heard was rightly given, even if "[he did] not speak every word in the form in which he was named to witness it," as long as the deviation did not affect the case (*Grágás* Ia 57). A plaintiff who incorrectly called people to serve on the panel of neighbors for his case did not lose his case as long as he swore that he called those he thought best qualified (Ia 62). This same provision reveals that Icelandic law was willing and able to consider states of mind. Lack of intent or lack of knowledge is a valid defense to a variety of actions ranging from errors in procedure (Ia 38–39, 43, 45, 53, 58, 62, 67, 91, 105) to substantive claims (Ia 127, 166–67, Ib 109, II 146). To this evidence we can add the negative evidence of the sagas, which shows virtually no failures in procedure leading to the voiding of claims (cf. *Band.* 5:317–18; *Njála* 60:152; see Heusler 1911, 108–9).[41] Saga cases turn on substance, the primary issue being the issue of justification, that is, whether the victim had forfeited his immunity, had fallen *óheilagr* to the defendant. And with the exception of *Njáls saga*,[42] saga descriptions of actual trials, though brief, show more colloquy and ad hoc argumentation than formal pleading (Heusler 1911, 108–9).

We shouldn't overstate the case. Traditional legal history wasn't exactly making up what it postulated about primitive legal process. Procedure was still a good nine points of the law. It required great skill to negotiate the maze of procedural rules. Errors were not cost free, even if they might not be sufficient to void one's claim. They gave the other side causes of action, mostly for fines of three marks, but on occasion for lesser outlawry. A man who called the majority of the panel of neighbors incorrectly was liable for a fine at the suit of his opponent (Ia 62) and one who called a man as a witness in court whom he had not formally cited to be a witness was liable for lesser outlawry (Ia 58). Testimony contrary to that already delivered or contrary to the verdict of a panel of neighbors was punishable by lesser outlawry (Ia 68). This last provision goes a long way to making the trial look like nothing more than a formal procedural exercise unless we consider that opposing issues could still be raised in two ways. One procedure for introducing conflicting evidence was to make that evidence the basis for a counterclaim pleaded as an independent cause of action. One saga example suggests that the two cases would then go forward at the same time (Glúma 9:33). In any event judgment would not be made in one case before the other had been presented. The other procedure was to put forth an affirmative defense, called a bjargkviðr or clearing verdict, by asking five of the nine neighbors on the panel (búakviðr) to answer defense submissions.[43] Why contrary witness testimony should have been so abhorred does not appear and I am at a loss to explain it.[44] It might have been to avoid the issue of perjury, which would have to arise unless it could be circumvented by such procedures.

The killing cases that are the usual fare of the sagas rarely show disputes arising over facts. The honorable killer always admitted his act. How else was the world to know that the repayment owed had been made, that honor had been satisfied? The proper functioning of the legal system and even the feud itself required wrongs to be made openly. Functional concerns, however, were not about to deter secret wrongs. When they occurred the laws provided for a "rational" investigative procedure, the housesearch, or rannsókn (Grágás Ib 166–68); but just as often recourse was had to irrational means of discovery: dreams, prophecy, divination, and witchcraft accusation.[45] Secret wrongs were especially discouraged, both by informal norms and by the law. A killing that was not announced properly was reclassified as a murder, a secret killing. The sanction for both killing and murder was full outlawry, but the murderer was deprived of any right to raise defenses of justification (Grágás Ia 154, II

348–49). And no one was lower than the thief, the secret appropriator of another's property. To sue someone for theft was so insulting to the defendant that the plaintiff who did not get a panel verdict in his favor was liable for slander at the suit of the original defendant, unless he openly affirmed at the outset of the action that he was summoning in good faith and not for the purpose of disgracing the defendant (Ib 162–63).

Facts were found either by witness testimony or by the panel of neighbors, except in a limited number of cases, mostly dealing with paternity, where the law provided for ordeal (Miller 1988a, 213n7). The Icelandic system of proof was remarkable for its almost total reliance on the knowledge and witness of neighbors, at the expense of more irrational modes of proof. Oaths and compurgation barely figure in the laws, although saga cases suggest they might have been resorted to in more cases than the laws provided for (see Maurer 1910, 549–56). The entire saga corpus preserves only ten offers of ordeal, only seven of which end up being performed (Miller 1988a, 213n9).[46] The rationalism of the fact-finding process should not be overemphasized, however. Many facts attained the status of fact by formal procedures. The aðili could attribute the wounds on a corpse by displaying the corpse before witnesses and formally assigning the wounds to various participants in the attack whether or not they had actually inflicted those wounds (Grágás Ia 152, II 310). It was also the búakviðr, the panel of neighbors, which found on the issue of state of mind where that was a necessary element of a claim or defense. Unfortunately, the sagas do not tell us how findings of mental state were made, but as discussed in chapter 2 regarding accident, it seems that intent was inferred from formalized actions such as whether the person had properly offered amends. Consider what the criteria for determining intent would be in the case of someone who sues for injuries he received while trying to separate people during an affray, but who in so doing ended up helping a man who had already forfeited his immunity for having wounded or killed someone earlier in the affray. Grágás says that in such a situation the peacemaker has incurred liability for outlawry for aiding the other and his (the peacemaker's) injuries are not to be compensated unless "he wished to separate them lawfully." A lawful separation was made out when "he can get a verdict that he would have separated them in the same way if the wounded man had inflicted such injuries on the other man as he had now received from him" (Ia 146, II 300). What actions on the part of the peacemaker would have shown his intention? It could hardly have been something as implausible as an offer of compensation to the very man whom he was suing to recover for the injuries he had received in the affray. In the absence of more evidence we cannot dismiss the possibility that the panel was informed of the peacemaker's allegiances and connections and inferred his intent from them.[47] In some of its functions the panel of neighbors undoubtedly resorted to local knowledge and personal experience as when, for instance, they were called to make appraisals and divisions of disputed property or to evaluate property damage (see, e.g., chapter 7, n. 6).

According to the laws, the judges decided cases on the basis of the formal proofs presented, either witness testimony or panel verdicts, whether plaintiff had made his case or defendant had made his defense (*Grágás* Ia 72–73). Their decision appears to have been both a function of the form in which the proof was presented and the substance of the proofs (*Band.* 6:321–25). Both laws and sagas, however, are quite obscure about the process of judging. The style of judging clearly had to be affected by the fact that the cases were heard, not by a single judge, but by a panel of thirty-six judges and by the fact that judges had no office and no special expertise, but were selected ad hoc for each Thing meeting. They did not appear to have been drawn from the class of legal experts and the criteria for selection were minimal: a judge had to be a male at least twelve years old, mentally competent, free, in fixed residence, and he had to have lived in Iceland for at least three years to be qualified if he had not learned the "Dansk tongue" in childhood (*Grágás* Ia 38). Intuitively and by comparison with examples in the anthropological literature (e.g., Gulliver 1963), we would expect a panel composed in such manner to reflect community values in their judgments and particularly when those values clashed with outcomes mandated by rules and ruled formalism (see Reynolds 1984, 23–25, 28–34). Community views were thus introduced into the legal process from at least three sources: by the panel of judges, by the panel of neighbors, and by the audience recruited by the litigants in the support-mustering process. If we are to credit *Njáls saga* (142:384–94),[48] it was the litigants themselves who made claims as to what the law was. When the claim was contested, the Lawspeaker was consulted to determine the rule, or, according to the citation law, recourse was to be had to written manuscripts (see p. 225).[49] When the answer was still unclear, the matter was put to the Lǫgrétta where it was decided by a majority vote of the chieftains, who also had the power when convened as the Lǫgrétta to make new law (*Grágás* Ia 212–14). It would thus appear that the judges had no formal powers of discretion to find the law when the law was not clear.

Except for the problematic example of *Njáls saga*, the sagas, unfortunately, do not care to present circumstantial accounts of court proceedings. But an occasional glimpse suggests that the multitude of formal requirements did not prevent ad hoc argumentation, involving explicit or implicit reference to law and right. Consider the following case, which illustrates the conjunction of concern for procedural form and substantive legal argument with force and intimidation. Sigmund and his father, Thorkel, as an excuse to expropriate a valuable field, had accused Glum's mother's slaves of stealing some sheep. Subsequently the sheep were found, but Thorkel and Sigmund refused to return the field, allowing Glum's mother to use it instead in alternate years. Glum had been away during these events. Soon after his return, he killed Sigmund while he was trespassing on the disputed field during the period when it was in possession of his mother. Thorkel convinced a substantial affine, the brother of his son's wife, to take over the killing case for his son. Glum's strategy was to defend by preparing an action against his victim Sigmund for theft and also summoning him to óhelgi,[50] the latter being the procedure for presenting the issue of justification for the killing. He also proceeded offensively by beginning an independent slander action against Thorkel for the initial false charge he had brought against the slaves. Glum mustered support at the Allthing. His adversaries pleaded their suit in such a manner "to make sure there were would not be any flaws in it." Glum commenced his action against Thorkel, and both cases were tried at the same time, at which point the saga notes parenthetically that "Glum had much support from his kin and friends."

> And when the defense was invited to present its case,
> Glum said, "Things have come to this pass: it might
> be known to many that you have ignored a flaw in the
> preparation of your case, because I killed Sigmund on my
> property and before I rode to the Thing, I summoned him
> to óhelgi." He named witnesses to his statement and so
> defended the charge. His kin supported him in such a
> way that Sigmund was judged to have fallen justifiably.
> Then Glum proceeded with the case against Thorkel.
> (Glúma 9:33–34)

The flaw in the plaintiff's case was not a procedural one, but a mistake of substantive law. Glum had killed Sigmund justifiably. Although Glum clearly made this point formally by bringing the action against the dead man, he also argued facts—"I killed Sigmund on my property"—with implicit invocation of the law underlying his claim, that is, a man stealing falls justifiably, óheilagr, if he is killed in the act (cf. *Grágás* II 384–85). A substantive rule of law determined the outcome of a dispute, not in an inscrutable way, but because the rule applied to properly pleaded facts. Of course the rule of law was assisted by the might of Glum's support. Just why the extra intimidation was needed is not clear. Was it directed at the judges because the sufficiency of Glum's *óhelgi* claim as an answer to the killing of Sigmund was in doubt; or was it directed at the panel of neighbors because Glum's facts were doubtful?

One saga episode gives a full account of an argument in which it is claimed that judges had the power to ignore procedural flaws in the interests of substantive justice. The plaintiff, Odd, made a procedural error in the preparation of his case that the defense threatened to use to invalidate the action. Demoralized, Odd returned to his booth; shortly thereafter Odd's father, Ofeig, took over the presentation of the case:

> [Ofeig] went to the North Quarter court and asked what was going on. He was informed that some cases had already been judged, some were ready for summing up.[51]
>
> Ofeig said, "Will you grant me permission to enter the court?" That was granted him and he sat himself down and asked, "What's happened with Odd's case? Has Ospak been outlawed?"
>
> They answered that he had not been outlawed.
>
> "Why is that? Was there not sufficient cause? Did he not kill Vali and steal before that?" asked Ofeig.
>
> "We don't deny that," they responded. "It's not happened because people prefer it that way, rather it's because there was a procedural flaw in the case; it was brought incorrectly."
>
> "What was the flaw, that it could be of greater value than the case itself? Have you not taken an oath?"
>
> They said they had.
>
> "Of course, and what was the oath you swore?" asked Ofeig. "Was it not 'I swear on the book that I give judgment that is most right and truest and in accordance with the law?' Thus have you spoken. Now what is truer and more right than to judge the worst of men a full outlaw, the man who did these deeds? But you have also sworn to judge in accordance with the law. That conflicts somewhat. But consider whether violating that one word of the oath, [law], is weightier than violating the other two [most right and truest]. It would seem to me more advisable to choose the way that would be considered appropriate by both God and men. . . . It is a grave

matter not to condemn to outlawry one who deserves to be condemned; people will speak well of you for condemning him." (*Band.* 6:321–24)

Ofeig did not just trust to the merits of his argument; he also bribed the judges. Was the bribe necessary because the substance of the argument was novel? The judges' oath was here claimed as empowering them to ignore some procedural law in the interests of substantive justice. The scene is proof of the conceivability of arguments based on equitable principles, at least by the time the saga was written in the mid-thirteenth century. And while the case suggests that the judges may have been nervous about tempering the undesired effects of legal rules with equity, they apparently had the power, within limits, to prefer substance to form. Whether such arguments were conceivable prior to the assimilation of Christian culture cannot be determined. My suspicion is that they could have, although one other scholar's suspicions are contrary.[52]

Other accounts of legal argument take place at the edges of the court, as part of the process of negotiation preceding the transfer of an action from law to arbitration. The terms of exile for a certain Olaf had provided that he was to retain his immunity as long as he was in the company or on the property of Thorgils; otherwise he could be killed with impunity (*Hafl.* 8:21). Sometime later Olaf was killed, not on Thorgils' home farm, but on land he had acquired subsequent to Olaf's exile. Thorgils brought suit claiming that Olaf had been killed in violation of the immunity granted him by the terms of his exile sentence.

> Both sides attended the Thing with large forces, and they were urged to reach a settlement. But Haflidi [the representative and distant affine of the killer] argued that Olaf had been killed as an outlaw while on other land than that stipulated for him. Thorgils asked whether or not the privilege accorded Olaf was that he should be inviolate "in my company or on my property."
> And thus they took issue. Then Thorgils said, "On what grounds do you claim Olaf an outlaw? I consider it 'my property' where I own land."
> Haflidi replied, "I will give Thorgils eight cow's worth for the sake of his honor and reputation, but I call it a gift and not a penalty." (15:32)

The critical information about the status of land on which Olaf was killed and when it was acquired is presented casually and needs to be reconstructed from random details (11:27, 29). Without this information, the brief argument quoted appears to be little more than a shouting match about a dispositive fact, but with it, the issue is one of law. The question is whether the burden to specify the precise sense of the word property in the original exile sentence belonged to the party seeking a definition limited to the factual state of the universe at the time the sentence became effective or to the party seeking the broader definition that included any property owned by Thorgils no matter when acquired. Haflidi's offer to settle shows that Thorgils had the better argument. In the absence of a specific agreement to the contrary, property meant what Thorgils said it meant: "my property" is "where I own land."

We even see, again in the context of arbitration proceedings, arguments based on the precedential value of prior cases. Not surprisingly, recourse was had to precedent when the result being urged was contrary to people's present sense of reasonableness. Thus it was that Sturla sought to justify his lack of measure in the compensation he adjudged himself for the injury Pal's wife inflicted on him (above pp. 158–59) by citing Haflidi's equally overreaching self-judged award in his dispute with Thorgils some sixty years earlier (Sturla 32:111; Hafl. 31:49–50; see below p. 278). Sturla's citation of precedent is not without an ironic awareness of its serviceability in the rhetoric of bad-faith justification: "Why should we deviate in our judgment from the example of that wisest of men, Haflidi Masson?" Haflidi, it should be recalled, headed the commission charged with transcribing the oral law into written form (see p. 224). The force of the precedent depends on it being Haflidi's example, the greatest of legal experts, and not another's. The force of the irony is derived from the fact that, even for the greatest of legal experts, the passion induced by slighted honor will outweigh the constraints imposed by norms of reasoned moderation in matters of self-judgment. But Sturla's irony runs deeper. He does not cite Haflidi's example without at the same time mocking Haflidi, "that wisest of men." By so doing, Sturla not only admits the existence of the norm of reasoned moderation he is about to violate, but he also subscribes to the judgment others have of those who violate it. This stance is the necessary requisite of the perverse delight Sturla takes in his overreaching. Sturla's awareness of all the significances of his action allows him to grace overreaching with self-mockery and hence to assume an ironic distance from his own actions. Part of the irony, however, is structurally present in the argument by precedent itself. That argument makes no distinction between good and bad prior example, only the anteriority matters. And it is precisely the controlling force conferred on mere anteriority that purports to absolve the present invoker of precedent of some of the moral responsibility for his judgment. Inasmuch as precedent necessarily pretends to fix the responsibility for decision making other than where in fact it lies, pretending, in other words, that it lies in the past rather than in the present, it is rife with ironic possibility.

These brief accounts and others like them (see, e.g., *G.dýri* 15:193) show a style of argumentation that assumes that rules should determine outcomes. All in all, the picture is of a legal style distinctly more developed and subtle than legal-historical orthodoxy has been willing to admit could exist before the advent of state administered justice, before the ability and willingness to find fact and to distinguish law from it. Icelandic law was not "wrapped in the judgment of God" (Milsom 1981, 43), it was amenable to rational discourse and sophistical manipulation. The Icelanders seemed to know the difference between law and fact, with each roughly (but only roughly) reflected in the different functions assigned judges and the panel of neighbors; but they did not take special care to distinguish them. Quite the contrary; the Icelandic style integrated fact into the statement of the law by weaving "a fine-patterned web of casuistry" (Grønbech 1932, 79). The laws took their form from facts. The casuistical style supported a fairly complex jurisprudence.[53] New facts made for new rules,[54] nearly all of which were amenable to some kind of sensible schematization with related rules derived from other factual situations. Early Icelandic law's obsessive fondness for the casuistic style shows that there is more than one road to legal competence. That legal proceedings themselves were deeply affected by the relative power of the parties is not to be attributed to a shortcoming in the law, but to the simple fact that there was no state apparatus to disguise better the relationship between the power of the parties and control of legal process (cf. von See 1964, 240–41).

The function and position of law in Icelandic society falls somewhere between two poles. Law in Iceland was differentiated from other social relations. It was not embedded in kinship and marriage, in production and reproduction. It stood apart with a life of its own. There was a distinct body of rules known as laws that were distinguishable from other norms of behavior that were not laws. There were courts to hear claims arising from breaches of legal rules, and there were means of identifying and changing these rules. In short, there was a legal system according to the criteria of H. L. A. Hart (1961, 89–106). These characteristics distinguish Iceland from those primitive cultures that have provided traditional legal anthropology with its usual subject matter. On the other hand, this weak autonomy of the law did not approach the level of autonomy that would satisfy theorists of autonomous social institutions (see, e.g., Luhmann 1982 and Kronman 1983, 173–75). No bureaucracy had removed law from the average farmers who still, like it or not, were the judges. Nor was there a discrete field of purely political action that allowed for at least some institutional separation of politics from law. True, there were legal experts consciously identified as such, but the expertise itself was not established autonomously, there being, among other things, no institutional control of standards for admission to the rank of expert. Law belonged to all free men, not abstractly, but as part of the great social occasions that were the annual Thing meetings. Legal proceedings, like horsefights, were spectator sports. The fans of both had sufficient knowledge of the game to understand and enjoy the contest. And in Iceland, the rules establishing the boundary between the world of the game and the world outside the game were often insufficient to contain the animosities the game engendered. But then the players knew that the boundary was porous. Their decision to play was informed with a knowledge of the range of possible consequences of playing. The difference between law and horsefighting was presumably that the latter, as a sport, was literally a game, and as such raised greater expectations about its separateness from life after the game. No one, however, expected law to be such or that it should have been so neatly demarcated from life.

# CHAPTER EIGHT

# Peacemaking and Arbitration

### Breaking Up Fights

If the sagas are tales of revenge, they are also tales of peacemaking and settlement. Not all dispute ended in the death, outlawry, or defeat of one of the parties. There were mechanisms to countervail the more violent aspects of competitive aggression. The give-and-take structure of feud meant that intervals of peace—of varying degrees of uneasiness—accounted for much more time than did vengeance and legal action. If peace means the absence of violence, then peace was in fact the norm; if it means the lack of anticipation of violence, then for people with recognizable feuding relations, peace was a phase of feud that had to be bargained for and earned.[1] For those segments of society disabled from feud by poverty, peace was like good weather: mysteriously present or absent, but beyond one's control. To the extent that the feuds of the powerful did not disrupt the countryside, the small farmer could remain aloof and even somewhat contemptuously amused by the heroic posturing of his betters. In a vignette in *Laxdœla saga* (49:152), a certain Thorkel prefers to watch from afar an ambush involving the chief contenders for power in the district, rather than warn the target: "To tell the truth, I could care less if they do each other as much harm as they wish. I think it a better course for us to find a good and safe place to get a view of their meeting and enjoy the sport."

If this scene gives us a rare and brief indication of hostility between classes of men, it also suggests that third parties of all classes had some obligation to prevent violent confrontation. In fact, the sagas are consistently clear that more than warnings were expected from uninvolved parties. There existed a strong expectation, bordering on the obligatory, that nondisputants who lived near to or were present at an affray were to separate the parties (e.g., *Glúma* 11:39; *Vatn.* 29:80). When Kalf intercepted and killed Hall, a man standing outside a farm above the field where the assault was taking place asked whether people were fighting in the field below. The answer came from a certain Jon who was complicit with the assailants: "'Some men are just playing around down there.' " The saga appends this significant observation: "And because [Jon] described things in that way, no one rushed down" (*Íslend.* 29:258). The sagas condemn men of rank who do not intervene to break up fighting. Snorri Sturluson's feeble efforts to stop a brawl involving his own thingmen merited harsh words from the man who finally managed to separate them by driving horses into their midst (*Íslend.* 33:263) And Mord Valgardsson's reprehensible character is confirmed by his refusal to respond to his servant woman's urgent call to separate combatants (*Njála* 54:138).[2]

Women as well as men were recruited to restrain combatants, sometimes dampening their weapons by throwing clothing over them (*Eyrb.* 18:36; *Glúma* 22:74; *Vápn.* 18:61). Peacemaking of this sort required strength and courage more than negotiating skills. One suspects, however, that these frontline peacemakers were assisted in their efforts by the expectation on the part of the combatants that they would be separated by bystanders. Clothing tossed on weapons could hardly restrain committed fighters for more than a few seconds if the will to fight were greater than the desire to cease fighting. The clothing was more sign than substance, like the bell signaling the end of a round, and it seems that the sign was not without significant cultural force. Violence in the feud, even in battle, was controlled violence. Armed encounters between feuding factions were of short duration with casualties rarely exceeding ten people.[3] One saga explicitly reminds us that the commitment to battle on the part of most of those mustered for action must have been indirect at best, unless they had their own scores to settle against the opposition: "Kodran went between the combatants and tried to separate them. It had gotten to the point that only those men were fighting who had prior grudges. By then most of them had broken off; they needed no more urging to separate" (*Ljós.* 24:80). In this same battle, the wounding of Kodran and the death of a servant are specifically invoked as the reason to stop fighting. Elsewhere the death of one man in an affray leads to the cessation of hostilities (*Íslend.* 4:232). Still, intervening to break up fighting was not a game. Women were injured (*Eyrb.* 18:36) and men lost their lives (*Grœn.* 5:287; *Ljós.* 24:81).[4] On the other hand, poor Thorkel (p. 259), who preferred to think of violent encounters as spectator sports, was later killed both for having failed to warn the victim of the ambush and for having dared to find the disputing style of his superiors comical (*Lax.* 52:160–61).

## The Aribitral Process: The First Stages
and Third-Party Intervention

Breaking up actual fighting was peacemaking at its most primitive. There were, however, significantly more complex and sophisticated mechanisms of achieving peace and attaining settlement. In Iceland, settlement was inseparable from the arbitration process. Arbitration is a procedure in which one or more people are selected and empowered by the principals to render a binding decision the principals agree to accept beforehand.[5] It thus contrasts structurally to other modes of managing conflict such as mediation, in which a third party intervenes in a dispute but is without power to impose an agreement; negotiation, in which the parties hammer out their own differences without the aid of third parties; blood revenge and self-help, which need no further explanation; and adjudication, in which a lawsuit leads to the judgment of a court (Nader and Todd 1978, 9–11). The arbitration process can include much negotiation and mediation preceding the submission of the dispute to the arbitrator(s). But saga evidence indicates that even settlements in which terms were bargained for and agreed to through negotiation were finalized as judgments of arbitrators. In the entire saga corpus, only one settlement is explicitly mentioned as having been achieved by negotiation without a judgment of someone formally empowered to decide (see *G.dýri* 3:165), although the circumstances of several other settlements, all of which occur in the same source, would seem to indicate a similar informality (*Reyk.*, chapters 10–14). I use arbitration broadly to refer to the agreement to submit the dispute to arbitrators, as well as the settlement finally articulated by them. This sense corresponds nicely to Old Icelandic *sætt*, pl. *sættir*, a term which can be variously translated as "arbitrated settlement," "agreement," or "reconciliation." I do not use terms like negotiation or mediation loosely, but in the precise senses, as represented immediately above, which they have come to have in dispute-processing scholarship.

Our knowledge of Icelandic arbitration comes almost entirely from the sagas. The laws have relatively little to say about it, except to restrict its range. *Grágás* thus provides, as we have had occasion to note in the preceding chapter (p. 228), that cases involving killings or severe wounds cannot be settled unless permission is first received from the Allthing (*Grágás* Ia 174, II 341; cf. Ia 108–9, 121, Ib 189–92, II 281–88). The sagas do not show any prosecutions for violating this stricture, and the numerous arbitrations in killing cases proceed as if there were no such rule. If these provisions had no effect on practice, they nevertheless indicate that some people, notably legal experts, were willing to claim a priority for formal legal resolution over purely private settlement. It is interesting to observe that *Grágás* was more committed to curbing the private resolution of disputes by arbitration than by blood vengeance, which, as we have noted, could be taken legally up to the next Allthing following the offense (see p. 192). Notwithstanding the law's jealous resentment of a procedure that invariably sanctioned wrongdoers less harshly than the law would provide, arbitrated outcomes outnumbered adjudicated outcomes by more than three to one in the saga record (see p. 236). There is little reason to distrust this ratio. We can readily believe that the sagas would overrepresent violent outcomes to nonviolent ones, but is there any reason why they should overrepresent arbitration to adjudication unless that in fact was the way things were? The preference could have been affected only minimally by the relative size of the class of disputes submittable to adjudication as opposed to those submittable to arbitration. The size of the classes was not in any meaningful way very different, for even if a dispute were not presently justiciable, it was never more than an insult or axe away from being cognizable by the courts.

As a general matter, cases submitted to arbitration were presented as specific claims, not as vague or generalized ill feeling. This did not, however, prevent power struggles and disputes involving complicated issues of relative status from going to arbitration, any more than the form of a lawsuit prevented feuding parties from using the courts as arenas of competition. Still, issues of competition and of relative rank had to be expressed as breaches of specific rules for which some penalty could be imposed or against which offsets could be calculated. This style for the most part restricted the ability of arbitrators to get to the crucial deep issues underlying the surface manifestation of the dispute. Nevertheless, an occasional imaginative and powerful arbitrator was able to fashion a judgment that reached well beyond the surface appearance of the dispute to its deeper structure. In one case, a systematic readjustment of relations between two competing kin groups was formulated by the arbitrator even though the dispute was submitted to him as a breach of a rule forbidding excretion on the Thing grounds and as actions for killings that arose from a fight over defiling the Thing (see *Eyrb.* 10:16–18; also *Egil* 81–82:280–88). The judgment left the killings uncompensated, but divided a chieftaincy between the factions and linked the sides by marriage. Judgments of this sort, however, were the exception. The usual practice, as we shall see, was to balance corpses on

each side, offset various claims with others, and make up the difference with compensation. When a wrongdoer's resources were insufficient to make up the difference, or when other circumstances
made it appropriate, arbitrators imposed various sorts of banishment, but without the panoply of disabilities that attended a judicially imposed sentence of outlawry (Heusler 1911, 144).[6]

Several systemic factors worked to move disputes out of the legal arena or violent phases of pure revenge into the arbitrational
mode. In some instances, the impulse toward settlement could come
from the litigants. Those desiring to dispose of a claim by compensation were for the most part constrained to go to arbitration since
compensation, according to the saga evidence, did not appear to
have been a remedy available at law in any other than minor property claims (Heusler 1911, 123, 219). Offers of and demands for compensation were thus the initial markers of the arbitrational mode.
The usual procedure was for the wrongdoer or his representative to
approach the injured person or some member of his group and offer
amends (e.g., *Reyk.* 12:184, 23:222; *Vápn.* 19:64; see Heusler 1911,
78n1). This was the protocol for indicating lack of hostile intent in
cases of accident (see p. 65), and for otherwise indicating a wish
to bring closure to the dispute. The precise significance of the gesture was, of course, much dependent on the context and especially
on the relative status of the parties. The offer might reflect either a
certain noblesse expected of the powerful in their dealings with
their weaker neighbors, or barely disguised contempt. When Gudmund the Powerful offered compensation to the brothers of Thorkel
Hake after having killed Thorkel, the offer was intended to convey
his sense that he need not fear blood or law at their hands (*Ljós.*
19:53). Weak offenders, on the other hand, might reveal their eagerness to settle by offering the other side self-judgment in hopes that
the more powerful wronged party would be moderate in his judgment (e.g., *Sturla* 25:99–100).

Not infrequently, however, it was the wronged person who took
the first step toward settlement. Most such instances clearly reflect
the weak position of the demandant, who knows his offender need
not fear him (e.g., *Háv.* 5:308–9; *Heið.* 8:231; *Njála* 12:39). But
other cases show that there is no necessary link between relative
inferiority of the offended person and the identity of the party who
initiated the settlement process. Other factors might also be at
work. Making a demand on the reticent wrongdoer could be undertaken as a tactical step to mold community opinion in favor of one's
cause, by proving one's own commitment to peace and the other's
truculence (*Heið.* 14:256–57). One case suggests that in some in-

stances a thingman might have to "exhaust his remedies," that is, he may have had to show that he had tried and failed to obtain satisfaction on his own from the wrongdoer, before seeking to enlist the support of his chieftain. Thus it is that Isolf requested compensation from the representative of the man who impregnated his daughter even "though he knew perfectly well that he would get only aggravation and no remedy" (*Ljós.* 22:66). But Isolf's action also suggests that the precise nature of the claim may have influenced which party was most likely to make the initial request for a compensatory settlement. The act providing the basis for a paternity claim, in contrast to the usual saga fare of wounds and killing, was not as likely to be openly acknowledged. This fact made the injured party's request for compensation also serve a double duty as a circumspect form of accusation, an accusation less likely to provoke hostility than one first appearing in the form of a lawsuit.

In many saga disputes, the will to avenge on one side and the will to resist settlement on the other, that is, the heroic high ground of uncomplicated honor, informed the consciousness of the principals. Settlement they knew there might eventually be, but they would not openly further its cause. Yet feud in some phase invariably found its way to arbitration, just as in other phases it found its way to law. Settlement was as much a part of the feuding process as were vengeance and outlawry. When, as was often the case, the impetus for settlement did not come from the principals, it came from third parties who intervened and succeeded in convincing the principals to agree to arbitration. The intervenor's role was not institutionalized in any one man, group of men, or office. This fact, however, did not prevent some people from acquiring reputations as peacemakers along with the prestige that attended successful intervention. These people intervened in disputes on their own initiative or at the request of nondisputants and disputants alike; and they were often selected as arbitrators both in disputes in which they had intervened and in those which were submitted to them after the intervention of others.[7]

The sources, on occasion, refer to peacemakers generically as *góðgjarnir menn*—men of good will. The term reveals the values associated with peacemaking; it describes the idealized intervenor as a person interested in the general good, a partisan of everyone rather than a disinterested neutral. The reality was often different. Intervenors pursued their own goals aggressively, at times almost cynically, for it was not lost on them that intervention in the affairs of others was a way to profit from others' embarrassments (e.g., *G.dýri* 3:164–66).[8] Yet many people were willing to undertake con-

siderable risk in the interests of peace without appearing motivated
by strategy and personal advantage.[9] As a rough rule, the more violent and potentially disruptive the interaction in which they intervened, the purer the motives of the intervenors. The urgencies of
time overrode selfish opportunism.

The chances of third-party intervention were greatly affected by
the disputants' choice of procedures and the location of the theater
of action. Intervention was more likely when the adversaries met
at the Things than when they met on a deserted lavafield in a
vengeance-taking expedition. In the field, intervention was fortuitous and depended on being observed. The intervenors were thus
likely to be local men of good will of the *bóndi* class and their servants of either sex. At the Things, attempts at intervention were the
usual fare in any serious confrontation, although intervention was
more likely at the Allthing than at local Things, if only because at
the Allthing there were certain to be enough people of sufficient
standing to be able to presume to intervene in other big people's
affairs. There, the intervenor's role was appropriated by the chieftains, the bishops, or other men of influence who often were not
even from the same Quarter as the principals. In cases held at local
Things, it was possible, for example in a dispute pitting two of the
district chieftains against each other, for there to be no one present
who was capable of pressuring the sides toward reconciliation (see,
e.g., *G.dýri* 3:163; *Ljós.* 10:131–33, 14:33).

The intervenor's identity was often a function of the identity of
the disputants. Not infrequently intervenors were people caught in
the middle, bound to both sides.[10] The untenability of their positions gave them the motive, and their structural position offered
them the means to mediate the dispute. Their plight might even
provide some of the reason for the principals to find settlement acceptable. One influential anthropological theory of the benign feud
postulates that the existence of a multitude of crosscutting ties created by exogamous marriage, friendship, residence patterns, and fostering, works to establish "peace in the feud" or at least to deter
violence within it (Colson 1953; Gluckman 1955b). The theory is a
bit too optimistic to explain the Icelandic feud adequately. The force
of the differences separating the principal disputants would often
greatly exceed the force of the ties binding them to their unfortunately situated middle man.[11] Nor were all people caught in the
middle motivated to make peace. Even Hamlet, after all, was capable of resolving his conflict in favor of violence; so were many
Icelanders. One especially cantankerous soul, finding his conflicting
duties of even weight, resolved his predicament by killing someone

on each side (*Eyrb.* 44:122). The fact, however, that crosscutting ties were not always able to forestall violence did not prevent people from seeking to create them, especially via marriage and fosterage. Most felt that peace stood a better chance when allegiances were confused and intertwined.[12]

The disputants themselves had much say in determining the identity of the intervenors as a consequence of the support-mustering process. When a disputant recruited support for a lawsuit, his conscious design was to enable victory or at least to prevent defeat. But at some level of consciousness he must have known when he recruited widely that the farther removed those he recruited were from him and his cause, the less commitment they would have to it, and the less interest in risking themselves in aggressive action unless that should happen to accord with their own agendas. Somewhat paradoxically, the support-mustering process, the recruitment of forces, that is, the very process of escalation, helped create the conditions that ensured the emergence of peacemakers. A principal could hardly have been too surprised when he found certain allies refusing to support his aggressive plans, pushing him instead into arbitrated settlement. Some principals were conscious of this and recruited people known for their skills as mediators. Such, for example, was the role Njal played in all of Gunnar's troubles (*Njála*).[13] Others were equally aware that if the move for peace were not to come from their own forces, they could activate the uninvolved to assume mediational roles simply by increasing the level of tension at the Thing meeting (*Ljós.* 17:41).

Once people stepped forward urging reconciliation, there still remained the problem of convincing the principals to leave off their aggressiveness and agree to submit the matter to arbitration, for no matter how much the principals on some level may have desired peace, the forms of honor usually demanded shows of firmness and aggression. The tactics used by intervenors to get agreement ranged from cajolery to threats of violence. Some intervenors offered friendship to the party they were trying to convince (*Lax.* 85:242; *Njála* 66:165, 122:309), or promised never to oppose that party in the future (*Njála* 66:166); others offered to forbear prosecuting claims of their own against one of the parties (*Njála* 145:411–12). Some were simply too powerful to say no to and would extract assent from the principals by threatening to oppose the side that refused to listen to them (*G.dýri* 3:164–65; *Grett.* 30:103; *Lax.* 87:246; *Reyk.* 6:168). Jon Loftsson attained such power in the late twelfth century that he was able to compel other chieftains to submit to his intervention and then to his arbitration of the dispute (*G.dýri* 18:200; *Sturla*

29:104, 34:113; see also *Lax.* 87:246). And others who were not as powerful would set out to recruit support for the peacemaking cause in much the same manner as did the principals for their causes. Consider this description of the preparations for a court of confiscation after Haflidi Masson had gotten an outlawry judgment against Thorgils Oddason:

> And when the time came to hold the court of confiscation Thorgils mustered nearly four hundred men. Haflidi had gathered from the north more than one hundred of the best men and well-equipped too. But in yet a third place the men of the district gathered together to intercede with good will. The leaders were Thord Gilsson and Hunbogi Thorgilsson and with them were other men of good will, Gudmund Brandsson and Ornolf Thorgilsson, accompanied by some two hundred men for the peacemaking. (*Hafl.* 18:35–36)

We see that it was more than just the feud or fear of it that sanctioned order. Order was not achieved only as a consequence of dyadic interactions that produced a reasonably ordered stasis. The community, that elusive collectivity of shifting membership made up of the third parties of the world, did more than just observe and award honor and dishonor via gossip and public opinion. They too put their lives on the line. At the very least, the peacemaker ran the risk of alienating powerful principals. The farmers who intervened between Sighvat and Kolbein incurred Kolbein's wrath (*Íslend.* 98–99:372–73). And in combat situations, as we saw earlier, separating antagonists subjected the intervenor to legal liability if his actions could not be shown to be wholly disinterested (see chapter 8, n. 4; also Miller 1983a, 328–32).

## The Role of the Clergy and the Effect of Christianity

Peacemaking was not something that had to be learned from Christianity, despite rather facile observations to that effect in the scholarly literature. The entire corpus of scholarship in dispute studies and conflict resolution has shown that all cultures develop means for resolving disputes, and peoples as disparate as the Cheyenne, Bedouin, Nuer, Arusha, and Ifugao did not need Christianity to have devised techniques of mediation and negotiation in the cause of peaceful order.[14] But Christianity was not utterly without effect. It created a class of people who, by profession, were to uphold the peacemaking cause, thus providing the first steps toward the institutionalization of peacemaking responsibility. These steps would have been virtually imperceptible at first since the clerical intervenors came from the same class of well-heeled chieftains and farmers from which lay intervenors came. Profession did not always prevent priests from behaving like other feuding partisans and those who emerged as peacemakers were on occasion also personally situated to have intervened even had they not been in orders (see, e.g., *Hafl.* 24:42). Sturla, for instance, was still sufficiently concerned that the bishop who was kin to Sturla's adversary would act like any other interested party that he made the bishop swear an oath to judge justly before he would agree to have him arbitrate the dispute (*Sturla* 10:75). The important thing to note was not that disputants would expect the clergy to act like laymen, but that despite this, clerical office created expectations that clerics would act as intervenors and arbiters in situations that might not otherwise have prompted them to intervene. That priests and men in lesser orders figured frequently in feud and combat (see, e.g., *Hafl.* 23:40) did not detract from the fact that priests and bishops also figured actively in the peacemaking and arbitration processes, even when their structural position relative to the disputants was not such as to have made them natural intervenors had they not been in orders.[15]

The other noticeable effect Christianity had on the peacemaking process was that it gave peacemakers a new stock of rhetorical devices with which to play their roles. Christianity helped improve the status of arguments urging forbearance, and even forgiveness, as against the competing demands of heroic honor. A politics of forgiveness might now be pursued with less cost in honor than before. Now, there could in fact be a politics of forgiveness. As an example, consider the manner in which a priest named Ketil, later to be named bishop, pleads the cause of settlement to the recalcitrant Haflidi, who had been refusing peacemakers' efforts to get him to submit to arbitration his claim for having lost some fingers to Thorgils' axe:

> "Your friends think it a grave disaster if there should be
> no settlement and the case not concluded in a good way.
> It seems to most people that things are hopeless, or
> nearly so. I do not have any specific advice for you, but I
> wish to tell you this parable:
>     We grew up in Eyjafjord and it was said we were a
> promising group. I married Groa, the daughter of Bishop
> Gizur, who was thought to be the best match. Word had
> it that she was unfaithful to me. I was greatly displeased
> by this; an ordeal was performed and it went well. None-
> theless, to my displeasure, the gossip persisted and be-

cause of this I became hostile to the other man. On one
occasion, when we met on the road, I attacked him. But
he dodged the blow and I ended up on the bottom. He drew
his knife and stabbed me in the eye. I lost my sight in
that eye. Then he—his name was Gudmund Grimsson—
let me up. The result seemed to me rather improbable; I
had twice his strength and I thought that this difference
was also reflected in other respects between us.

I wanted to avenge this at once with the support of my
kinsmen and get him outlawed. We prepared the case,
but some powerful men aided him in the action and they
quashed my suit. (Now it may be that similar people will
support Thorgils even though your claim is more just).

At this point they offered compensation for the claim.[16]
I considered what had happened to me, how grave it was,
and I refused the offer. I saw that the only salvation was
to entrust the claim to God's mercy, because when I had
made the decisions everything had worked against my
reputation. . . . When I considered my reputation, I realized then that no compensation would be offered adequate to restore my honor.[17] I decided then, for God's
sake, to give Him my claim. I knew that I would receive
in return what would be most favorable for me. I invited
Gudmund to my home and he stayed with me for a long
time after.

Then the gossip and people's evaluations switched
around. And since then everything has worked more to
my good luck and honor than before. I believe that God
would do the same for you." (*Hafl.* 29:47–48)

Haflidi was persuaded by Ketil to soften his position and agree to
settlement. Haflidi, however, was not moved to give up his claim;
he obtained self-judgment and adjudged himself an amount which,
as we have seen (p. 255), became legendary in matters of overreaching.

There are some noteworthy features of Ketil's parable that require
comment. Ketil, it should be observed, does not adopt an unambiguous position on the virtues of forgiveness and passivity. Ketil is a
politician as well as a homilist. And like many other Scandinavian
churchman, he knew vengeance was a duty that had its time and
place (Foote 1984, 53–54). His argument is that his case, and by
implication Haflidi's, were not sure things; and given that fact, for
political reasons, vengeance may not be the most sensible course to
pursue. The goal instead is to determine the best strategy to mini-
mize the prospects of further losses of honor beyond those already

incurred by the loss of some fingers or an eye. For even more central to Ketil's parable than forgiveness and trust in God is the fact that his claim was a weak one, at least a lot weaker than he originally thought it was. Gudmund Grimsson, who had been cleared already in the adultery matter and had been set upon unawares, was thus able to find powerful people to aid in his defense.[18] And Haflidi's opponent, as Ketil interrupts his narrative to remind Haflidi, may well be able to do the same. One of Ketil's points is that the injured person is likely to overvalue his injuries and hence not always be in the best position to evaluate his case properly. But the chief point is that *practical* advantages can accrue from conciliation, not just to the community but to the person who is willing to forgo absolute enforcement of his rights. Ketil is not advocating concession as a universal principal of dispute resolution. The parable he tells situates his argument socially and conditions its applicability to specific contexts. With a losing case like Ketil's, one should cut losses by forgiving the claim and the adversary. And even with a better case, like Haflidi's, forgoing the execution of an outlawry judgment in exchange for damages in an arbitration proceeding made good tactical sense, if the aggressive prosecution of the case would aid the adversary's cause by alienating significant segments of the community. The argument is a simple one and sufficiently commonplace that one wonders if it needed the veneer of God's special favor to Ketil to make it work.

Presumably Ketil's arguments could have been made without recourse to God and Christian values, but, then, by this time, it may have been almost impossible to conceive of such arguments independently of Christian themes and Christian figures. Christianity provided a ready rhetorical fund to draw on for these kinds of arguments and an entire body of hagiographic and homiletic literature to buttress the rhetoric with examples of heroic passivity and the benefits of forgiveness. Once Christianity became established, it would have soon become difficult for clerical peacemakers not to invoke these motifs to aid their cause, while both secular and clerical peacemakers would still continue to invoke the secular values of societal order (*Prest.* 2:119–20). Christianity also, of course, armed clerical peacemakers with a new class of threats to urge disputants to adopt more conciliatory modes. Ecclesiastical ban was not without effect; people would avoid it if they could (*Hafl.* 28:46; *Íslend.* 24:252), although one still sees many Icelandic disputants no more fearful of hellfire later than axes now (e.g., *Hafl.* 22:40; *Íslend.* 25:254; *Þorg. sk.* 57:198–99).

## Achieving Settlements: Form, Content, and the Sanctions Behind Them

As we have already noted, there is much evidence to suggest that the principals were in many cases quite pleased with the opportunity to settle. Yet, honor often demanded that the claimant not look too eager for settlement.[19] The claimant's goal was to make his concession look like a gift both to influential intervenors with whom he did not wish to quarrel and to the community as a display of willingness to value communal order higher than personal interest. He did not wish his actions to be interpreted as motivated by either greed for compensation or fearfulness. The concession, in other words, had to look as if it were made to third parties and only indirectly to his opponent.[20] The peacemaking process, the interactions between principals and intervenors, had thus a certain ritual quality of predictable rhythm. The claimant must first repel suggestions of peace, but if all went smoothly, initial categorical opposition would eventually give way by degrees to resigned acceptance or gestures of magnanimous forbearance. Moreover, certain members of the claimant's support group would act as hotheads, just as others would act as conciliators. The claimant could thus appear to maintain a respectable middle ground or deflect some of the responsibility for his own decisions as he leaned now to one, now to another faction of his own support group. One should not, however, confuse predictability with certainty, nor the existence of rhythm with triviality. The stakes were high and at any moment the peacemaking cause might fail. In fact, it was the very real possibility of failure that made the ritual work, that gave it the ability to convince others that what motivated the claimant was not fear or avarice. For if the claimant suspected that the observing community doubted his mettle, the predictable rhythms of the settlement dance could abruptly cease to be replaced by a dance of a different beat (e.g., *Njála* 122–23:309–14).

Intervenors were assisted in their efforts to bring about settlement by the strategies of the principals themselves, who often openly admitted that settlement was their goal. Then as now people were aware that lawsuits had a settlement value. After initial informal attempts to arbitrate had been rejected, plaintiffs often prosecuted lawsuits with the sole intention of coercing recalcitrant defendants to agree to submit to arbitration. Such appears to have been much of the motivation behind old Thorbjorn's decision to prosecute Hrafnkel for the slaying of his son (*Hrafnk.* 3:106–8, above p. 242). Likewise, defendants would prosecute plaintiffs using counterclaims arising from the incident in dispute, new claims arising from serious errors in procedure, or claims obtained by formal assignment (*handsal*) from others (e.g., *Njála* 64:160–61). Although in this fashion both sides succeeded sometimes in outlawing each other (*Sturla* 9:74, 19:87), the prospect of such an outcome usually induced the parties to submit to arbitration. As an example, consider the following: Geir had brought four killing cases against Gunnar, of which two were invalidated (*Njála* 56:142–46).[21] Thereupon, Gunnar quickly announced his intention to prosecute Geir for wrongful preparation of a case, which carried a penalty of lesser outlawry. At that moment, Njal, a supporter of Gunnar, stepped forward urging settlement:

> This must not happen because it would lead to increased tensions in the dispute. Each of you, it seems to me, has much substance in his case. Some of the killings, Gunnar, you have no defense for and you will be outlawed for them; but you have raised an action against Geir so that he too will be outlawed. You, Geir, know that there is still another outlawry action pending against you. It won't be dropped if you will not follow what I say.

A chieftain who supported Geir then came forward and also urged settlement. The result was that the dispute was submitted to the arbitration of six men. The award held Gunnar to money compensation for some of his victims with no outlawry or exile for either Geir or Gunnar.

Even in those cases in which both sides were outlawed, postjudgment arbitrated settlements could arrange for the release of the judgment (*Sturla* 10:75, 19:87). Both Sturla and Einar had brought actions against each other and each had powerful backing:

> Some people sought to arrange a settlement, but nothing came of it. The cases went to judgment and each was able to outlaw the other. But when it came time for the dissolution of the Thing, people thought it would promote disorder if the cases were sent back to the local district disposed of in this fashion. Men then intervened and it so came about that the cases were to be submitted to the arbitration of Klæng the Bishop and Bodvar Thordarson. The matter was concluded right away, although Sturla thought the judgment was unfavorable and lacked proportion. The outlawry sentences were released. (19:87)

Third-party pressure, insufficient to deter the principals prior to judgment, had been given an assist by the consequences of having not settled earlier.[22]

Cases like these reveal that the structure of Icelandic dispute processing cannot be fully explained as a cumulation of disputant choices (cf. Collier 1973, 250–51; Barth 1965, 1–4). These choices, as we have seen, were much constrained by the choices of nondisputants as well as by norms that limited the range of viable options. Brief notices throughout the sources suggest that arbitrated settlement was the expected outcome of, among other things, property divisions following divorce (Njála 8:27) and disputed mercantile claims (Ljós. 14:32–33). And claimants breached well-established norms if they pressed such matters toward legal judgment. Arbitration was also the likely outcome when the prosecutor was a proxy for the true claimant, at least in those cases where the proxy did not choose to make the case a vehicle for his own aggressive designs. To refuse to settle when settlement was expected was one of the classic traits of the ójafnaðarmaðr, literally the "uneven man," the unjust man or the man without measure. In other words, the demands of honor did not in every case require even a show of initial reluctance to settle. In one instance, a disputant's refusal to arbitrate a mercantile claim led people to infer correctly a darker motive to his actions: "People felt that the case had been prosecuted with great vigor; many suspected that there was something more to the hostility than met the eye" (Ljós. 14:33).

The litigant perspective, however, is useful and indeed crucial to understanding the processing of specific cases; it is also one of the ways the sources account for the course of a dispute.[23] Hence the sagas type some characters as "settlers," while others are cast in the heroic mold: they will settle, if at all, only after they have satisfied their blood urge.[24] Still others are litigious and overbearing, using lawsuits as vehicles for the harassment and subjugation of others.[25] And even though pressure by third parties and opponents, if strong and insistent enough, could force most to alter their tactics and reassess their goals in spite of the predispositions of their personalities, astute disputants made their choices with the knowledge that the disputing process entailed working with and around specific third parties and the general community.

The prudent avenger and the wise litigant anticipated the likelihood of arbitrated settlement. Avengers who did not have technically sufficient legal justification for their vengeance killing knew that they would have to pay an arbitrated compensation award, if they were fortunate enough to avoid an outlawry sentence; even those who had sufficient justification were often constrained to pay. There are examples of disputants and would-be avengers collecting and setting aside funds earmarked for satisfying the compensation assessment they anticipated incurring in the next round (see *Ljós.* 5:20 and *Njála* 70:173, 74:180). But the prudent avenger also took care to insulate these funds lest he were outlawed. Thus the funds collected in the cases just cited were kept in the possession of an adviser for no other reason, it seems, than to keep the property out of the clutches of the judgment creditor on the chance that the outcome were outlawry rather than the arbitrated settlement they had planned for (see Andersson and Miller 1989, 176–77nn99–101). More than just money was set aside in anticipation of arbitrated awards. In one of his many defenses of Gunnar, Njal drew on a repository of unprosecuted claims, both his own and ones he was able to obtain from others, and arranged their transfer to Gunnar (*Njála* 64:160–61; cf. Lehmann and Carolsfeld 1883, 64–76). These claims were not needed to defend against the legal action, since Njal had already provided Gunnar with a valid defense sufficient to void plaintiff's action; they were prepared to be used as offsets to reduce Gunnar's monetary liability in the arbitrated settlement that Njal foresaw would be pressed upon the principals by intervenors once the plaintiff's case has been invalidated (66:164–66). Njal's foresight was less a matter of the prescience the saga attributes to him than of the skillful orchestration of the intervention of third parties whose entry into the dispute he could virtually assure simply by threatening to let the law take its course. Examples like these demonstrate a cool litigant awareness of the probability of an arbitrated outcome once a dispute found its way to the Thing. They also suggest a warm appreciation of the unpleasantnesses that lay in store if there were to be no *sætt*.

The attractiveness of arbitration as an outcome probably owed less to its virtue than to the grimness of the alternatives. "Lumping it" was simply not available to the honorable man, and the two modes that were, blood and law, were fraught with danger. Vengeance-taking was obviously risky business for the avenger and the targeted expiator alike and the law, as shown in the previous chapter, was often no less so. But the dysfunctions of legal process also had their functional aspects. I do not mean to suggest that the origins or continuance of the Icelandic legal style owed anything to accidental functionalisms; nevertheless, the fact was that the legal process provided two and perhaps three different occasions—summoning, trial, *féránsdómr*—where the parties would have to meet, accompanied by substantial numbers of recruits or simple bystanders from whose ranks people might come forward urging, even compelling settlements. Not all meetings of disputants, in other words, need be cause for strife. In those disputes where for various reasons, like geographical distance or lack of crosscutting ties, no peacemakers emerged in the neighborhood, forcing the dispute into the Things gave the uninvolved or peripherally involved free farmers and chieftains, who for the sake of convenience, if not precision, I shall refer to as the "community," a convenient opportunity to have their say in the matter. And substantial segments of the community usually desired some kind of reconciliation, if for no other reason than to avoid the vexations of being expected to separate combating disputants, of suffering the depredations of outlaws on their livestock (*Eyrb.* 59–62:162–67; *Sturla* 7:69–71), or of having the outlaw's dependents become a charge on the district (*Hafl.* 4:14; *Grágás* Ia 86–87, 113, 115; see above p. 152).

Orthodox dispute-processing scholarship postulates that conciliatory settlements are more desirable than legal judgments in small face-to-face societies (e.g., Gluckman 1955a, 18–24; Gulliver 1963; Nader and Todd 1978, 12–14).[26] At law a party won or lost, and losing in Iceland meant outlawry if a defendant and humiliation if a plaintiff. A defeated defendant had little interest in complying with a judgment ensuring his death; a defeated plaintiff would resort to vengeance when the opportunity arose (e.g., *Eyrb.* 26:65). On the other hand, arbitrated settlements, without exception in the surviving sources, imposed punishments less severe than full outlawry (Heusler 1911, 130–44 and 1912, 47);[27] this concession presumably increased the likelihood of compliance. In spite of being severely confined by the limits imposed by the stipulations of the parties, or by the strategies of disputants who were interested more in defining hostile relations than in ameliorating them, arbitrators could attempt to fashion awards that took some account of workability and the likelihood of compliance. Consider the colloquy of those appointed to arbitrate the case against the Njalssons for slaying Hoskuld Hvitanessgoði:

> Snorri the chieftain said, "Now we twelve arbitrators to whom this case has been submitted are assembled here. I wish to beg of you that we do not provide the basis for difficulties that would prevent them from being well-reconciled."
> Gudmund said, "Would you adjudge district banishment or exile abroad?"
> "No," said Snorri, "because such sentences are often

disregarded, and that leads to more killing and further disagreement. I wish to award money damages so high that no man will have been dearer than Hoskuld." (*Njála* 123:311)

Awards were also able to reflect implicitly considerations of fault, excuse, justification, moral character, and social status of victims and principals. Compensation amounts would thus be adjusted accordingly, as would the length (in time) and breadth (in land area) of exile sentences. Fault, intent, and justification could also be raised in lawsuits (see p. 248); but there, in claims involving death or injury and in serious property claims as well, it was full or lesser outlawry or nothing. Monetary damages for injury or killing were not available at law, as they were in arbitration.[28] It was more the poverty of types of legal remedies, not the inability of the law to evaluate inconsistent or conflicting rules, or deal adequately with facts, that made arbitrated settlements preferable to legal judgments. Arbitration was also a more efficient way of handling the multiple claims that arose in a general affray or in a series of hostile encounters. Rather than requiring principals to summon, call neighbors and witnesses, and plead several separate claims and counterclaims, the arbitration process allowed for joining all the various claims in one balancing and accounting, thus bringing some kind of closure to complicated hostile interactions.

The peacemaking and arbitration process also increased the number of people who had a direct interest in enforcing compliance with the award. As noted above, intervenors, and arbitrators too, would promise friendship, support, at times even enter into marriage and fostering arrangements with one of the parties (*Eyrb.* 10:18; *Sturla* 34:113). Arbitrators themselves could contribute to the compensation awards or stand surety for their payment (e.g., *Njála* 123:311, 145:412). Violation of the settlement could thus mean not only the renewed hostility of the other party but the new hostility of the peacemakers and arbitrators and their kin (*G.dýri* 18:200).

We should not, however, overestimate the success of arbitrated settlements. They too had their problems of enforcement. Sentences of district exile or three years abroad were not always happily accepted or even disgruntledly adhered to. A person under a sentence of banishment might not be able to find passage within the allotted time (*Hafl.* 9:22) or might simply refuse to leave (*Glúma* 19:66; *Njála* 75:182–83; *Reyk.* 13:187–91). Monetary awards, if made payable immediately, solved the problem of collection but requiring immediate payment also severely limited the amount that could be awarded to satisfy the seriously aggrieved plaintiff. Even the stylistics of arbitrated awards reflected a certain lack of confidence in the likelihood of compliance. The typical arbitration award in which multiple claims were settled balanced corpse against corpse, insult against injury, so that in the end little wealth need exchange hands, thus assuring compliance by removing all opportunity not to comply. It was by such a feat of bookkeeping that Snorri Sturluson's corpse was compounded for. Orækja, Snorri's son, was assessed 500 hundreds for attacking Gizur, Snorri's killer, who in turn was assessed 300 hundreds for having earlier attacked Orækja. And Gizur was to pay 200 hundreds for having killed Snorri to balance the account (Íslend. 157:470). It's hard to believe that such awards could ever have assuaged grief or ameliorated disrupted relations (e.g., Grœn. 6:290). But if wealth was not always changing hands, honor was. Even if the profits were only "paper" profits, it made a difference that Snorri was judged worth 200 hundreds, an extremely high wergeld,[29] rather than some lesser sum, just as it mattered who was balanced off against whom.[30]

There is more than just philological significance in the fact that the term mannjafnaðr—the comparing, matching, "evening" or balancing of men—is applied to the pairing of corpses in a settlement (Heið. 37:318–19; Grœn. 6:290), as well as to a formal competitive verbal duel in which two men compare themselves or their patrons with respect to valor and prestige.[31] The image of man-balancing coincides with the dominant image of the balanced-exchange model of the feud, the notion of balance itself being one of the key organizing symbols of the culture (see Ortner 1973). In balance lay the only hope for closure of disputes. And in the formalized balancing of man against man or of man against property, we see one of the few explicit indicators of rank in a society virtually without formal ranking. One's value in the social universe was finally fixed by whom or what one was compared to in death. The author of Njáls saga, for instance, shows his and the community's grand estimation of the glowering and flawed Skarphedin by balancing him against his victim, the peaceful, righteous, and beloved Hoskuld (145:413; cf. Glúma 23:80–81). Elsewhere arbitrators struggle to determine who to balance against whom and are constrained to recognize the disparity in quality of victims by balancing two corpses against one, or adding a rape that had occurred to even up the difference between the corpses (Heið. 37:318–19; Hallfr. 10:193).

The wrongs on each side, of course, were not always capable of being balanced and movements of property or people had to make up the difference. Sentences of exile for various durations, or limited exile from certain bounded districts were most frequently the lot of lesser men, although there are notable exceptions in which well-established men had to go abroad (e.g., *Heið.* 37:319; *Íslend.* 157:471; *Njála* 74:180). Financial assessments were usually made against those who had the ability to pay or who had a chieftain, thingmen, friends, or kin to call upon for assistance. Typically big men were able to make their willingness to submit to arbitration contingent upon stipulations that denied the arbitrators any authority to adjudge exile or the loss of a chieftaincy or home estate (e.g., *Lax.* 71:210; Heusler 1911, 89). Such stipulations limited the arbitrators to awards of moveable property, although these at times could be quite substantial. Those awards that were paid in full were often partially or wholly funded by third parties.[32] Thorgils Oddason was thus able to get commitments from his friends and kin as well as "great gifts" from a wide array of people throughout the country to discharge the eighty hundreds Haflidi assessed against him, to be payable

> in land in the North Quarter, gold and silver, Norwegian wares, ironwork, fine livestock not less than one cowvalue in worth, and gelded horses—a stallion on condition he was accompanied by a mare, or a mare on condition a stallion went with her, but no horse older than twelve or younger than three years. Payment was to be made at the door of Haflidi's booth, or borne to his home and he himself was to appraise its value. (*Hafl.* 31–32:49–50)

The specificity with which Haflidi set the payment terms showed that he was serious about getting paid; he also had Thorgils find three wealthy sureties.[33] The alacrity with which Thorgils was able to acquire the assets to pay shows that community input into peacemaking need not only take the form of intervening in disputes by mediating and arbitrating, but could also be manifested by making it possible for judgments to be fulfilled. Haflidi's award was excessive, but Thorgils was able to acquire greater honor by discharging it without complaint. At some time Thorgils would have to repay these debts, but probably not quite in the amount he had received, since the contributors would recognize that by making peace and by complying with the judgment he had already paid them a valuable consideration when he acceded to their desires to take the peaceful course.

In other cases people registered mild surprise that stiff awards were honored. Consider the remark of Jon Loftsson's son commenting on the last arbitration his father made before dying:

> I do not know which is the more remarkable: the causes that were submitted to his judgment or those judgments he last made. Those very steep judgments that people thought would never be paid and that would thus lead to a collapse of the settlement have all been discharged.
> (G.dýri 18:200; see also Bjarn. 34:211)

The arbitrator's skill lay in manipulating the rather constrictive conventions governing the content of arbitrated judgments in such a way as to satisfy the aggrieved without alienating the wrongdoer into noncompliance. The conceptual problems were never difficult; the skill of fashioning workable judgments was simply the ability to recognize what amount would be deemed acceptable to both parties and what types of exile would be considered reasonable against whom. Arbitrators were not without guidance on these matters, since both monetary amounts and exile sentences followed fairly well-established norms; moreover, the arbitrators were usually well informed of the principals' positions, these having been the subject of haggling prior to the submission of the case to them (Bjarn. 34:208–10; Heið. 37:318–19).

Workability should have been the arbitrators' chief concern, but at times self-interest or conflicting demands could lead to imprudent judgments. If, however, the first award wasn't honored, there would no doubt soon be opportunity to devise a better one. Consider, for example, the following case. After a succession of broken settlements, and after having twice succeeded in outlawing each other, Einar and Sturla engaged in a general affray with wounds and killings on both sides. Both prepared lawsuits and prosecuted them at the Allthing. Their friends intervened with the result that the cases were submitted to the arbitration of Jon Loftsson and Gizur Hallsson, influential and powerful goðar. The saga then describes the general principles which the arbitrators applied to the case: "And they fashioned the awards in the way they thought most likely to lead to the settlements being honored; not like those overreaching awards which had previously been arbitrated" (Sturla 22:94–95). The terms are not given; it is only mentioned that actions were settled and people "went home and were reconciled for now." The success of the award lay both in resolving several serious lawsuits and in assuring that the award itself would not provide a new source for conflict. This meant the terms had been acceptable to both parties and undoubtedly were immediately fulfilled. Some arbitrators provided incentives to comply within the construct of the award. Sæmund Ormsson thus announced that for each ounce paid pursuant to his decision, one ounce would be remitted (Íslend. 162:475).[34]

Even though settlements were hardly self-enforcing, breaches were not taken lightly. Settlement breaking was distinguishable from refusal to comply with the initial judgment. The settlement breaker was the wronged party who, in his own person or by proxy, had received compensation or obtained the exile of his adversary and then resorted to self-help when the opportunity presented itself. The noncomplier had never quite accepted the validity of the award or at least had never accepted its benefits. A settlement-breaker breached firmly established norms, so powerful that they even overrode the obligation to avenge one's father. The scene is Norway, and Halli, an Icelander, is before King Harald Hardrada:

> The king asked, "Is that true, Halli, that you have not avenged your father?"
> "It's true, my lord," said Halli.
> "Why then have you come to Norway?" asked the king.
> "It so happened, my lord," said Halli, "that I was only a child when my father was killed. My kinsmen took up the case on my behalf and reached a settlement. And among us it is not thought very becoming to be called a griðníðingr." (Sneglu-Halla þ. 278)

The griðníðingr[35] was the betrayer of a truce, one of the lowest of the low. People preferred to avoid the designation if possible (e.g., Njála 68:169, 75:183). The norm against settlement breaking was so strong that we even see one person concerned that duress would not excuse his failure to adhere to a "forced-settlement" (Þorg. sk. 18:133). And if shaming was an insufficient sanction, there were others.[36] The usual sanction was the resumption of hostilities. Some settlements explicitly provided that if the terms were not fulfilled, the offender could be justifiably killed (Njála 74:180). The underlying claim could still be sued on, and there is some evidence that the breach itself supported an independent cause of action (Sturla 9:74). In one case some "griðníðings" were placed under ecclesiastical ban (Íslend. 176:500).

One especially troublesome issue regarding breach was precisely who was bound to adhere to the settlement. How many people beyond the actual participants were included? The evidence, such as it is, is difficult to assess. In one instance a man who was out of the country was not considered a part of the settlement that his brother was party to for their father's death (*Reyk.* 16–17:203–4). In *Njáls saga*, a father purported to bind his absent sons (43:110–11; 99:254) and a sister's husband was judged to have broken a settlement in which only his wife's brothers had participated (98:249). Certain people expressly declared themselves not bound, presumably because there would have been doubt otherwise (145:409). A case we have already discussed in various contexts preserves a disagreement between the principals as to who is to fall within the ambit of the settlement:

> And when Pal arrived Sturla said, "How many people do you wish to include in our settlement, so that you will vouch for them?"
> "Me, my sons, and my wife," said Pal.
> "Any others?" asked Sturla.
> "Hermund, his son, and Torfi," answered Pal.
> "You wish to include them; then I wish to exclude them because you are now proving just who has been treacherously opposed to me." (*Sturla* 32:111)

Sturla is evidently concerned to preserve his right to attack Hermund and Torfi without being deemed to have violated the accord. We see some chieftains presuming the power to bind third parties by their settlements (*Vall.* 9:259; see Andersson and Miller 1989, 284n265). In the later years of the commonwealth in which the settlements of the big players look more like treaties than discrete resolutions of specific claims, nonparticipants are expressly bound by their leaders (e.g., *Þorg. sk.* 31:158; see Heusler 1912, 55).

According to the saga record, settlements were honored often enough that people would register disappointment, if not quite shock, when they weren't. Much compliance, however, was technical compliance: people paid the assessed compensation and fulfilled the terms of exile sentences, but there was little peace in their hearts. Settlements could not prevent new incidents of hostility, arguably unrelated to the original incident, from arising (*Njála* 43–44:111–15); nor did they prevent one party from claiming the other side had broken the settlement or from manufacturing new claims so as to provide an acceptable justification for renewed hostility (*Íslend.* 46:294–96; *Njála* 91–92:225–32; see Miller 1983a). Because so many arbitrated settlements took place in the context of feud, they could not always achieve permanent peace. They bought time. They tended to be concerned less with the establishment or re-establishment of good relations than with bringing some sort of closure to particular grievances (cf. Gluckman 1955a, 78). As we noted at the beginning of the chapter, few settlements got to the underlying causes of a dispute; the arbitrational style of balance and compensation was not quite up to it. Provisions for exile could do much to reduce future hostility by forcing a separation of the factions, but the success of this resolution ran up against the fact that exiles of big men were hard to impose without their prior agreement.[37] Yet settlements could manage to delay crisis and turn the feud to a dormant phase for the present; and that was a goal that most felt well worth pursuing. Despite the shortcomings of arbitrated settlements, they were perceived by a substantial segment of the community to be more likely than either self-help or legal judgments to lead to peace, even if that peace were only temporary.

Indeed, so pervasive was the feeling that cases were better concluded in agreement than judgment or dismissal that we see litigants refusing to put forward absolute defenses, using them instead as leverage to induce the other side to enter into some kind of arbitrated settlement. Njal, again acting on Gunnar's behalf, obtained a favorable clearing verdict (see p. 249) from the panel of neighbors and "he said he would submit the verdict unless the plaintiffs agreed to put the case to arbitration" (Njála 74:180). Many goðar then also urged settlement and the case was submitted to a panel of twelve arbitrators, with the result that Gunnar, who had an absolute legal defense, was still adjudged liable for compensation and a three-year banishment from Iceland.

Any realistic hope for peace required concessions from both sides; at least such was the case when the parties were of roughly the same strength. Victory at law, as everyone knew, was simply perceived as another offense in the feuding process which would elicit repayment at a later date. The kin of a dead man, on whose behalf an outlawry action had failed because the killer had a valid claim of self-defense, were still aggrieved; they had suffered loss, and they themselves had done nothing to forfeit immunity vis-à-vis the killer. They had to have something to show for their loss if they were ever to let matters rest, even if there was no adequate legal basis for compelling recompense. Njal knew that the chances for Gunnar's future peace and safety would be much improved if he paid something now, as part of a settlement mutually agreed to, rather than later, when the kin of his victim might try to extract it from him unilaterally. Justifiable killing always absolved the killer completely at law, but, in arbitration, legal justification was not sufficient to prevent compensation awards where they were deemed necessary to ensure the injured party's compliance with the judgment (see Heusler 1911, 63–64). These sentiments were articulated explicitly in one case:

> I will offer to judge your dispute with Thord because things cannot continue the way they are. Though you have killed with legal justification men who had forfeited their immunity, you will be involved in more conflict if there is not some compromise in these cases. I will tell what I would award. You shall pay some compensation, though it may be less than they desire, and I will make up the difference so that they will think their kin well compensated for. (*Bjarn.* 27:187)[38]

But if the desire for peace prompted terms reflecting concessions and compromises of absolute rights, power differences between the parties often cut the other way. This should hardly be surprising since bias was built into the arbitration system to the extent that the identity of the arbitrators would reflect the connections and relative bargaining strengths of the parties. Some arbitrated awards, as a result, especially those made pursuant to a grant of self-judgment, conceded precious little (see, e.g., *Bjarn.* 34:209–11; *Egil* 82:287–88).

To the transactional, functional, and structural considerations already noted we should add another of a different quality. That is, we do not know how much the ideals of peacemaking, of settling disputes by *sætt*, whose virtues were invoked by intervenors,[39] were able to influence the principals independent of cruder factors such as the identity and power of the intervenors and the risks of alienating them by not acceding to their requests. The ideologies of peace and vengeance were frequently at odds. In one sense, the peacemaking cause was at a structural disadvantage compared to the forces of vengefulness. Peacemaking was reactive. People spoke of its virtues only when its virtues were threatened. There did not seem to be an ubiquitous consciousness of the peacemaking discourse. The discourse of vengeance, on the other hand, was always in the air. The economy of honor, of which all were conscious at all times, would have it no other way. Nevertheless, the cause of peace was something people tended to favor when their own honor was not directly in issue. This meant that the pool of people favoring peace was invariably larger than the pool actively wishing strife on any particular issue. The problem was how hard those favoring peace were willing to work for their wishes and whether, even if they were willing, they were situated so as to be able to effect them.

Our discussion is best rounded out with a consideration of specific cases. They help provide some sense of the range of possibility in the settlement process and the subtle significances that context imparts to structured action; they also give a feel for the rhythms of the processes we have been discussing.

## Case I: The Meanings of Self-Judgment
### (Njáls saga chapter 38)

The following case occurs in the course of a feud which we have touched on before in a different context (above p. 183). The account is somewhat stylized, but it is well within the range of possible behaviors appearing in numerous other saga accounts and in studies of dispute processing in stateless societies. The case's chief virtue is that it is neatly circumscribed, or at least circumscribable, and can be presented without gross oversimplification in fairly short space.

Gunnar and Njal are substantial householders; they are neighbors and good friends. Their wives, however, have been bitter enemies ever since a quarrel over seating arrangements at a feast. Insults were exchanged there and over the course of the next few years so were killings of slaves and servants. In the particular incident that concerns us, while Gunnar and Njal are away attending the Allthing, Gunnar's wife Hallgerd sends one Brynjolf, her kinsman and a member of her and Gunnar's household, to kill Atli, a member of Njal's and his wife Bergthora's household. Atli had the year before killed a servant of Hallgerd's at Bergthora's request. Brynjolf carries out his task and rides home to tell Hallgerd, who in turn sends a man to the Allthing to tell Gunnar.

Gunnar, accompanied by his brother, goes to Njal's booth to inform him of the killing and offers him compensation in an amount which "you yourself shall judge." This offer is in accordance with the procedure adopted by the two men for the two killings already encompassed by their wives. In those cases each victim was valued at twelve ounces of silver, in the saga's terms a "slave payment." Njal responds to Gunnar's offer by recalling their past agreement not to quarrel between themselves, "but nevertheless I cannot adjudge Atli as a slave." Gunnar says that that would be acceptable and extends his hand to Njal, who takes it and names witnesses that they agreed to these terms. Njal then awards himself a long hundred (120) ounces of silver which Gunnar pays immediately. The saga notes the response of third-party observers: "Many of those who were there said they thought the award excessive." Gunnar responds angrily that full compensation had been paid for men less brave than Atli. With that the meeting breaks up.

The negotiations between Njal and Gunnar are not complicated. As Njal notes, the two have already agreed to maintain their good relations, agreeing to agree, so to speak; they have a history of settling quickly for the deaths of their servants and of using the same procedure to arrive at the settlement. The procedure is called *sjálfdœmi*, sometimes *eindœmi* (*Bjarn.* 29:191), meaning self-judgment, sole judgment. As its name indicates, it is the grant of power to one principal by another to arbitrate the dispute to which he is a party. The negotiations here, brief as they are, involve two separate issues. First, the selection of the procedural mode within which the dispute is to be processed. Gunnar's offer and Njal's acceptance of self-judgment settles that. The final award will be an arbitrated one, its exact terms to be in Njal's power. Orthodox definitions of arbitration, which make the presence of a third-party decision maker necessary, need to be readjusted to accommodate self-judgment (e.g., Nader and Todd 1978, 11).[40] The Icelanders themselves made no distinction. Both self-judgment and triadic arbitrations were called *sættir* and were opposed as such to legal judgments and vengeance (e.g., *Lax.* 85:242; *Njála* 43:110–11, 45:118).

The second issue has to do with delineating the arbitrator's power and establishing an acceptable range of terms for the judgment. There is little haggling here. Gunnar's original offer is not as unbounded as it may seem. By offering Njal compensation in an amount Njal is to determine, Gunnar has already eliminated several possible outcomes: among these are the outlawry or exile of either Brynjolf or Hallgerd, or the forfeiture of particular pieces of property. The offer is specifically to assess a general monetary award, with only the amount to be left to the judgment of the arbitrator. There is also some doubt that the amount itself has not been implicitly agreed to by the past practice of accepting slave payment for the killing of their servants. Njal, in fact, wants the issue clarified and gives Gunnar the chance to rescind the offer of self-judgment if an award greater than twelve ounces will not be acceptable to him. The reaction of the bystanders to an award ten times greater than their prior settlements, as well as Gunnar's defensive justification of the propriety of the award, suggests Njal had violated the norms governing the amount of compensation for someone of Atli's position. Gunnar, however, complies immediately. If Atli's status does not merit the amount then his character does: "men not as brave as Atli have been paid for with full compensation." The saga is not exactly clear about Atli's juridical status,[41] but it gives more than enough indication of his fearlessness and loyalty to Njal and Bergthora. It is these qualities that led Njal to have granted Atli's request earlier that spring not to accept a "slave payment" for him if he should be the target of Hallgerd's hostility:

> That spring Njal spoke with Atli: "I wish that you
> would attach yourself to a household out east in the
> fjords before Hallgerd does you in."
> "That doesn't scare me," said Atli, "and I would rather
> stay here if I had the chance."
> "That's not very advisable," said Njal.
> "I'd rather die in your house," said Atli, "than change
> masters; still, I wish to ask you this: if I'm killed, don't
> let me be valued at a slave's rate."
> "You will be compensated for as a free man," said Njal
> ... and he took him into the household. (38:99–100)[42]

The content of Njal's award was thus not only determined by his negotiations with Gunnar, but by negotiations entered into with the victim at the time he was taken into the household. Njal's promise to value Atli as a free man, however, was clearly not a matter of community knowledge. Hallgerd, for instance, thought him a slave when she chided Gunnar later: "'Did you pay a hundred of silver for Atli, judging him at a free man's rate?' 'He was free before,' said Gunnar." And apparently the bystanders' disapproval of Njal's judgment was based on the same misinformation. Whatever Atli's precise status, the judgment effectively freed him posthumously if Njal had not properly manumitted him earlier.

The exact significance of self-judgment depended on the context. The state of relations of the disputants was one important factor. Between friends like Gunnar and Njal, the granting of self-judgment was a confirmation of their friendship and mutual trust; above all it was an indication of their wish to settle quickly each flare-up of trouble between their households. But where the relations of the disputants were hostile and the intent was to continue to define their relations in this way, the granting or, more often, extortion of self-judgment was a marker of the relative status and bargaining power of the principals. This significance of self-judgment was consciously acknowledged and clearly articulated by disputants, their supporters, and peacemakers alike (e.g., *Hœn.* 7:20, 12:34; *Íslend* 93:364; 103:378; *Qlk.* 1:85). One man actually refused an offer of self-judgment because, he felt, it would allow his opponents the opportunity to justify noncompliance by claiming they were under duress. He instead proposed that the sides each name an equal number of men to an arbitration panel (Þorg. sk. 70:214).

It is helpful to think of self-judgment as having two aspects: the grant of power and the determination of the award. The grant is in itself a form of compensation, the specie being in units of prestige and honor, and the party receiving it accepts it in his role as principal. But once the power is assumed, the principal becomes an arbitrator, and he is expected to behave in accordance with the general norms governing third-party decision makers, as well as any specific limitations negotiated prior to the transfer of the power. To oversimplify greatly, the award should have some element of forbearance in consideration that a payment of much value, the power itself, has already been made. The expectation of forbearance and moderation led some grim-minded disputants to refuse to accept offers of self-judgment, preferring instead to let the law or the feud take its course (Lax. 85:242; Njála 49:127). Some disputants could play off these expectations for grand effect. Thorgils accepted an offer of self-judgment from his kinsman Sturla, against whom he had been opposed, and awarded himself a substantial, if not overreaching sum. He then took Sturla by the hand and said:

> Now kinsman, you have given me self-judgment and thereby done me honor. I have held you liable for a large sum, but not more than I think was my due. I am also fully aware of your straitened circumstances. I do not want this debt to be a cause of further disagreement between us. I am thus releasing you, kinsman, from the entire judgment; neither I nor my heirs will ever claim it, however we get along, for better or worse. (Þorg. sk. 31:159)

Thorgils' gesture was much more dramatic than either simply refusing the power of self-judgment or judging a mild compensation would have been. By first realizing the dangerous possibilities inherent in empowering the enemy to be the judge in his own case, and then dispelling them with gracious condescension, he was able to elicit despair and gratitude in rapid succession: all in all, only a slightly subtler version of arming an entire firing squad with blanks and only a little less humiliating to the target of the display.

Even in a case between friends, like that of Njal and Gunnar, the announcement of the self-judged award was more than just a ritualized reiteration of a settlement already arrived at by negotiation. The negotiations did not specify the precise terms of the award; the parties negotiated the limits of the arbitrator's discretion and powers, the range of acceptable awards, and the identity of the arbitrator. The limits imposed by the principals on the arbitrator's discretion could at times leave him with little room for maneuvering, most of the terms having already been set by the principals as a condition of their agreeing to submit to arbitration (Heusler 1912, 53–54). But there was always some amount of discretion in the arbitrator to determine, if nothing else, the amount of money compensation due, or to declare, in cases where multiple killings occurred on both sides, whose death was to balance against whose. As limited as the arbitrator's power may have been on occasion, there was, as a general rule, no agreement, nor any terms to adhere to until he articulated them. As we noted at the beginning of the chapter, this is a typical feature of Icelandic settlements. Disputes which could have gone to law or had already found their way to court generally did not get resolved solely by negotiation. Negotiations that did not lead to some form of award, announced as such by someone given the authority to determine the precise terms of the agreement, were failed negotiations. Occasional attempts were made by wrongdoers or their representatives to avoid the form of arbitration by trying to characterize whatever transfer of wealth was to be made as a gift rather than as compensation. The claimants, ever alert to the adjustments of honor at stake, invariably preferred to take less and have the transfer classified as compensation (Hafl. 15:32; Hrafnk. 3:106).

The self-judgment procedure allowed negotiations, dyadic in form, to be assimilated to the form of arbitrated settlements by allowing one of the parties to play two distinct roles, principal and arbitrator. The arbitrational mode was thus able to attract to itself not only disputes originally processed in the highly formalized legal system, but also those disputes initially processed in a less structured negotiational mode. Self-judgment, Janus-like, looked two ways: to legal judgment and to arbitrated settlement. In substance, self-judgment could be as harsh as a legal judgment. This recognition led certain overbearing claimants to equate them, seeing either as an equally desirable way of humiliating their opponents or expropriating their property (e.g., Band. 7:327; Hœn. 7:20, 12:34). Stories of overreaching and excessive self-judged awards are the best-known cases in the sagas (Egil 82:287–88; Hafl. 31:49–50; Sturla 32:111, see above p. 255). In form, however, self-judgment was a sætt, an arbitrated settlement. As such it confirmed the values of the peacemaking ideology: that sætt, mutually agreed to, was preferable to a legal judgment or blood. This significance of self-judgment, as well as the expectation that the judgment should be moderate, helps explain why claimants were occasionally reluctant to accept self-judgment and why third parties were eager to convince reluctant claimants to accept it (*Lax.* 85:242; *Njála* 49:127–28, 51:132).

The darker side of Gunnar and Njal's settlement is that it was little more than a symbol of peace, a formalized reaffirmation of their friendship. Their wives, Bergthora and Hallgerd, the real disputants, continued to fight; within a year Brynjolf was dead at Bergthora's bidding.

## Case II: The Interplay of Self-Help, Law, and Peacemaking (Eyrbyggja saga *chapters 30–33*)

In the preceding case one of the principals sought out the other, with the intention of negotiating a settlement of the troubles that had arisen, and succeeded in arriving at an agreement. In this case negotiations fail and the parties process the dispute by going to law. The outcome, however, is not a legal judgment but an arbitrated settlement. The case allows us to make some small observations about the relations of legal rules and arbitrated settlement.

Thorolf Lame-leg was a troublesome, overbearing sort. He had one son, Arnkel, a powerful, well-respected chieftain established on a neighboring farm. Thorolf owned a meadow in common with Ulfar, a wealthy freedman. Thorolf had taken hay belonging to Ulfar and denied Ulfar's claim for payment. Ulfar had then sought out Arnkel to intervene on his behalf. The upshot was that Arnkel paid Ulfar the value of the hay and self-helped himself to seven of his father's oxen after his father had refused Arnkel's request for reimbursement. During a Yule feast at his farm, Thorolf got his slaves drunk and promised them their freedom if they would burn Ulfar in his house. Six of them set out to do it, but the flames were seen at Arnkel's place and people from there captured the slaves and quenched the fire. The next morning Arnkel took the slaves out to a headland and had them hanged (*Eyrb.* 30–31:81–84).

Ulfar's fear for his life then leads him to transfer formally all his property to Arnkel in return for Arnkel's protection. The arrangement, called an *arfsal* (literally, transfer of inheritance rights), allowed Ulfar to retain a life interest in his property but the estate was to pass to Arnkel at Ulfar's death.[43] Thorolf, on his side, makes an attempt to get Arnkel to pay compensation for the slaves but his son "flatly refused to pay a single penny for them" (31:84–85). Thorolf then sets out to recruit support for his claim. He goes to Snorri, a chieftain who already has been several times opposed to Arnkel in legal actions to which each had been recruited. Snorri and Arnkel were at this time the two leading competitors for power in the district, and their relations were hostile but not openly violent. Thorolf asks Snorri to take up the legal action for the killing of the slaves, offering him a portion of whatever compensation they received for them. Snorri is reluctant to get involved in the troubles between father and son, but not so reluctant as to refuse Thorolf's offer to transfer to him some valuable woodland in return for Snorri's taking up the prosecution.[44]

Snorri prepares the case for the district Thing. Both sides attend with numerous supporters. The case goes to court and Arnkel defends by calling for a *bjargkviðr*—a clearing verdict—from the panel of neighbors (see p. 249), putting forward as his defense that the slaves were caught in the act of setting fire to a dwelling, thus privileging his killing them. Snorri concedes that the slaves could have been killed justifiably at the place of action, "but when you took them over to Vadilshead and killed them there, they had not, I think, forfeited their immunity (*óhelgi*) at that place."[45] Snorri is able to invalidate the *bjargkviðr* and would have gotten a judgment in his favor, yet before it is submitted to the judges, "men came forward in order to reconcile them, and it was agreed that the brothers Styr and Vermund should arbitrate. They judged twelve ounces to be paid then and there for each slave." Arnkel complies. And everyone goes home mad.

This case provides a typical example of how disputes in the sagas escalate and expand. The support-gathering process often created new sources of conflict or connected preexisting disputes into complicated networks. Principals and their supporters were aware of these possibilities and much of the politics of support gathering lay in astutely using the hostilities of others for processing one's own disputes. But for now we are concerned with the narrower issue of why this particular claim for compensation ends up in court and why, once there, it is settled by arbitration.

The way in which the dispute was processed owed a lot to the choices made by the disputants and their supporters at critical junctures in the dispute. Arnkel chose to deny his father's claim for compensation for the slaves; Thorolf chose to enlist Snorri to pursue the claim at law; and Snorri decided to take it up. There was also something in the context of the dispute and the structure of relations between the disputants that made it unlikely that third parties would intervene unless the dispute was aired at a public assembly. For one thing, neither Thorolf nor Arnkel had brothers. Their kin group was very small and its other members, Arnkel's sisters and

sisters' sons, either lived at a distance, had been outlawed and ex-
iled, or were of insufficient stature to merit any notice in the saga
beyond the mere mention of their existence. Thorolf had a wife,
but she was not Arnkel's mother, who had been dead some years
(20:54). There were thus no kin or affines at hand who had an interest in father and son keeping good kinship. In addition, since father and son lived on neighboring farms, meetings for negotiations
looked more like casual visits than expeditions and hence would go
unobserved. Few men need be gathered for the trip and what accompaniment there might have been would be household men rather
than neighbors. That is, during negotiations there would be few if
any bystanders of sufficient rank to serve effectively as intervenors.

The dispute between father and son was more than an affair about
slaves. Both were seeking to redefine their relations; going public
with the dispute was a way of accomplishing this.[46] Arnkel had an
interest in distancing himself from his troublesome father in order
to show his thingmen and clients that his kinship with Thorolf
would not stand in the way of meeting the obligations he had undertaken to them. Opposing Thorolf in a lawsuit would serve this purpose. Arnkel, presumably, could predict that denying his father
compensation might lead to legal action. He knew that Thorolf was
not the sort to process a dispute by "lumping it." Thorolf, on the
other hand, resented his son Arnkel supporting his client's claims
against his father and he was jealous of his son's prominence and
prestige as well. Father and son had independent neighboring estab-
lishments and their relations look more like those of competing
neighbors than close kin. Although both stopped short of a formal
repudiation of their kinship ties, Thorolf made several gestures in
that direction. He apparently shifted his Thing attachment from
Arnkel to Snorri and, by transferring the woodland to Snorri, he attempted a partial disinheritance of his son.

Thorolf's actions could also be accounted for in a way wholly
consistent with the simple goal of getting payment for his slaves.
Even though the formal action for killing the slaves would not
have yielded a money judgment, but rather full outlawry,[47] the
aggressive prosecution of a lawsuit could force his son to accept
an arbitrated settlement in which money compensation would be
awarded. Still, to make the prosecution of the case sufficiently
threatening to be able to compel his powerful son to accept arbitration, Thorolf needed the support of an equally powerful man. Snorri
not only provided the skills of a legal expert, but as a chieftain he
had the thingmen to ensure the case would be heard and not forcibly
overthrown. If, however, Thorolf's goal were recompense he could

have accomplished that just as well by self-help, a mode of dispute-processing to which Thorolf was no stranger. When Thorolf chose law rather than self-help and chose to seek support from Snorri, his son's chief rival, we get some indication that his goals were more oriented toward the relations themselves than to any specific material interest.[48]

For his part, Snorri was initially reluctant to take up Thorolf's claim. He admonished Thorolf, referring to the norms of keeping good kinship and deferring to one's superiors: "You should not prosecute because you and Arnkel should be in agreement on all issues and because he is better than you" (31:85). But Snorri, as Thorolf reminded him, was "no friend of Arnkel's"; he also greatly desired the woods at Crow's-Ness that Thorolf offered to transfer to him. The saga writer seems to attribute Snorri's involvement mainly to greed, yet his reasons were as much political as avaricious. His relations with Arnkel were clearly defined, and they were hostile. The present opportunity to embarrass his rival as well as obtain some claim to a portion of Arnkel's inheritance was too good to pass up.

The dispute goes to law then because the three chief actors either actively want it to or don't mind that it does. Once it is in court, however, unnamed men intervened urging reconciliation at the moment Snorri was able to invalidate Arnkel's defense. Had Snorri submitted his case to judgment, the rule he invoked—that the slaves could only be killed with impunity at the place of action—would have dictated the outcome: outlawry for Arnkel. No one intended this result. Even old Thorolf assumed the action would only lead to money compensation, hence his earlier offer to pay Snorri for his support with a portion of the compensation the case would yield. But the threat of a legal judgment served two important functions. It provided the pressure needed to get Arnkel to agree to a settlement and it was a cue for nondisputants to intervene. The community had no desire to see the district thrown into turmoil for the price of a few slaves. Snorri, on his part, had no wish to enforce a judgment against the powerful and popular Arnkel, especially on behalf of the unpopular Thorolf.

The disputants could be fairly certain of peacemaker intervention at this stage of the case. More disturbed the community than the threat of violence. There was also a strong sense that the entire proceeding was inappropriate. It was a serious breach of the norms of good kinship for fathers and sons to take each other to court. People had taken a dim view of Snorri's agreement to prosecute Thorolf's claim: "Thorolf rode home well pleased with the arrangement, but others showed little approval for it" (31:85). Even Snorri, as noted

earlier, was initially reluctant to get involved in what he referred to
as a "dispute between father and son." But at the Thing that amor-
phous collectivity, the community, was assembled and it wanted
some symbol of reconciliation—the dropping of the lawsuit, the
agreement to submit to arbitration—though all knew that the reconciliation would be symbolic only. The actual terms of the arbitrated award did not concern the intervenors so much as the fact
that the case was to be arbitrated. The transfer of the dispute from
the legal to the arbitrational mode was itself a socially significant
act, an affirmation of the peacemaking ideology.

The source gives the identity of the arbitrators—the brothers, Vermund and Styr. We do not know if they were among the men of
goodwill urging an agreement but it is significant that they are
structurally situated so as to have an interest in reconciling the
parties. Each is bound by affinity to an opposing side. Vermund was
Arnkel's sister's daughter's husband and had been allied with Arnkel
in lawsuits against Snorri on several occasions, while Styr was
Snorri's wife's father and had, prior to the marriage of his daughter
to Snorri, vowed to support Snorri in lawsuits (21:54, 24:60, 27:69,
28:75).[49] The text does not describe how Vermund and Styr arrived
at their award, but it appears to have been largely influenced, if not
exactly determined, by a rule governing the compensation due for
the killing of slaves. Later in the same saga, and confirmed in another source, we find the following:

> That was the law in that time that if a man killed an-
> other's slave that man should take slave payment to the
> owner's home and start his journey before the third sun-
> rise after the killing; the price should be twelve ounces
> of silver. If the slave payment were thus lawfully made
> then no action lay for the killing. (43:118; *Egil* 81:282)[50]

Vermund and Styr were not especially imaginative in their decision.
They awarded twelve ounces for each slave to be paid immediately.
The only deviation they showed from a straightforward application
of the above rule was to waive the three-day time limit, which in
turn necessarily substituted a money penalty for the outlawry penalty required by the killing case.

There is one aspect of the award that illustrates a point touched
on earlier: it is noteworthy how narrowly the arbitrators defined the
subject in dispute. To them it was purely about killing slaves. The
range of relevance was no broader than it was in the original legal
action. They either were not given the authority or they did not

pretend to judge issues not explicitly raised by the pleadings in the case. They did not, for instance, take Thorolf's soliciting and plotting into account at all. They apparently did not consider the slaves' wrongdoing either, although that might have had much to do with prompting people to intervene to prevent the case from going to judgment. Once the arbitrators took up the case they judged the issue as they would any killing of a slave for which no justification was available.

Yet within these somewhat constrictive confines, arbitrators could use the occasion to assert implicitly other norms they felt were relevant to the dispute. If there is a hidden message in Vermund and Styr's arbitration, it lies in judging Arnkel liable for the full twelve ounces set forth by the rule and not some lesser amount reflecting an offset for any wrongdoing on either Thorolf's or the slaves' part. They are telling Arnkel in effect that the rule they are basing their award on should have governed the behavior of father and son in the three days after the incident and that Arnkel should have used it to preempt his father's recourse to law. Then, too, Vermund and Styr know that the substance of the dispute has more to do with the relational dislocation of father and son than the price of some slaves. Although it was possible to deal with relational problems like this by arbitration, to have done so here would have required more powers than the arbitrators were granted and also a context that raised the underlying problems more distinctly. It may be, however, that Vermund and Styr's judgment should be attributed to nothing more than the ease with which a well-established and conveniently relevant rule can be invoked to settle a claim to which it arguably applies. Yet even then, whatever may have been the intention of the arbitrators, the very application of the rule makes the argument for its own propriety and virtue.

The award, although complied with immediately, did not succeed in establishing good relations among the parties. "After that people left the Thing; Arnkel and Snorri were ill-pleased with the outcome, but Thorolf even more so." This failure can hardly be blamed on the arbitrators. The parties were more interested in continuing hostilities than in settling them.

## Case III: Closure (Guðmundar saga dýra chapter 6)

Gudrun was a beautiful woman whose attractiveness was augmented by having inherited a farm from her father. Her first marriage was not a happy one, but mercifully her husband drowned after three years. She next married a certain Hrafn. The marriage did not have an especially auspicious beginning. On the night of the wedding, when Hrafn was led to her bed, in accordance with the rules of proper marriage (*Grágás* Ia 222, II 66), she jumped out. She did not get on well with her new husband either, and so she left and lived in various places. She eventually returned to her husband, but not before she had attracted the attentions of Hakon Thordarson, who continued to pay her frequent visits all winter at her husband's residence. One day Gudrun told Hakon she did not wish him to continue coming by as long as Hrafn, her husband, was alive, "but you can do as you think afterwards." Hakon soon speared Hrafn who, nevertheless, managed some parting witticisms before dying (*G.dýri* 5:169–70).

The chieftain Gudmund dyri took over the defense of Hakon since Hakon was his brother's son. Several other chieftains were anxious to take up the case against him because "they thought Gudmund dyri had risen high enough." Gudmund realized that the case would provide his competitors with an excellent opportunity to assume the moral high ground in a dispute with him. They would be seeking justice for the treacherously slain husband, while Gudmund would be forced to stake his honor in an unpopular cause. He acted quickly, sending a messenger to Erlend, Hrafn's brother, to whom the cause of action belonged, inviting Erlend to see him to receive a generous compensation. Erlend went to meet Gudmund accompanied by two priests, named Flosi and Bjorn. When they arrived Gudmund sent for his brother Thord, the father of the killer, and his sons. Gudmund proposed a settlement.

> But Thord said he was not willing to pay compensation
> for Hrafn unless Gudrun paid half. Thord said she had
> conspired and planned Hrafn's death. But Gudmund
> [Gudrun?][51] did not want that spread about. They agreed
> that Flosi and Gudmund should arbitrate. They awarded
> fifteen hundreds for the killing of Hrafn in three-ell
> ounces and Gudmund paid every ounce immediately.[52]
> He also handed over two tracts of land west of the heath . . .
> and he bestowed gifts on them all when they left. . . .
> The chieftains were not aware of this until the matter
> was concluded. (6:171)

The case follows well-established forms. The wrongdoer or his representative approaches the proper plaintiff with an offer of settlement. They meet and negotiate the ranges of possible settlement; once the ranges have been determined, arbitrators are selected and a judgment is made. What is noteworthy about the case is the political concern that motivated its being processed so smoothly. Here permanent settlement was achieved in the face of contextual circumstances that favored the expansion and transformation of the dispute. Other chieftains were only too willing to take up the claim of the victim's kin. But Gudmund was able to outmaneuver them and resolve the dispute before they could get involved. This case gives an explicit indication of how much the mode of resolution and the form of processing of any particular claim, even among small people, was dependent on a host of factors having nothing to do with the event that formed the basis of the action. Any wrong was capable, given the right set of circumstances, of attracting to it the power struggles of the region, much in the manner unformed moisture coalesces around a dust particle, finally getting heavy enough to fall as a raindrop. And as one saga makes clear, when it rained in Iceland there could be drops of blood mixed in (*Eyrb.* 51:140).

The case of Hrafn's death shows, however, that particular grievances could be settled once and for all when they were not subsumed into the larger disputing strategies of feud. It also reveals something rather important about the confidence disputants might have about certain settlements. Gudmund's maneuver is only the astute move it turned out to be if in fact the settlement he achieves with Erlend will be able successfully to remove this embarrassing incident from the stock of claims available for his adversaries to use against him. This suggests two things: (1) either Gudmund had confidence that the settlement with Erlend would be honored or (2) that if it weren't, the fact of violating the settlement would shift the justice of the underlying claim sufficiently so that it would not embarrass Gudmund to have to defend it. In any event, Gudmund's actions give a rather strong claim for the virtues of some arbitrated resolutions.

As a concluding matter of some human interest, Gudrun and Hakon did not get to live happily ever after, although the reasons for that were not a consequence of having murdered Hrafn. The saga records that once Hakon won Gudrun's hand he never trusted her; he was hard on her, saying that "her men friends would never bury him." But Hakon was not able to watch her as closely as he wished. He did, in fact, end up being killed by one of his wife's ex-lovers, although his death was not related to the sexual liaison but rather to Hakon's having participated in an attack in which a chieftain was burned to death. Consider Hakon's last words to the man who volunteered to be his executioner: "I took you in when you arrived in Iceland without a penny to your name and I gave you food and lodging. Moreover I endured your sleeping three times with my wife Gudrun" (18:199).

## Conclusion

Two of these three cases were incidents in protracted hostile relationships that continued in spite of the settlements reached in the
particular issue at hand. In the other case, the settlement brought
closure to the dispute because someone actively prevented it from
becoming part of protracted hostile relationships. Other cases could
have been selected to show settlements that resolved a dispute and
concluded the matter for good. But such settlements often worked
less because of any special virtue in their terms or because of any
special peaceful propensities of the disputants, than because the incidents were discrete and had not been integrated into the feuding
process. Fairly enduring arbitrated settlements were the expected
outcomes of those cases between people of no great power or middling wealth when, for reasons wholly extrinsic to the dispute, the
matter did not happen to provide a vehicle for bigger people to pursue their feuds and competitions with each other. If the parties
lacked the means or will to engage in prolonged hostility, settlements would bring closure to the affair.[53] We should not suppose,
however, that some prior state of good relations was restored between the disputants, if there ever was such a state. But even though
the parties might seldom really forgive each other in their hearts,
they, at least, felt constrained to avoid disruptive behavior on account of those feelings.

It was mostly otherwise with settlements that punctuated the
course of the feud. They seldom resolved the underlying hostility;
they purported to close only the last exchange of wrongs, by giving
a public emblem of the scores achieved in the last exchange. When
it was convenient for the factions to revert to hostile phases of feud,
they would do so, although, as we noted, they usually took care to
characterize the new moves as retribution for some new wrong or
some prior unsettled claim that could be recalled or reinterpreted to
provide the justification for new aggression. If nothing else, the existence of a prior settlement put the feuding parties to the effort of
finding independent justification for new hostility, so as to avoid the
ignominy of being known as a settlement breaker.

But my purpose is not show that arbitration didn't work, even in
the feud. It clearly had definite short-term advantages of which all
were aware. Wronged parties could claim some measure of satisfaction from them, while wrongdoers were spared the prospect of full
outlawry and, in most cases, the avenger's axe as well. Kin, friends,
neighbors, and thingmen and *goðar* to the principals could avoid the
duty of attending the court of confiscation or the claims of avengers

and vengeance targets upon them for support. An arbitrated settlement postponed some annoying responsibilities and some very real dangers.

For some, settlements had a therapeutic effect. Gunnar and Njal's settlement (Case I) confirmed their friendship. The grant of self-judgment and the compensation paid in accordance with it were themselves acts of friendship. To the unnamed men in Case II who urged the arbitrated settlement of the dispute, the values of peace and good kinship were reaffirmed by the terms of Vermund and Styr's award. The compensation Erlend received (Case III) assuaged some of the social and psychic dislocation caused by his brother's death even though the payment came from a source that had no liability for causing the harm. The therapeutic aspect of settlement gave something to everyone: the wrongdoer got his life, the complainant still had something to show for his loss, and the community got peace and order, either in symbol or in fact. And even though the complainant would perhaps have gladly exchanged therapy for the catharsis of revenge, it was not always within his power to determine the outcome of the dispute unilaterally.

I have suggested that there were several factors, operating at different levels of categorization, that led to the processing of disputes in the arbitrational mode: the presence and strength of third parties urging settlement, the difficulty of achieving resolutions of any sort through vengeance or legal judgment, the relative strength of the parties and their ability to engage in classic feud, the substance of the claims being processed, and the choices and goals of the disputants and their supporters. The ideals of peace and reconciliation received a nice assist from the grimness of the alternatives. The law placed a maze of procedural obstacles in the way of the outlawry judgment, the only punishment it knew in serious cases. When the sides were of equal status and rank, outlawry judgments were hard to get and hard to enforce once gotten. Functionally, one of the law's main successes was that it provided the arena, and often the motive and means, for the parties to force disputes out of the legal mode and into the arbitrational one.

Culture wide, the ideals of peace invoked to get parties to accept arbitrated settlements were in constant competition with the ideals of revenge. The norms of these competing ideologies were accepted by the culture; and they came into frequent conflict. But when things went well that conflict was regulated and, within bounds, fairly predictable. Widely held norms, both customary and legal, recognized that vengeance was appropriate in some circumstances and not in others. Peacemaking, mostly as a consequence of the support-mustering process, was inextricably part of the very structure of vengeance and hostile legal action. Settlements themselves were bound up with violence in two fundamental ways. On the one hand, they were often merely a phase of the very feud they purported to settle, the visible means of scorekeeping that gave a clear picture of whose turn it was next. On the other hand, it was the prospect of new or renewed feud that ultimately provided the sanction behind the settlement. To borrow from J. M. Wallace-Hadrill's description of the Merovingian feud, settlement "necessarily hover[ed] on the edge of bloodshed" (1962, 147).

I hope my view of arbitration has neither been too positive nor too carping. I worry because it is easy to be seduced by certain romantic tendencies in much of the classic anthropological and sociological dispute-processing literature (see Cain and Kulcsar 1981–82), a literature which has greatly formed my own views. The negative view of arbitration and the other nonadjudicatory modes—mediation, negotiation, etc., that is, those modes commonly grouped together as ADR, or "alternative dispute resolution"—has even longer academic credentials. It still survives in American law schools, where adjudication is valorized as against the "alternative" modes because it is supposedly more ruled, less subject to infinite negotiability and power differences between the disputants, and evolutionarily more advanced than less formal modes of conflict resolution. Both views, positive and negative, are ethnocentric and unhistorical. If we wish to recover native sensibilities I think we would do well to recall that vengeance, whether in its pure form or legitimated as the enforcement of an outlawry judgment, was a frightening prospect for avenger and wrongdoer alike. Vengeance-taking was no easy task; it involved risks many were understandably reluctant to incur. Its difficulty and the thinly disguised averseness of avengers to undertake their grim duty is the main theme of a good portion of the saga corpus (Miller 1983b). Honorable settlements must have occasioned as many sighs of relief from reluctant avengers as from anxious wrongdoers and their kin.[54]

# CONCLUDING
# OBSERVATIONS

In the last chapter we had occasion to discuss briefly the term *mannjafnaðr*, a word meaning literally "man-evening" (Old Norse *jafn* is cognate with English *even*) and used to mark the comparison or balancing of men in death as part of an arbitration settlement or in life as part of a formal verbal contest in which the relative merits or demerits of two men were the subject of contention (see p. 277). In each case the worth of a man, the condition of his honor, was weighed and quantified. There is an inherent ambiguity in this process. When two men were matched in death as part of an arbitrated settlement they were equalized, symbolically at least, even if the parties might still continue to reconstruct and deconstruct posthumous reputation. Neither was judged preeminent to the other, the life of each had the same value. When, however, the comparison was made in life, the point of the *mannjafnaðr* was to determine precedence. If one aspect of the *mannjafnaðr's* balancing was the very form of the cultural values of reconciliation and peace—the image of social measure—the other aspect was the quintessence of the competition for scarce honor—the image of strife and discord. The first aspect suffused the concept of the *ójafnaðarmaðr* with its moral negativity: he was the "uneven," unbalanced, or unjust man, the man who refused to be bound by the rules of balance and equivalence in the disputing process. The second aspect is what informed one saga writer's description of a feast at which a comparing of men took place:

> There was much merriment and people talked about comparing men, who was the best man in the district or the greatest chieftain. And people were not in accord, as is so often the case whenever people engage in a comparison of men (*mannjafnaðr*). (*Eyrb.* 37:98)

Each aspect of comparing—the balance in equipoise, the balance tilted—was itself infected by its antithesis. In arbitrated settlement, the balancing of men and their injuries needn't always be weighted evenly. Differences in rank could be memorialized just as well as equality. And not all comparisons of living men need prompt more discord than accord. The fact that, in the passage quoted above, the comparison of men was entertaining, a topic for convivial gathering, is itself a reminder of how closely enmeshed were the sociable and unsociable, feast and feud.

The paradoxes of weighing are also played out in the native model of balanced exchange in feud. The notion of getting even, as the semantic burden of the modern English phrase "getting even" suggests, is not the most benign of sentiments, nor is it all that easy to administer as a principle of justice. For it was by getting even that one established the inviolability of one's honor, that is, by getting even, paradoxically, one person reasserted superiority relative to the other.[1] And as we pointed out in chapter 1, honor too involved a similar paradox, requiring equality among the players in the game at the same time that the object of the game was to undo the basis for equality. Similar ambiguities existed in the world of gift-exchange where getting even did not usually mean requiting like for like. One had to do something more to do honor to oneself and also to one's recipient. To these ambiguities we can add the uncertainties occasioned by the relativity of value and the shifting definitions of what precisely it was that needed to be paid back: just how was one supposed to know when measure had requited measure when there was no measure of measures?

There is thus a fair degree of consistency in the types of ambiguity in the key cultural concepts of balance, reciprocity, honor, and the comparing of men. Can we make anything of these consistent ambiguities? Do they have a life of their own independent of the academic construct that brings them to the fore? There is some reason to think so. The ethnographic record would seem to indicate a cross-cultural correlation between the values inherent in honor and the existence of feud. While not all societies who value honor will feud, few which feud won't have honor as a central cultural value.[2] And in Iceland, at least, honor was largely congruent with man-evening, the comparing of men. It just might be that the very comparing of men, that is, honor, with its inherent ambiguities, was much of what drove the feud, bearing some kind of causal relation to it. In any event, the nervous contradictions of demanding balance only to deny balance structured the meaning of a significant portion of experience in the saga world.

Honor, however, was much subtler than we are inclined to think. Available to the honorable person was an expansive range of practical activities, with more than enough room available for sharp practice, tactic, and strategy. Honor was more than just the pure heroic warrior ethic, although at root it still meant "don't tread on me." We are talking about honor among farmers, who worried about their livestock, land, and lawsuits. The particular content of honor was not the same in this setting as it was on longships. Reputations inhered in one's skill in law, in the quality of one's land and herds. Honor translated into practical advantage. It could even be practicality itself. It meant good marriages for oneself and kin; It meant active involvement in a number of exchange cycles with other people of honor, whether the exchanges were of gifts or of insult and injury. Honor, above all, meant relations of reciprocity with other honorable people. The life of honor could thus accommodate peace and peaceful resolution. This is captured lexically by the extension in the plural of Old Icelandic sœmð, "honor," to mean "compensation payment." The word thus embodies an argument on behalf of the honorableness of honorable monetary settlements, an argument that we know was made. But we also know that the bloody counterargument was still available and more than respectable in a wide range of settings. A person, after all, should not like to "carry his kin in his purse," and any waiver of blood revenge could only be honorably made if one was able to indicate one's future inviolability at the same time. It could be said that honor is the ability to make others believe that you will indeed be tough the next time, in spite of present discomfitures.

Rather than resume the substance of this book as its author, let me step back from the work and react as a reader to the society depicted here. How do we respond to it and how do we end up describing its essence? Was it violent? If so, was it more violent than other cultures? Than ours, for instance? How can we possibly know; how can we possibly measure violence anyway? Homicide rates, only the crudest of indicators at best, are not recoverable in medieval Iceland, since we know neither the number of homicides nor the number of people. Homicide rates don't begin to capture the systematic violence directed toward children, women, slaves; they don't take into account the fear of violence. And none of these things are any more measurable now than they were then. Should the measure of societal violence also take into account the acclimatization that might inure people to violence? That pain might be something universal to the human condition does not tell us if the same act causes the same amount of pain in different times and in different places. How do we factor in saga Iceland, where, apparently, verbal insult could cause somatic responses as painful as those caused by physical assault, where words could hurt more than sticks or stones? Is such a culture more violent because to the pain of blows we must add the pain of words? Or is it less violent because some pain has its origin in mental rather than physical causes? If we judge early Iceland violent, is it because the sagas appear so unembarrassed, so matter of fact about acts that appall us? Or does it seem violent because the typical reader of this book, like myself, couldn't endure the fear and anxiety we imagine we would feel at the prospect of having no state to enforce our rights for us or to protect us from those bent on enforcing their own? In other words, does their culture seem more violent because the responsibility for actually doing acts of violence was more evenly distributed than it is now, there being no state agents to delegate the dirty work to or to claim a monopoly on the dirty work? One reader of this book in draft offered the view that if he had had doubts about the idea of progress in history before, they had just been dispelled. He was troubled by what he felt was the amorality of my account, the sympathy he believed I felt for the people and their culture, a violent and anarchic society. In his view, if this is what the minimalist state would tend toward, then that constituted a refutation of the justifiability of the minimalist state.

But could we not also describe the culture as fairly stable with violence rather constrained or at least almost always constrainable to reasonable levels? There are still scholars willing to accept a soft-on-feud view, which sees it as a "cohesive force" in Black-Michaud's terms, or sees it as promoting nonviolent stability by being so replete with conflict that conflict itself ends up in gridlock; this is the paradox of Gluckman's "peace in the feud." There is also the discounting some readers will supply for the fact that the legal and narrative sources used to construct this history would tend to be biased in favor of good stories, hence violent stories. We don't even have to discount that much. The sagas do it for us, letting us know that the violence of feud was not a daily occurrence (although we know next to nothing of violence within the household). If we add up time and killings in these stories we find that the impression of excessive violence is often a function of the compression of narrative time. The frequent saga refrains of "nothing happened that year" or "everything was quiet for a time" condenses long periods of time into very few words, the time in which animals were tended, hay was mowed, cloth was woven, etc. The sagas do not show people *continually* living with the anticipation of violence, rape, or expropriation that many American urban dwellers must live with daily.

How would a feminist react to early Iceland—a libertarian, a communitarian? I can't suppose to speak on their behalf, but I would suspect that there is no reason why the Iceland I have painted couldn't equally disappoint and appeal to them without any necessary correlation between the politics of the reader and the favor or disfavor they might choose to bestow upon the culture. The saga world is mainly a world of men, but women figure larger in it than they figure in many societies before or since. Jurally and actually, they were less disabled than their continental counterparts of equivalent social ranges. Above all, the sagas did not like weak women any more than they liked weak men. Intelligence, health, beauty, and toughness were attributed in a surprisingly gender-neutral fashion in this literature. Virginity was a nonissue. The sagas did not put women on pedestals. It was women who put men there and then goaded them into maintaining their precarious stance aloft if they showed an inclination to descend. What a refreshing relief to meet the women of the sagas after a lifetime of reading of romantic heroines, or of Marys and Eves. But if Icelandic women may have had it better than did their more degraded sisters on the continent, this, for some, is still no reason to credit Icelandic society for such small favors. The world of the sagas was enough of a man's world that I could not have adopted nonsexist pronouns without seriously misrepresenting the reality I was trying to reconstruct. When I use the male pronoun it means a man, not mankind. And one might suspect that among the class of people the sagas are not especially interested in, the servants and the poor, the lot of women was somewhat worse than the lot of the men, if only because the women had more to fear from their male counterparts in the way of violence than the men did from women.

Libertarians might have reason to be suspicious of a society that draws them like a siren. Here they have a society with no coercive state seeking to redistribute wealth or entitlements. Here rights are for the most part privately created and all are privately enforced. But "private" enforcement does not mean much when there is no "public" alternative for it to be compared to. Can the "private" as an analytic category exist unless it is paired with and distinguished from "public?" The very pairing itself is a part of the history and theory of the state; it only makes sense in the context of the coercive state. There was thus no "private" enforcement of rights in Iceland. There was simply enforcement by people seeking aid from the various overlapping social solidarities they could claim connection with. And none of these solidarities, except perhaps the chieftain-thingmen association, had as its central motive the enforcement of rights. Kin groupings and household groupings were more complexly motivated. At the same time there is a suggestion that the reason there is no state is because there is not enough wealth to support it, not because, as some libertarians might suppose, of objections to certain necessarily redistributive aspects of the state (cf. e.g., Nozick 1974). It is not the have-nots, after all, who invented the state. The first steps toward state formation in Iceland were made by churchmen, who had the model of the Roman church and Rome itself available to them and by the big men intent on imitating Norwegian royal style. Early state formation, I would guess, surely tended to involve redistributions, not from rich to poor, however, but from poor to rich, from weak to strong.

People of communitarian tendencies also have reason to be attracted and repelled. The attraction is the limited role of lordship, the active participation of large numbers of free people (mostly men, but women too in a nontrivial way) in decision making within and outside the household. The economy barely knew the existence of markets. Social relations preceded economic relations. The nexus of household, kin, Thing, even enmity, more than the nexus of cash, bound people to each other. The lack of extensive economic differentiation supported a weakly differentiated class system. And if low societywide productivity meant some material deprivations, these deprivations were more evenly distributed than they would be once state institutions also had to be maintained. On the grimmer side, there were still startling disparities in access to resources. Men were net beneficiaries of women's productive and reproductive capabilities. In the Settlement Age the free could appropriate the labor and lives of slaves. And if the juridical slave disappeared sometime in the twelfth century it can hardly be said that the lot of later day laborers and vagabonds could have been much better. If we were troubled some by measuring violence across time and space, how do we measure things like quanta of misery? Was an impoverished Icelandic tenant any better off than an Angevin serf of the eleventh and twelfth century? The Icelandic tenant seemed to endure a more ecologically and less socially imposed precariousness than the Angevin serf. But do the same presumably pathetic average caloric intakes mean something different when one is juridically free or when one is bound? The serf, we may presume, suffered greater chagrin, akin to the torment of Tantalus, seeing most of the fruits of his labors consumed by others within his sight and just beyond his reach. We still think, intuitively, that there is something more immoral about starving in a wealthy society than starving in a poor one. The serf also suffered more for the feuding style of the counts and castellans. The Icelandic feuding style, at least until the last decades of the commonwealth, and unlike its French analogue (see White

1988), tended to spare the productive units of the poor. But such small virtues have their costs too. Was the benefit of a *relatively* (I must emphasize relatively) nonexploitive society bought at the price of production levels so low that there was little to expropriate? To the extent that answers depend on hard numerical data we will never know.

Those people committed to the rule of law will have to find in medieval Iceland an interesting limiting case. The often unquestioned assumptions that law depends on the state either for its existence or for its efficacy might have to be justified more fully. In any event, theoretical musings on the origins of law and the state of nature might benefit from knowledge of this remarkable instance of social and legal form in the absence of a coercive state. Law in Iceland was pervasive, complex, purported to be regular and uniform in application over the ranges it claimed for itself. Although some of the claims sounded rather hollow, as when it purported to prohibit out-of-court settlements in serious cases unless leave to settle had previously been granted by the Lǫgrétta (*Grágás* Ia 174, II 371), it still recognized its limits in the face of blood revenge, which it countenanced within fairly generous limits. The limits of law might well have been clearer to these people than they are to us, because they would not have been tempted to confuse the category of law with the category of the state and not because there is any necessary reason why law as law should be more limited without the state than with it. And could it be that the prospects for law's legitimacy were better in this minimal setting because law might have been perceived as less a vehicle for enforcing the interests of those whose particular interests the state primarily advanced? Did the powerful in Iceland control law in the same way that they control it in state settings? Or are the mechanisms of dominance as regards law substantially different? Whatever the limits of Icelandic law, and despite the lack of state enforcement, we have seen that people learned law, cared to have it on their side, used the legal forums, and bargained in the law's shadow. The Icelandic example reveals the force of law as a legitimating entity in a society in which legitimacy was something that was not firmly fixed or complacently assumed.

Incurable romantics might find saga Iceland to have a kind of gruff quaintness that is not without considerable charm. I must admit I fear the undermining of my critical sensibility by the attractiveness of the saga style, with its ability to imbue homely action with a sense of the heroic, with its ability to praise imperceptibly and hence subtly the honorable life well lived. Many of the men and women I admire—Skarphedin, Egil, Bergthora, Hallgerd, Hvamm-Sturla, his son Sighvat—I must remind myself probably would make worse company in life than they do in books where their dullnesses are suppressed and their excesses mediated by the considerable skills of the saga writer. A significant portion of their charm is their absence, their distance in time. The people I have named were all intelligent and witty, but Skarphedin, even when properly behaved as indeed he usually was, inspired uneasiness in his closest friends, and Egil, great poet that he was, was also something of a psychopath. While a modern might find some cause for nervous laughter in his purposefully vomiting on the face of a niggardly host, if not in his gouging out the unfortunate man's eye a few hours later, the fact is that this was the kind of man whom anyone ending up in academia was unlikely to seek the opportunity to socialize with. My own romantic propensities are well checked by a firm belief that it would have been my luck to have lived as poor Skæring Hroaldsson did, whom we met in the preface of this book: a minor cleric, for a while without hand, and finally without head.

# ABBREVIATIONS

Frequently cited sagas and other primary sources are abbreviated in the text as follows:

| | |
|---|---|
| *Aron* | *Arons saga Hjǫrleifssonar* |
| *Auðun* | *Auðunar þáttr Vestfirzka* |
| *Band.* | *Bandamanna saga* |
| *Bjarn.* | *Bjarnar saga Hítdœlakappa* |
| *DI* | *Diplomatarium Islandicum* |
| *Drop.* | *Droplaugarsona saga* |
| *Egil* | *Egils saga Skalla-Grímssonar* |
| *Eyrb.* | *Eyrbyggja saga* |
| *Finnb.* | *Finnboga saga* |
| *Fóst.* | *Fóstbrœðra saga* |
| *G.dýri* | *Guðmundar saga dýra* |
| *Gísli* | *Gísla saga Súrssonar* |
| *Glúma* | *Víga-Glúms saga* |
| *Grett.* | *Grettis saga Ásmundarsonar* |
| *Grœn.* | *Grœnlendinga þáttr* |
| *Gunnl.* | *Gunnlaugs saga ormstungu* |
| *Gunn. þ.* | *Gunnars þáttr Þiðrandabana* |
| *Hafl.* | *Þorgils saga ok Hafliða* |
| *Hallfr.* | *Hallfreðar saga* |
| *Háv.* | *Hávarðar saga Ísfirðings* |
| *Heið.* | *Heiðarvíga saga* |
| *Hrafnk.* | *Hrafnkels saga Freysgoða* |
| *Hrafn Sv.* | *Hrafns saga Sveinbjarnarsonar*; cited to the *Sturlunga saga* version when followed by "St.," otherwise to independent version |
| *Hœn.* | *Hœnsa-Þóris saga* |
| *Hungr.* | *Hungrvaka* |
| *Íslb.* | *Íslendingabók* |
| *Íslend.* | *Íslendinga saga* |
| *Land.* | *Landnámabók* |
| *Lax.* | *Laxdœla saga* |
| *Ljós.* | *Ljósvetninga saga* |
| *Njála* | *Brennu-Njáls saga* |

| | |
|---|---|
| *Oddav.* | *Oddaverja þáttr* |
| *Ǫlk.* | *Ǫlkofra þáttr* |
| *Pál.* | *Páls saga byskups* |
| *Prest.* | *Prestssaga Guðmundar góða* |
| *Reyk.* | *Reykdœla saga* |
| *Sturla* | *Sturlu saga* |
| *Svín.* | *Svínfellinga saga* |
| *Vall.* | *Valla-Ljóts saga* |
| *Vápn.* | *Vápnfirðinga saga* |
| *Vatn.* | *Vatnsdœla saga* |
| *þ.* | *þáttr* |
| *Þórð.* | *Þórðar saga kakala* |
| *Þorg. sk.* | *Þorgils saga skarða* |
| *Þorst. hv.* | *Þorsteins saga hvíta* |
| *Þorst. stang.* | *Þorsteins þáttr stangarhǫggs* |

## Other Abbreviations

| | |
|---|---|
| ModE | Modern English |
| ModI | Modern Iceland |
| OE | Old English |
| OI | Old Icelandic |
| OIr | Old Irish |
| ON | Old Norse |
| PrmGmc | Primitive Germanic |

# NOTES

## Prologue

1. For a discussion of the effects of Christianity on the style of dying see Sveinsson (1953, 78–82).

## Chapter One

1. For a useful and more detailed account, in fact the best account available to date, see Jóhannesson (1974); see also Hastrup (1985). Brief introductions abound; for a competent recent one abstracted mostly from Jóhannesson, see Sawyer (1982b).

2. The arrival of three such characters in Cornwall in 891 was considered as strange an event to the writer of the *Anglo-Saxon Chronicle* as the appearance of a comet a short time after:

> In this year . . . three Irishmen came to King Alfred in a boat
> without oars, from Ireland, whence they had stolen away be-
> cause they wished for the love of God to be on a pilgrimage,
> they cared not where. The boat in which they set out was
> made of two and one-half hides, and they had taken with them
> provisions for a week and after a week they came to land in
> Cornwall and soon went to King Alfred. . . . And in the same
> year after Easter . . . appeared the star which in Latin is called
> *cometa.* . . . (Garmonsway 1953, 82)

3. The numbers in the source are given in round "long" hundreds (i.e., 120) of seven, ten, nine, and twelve hundreds respectively. By expanding them into decimals, I have given them a spurious look of precision they in fact do not have. Estimates of the population of medieval Iceland are all ultimately derived from Gizur's enumeration, but are no more than rough guesses. These estimates seem high when compared to the 50,358 souls counted in the first comprehensive census taken in 1703 (Gunnarsson 1980a, 4). But that census was preceded and prompted by a decade of severe famine in which mortality greatly exceeded fertility. And when we consider that many regions of Europe did not reattain population levels of the early

fourteenth century until the end of the eighteenth, the Icelandic numbers and guesses do not seem too absurd.

4. *Kristni saga* (14:30) tells that one of the ships that was wrecked had place (*rúm*) for twenty-seven pair of oars. The ship probably received special notice because of its substantial size. It is, however, by no means certain that the ship had a crew to match the number of rowing positions. The number of *rúm* was a conventional way of noting a ship's length and need not necessarily correspond with the number of people taking passage on it. The number of unexpected winter guests could have ranged anywhere from five hundred to twelve hundred with the lower limit having somewhat more plausibility than the higher. We are in all likelihood talking about no more than eight hundred extra people.

5. I place "public" in quotes to signal my uneasiness with a category that brings with it many anachronistic and misleading associations. The public/private distinction must mean very different things in the context of stateless or weak state systems than in the context of the bureaucratic state. In Iceland, public meant the world outside the household. It did not indicate a sphere of governmental activity as opposed to a sphere of nongovernmental "private" activity. The use of either public or private in this work is meant only to indicate loosely a difference in the location and intended scope of relevant actions, that is, whether they are intra- or extrahousehold or intended to engage the reaction of few rather than many.

6. The polity that existed from 930-1262 has been variously called a commonwealth, republic, or freestate. All are anachronistic. "Freestate" suggests the existence of statelike institutions that did not in fact exist; "republic" suggests a Mediterranean analogue, which is more misleading than instructive. I opt for commonwealth only because, for the modern American at least, it comes without any greatly misleading associations. Its slightly archaic quality, if not serving us well, nevertheless serves us better than the alternatives.

7. There are several obscure indications that there were to be Quarter courts that met at Quarter Things, but it is uncertain to what extent these were ever convened. See *Grágás* II 356; *Glúma* 24:82; and Maurer (1910, 324–25).

8. *Grágás* is explicit as to the number of judges that sat on the courts at the local Things (Ia 98). The exact number of judges as well as the arrangement for their selection for the Quarter courts at the Allthing is less certain, but is deemed by reasonable inference to have been as indicated in the text to which this note is appended (see Jóhannesson 1974, 66). The ancient and full chieftaincies are explained by the laws as those "which existed when there were three Things in each Quarter and three chieftains in each Thing" (*Grágás* Ia 38). This is somewhat difficult, but it is usually accepted that the designation was meant to distinguish those chieftaincies clearly in existence prior to the division of the country into quarters in the 960s from those created at that time as part of the establishment of a fourth local Thing in the north and the subsequent creations of additional chieftaincies

in the other Quarters to equalize representation in the Lǫgrétta (see further Sigfússon 1960).

9. Recall that only the holders of "ancient and full chieftaincies" had the power to name people to the Quarter courts. See preceding note.

10. A coarse woolen cloth used as a measure of value and medium of exchange.

11. The usual explanation for the development of a unified law is a functional one. The settlers did not all come from the same "laws" in Norway and the confusion of such legal diversity provided the impetus for the idea of one law for the new colony (see Jóhannesson 1974, 37). It should be noted, however, that there is evidence that district Things might establish price lists that were to govern the maximum allowable price on various goods bought and sold in the district (see Gelsinger 1981, 39–44; DI I 315–17; and also Grágás Ib 72–73).

12. As far as we know, social and economic arrangements were the same throughout the island. But the uniformity might well be a function of the blurriness of the evidence. There do not appear to have been regional dialects in the middle ages and this confirms the view to be constructed in chapter 4 regarding the mobility of the population. (It is part of modern Icelandic ideology that the Icelandic language is undifferentiated geographically and socially and that those people who show "dialect" are said to be ill with such contagion as the dread "dative disease" [G. Pálsson 1989]). Still there is a mildly disturbing detail in Ljós. 8:47 in which a person from the Eastfjords is said to resemble the men who come from the west from Halfdanartongue. The reference might be to nothing more than a fortuitous physiognomic likeness to the kin group that lives at Halfdanartongue, but it also might indicate local distinctive variations in dress or manner.

13. On the conversion see generally Jóhannesson (1974, 124–38); also Aðalsteinsson (1978) and Strömbäck (1975).

14. Kirsten Hastrup (1982, 1984), in a convincing argument, believes that an Icelandic ethnicity, as distinguished from a general Norwegian or Scandinavian one, had arisen by the early twelfth century. In any event, the family sagas of the thirteenth century depend on it, and it seems that one of their chief purposes is to assert the uniqueness of the Icelandic experience and the Icelanders' consciousness of it. See also Andersson and Miller (1989, 236n197).

15. For various treatments of chieftains' wealth, see Byock (1988, 77–102), Karlsson (1980), and Þorláksson (1979, 1982).

16. The stórbœndr generally were those churchowning farmers who had access to tithe income. In the last years of the commonwealth, we see arbitration awards explicitly reflecting the ability of people to pay. In one award stórbœndr were distinguished from those farmers eligible to pay the Thing attendance tax, the former assessed five hundreds, the latter three hundreds, for their offenses (Þórð. 8:17–18).

17. A hrísungr is the child of the bushes (hrís); a hornungr the child of the corner (horn), a bæsingr the child of the cattle stall (báss). All these

designations partake of an underlying symbolic construct that contrasts the human world situated inside and at the fire with an outside world of outcasts or animals. A child born of a slave and free woman, though meriting no colorful status term, was also ineligible for heirship (*Grágás* Ia 224, II 68), but apparently was free (Karras 1988, 51). The laws, however, do not mention the status of the offspring of a free man and a slave (see further Karras 1988, 117, 172).

18. I confine myself to a brief social-structural treatment of honor suitable for the limited purposes of this introduction. I have thus not included a discussion of the relevant terminology. I sketch here a rough model that, in fact, is not quite up to representing the situational subtleties and the shifting contents of honor's possible significances. The topic merits a book of its own. Some qualifications to the model will emerge in the chapters that follow. The social economy of honor has been ably studied and discussed in the anthropological mode by Bourdieu (1966), Pitt-Rivers (1977), and Dresch (1989). I am generally indebted to their work.

19. In the example in chapter 2 the gain in honor by both principal adversaries appears to have been funded entirely by the failures of lesser-ranked members of their own constituencies: old men, women, servants, and clients (on the significance of this, see p. 75). I do not deny that in an honor-driven society many social interactions can be bounded in such a way to produce utilities greater than zero (cf. Schelling 1984, 270–76). Saga Iceland, for instance, valued the amicable resolution of disputes (see chapter 8). It is my point, however, that in a society in which honor is highly valued such local optima are just that, local.

20. Consider in this regard the seventeenth-century observation of the earl of Derby: "Undertake no suit against a poor man . . . for then you make him your equal" (cited in Herzog 1989, 132).

21. I do not mean to suggest that it was impossible for someone to rise through the ranks. The loyal and courageous slave might win honor as well as freedom (e.g., *Lax.* 16:36–37), but these were exceptional cases.

22. *Landnámabók* is a remarkable and problematic source. Presumably compiled in the twelfth century, it survives in recensions dating from the last quarter of the thirteenth century. The book describes the land claims of some four hundred of the original settlers. It is a repository of much genealogical lore and local tradition. And while it is reasonable to assume that much of the material it contains was invented or molded to legitimate landholding arrangements at the time of its composition, it is generally believed that it also preserves much reliable information about the settlement period. (See Benediktsson 1968, 1969, and Rafnsson 1974).

23. On exposure of infants in Iceland compare Clover (1988) and Boswell (1988, 285–91). On the significance of the prohibition against eating horsemeat, see Á. Pálsson (1932), Steffensen (1967–68), and Boswell (1988, 289–90).

24. *Eyrbyggja saga* (49:136) accounts (fancifully it seems) for church-building activity immediately following the conversion in the following

manner: "People were quite eager to build churches because the clergy promised that a person would have the right to room in heaven for as many people as might stand in the church he had had built."

25. The one-percent property tax assumes, clearly, a base return on capital of ten percent, which in fact was the legal interest rate (Grágás Ib 140, II 213); see generally KLNM (18:287–91).

26. Nevertheless, the law required the person who possessed the church to have written evidence of any donations to his church and he was further prohibited from converting any of the property under pain of lesser outlawry at the suit of anyone who wished to prosecute (Grágás Ia 15, II 17). These provisions in no way interfered with the transmission of the church and its endowment to the heirs of the present possessor. The church inventories at times explicitly indicate that the property was to pass by inheritance or was to provide for the support of the owner's dependents (Hastrup 1985, 194, citing DI I 278, 180, 203).

27. Those who became monks seemed to lead celibate lives. Although one monastery (Thingeyrar) played an important role in the development of historical writing, the six or seven houses did not figure prominently in disputes or in the networks of power. (See further Jóhannesson 1974, 192–200, KLNM 8:544–46 and Stefánsson 1975, 81–85).

28. Thorlak did not have the apparatus available to administer the churches he claimed. Those churches ceded to him were granted back as fiefs with practical control still remaining with the prior owner (see, e.g., Oddav. 18:281).

29. See Hastrup (1985, 228–32) for a discussion of the effects the new order had on the organizing metaphors of the culture.

## Chapter Two

1. Konungsbók is conventionally cited to the pages in Finsen's 1852 edition as Grágás Ia and Ib; Staðarhólsbók is cited to his 1879 edition as Grágás II. The relationship between the manuscripts is unclear. Both manuscripts share many identical provisions and a substantial number of other provisions show only minor scribal and editorial variation between them. But the arrangement of the provisions varies considerably and each manuscript contains substantial material not found in the other. The conventional view is that the manuscripts are derived from a common exemplar, assumed conjecturally to be the scroll compiled in 1117 by the group of experts under the direction of Haflidi Masson (see p. 224). In general Konungsbók is less circumstantial than Staðarhólsbók, but it contains provisions, notably Baugatal (see p. 144), that do not appear in Staðarhólsbók. Texts of more fragmentary manuscripts duplicating provisions in the two main codices are assembled in Finsen (1883), conventionally cited as Grágás III.

2. According to Grágás, a new law's proper enactment required that it be announced at the Law Rock the first summer by the Lawspeaker. New laws

were to be valid for only three years unless they were included in the Law-speaker's recital of the laws every third year (*Grágás* Ia 37; cf. III 443). It is conceivable that expired new laws found their way into the *Grágás* manuscripts. See also p. 231 and chapter 7, n. 23.

3. On the sagas and saga scholarship, see generally Andersson (1964, 1967), Clover (1982), and especially Clover (1985), which provides a comprehensive review of the main scholarly debates and trends that have occupied saga literary studies since 1964. For a review of earlier scholarship see Andersson (1964). Schach (1984) is a readable and reasonable introduction to the family sagas. Bragason (1986) provides a competent introduction to the problems in *Sturlunga saga* scholarship. The classic comprehensive literary critical treatment of the sagas remains W. P. Ker's brilliant *Epic and Romance*, the first edition of which appeared nearly a century ago.

4. One should also note the existence of the kings' sagas (*konungasögur*). These are Icelandic productions but are devoted to non-Icelandic events. As their name implies, they are largely biographies of Scandinavian kings. Nevertheless, as a matter of literary history, the kings' sagas are inextricably bound up with the family sagas. Some family sagas and many shorter stories of Icelanders (*þættir*), for instance, are found in manuscript environments interwoven with the histories of Norwegian kings. Unlike the family sagas, which are all, with one possible exception, anonymous, as indeed are most of the sagas of the *Sturlunga* compilation, the authors of a good portion of the kings' sagas are known. For a discussion see Andersson (1985) and Clover (1982).

5. Nevertheless, attempts have been made to distinguish them in this way. W. P. Ker, for instance, would classify the family sagas as epic and the secular contemporary sagas as history (1908, 246–69).

6. A few of the family sagas—such as *Grett.* and *Háv.*—are believed to have been first written as late as the fourteenth century. One of the contemporary sagas—*Svínfellinga saga*—might be as late as 1300. For an introduction to the subject of dating the sagas see Sveinsson (1958) and for a review of recent developments see Clover (1985, 247–49).

7. Part of *Hrafns saga Sveinbjarnarsonar* is included in the *Sturlunga* compilation, but the complete saga is preserved separately. *Arons saga Hjǫrleifssonar* is not included in *Sturlunga*. See section I.B. of Works Cited for the sagas of the *Sturlunga* compilation and for a recent discussion of the stylistics of the compilation see Bragason (1986).

8. The sagas in *Sturlunga saga* set in the twelfth century are *Þorgils saga ok Hafliða*, *Sturlu saga*, and *Guðmundar saga dýra*.

9. The Icelandic school, most frequently associated with the name of Sigurður Nordal, is a common designation used to indicate both the scholars responsible for producing the fine Íslensk fornrit editions of the sagas (1933– ) and also the type of scholarship evidenced by the lengthy introductions to these volumes. The work of the school was distinguished by its attention to traditional methods of source and manuscript criticism. Questions of relations among manuscripts, literary relations among saga texts, dating, questions of authorship, took precedence over sociological or artistic

matters. The school represented orthodox literary opinion for some thirty years until the emergence, in the 1960s and 1970s, of work that focused on the formal qualities of saga structure and its narrative style. These writers—mostly German and American—also rejected the claim of the Icelandic school that the sagas were composed much in the matter of novels in the thirteenth century. They postulated connections between the extant sagas and earlier oral forms, or they sought to connect the sagas with continental medieval literature. Icelandic scholars, too, are starting to reassess some of the claims of the Nordalian school. Óskar Halldórsson (1976), among others, makes a case for not being so hasty to reject the sagas as repositories of genuinely antique material preserved in oral tradition; see also Kristjánsson (1986, 196) and Ólason (1987). Again see Clover (1985) for a comprehensive review of this scholarship.

10. The history of early Icelandic social and legal history is not the happiest one. On the positive side, masterful work was accomplished by scholars working in the philological and legal historical tradition of the Rechtsschule in the latter half of the nineteenth and early decades of the twentieth century. The works of Finsen, von Amira, and Maurer remain valuable to the student of legal history, even if some of the questions that obsessed them seem strangely inconsequential now. To the modern these scholars seem a little too devoted to rules and juristic categories, their instincts irrevocably jural rather than social. Such, however, was not the case with Andreas Heusler whose inspired works on law in the sagas remain to date the best works on Icelandic legal and social history, even if his main thesis about the genuine antiquity of family saga legal process cannot be maintained (Heusler 1911, 1912). But Heusler's historical writing produced no school of followers and to this day no social or legal history of Iceland comparable to its sophistication, insightfulness, and scope has been produced. The last ten years, however, have seen the beginning of renewed historical interest in saga society and the social context of the sagas. The first attempt was by Preben Meulengracht Sørensen (1977). Other Danes followed, notably the anthropologist Kirsten Hastrup (1985). American scholars too have moved in this direction, although the fundamental sensibilities of most of these scholars (Jochens and perhaps myself excepted) are literary rather than sociological. See Andersson (1984), Andersson and Miller (1989), Byock (1982, 1988), Clover (1986, 1988), Gade (1986, 1988), Jochens (1980, 1985), and Miller (1983a, 1983b, 1984, etc.). I hope not to have offended Jochens, a Dane, and Gade, a Norwegian, by including them, but they qualify for the list as members of American academe. The cultural history of saga Iceland, to the extent it can be separated from pan-Germanic and literary history, has not been an especially fruitful area either. The field is still dominated by Grønbech's classic study of Teutonic culture (1932, Danish orig. 1909–12). Excellent contributions to this field were made by Gurevich in the 1960s and most recently the work of Hastrup (1985) promises renewed sophisticated activity. Cf. also Steblin-Kamenskij (1973).

The paucity of social historical scholarship of early Iceland can be explained by several factors: (1) Icelandic social history was never likely to attract great numbers of researchers. (2) The discredit of the Rechtsschule style as a consequence of Nazism did something to discourage non-Icelandic researchers from the field. It had the dual effect of distancing Scandinavians from the interests of German scholarship and of delegitimating German interest in early Scandinavia. (3) Surely, the debate over the "historicity" of the family sagas was also a factor. Scholars associated with the Icelandic school viewed the family sagas as fictional creations of the thirteenth century and they rejected them as valid historical sources for the study of the Saga Age some two to three centuries earlier. If the family sagas contained anything of use to the historian, it was for the thirteenth century, the time in which they were written, not for the time they were written about. The criticism is sensible enough and one to which I largely subscribe, but the claim did not lead to an improvement in the quality of social historical scholarship of the thirteenth century. Some of the reason was that Icelandic scholars really never were interested in social history. To them history was biographical and political and so the question of the historicity of the family sagas centered solely on the issue of whether they were accurate chronicles of actual events. (Jon Jóhannesson [1974] is a partial exception and evinces interest in economic history and some social matters. More recent Icelandic historical work has become more socially oriented but has never really broken with the biographical, political, and institutional orientation of the native historical style; see, e.g., Karlsson [1972, 1980], Þorláksson [1979, 1982, 1986]). Since the family sagas were unreliable political histories, Icelandic historians turned to the bishop's sagas and *Sturlunga saga*, which continued to be culled to construct the political history of the twelfth and thirteenth centuries. But the narratives of the contemporary sagas are no less fictional than the family sagas. The bishops' sagas adopt the conventions of hagiography and the contemporary sagas use the same conventions of style and form as the family sagas (see Bragason 1986). Certainly those contemporary sagas set in the twelfth century raise the same questions about the present-ness of narrative content as the family sagas do. And the events of those sagas in the *Sturlunga* compilation, which were composed fast on the events they describe, are "no more verifiable than the events of the family sagas" since the only evidence of these events is *Sturlunga* itself (Clover 1985, 255). The relationship, in short, of each genre of saga to the "real" world, as well as the relationship between the "fictional" and "historical," is more complex than the terms of the debate allowed. For those interested in pursuing the matter beyond the discussion I have given it, see Andersson (1964, 41–50) and Clover (1985).

11. Still, some very able historians (I have Peter Sawyer primarily in mind) stick fast to hard evidence, preferring archaeology to the sagas, granting artifact status to coprolite but not to written words. Such preferences have baffled historians in related fields. Patrick Wormald (1982, 129–31), for instance, wonders why historians of the Viking Age fall "back in despair on the archaeologists" rather than make use of the Scandinavian saga sources; he sees in their overly pessimistic view of their sources a "failure of [scholarly] nerve." Wormald is directing his argument to those who are reticent

about using late sources to study periods significantly earlier than their composition. He apparently would find the failure of nerve even harder to fathom if these sources were being used to reconstruct the society that produced them. See also John Boswell's reasoned discussion and defense of literary sources for social historical work (1988, 1–24).

12. One learns quickly to discredit certain excesses demanded by the heroic style. Heroes must triumph against impossible odds and be slow to give up the ghost when they are finally overwhelmed. The occasional ghost and the ubiquitous presence of prophetic dreams might trouble the modern somewhat, but it should be clear that such excesses also have a story to tell about beliefs and values.

13. For a general introduction to this literature see Roberts (1979); see also Gulliver (1963) and Comaroff and Roberts (1981).

14. There was a category of literary artifice recognizable by twelfth- and thirteenth-century Icelanders as artifice, but it did not include the family and contemporary sagas. Sagas of the more fantastic and fabulous variety were deemed *lygisǫgur*, lying sagas; see *Hafl.* 10:27 and Foote (1984, 65–83).

15. I am well aware of how culture-bound the notion of plausibility may be, and there is always some risk that that type of plausibility that is simply a function of consistency can also be the plausibility of the paranoid. Thus the importance of comparative materials. They obviously cannot help tell us precisely what happened in Iceland, but they can help the researcher get a fix on the quality of some of his or her judgments that are based on the surviving Icelandic evidence.

16. The family sagas, for instance, show significantly less mutilation and maiming than *Sturlunga* while at the same time their descriptions of combat show the hero's sword slicing through torsos like a hot knife through butter. High mortality in combats pitting small numbers against each other is in keeping with the grander heroics of the family sagas. Gunnar and his two brothers in *Njáls saga* (61–63:153–59), a family saga, are thus able to kill fourteen of the thirty attackers who ambush them, whereas the decisive encounter between Sturla and Einar in 1171 in *Sturlu saga*, a contemporary saga, pitted fifteen against sixteen and yielded only four dead, three on one side, one on the other (20–21:89–94). Some commentators believe that the much more frequent depiction of women in the family sagas as grand goaders and inciters with considerable power in determining their marriages is a fiction of the thirteenth century reflecting clerical influences (Heller 1958; Jochens 1980, 1986). For my contrary views on this matter see pp. 212–14. It is nevertheless incontrovertible that women do not figure as prominently in *Sturlunga* as they do in the family sagas. It is also true that *Sturlunga* shows looser marriage arrangements than the family sagas. While concubinage elicits no sense of abnormality or cause for censure in the family sagas, it is still less frequently in evidence than it is in *Sturlunga* where it is widespread.

17. There are other similarities noted by Heusler in the style of law and disputing in the family and contemporary sagas. A partial list includes the

susceptibility of legal rules to negotiability, the primacy of kin obligation to legal obligation when these two conflicted, the tendency of leaders to be punished more leniently than their followers. Also no evidence exists in either type of saga that the *Grágás* rules regarding *vígt*, "the right to kill" (see p. 192) were adhered to, etc. (Heusler 1912, 22, 24, 26, 31; Ingvarsson 1970, 74). In both sources lawsuits are considered as tactics in the context of feud; summoning is a dangerous procedure; and full outlawry only appears as a consequence of legal judgment, never as an element of arbitrated settlements. Significant too is that the ratios of different types of sanctions administered are virtually the same in both sources (Heusler 1912, 62, 72, 81–82).

18. The sagas, both family and contemporary, have views on what constitutes a life well-lived, or a character worth emulating. There is an exemplary quality to many saga accounts. But I do not find this especially troublesome, since the sagas, carefully read, also tend to provide the bases that allow us to recognize the exemplary when we see it. We are seldom totally without any basis for making reasoned judgments on these matters, even if we must proceed warily and with somewhat limited goals.

19. In general, Heusler's study comparing the feud in the family sagas and *Sturlunga* sagas finds more continuity than change, despite his efforts to accent the differences at the expense of similarities (see Andersson 1964, 44). If Heusler had distinguished between those contemporary sagas set in the twelfth century and those set in the thirteenth, many of the differences he discovered, both technical and substantive, would have been confined to the sagas describing thirteenth-century events. It is also easier to note variation than it is to note likeness, for small likenesses are distinctly less salient than small differences. I list a sample of the differences in addition to those already noted in the text: Raiding as a means of discomfiting the opposition is much more prevalent in all *Sturlunga* (see Heusler 1912, 30–34). More technically, the contemporary sagas show people being compelled to swear oaths, a rather rare procedure in the family sagas (27–28). A procedure noted in the laws of appointing an "oddman" for breaking deadlocks among arbitrators is confirmed by one example in *Sturlunga*, but nowhere in the family sagas. There is also greater evidence of forbearing and forgiving legal claims (56), but only the sparest evidence of *óhelgi* claims (see below chapter 6, n. 16) (36). There are other very technical legal differences of no great consequence that I pass over. The effects of idealization do not explain variations like these. The past, for instance, is no more golden for not having had evidence of "oddmen" or for having had more *óhelgi* claims than the present. Such differences between the two genres of saga may actually mark the preservation of genuinely antique knowledge.

20. The translation is my own, although I have consulted and adopted readings from Hermann Pálsson's translation in *Hrafnkel's Saga and Other Stories* (1971b, 72–81). For earlier comments on and explications of the story see Pálsson (1971a, 75–79), Schach (1977), and de Vries (1967, 448–49).

21. Jón Jóhannesson, the editor of the standard edition, bases his dating

on the genealogies that are appended to the end of the story. He assumes that the story is later than the death of the last living person listed there who died in 1241 (Jóhannesson 1950, xxxiii). For the *terminus ad quem* he assumes the genealogy would have included a certain one of Bjarni's descendants who became the bishop of Skálholt in 1269 had the story been written after that date. The dating assumes that the genealogy was not an interpolation or artificially truncated. It is, however, likely that the story is later than *Vápnfirðinga saga*, dated in a similarly impressionistic manner to 1200–40 (Jóhannesson 1950, xxvi–vii), with which it shares one of its main characters—Bjarni of Hof. The story assumes the reader is quite familiar with Bjarni and his history. He is thus introduced without genealogy, which is very unusual for a central saga character of chieftain rank, and several significant allusions in the story depend on a knowledge of Bjarni's prior kin troubles and his fight at Bodvarsdale, which are dealt with in *Vápnfirðinga*. The social concerns registered in the saga are consistent with any date from roughly 1225–1270.

22. Thorarin and Thorstein make no clearly identifiable appearances in other sagas.

23. As is clear from the story and also from *Vápnfirðinga saga*, Bjarni is a chieftain. It is not clear, however, that Thorstein or Thorarin are his thingmen, although they would have found it difficult not to be since they lived so close to Bjarni. There is a tone of exclusiveness to the only reference to Bjarni's thingmen in the story that does not seem to include Thorstein: "Your thingmen don't think there's much support to be looked for from you when you leave these things unavenged." But had Thorstein been attached to another chieftain, it is quite likely that Thorstein would have sought to involve him in the case, or, for that matter, that Bjarni would have preferred to deal directly with his chieftain. On balance it seems that Thorstein is Bjarni's thingman.

24. Benches usually ran down the long sides of the main farmhouse room. They provided seating for meals and sleeping platforms at night for household members.

25. The reading is conjectural. There is a lacuna of about three words length in the manuscript that is sensibly emended thus: [*ok hvárt bœta*] *muntu þá vilja yfir*, which, strictly speaking, should be rendered "and then whether you will be willing to compensate for it." I have purposely let the request for compensation be general rather than have it refer specifically to the second alternative in Thorstein's question. This is somewhat tendentious, but I admit to being influenced by the laws that would require compensation in the case of unintentional damage also.

26. The suit would have been properly brought at the local Thing in Bjarni's district or at the Allthing (*Grágás* II 356). There was a district Thing in Sunnudale but according to *Vápnfirðinga saga* (14:53), it was disbanded by the farmers of the region, who were fed up with the feuds between Bjarni and his kinsmen. It appears that it was never again reestablished, and if we are to give any credit to internal chronologies across sagas, this would have occurred before the events related here. There were other district Thing

sites in the East Quarter where the action could have been heard (Jóhannes-son 1974, 80–81).

27. This is an obscure observation. The turf walls of an Icelandic farm-house could be as thick as four to six feet. It is entirely possible that the kitchen was not attached to the main building or that a temporary unroofed outer building was used as a kitchen for singeing sheep's heads to save people from the smoke and odors of burning wool (personal communication from Kevin Smith).

28. The sheep's heads are being singed of hair in preparation for eating. The insult works two ways: it registers the complaint that Thorstein stands higher than Bjarni's servants inasmuch as a gelding is worth more than a lamb, and it likens Bjarni to a gelding whose manhood is suffering because of the way he has handled his business with Thorstein.

29. See *Vápn.* 18 : 61–63.

30. Rannveig is known from *Vápnfirðinga saga* (14 : 51), where it is noted she had been married before and had a son by that marriage.

31. The text has *einvígi*, which is a rather free-form duel. It contrasts with the more structured *hólmganga*. It would seem that this duel involves taking turns giving blows: "It was up to Bjarni to take the next stroke. . . ." See Bø (1969). Jón Jóhannesson (1950, 74n3) notes that there is today a hill and a little brook where the saga says the fight took place. On *hólmganga*, see further Ciklamini (1963) and Jones (1932).

32. An identical offer is made by Bjarni to the father of two men who fell on his side at Bodvarsdale (*Vápn.* 18 : 63). That man too was not about to give up his independence: "I am greatly grieved by the death of my sons, but I still think it better to have lost them than that they should be called cowards like some of your companions. But I am still satisfied with my own household so I will not move to Hof. But I wish to thank you for the offer anyway." See also *Þorst. hv.* 7 : 17.

33. Old Icelandic *fretkarl*; the translation is literal.

34. Thus the MS. It is probably an error for Sutari, that is, Sutri (Jóhannesson 1950, 78n2).

35. The announcement of the killing is required by law. The killing was to be published at the first farm where the killer could make the announce-ment without fear for his life. Refusal to comply resulted in a classification of the killing as a murder, with the consequence that any affirmative de-fenses available to the killer were voided (*Grágás* Ia 153–54). For another black-humored announcement see *Njála* 37 : 98.

36. Pálsson (1971a, 79) also believes that the woman servant "deliber-ately withholds the information that Thorstein killed Thord in order to give Thorstein time to get away."

37. The confusion was partly resolved by marking namesakes as "the old" or "the young." These were nicknames of genealogical position and were often conferred posthumously to distinguish their bearers from name-sakes in former or later generations.

38. The commonness of people having the same name prompted an ex-

pression—*nafni*—to refer to people who bore the same name. See *Njála* 69:169–70 for instances.

39. A general discussion of early Icelandic nicknames is available in Steffensen (1967–68, 179–91); see also Hale (1981). Nicknames could change over time. Harald Finehair of Norway was also known as Harald the Shaggy, depending on which part of his career the writer was focusing. According to legend, Harald took a vow never to cut or comb his hair until he had all of Norway under his control. Ten years later, when it was time to comb and cut his hair, people were quite surprised to discover he really did have a fine head of hair. At the occasion Jarl Rognvald gave him his new nickname (*Heimskringla* I:123). Nicknames might be conferred and not stick. In at least two instances in the sagas it is considered noteworthy that they did and in both cases they were more or less formally conferred and of positive signification (*Fóst.* 11:171–72; *Lax.* 16:39).

40. Some nicknames were evidently ironic in the same manner that a large person might get the name Tiny today. This might account for the discrepancy in the introduction of a certain Thorbjorn the Frail (*skrjúpr*), who is described as "large in size and of great strength" (*Lax.* 11:21).

41. The scene also shows that tasks were typed by social rank within genders. Servant women, not the householder's wife, were to milk, nor was mucking a job for the household head. See also *Njála* 120:305.

42. See Gade (1986) and Meulengracht Sørensen (1983) for recent informative discussions of sexual insult (*níð*). The person playing the phallic role in the coupling was seen as a humiliator, although as one source says "neither [participant] had it so good but the one who stood in front had it worse" (*Bjarn.* 17:154–55).

43. It is interesting to note that medieval English juries were quite willing to find that victims "stumbled into the weapons of another" as a way of nullifying the effects of a severe law of homicide that allowed little consideration of extenuating circumstances on behalf of the defendant; see Green (1985, 38–46). We have no examples of Icelandic panels of neighbors using "accident" as a way of extending the range of justification defenses. Given that Icelandic law had rather generous views of justification, the fiction was not needed.

44. One *Grágás* provision denies any defense of mistake or lack of knowledge to a person who measures or counts cloth incorrectly *if the error exceeds twenty ells* (II 262–63, Ib 249). In matters of trespass by animals the extent of damage also was reflected in the gradation of punishments. As a general rule the penalty was a three-mark fine for damage of less value than five ounces, lesser outlawry for damage greater than five but less than the value of cow, and full outlawry for damage greater than a cow's worth (II 429). With the usual standard of six ells to a legal ounce and eight ounces to the mark we can discern that the person who miscounts by twenty ells is being punished for his presumed intentions rather than for the value of his conversion.

45. For a fairly extended description of a horsefight see *Glúma* 18:61–62.

46. Saga cases show that in order to avoid the risks of vicarious liability of this sort Thord would have to take overt and unambiguous steps to repudiate Thorhall's and Thorvald's slander (see Miller 1983a, 330–31).

47. Unlike the early Germanic codes, the Icelandic laws contain no schedule of prices for body parts and various types of bodily injury. The cost of a limb or an eyelid was a matter for negotiation and would be awarded as part of an arbitrated settlement, not pursuant to a legal judgment; see further chapter 8.

48. For example, in one case in which one of A's men mistakenly slaughtered B's sheep, A immediately offered B his choice of *vaðmál*, another sheep of his choice, or the carcass of his own animal. For other reasons, all the offers were rejected and a suit was prepared for wrongful slaughter instead (*Hrafn Sv.* 6:646–47).

49. Although by no means the only case of a disputant having to "lump it," Thorstein's attempt to classify his injury as accidental is the only case of accident in the sagas that I have found in which the injured party, rather than the injuror, made the categorization of accident; cf. *Njála* 53:135.

50. There are several saga cases that show that people were not above taking strategic advantage of this procedural restriction. It could provide the unscrupulous victim of an "accident" with an outlawry claim when the underlying facts did not support it. And these were always serious matters, even if the wrongdoer still had his defense of accident. In one case the "wronged" party actually staged the accident so as to acquire a lawsuit against the other (*Hrafn Sv.* 6:646–47); in another the victims of the accident were delighted at the opportunity it afforded to dispossess the wrongdoer of his property (*Qlk.* 1:85).

51. The Icelandic practice in this regard contrasts significantly with provisions in the twelfth-century Norwegian Gulathing law, where it was up to the injured person to make the determination regarding intent:

> If two men are shaping timber and the ax flies out of the hands
> of the one and the other is killed thereby, then the injured man,
> if he is still able to speak when men come to him, shall have
> the [decisive] word; and it shall be counted accidental slaying
> only if he wills it. But if he is not able to speak, his heir shall
> have the [decisive] word. (cap. 169, tr. Larson 1935, 135; see
> also caps. 175, 177)

See generally the discussion in von Amira (1895, 2.404–15).

52. *Hrafn Sv.* 6:646–47 (this case ended in blood also, but it was not the "accident" that provided the grounds); *Qlk.* 1:85.

53. Carol Clover (personal communication) rightly would call special attention to the fact that the servant explaining the reason of Bjarni's course of action is unnamed. His anonymity serves to detach his observation from the particular and elevate it toward the authorial plain. In this way the author lets us know he agrees with the sentiment expressed.

54. See the disapproving representation of Gudmund the Powerful's aggressive response to the violent death of his good-for-nothing servant (*Ljós.* 20:56–58). He even shows a willingness to burn down a farmhouse his wife is in to avenge the killing.

55. Although the propriety of response depends on the vagaries of context, the killing of a servant by itself should lead to an arbitrated settlement, either after or without the prior initiation of a lawsuit, with compensation assessed to the killer's party. Saga cases illustrating the point are numerous. See, e.g., *Njála*, chapters 36–43; *Ilufl.* 5–6.17–18. When settlements are reached, however, the wrongdoer's position is represented by someone more the claimant's equal, that is, by either his chieftain or his head of household. In this case it seems that the disparity in rank between Bjarni and Thorstein, coupled with the fact that Thorstein is left to represent himself, significantly constrains the form the dispute takes.

56. See the discussion in chapter 5 on the usual ways of repudiating unwanted household members and kinsmen. This case fits well into the general Icelandic pattern of pleading faintly after others had disposed of the offending person.

57. Bjarni and Thorstein are at the extremes of disparity in which honor was likely to be expressly and intentionally gaged. Bjarni, in fact, is at first unwilling to admit that Thorstein's actions have engaged his honor. (We have postulated that this was for reasons of sensible district management.) It is his wife, his thingmen, and his servants who force him to recognize a point of honor between Thorstein and himself. The irony is that the disparity was merely superficial: Thorstein was a man of honor and more than proves himself a proper opponent for Bjarni. That Bjarni recognized this long before anyone else is one of the chief factors making for Bjarni's appeal. Still, the differences in rank between the two and the corresponding differences in honor this tends to imply merit Thorstein's deference. More subtly, he is well aware that Bjarni risks disparaging himself and his deference is meant to take no special advantage from Bjarni's risktaking in that regard.

58. *Egil* 81:280–81. In *Íslend.* 80:343 a certain Brand tricked Dagstygg into exchanging clothes and horses and axed him when he was pulling his shirt over his head.

59. See p. 33 above, where Jon Loftsson's response to the killing of chieftains by people of lower rank is noted.

60. Nevertheless, a person risked losing face if he made too many fruitless expeditions to hunt down his outlaw. The longer an outlaw held out the greater the admiration he elicited from the uninvolved; see, e.g., *Grett.*, *Gísli*, and *Aron*.

61. On the real possibility of glitch in routinized and ritualized interaction, see Bourdieu (1977, 5).

62. Cf. Karlsson (1980) with Þorláksson (1979, 1982) on chieftain wealth and material needs in the middle decades of the thirteenth century.

63. The author does not entirely disapprove of the new arrangement. This is the point of his suggesting that both Thorstein's and Bjarni's honor is

enhanced. The concord between Bjarni and Thorstein surely is meant to contrast favorably with the contentiousness of the old Viking, Thorarin. Still, the benefits are not achieved without cost, and the author shows he knows this by giving old Thorarin his powerful speech on chieftainly rapacity that rings true. Thorarin is something more than St. Paul's old man who must be rejected for the slicker new man with new ways.

## Chapter Three

1. Ospak's answer makes ironic use of legal formulae, which couple *gefa, gjalda,* and *selja* to represent the means of alienating property (see *Grágás* Ib 123, II 411). The fact that the goods could have been paid as well as sold is a reflection of the ambiguities that arise when money substances, like *vaðmál,* also have use values.

2. I refer only to *inter-vivos* transfers, in which the parties to the exchange meet or know the identity of each other; acquisitions by inheritance and by finding are thus excluded.

3. See *Grágás* 1b 164. I translate *rán* variously as raid and forceful taking. For a good discussion of the distinction between theft and *rán* and the moral and social values associated with them see Andersson (1984, 497–98).

4. *Gjalda* (verb) describes generally the act of requiting an obligation; it can refer to the debt repaid to a creditor, the price given to a seller, the countergift returned to the giver, and frequently the compensation of a wrongdoer paid to an injured party. Whatever the precise meaning of *gjalda* here, Ospak's sense is clear; he is denying that the loot had been freely offered him or that it was taken in satisfaction of a prior claim.

5. General treatments of the early Icelandic economy have attended well to domestic production, but less so to domestic distribution (see, e.g., Jóhannesson 1974, 288–335). Discussions of exchange focus almost exclusively on long-distance transactions of distinctly mercantile character. See Gelsinger (1981) and *KLNM* 6:118, 127, 138; 11:454. Recent particular studies have focused narrowly on the size of chieftain wealth; see, e.g., Karlsson (1980) and Þorláksson (1982). These articles are mostly political and institutional in focus and rather cursory in social and economic analysis; similarly Byock (1988). Historians must await the results of regionwide social archaeological studies only recently begun. It would be hoped that they might help reveal the extent and substance of exchanges between farms.

6. The legislation has been assigned to the year 1265, but that date has been disputed. Sveinsson (1953, 57) would date the enactment to 1321.

7. One person made more money than friends selling ale at the Allthing (*Qlk.* 1:83). The laws allow a person to transport a half *vætt* (forty pounds) of wares to the Allthing without violating Sunday prohibitions on work (*Grágás* Ia 24, II 29). A farm bearing the name Kaupangr, meaning market, was located within a mile of the site of the Vodlathing (see Beck 1987).

8. There is no mention of a special market peace independent of the peace of the Thing or churchpeace, although evidence from the rest of Scandinavia suggests that such a peace could well have existed (see Lehmann 1893).

9. The image of the submerged or embedded economy is Karl Polanyi's formulation, derived in large part from Malinowski's work. See Polanyi (1944, 43–55); also Sahlins (1972, 185–275) and Bourdieu (1977, 159–97). Among historians, see Finley (1973).

10. There is an extensive anthropological literature on competitive gift-exchange. See, e.g., Mauss (1967), Codere (1950, 62–97), Young (1971, 189–227), and Brown (1979, 712–33) and the works cited therein.

11. See, e.g., Malinowski (1922, 176–91). More recent influential constructs can be found in Sahlins (1972, 185–230) and Gregory (1980, 1981).

12. Such redefinition was what lay behind the dispute over driftage rights in Grettis saga (11–12:26–33); see also Egils saga 82:287–88.

13. See, e.g., Reyk. 9:173: " . . . keypti Vémundr þegar viðinn, þann er hann hafði áðr falat" ("Vemund immediately bought the wood that he earlier had sought to purchase").

14. We must not let our exercise in modeling obscure the fact of a messier reality. In fact, the buy-sell mode in the modern world of business often implies continuing relations between vendors and purchasers, and, indeed, the whole universe of honor can figure in the mercantile world too (Rosenwein 1989, 98–99). To account better for the complexity of reality, Barbara Rosenwein would place the pure form of the market and gift economies at two ends of a continuum. "[The continuum] begins at one end with 'pure' profit and at the other with 'pure' honor; that is, at one end with material motives and at the other end with social" (1989, 130–31). It is thus the motive of the transactors that locates the transaction on the continuum. I would qualify Rosenwein's continuum slightly to accommodate better the fact that the language of exchange types is relatively discrete. People do not usually say 'sell' when they mean 'give.' The idiom of exchange forces the transactors to define rather particularly the discrete category in which they think the transaction belongs, whether gift, sale, loan, or raid. It may be that motive is the best way to determine the precise nature of any transaction, but motive will often be accessible to the outside observer only as it was expressed in rather unnuanced language.

15. The classic treatment of gift-exchange is Marcel Mauss', The Gift, which takes its epigraph from Hávamál. Bourdieu's brief treatment is particularly insightful (1977, 4–8). Historians were rather late in making use of this literature (see the discussion in Rosenwein 1989, 125–30), but it has been well assimilated by medievalists for nearly two decades (see, e.g., Duby 1974, 48–72 and Little 1978, 3–8). There have appeared recently several very able studies of the social relations established by lay gifts to saints in the tenth and eleventh centuries, which are greatly indebted to Maussian ideas (see Geary 1986, Rosenwein 1989, and White 1988). In the Germanic context, see especially Gurevich (1968); also Fichtner (1979) and Kuhn (1980).

16. Grágás purports to legalize the repayment obligation where the recipient has promised to repay. The amount owing is to be determined by a panel of five neighbors (II 84–85); Grágás Ia 247 is less clearly to the same effect. The sagas, to my knowledge, show no prosecution based on these provisions. Moreover, the context in which they appear—that is, in sections

setting forth limitations on the power to give without the heir's consent and giving the heir an action to set aside gifts that wrongfully disinherit him—suggests they are intended to confer a cause of action on the heir of the giver, rather than on the giver himself. In the sagas, however, there are firm normative statements about the obligation to return a gift (e.g., *Njála* 44:114; *Hafl.* 15:32).

17. In distinguishing the differences between "commodity-debt" and "gift-debt," Gregory (1981, 125) notes that the amount of the latter is "always measured at its historic level at the time of the gift and no interest accrues." A return in an amount greater than the original gift constitutes a new gift-debt, not interest on the original sum (see also Gregory 1980, 638–39). While Gregory's distinction was derived from ethnographic data assembled from communities practicing ceremonial cyclical exchanges, he argues its validity to "gift-economies" generally. The Icelandic materials are basically consistent with his point.

18. See Duby's discussion of 'necessary generosity' (1974, 56, 68–69); also Bloch (1961, 206).

19. Such misrecognition can be fruitfully considered in light of Jon Elster's discussions of wish fulfillment, self-deception, and his general theory of byproducts (Elster 1983).

20. The subject of Icelandic money and ways of expressing value is complicated; reasonably clear introductions are available in Jóhannesson (1974, 328–35) and Gelsinger (1981, 33–44). There were caloric money substances. Cows were used as a measure of value and certain animals might also figure as a means of payment. See, e.g., the terms of the award in *Hafl.* 31:49–50, quoted on p. 278 above.

21. Otkel's inability to recognize the quality of people and the advice they give is effortlessly symbolized by the author's noting that Otkel did not have good eyesight (49:128). Others who see Skammkel recognize immediately that he looks like he is up to no good (see, e.g., 50:129). The effect of the detail about Otkel's nearsightedness is to shift the ultimate responsibility for the course of action from Skammkel to Otkel.

22. When Otkel sought to acquire Melkolf the slave from his brother Hallbjorn, he did not ask his brother to give him the slave but offered to buy him first, just as Gunnar offered to buy the hay before he asked for a gift. But Otkel was dealing with a brother, Gunnar with someone to whom he has no close connection, nor are the goods comparable. Still, there is the suggestion that Gunnar's etiquette was correct when he offered to buy before he requested a gift. Even King Harald Hardrada of Norway observed these forms when asking an inconsequential Icelander named Audun for his bear:

> The king said, "Will you sell us the animal for the price you
> bought it?"
> [Audun] answered, "I prefer not to, lord."
> "Then do you prefer," said the king, "that I give you twice
> the price . . . ?"

"Lord, I don't prefer that," he said.
The king asked, "Will you give it to me then?"
He answered, "No, lord." (Auðun. 1:362)

One suspects that Harald, not known in the sources for his generosity, was motivated by a desire to come by the bear in the cheapest manner possible.

23. The statement needs to be qualified to reflect the difference between musters specific as to purpose and those of general intent. In the last decades of the commonwealth, the mere ability to muster significant numbers, even if the expedition was broken off, was a sign of power (see Þórð. 19:39–40).

24. Some provocative materials on the relation of wergeld payments to gift-exchange in another ethnographic context are discussed in Feil (1979).

25. The companions were not necessary to witness a sale, although they might be necessary to witness other claims—insults and injuries—that might arise. Except in transfers of land, seagoing vessels, chieftaincies, and betrothals of women (sic Grágás Ib 75), a valid sale could take place without witnesses. The companions were of sufficiently high status to do honor to Otkel and the expedition. These were not servants whose only purpose for attending—to help bear the purchased fodder home—would evidence a presumption on Gunnar's part that would deny Otkel the opportunity to display graciousness.

26. Note the like sensitivity of Ketil, who agreed to accept liability for debts incurred by his household member before the debtor had joined his household, only if the summoning of the debtor were carried out with few men (Gunn. þ. 1:198).

27. Háv. 15–16:343–45 (food); Hœn. 5:13–16 (hay); Íslend. 69:324 (food), 79:341 (cloak); Lax. 37:102–5 (horses); Reyk. 1:153 (firewood).

28. Would-be buyers, as was to be expected, did not react well to refusals to sell: e.g., Hrafn Sv. St. 13:216 (horse); Íslend. 32:261–62 (sword), 104:380 (food); Vápn. 4:29 (valuables); Vatn. 17:48 (sword).

29. Cf., however, Campbell (1964, 211–12). Among the Sarakatsani shepherds of northern Greece, thieving is so generalized and institutionalized as to form a system of reciprocities.

30. Although Hallgerd's theft is attributed to a flawed character by the saga and commentators alike (Njála 1:7, 48:124; e.g., Andersson 1984, 504–5), it should be noted that her response is determined, to some extent, by the role relegated to women in the disputing process. Women were under strong social and legal constraint, in matters of rights and honor, to act through men. Hallgerd, at this juncture in the saga, has been deprived of her influence over the free men of Gunnar's kin group and her household while her own kinsmen live at another end of Iceland. She had earlier found that her husband was impervious to her goading (45:118). She is thus without means to organize an avenging raid on Otkel's farm. But while Gunnar is away at the Allthing she can order a slave about and he is more likely to succeed at a furtive taking than at an open and notorious one.

31. Hallgerd is liable for her own wrongs and her property would be sub-

ject to confiscation should she be outlawed (*Grágás* II 350). Gunnar is summoned in his own right for having benefited from the use of stolen property (see *Grágás* Ib 163; also *Drop.* 5:150).

32. Cf. Firth's account of people's reactions to severe famine in Tikopia (1959, 75, 82–84). The Tikopia maintained the social framework of their exchange system in spite of famine. If food was transferred it was by gift, not by sale; there was no profit taking. Good manners remained. Still thieving increased and there was a contraction of peripheral social relations, although people still continued to voice the norms of sharing and norms against thieving. "The Tikopia avoided where possible their general responsibility or undefined responsibility for kin during the famine, but showed no disposition to reject responsibility which had been specifically defined by undertaking." But households where food was not desperately short would "link ovens" and pool supplies. Food only stopped being shared with nonhousehold members when the situation was desperate. The general food shortage described in *Njála* does not appear to have reached anywhere near these proportions. The famine seems to have been short and localized.

33. In this passage "money" translates Old Icelandic *fé. Fé* was used to refer to money substances and generally to property, but it also meant sheep or livestock and is so used later in the passage we are discussing. The ambiguity in *fé's* sense is paralleled by the development of *pecunia* in Latin, as well as Old English *feoh,* ModE *fee* (see Murray 1978, 58). The Latin and English terms eventually lost their associations with livestock and became unambivalently monetary. Not so Icelandic *fé,* the double sense of which still survives. The tenacity of the connection of animals, property, and money in Iceland bears witness to, among other things, the late development of towns. In any event, to translate money here may be slightly tendentious and anachronistic; "property" is perhaps better. Yet it is clear that what is meant is whatever would be given as a payment for the hay. The means of payment was, as the passage shows later, open to negotiation. It could be in money substances like silver or *vaðmál,* or an exact exchange of hay for hay.

34. In this regard, consider that one of Blund-Ketil's offers of payment is to transfer a like quantity and quality of hay the next summer. In Gregory's model (see above chapter 3, n. 17) such payment is one of the markers of a gift since no consideration is given for the delay in repayment. But there is in fact consideration here. The guarantee to repay the same amount of hay later in recompense for the hay taken now is an offer of insurance. Thorir, however, prefers to self-insure.

35. See Jóhannesson (1974, 319–20). Norwegian and Orkneyian merchants did not always acquiesce peaceably to *goðar* who attempted to exercise this authority (see, e.g., *Íslend.* 15:240, 35:270; *Hœn.* 2:8–9).

36. On the technical legal issues raised by certain particulars in the account of this case, see further Maurer (1871, 189–95).

37. Recall Gunnar's "I won't take part in a raid" in the first case and Blund-Ketil's response to Thorir's suggestion that Ketil had the power to take forcefully: "This is not the way to go about it."

38. See *Árna saga* 28:718; Jóhannesson (1974, 171–78, 182–86). Such is the desperate state of the evidence with regard to dating the sagas that the dispute over the *Jónsbók* provision has been used to date *Hœnsa-Þóris saga* to sometime after *Jónsbók's* introduction (see, e.g., Berger 1976, 7–11 and cf. Nordal 1938, xxxi). In any event, the provision was not all that revolutionary an innovation. *Grágás* already had provided for forced sales of hay to travelers on the way to baptize an infant (Ia 4, II 2).

39. On the wife's rights to her marital property upon divorce, see chapter 5 n. 23.

40. On the contradiction of proverbs regarding food sharing, see Sahlins (1972, 125–28) and cf. *Hávamál*, sts. 3, 35, 67.

41. No provision in *Grágás*, however, makes the legal classification of the type of taking depend on the size of the party as does, for example, a law of Ine, King of Wessex, in the late seventh century: "We call 'thieves' a group of less than seven, from seven to thirty-five is a 'raiding party' (*hloð*), after that it is an 'army' (*here*)" (*Ine* cap. 13.1).

42. The gift, it turns out, was as unwelcome to Thorleik as it was to Eldgrim. Relations had never been good between Thorleik and his uncle and the unsolicited favor so greatly angered Thorleik that he sought out Kotkel and his family to use witchcraft against Hrut. Thorleik's reaction shows that gift-giving was not to be entered into unilaterally without some prior indication that the intended recipient would welcome the gift and be willing to incur the obligation to requite it. In *Egil* (78:272), for example, Egil's initial reaction to an unsolicited gift is to try to kill the giver.

43. See *Hrafn Sv. St.* 13:216 where a failed attempt to buy a horse leads to a similar conclusion.

44. The fine dividing line between intergroup trade and war has long been noted in ethnographic accounts. See variously Thurnwald (1932, 164), Lévi-Strauss (1943), and Sahlins (1972, 302–3). On the origins of the peace arrangements made for marketplaces, see Lehmann (1893); also Dalton (1975, 101–9).

45. *Band.* 1:296 indicates that persons owned shares in ferries involved in local carrying of fish, whales, and driftwood. There is no indication of the status of such persons, except that one, Odd, was fifteen at the time and not himself a householder.

46. Cf. the amicable partnership of Kalf and Kjartan (*Lax.* 40:114, 44:134) with the troublesome one of Thorstein and Einar (*Þorst. hv.* 3–4:8–9). *Grágás* (Ib 67–69) has procedures for buy-out in the event of a disagreement between partners in an oceangoing vessel as to when or whether to sail (see also Gelsinger 1981, 29–32).

47. Friend, OI *vinr* and friendship, OI *vinátta, vinfengi*, often bore a formal sense that did not necessarily indicate the presence of psychologically based affections. As between equals, friends were those with whom one was formally allied. Friendship also indicated various types of patronage relations. Thingmen and chieftain were thus friends (*Ljós.* 1:3, 22:64), or likewise a freedman and his patron (*Eyrb.* 32:87), a big man and a widow (*Þórð.*

44:81). Kin could undertake explicitly to be friends in an effort to patch up prior disaffection (*Eyrb.* 33:91). Grants of friendship were made by big people to lesser people (*Glúma* 11:37), or requested by lesser people of their superiors (*Njála* 51:132). See further Charles-Edwards (1976, 180), Byock (1982, 42, 95), and Miller (1983a, 339–40).

48. *Grágás* Ib 143, II 217: "and if he wishes to pay with a slave two ounces worth for an ounce's value [of vaðmál] and he shall have the right to redeem the slave during the next half-year if he raised him." The right to redeem is evidently restricted to slaves who have not already figured in prior transactions, either as a means of payment or as the object of purchase.

49. Unlike sales of goods, sales of land are commonly noted without much ado; see, e.g., *Drop.* 2:140, 3:144, 4:147; *G.dýri* 3:166; *Lax.* 32:86; *Hrafn Sv. St.* 13:216; *Njála* 90:225; *Sturla* 2:64, 3:65, 15:81. The fact that land sales can be easily found is not, however, very good evidence that there were not sales of goods just because they are hard to find in the sources. One would expect the sagas and especially those episodes taken from *Landnámabók* to show a concern for land titles. Transfers in land needed to be accounted for in order to give sense to the plots and sense to the present state of land occupation. No such concern would motivate an author to note sales of goods. But elsewhere the evidence of land sales suggests that it may be the brevity of the account rather than the smoothness of the sale that made for the uneventfulness of the transaction; see, e.g., *G.dýri* 9:178; *Háv.* 14:337; *Heið.* 38:320, 41:324; *Íslend.* 79:341; *Lax.* 24:67, 47:147, cf. 75:218–21; *Reyk.* 1:151; *Sturla* 6:68.

# Chapter Four

1. This view is most frequently associated with the name of Peter Laslett who drew heavily on the work of John Hajnal. Laslett's methods and results are still the subject of active debate, which is at times quite acrimonious (e.g., Laslett 1987). For an exceptionally lucid critique of Laslett's influential introduction to *Household and Family in Past Time* (1972), see Berkner (1975), also Wheaton (1975) and the additional qualifications of Kertzer (1989).

2. The tenacity of the complex household is in part a function of the common tendency of a researcher to assume the validity of the older orthodoxy for any period prior to the one of his or her expertise. It's easy to see why. Doing so saves the often impossible task of becoming expert in ever earlier times in an infinite regress back to Eve. It also tends to inform dull description with some polemical energy and to satisfy our careerist and guildish impulses, which make it crucial to have the great change take place on our own turf. We thus find that we all work in the most significant of times purely by accident. But the impression given by the whole body of work undercuts the claim of each individual performance.

3. On *búðsetumenn* see *Grágás* II 145–46; *Njála* 142:386. Jón Jóhannesson (1974, 347–49) assembles what little information there is; see also Hastrup (1985, 108–11). Our only evidence of the precariousness of the tenure

of the *kotkarl* or cotter must be extracted from a simile recording the reluctant parting of an old chieftain from his land: "Glum sat in the highseat and did nothing to prepare for his departure, even though he was called to do so. He had the hall decorated with tapestries; he did not want to depart his land like a *kotkarl*" (*Glúma* 26:89). There are only two mentions of *hjábú*, or dependent households, in sources dating from the commonwealth period. In one a woman is said to have had a *hjábú* and a cow for the winter (*Íslend.* 141:440). Her small establishment is located on the farm of her daughter's husband. The etymology of *hjábú* (literally "beside-house") suggests that the older woman was not housed in the main building but in a small detached structure somewhere on the estate. An inventory for a church, dated conjecturally to the early thirteenth century but perhaps later, requires tenants, *hiábúðar menn*, and their servants (*hjún*) who occupy certain parcels of land to pay their tithes at the church. Landowners and their servants, on the other hand, are entitled to discharge their tithes at their homes. It should be noted that the passage envisages the possibility of servants who have ratable property and that such servants might be attached to tenant and cottager households (*DI* I 402).

4. My modifications of the terminology are mostly implicit. The data itself will provide new and varied sense to the terms.

5. "Joint" in Hajnal (1983, 68–69, 77–78) corresponds, for the most part, to Laslett's "multiple" (1972, 28–31). Laslett's "multiple" household allows one of the two or more conjugal units to be a widow and her children. I make no arguments that depend on the slight distinction in definition.

6. It seems, however, that in fact most complex householding arrangements involved kinsmen and affines.

7. I am extending the household to include what Laslett and Wall call the "houseful," that is all those residents who are not spouse, child, relative, or servant of the household head (Wall 1983a, 35; cf. Berkner 1975, 726). The "houseful" adds nothing to understanding Icelandic householding and it seems that the concept was devised to make up for an overly restrictive definition of household. In any event, our information is seldom circumstantial enough to know whether residents are kin to the head or not.

8. *Félag*, the etymon for ModE *fellow*, means literally a laying together, a pooling of property, a partnership (Cleasby and Vigfússon 1957, s.v. *félag*). Similarly, a *félagsbú* implies a jointly managed economic enterprise situated at one farmstead.

9. An earlier form, *búandi*, shows the clear link to *bú*. *Bóndi* is the present participle of *búa*, "to have a household."

10. Servants are variously indicated as *griðmenn*, *griðkonur*, *húskarlar*, *heimamenn*, *heimakonur* (homemen, homewomen). The laws generally refer to servants as *grið*-men and women, occasionally indicating male servants as housecarls. The sagas are somewhat casual in their use of *heimamaðr*, which, although generally synonymous with the legal terms, need not always indicate someone of low social rank; like *griðmaðr* it referred to someone formally lodged (*á vist*) in another's household, but, unlike *griðmaðr*, he was not necessarily in service there. See, e.g., Thorvard, a

chieftain, who is called a homeman of Kolbein (*Íslend.* 177:501) and below chapter 4, n. 23.

11. This also suggests that access to householder status was not especially difficult to achieve and did not depend on coming into a farm.

12. The text of the provision is as follows:

> If two men have a household together and one of them owns the land and the other is a tenant, the landowner is to be called. If two landowners have a household together or two tenants who are eligible to serve on a panel, he is to call the one who owns the greatest portion of the household. But if they have equal shares in the household, then he may call whichever he pleases, even though they keep no serving man. If two men who have to pay the Thing attendance payment [see p. 25] have a household together and do not have a serving man, then one of them is rightly called to serve on a panel. The other—given that he is capable of earning at least his food—is to contribute to all the necessary outlay in proportion to the share he has in the household.

The same provision, several lines later, contemplates the presence of a married daughter and her husband living with her father:

> For the household of a man incapable of attending the Thing four men may be rightly called if they have their settled home there: (1) the man's son, (2) his stepson, (3) the near affine who has married his daughter, and (4) his legal foster-son who the householder has brought up.

13. *Bú* appears in the singular in this passage. If we were dealing with discrete households at the same farmstead we might expect to find the plural.

14. Both men in this passage have to be *bœndr* or the passage is without motivation, since in order for there to be a problem about whom to call, both would have to be eligible to be called, that is, *bœndr*.

15. There is some archaeological evidence of small pit-houses separated from the main hall dating from the tenth century, but found in later sites also, that might have served as bathhouses, weaving rooms for the women, or possibly slave quarters (Ólafsson 1980). See also Gestsson (1976), Eldjárn (1961), Grímsson (1976), and Karras (1988, 82).

16. Thus *Grágás* Ia 126 provides that

> if men share a household and one of them takes in an outlaw and the other is unwilling, then the one who is unwilling is to name witnesses to witness that he is unwilling and that it is with his disagreement and report it to five of his neighbors.

> Then he is not liable for sharing living quarters with an outlaw
> as long as he gives him no other assistance.

See further chapter 6, n. 32.

17. See, e.g., *Grágás*, which provides rules for Thing attachment where a *bóndi* marries a woman who has a *bú* (Ia 139); for men eligible to represent a household headed by a woman (Ia 161); for governing the killing of foreigners who are lodged in her household and for the disposition of their property (Ia 173, II 340, Ia 229). The sagas confirm the existence of households headed by women, usually widows, but also unmarried heiresses; see, e.g., *Njála* 18:52 (Unn) and *G.dýri* 5:168 (Gudrun Thordardottir). One more matter of brief note: Sturla Sighvatsson's household at Saudafell includes, among others, his wife and his wife's mother. Both are designated with the title *húsfreyja* (*Íslend.* 71:327). Although the mother-in-law might simply bear the title as an honorific and a reflection of past status, this is not altogether clear. Could it be that the wife's mother has sufficient wealth to qualify as head of a separate juridical household?

18. *Grágás* Ia 129: "If a man has not found places for the people he has to provide for on the last Moving Day, he is to be fined for each one of them and the case lies with anyone who wishes to prosecute."

19. Saga evidence suggests that many of these were loose marriages; see, e.g., *Ljós.* 13:16–17 (marriage); *Hrafn Sv. St.* 14:218 (concubinage); *Sturla* 4:65 (concubinage); *Njála* 39:103 (concubinage). For a discussion of slave marriage, see Karras (1988, 116). One of Hajnal's essential features of northwest European household formation is the circulation of young people between households as servants *before* marriage (1983, 92–99). Service of this sort, he observes, did not exist in joint-household systems such as in India. Some of the servants in early Iceland were in service of the northwest European kind, but many did not appear to be. Servants often seem to have been poorer kin of the household head and many of these constituted a fairly permanent underclass. Although early Iceland did not have a joint-household system in the manner of India, neither was it yet a society whose householding arrangements were typified by the northwest European model (see Wall 1983a, 60).

20. The laws contemplate separate households for a husband and wife, each of whom must find household attachment: "If a man has a wife, he shall have gotten her a position and informed her of it at the latest on Thursday when seven weeks of summer have passed. If to her knowledge a place has not been found for her by then, it is lawful for her to join a household where she pleases" (*Grágás* Ia 129). Likewise: "If a servant marries and each of them lives in different places, each is to stay in the place where they have their home if they are tied to particular jobs" (Ia 135). Marriage without coresidence is rare in Europe, if not always so in ethnographic literature (Wheaton 1987, 290).

21. According to the laws, the primary liability for servants belonged to their kin although the householder whom they worked for was obliged to keep a sick servant for half a month if he or she did not need tending (*Grá-*

*gás* Ia 134). A landlord was obliged to maintain his tenants until the next Moving Days if their means failed them (Ib 172, II 250).

22. Life-cycle service appears to be what Isolf intended for his daughter by sending her to Eyjolf (*Ljós*. 22:64), although some of these arrangements must have been scarcely distinguishable from concubinage; consider, for example, the succession of housekeepers that Thorgils skarði took in (*Þorg. sk*. 27:151–52; see also *Háv*. 1:291).

23. See also *Sturla* 20:89 and *Þorst. hv*. 3:6. It is of some interest that Solvi is provided with a patronymic. The sagas do not care to give us much detail about servants; they are frequently unnamed or, if named, they are often without patronymic, although in this matter *Sturlunga saga* is more likely to provide a patronymic than the family sagas are. The presence of a patronymic is likely to indicate a *bóndi*'s son and thus, perhaps, a life-cycle servant. See, e.g., what appear to be life-cycle services in *Sturla* 12:78 (Hall?), 15:82 (Thorleif); *Ljós*. 9:128–31 (Brand). Younger brothers and kinsmen of the powerful Sturlungs could be homemen to their seniors; but these were short-term arrangements, and although they might be called homemen, they were unlikely to have been servants in any meaningful sense (*Íslend*. 81:344, Kolbein and Orækja); see above chapter 4, n. 10. Nevertheless Sturla Sighvatsson can at least contemplate reducing some of his powerful kinsmen to service (*Íslend*. 125:407–8).

24. Specific saga instances of girls in extrahousehold fosterage are rather rare. I know of two (*Hœn*. 11:32; *Reyk*. 28:238) or three if we include the late *Víglundar saga* (7:75). With the sense of widespread fostering derived from the sagas, compare the 1703 census, which had 77.8 percent of children age 0–14 living at home (Gunnarsson 1980a, 9). This percentage indicates a significantly higher prevalence of fostering than the number suggests at first glance. If fostering, say, were most favored between the ages of ten and fourteen, the census grouping of 0–14 is simply too broad to reflect adequately how widespread fostering was. In other words, it is not the case that any one child in 1703 had only a one-in-five chance of being fostered for some period of his childhood.

25. According to *Grágás* all fostering of whatever type had to be paid for, either by paying the fosterer directly or by giving him support and protection (II 133–34, 136–38). It was thus provided that even in those fosterings that arose from the obligation to care for poor kin, the relative, or the heir of the relative, who had borne the cost of maintaining a poor child or kinsman could recover against the child the outlay (*fóstrlaun*) if the child ever came into any property (*Grágás* II 136–38; see chapter 5, n. 20). The sagas, it should be noted, give us no examples of suing to recover the *fóstrlaun*, although it is forced extralegally from one father to recompense the couple who raised his abandoned child (*Finnb*. 6:262). There is, however, an ironic use of *fóstrlaun* that suggests its recovery was not unusual. Thus, after Bolli had killed Kjartan, Thorgerd, who was Kjartan's mother and Bolli's foster-mother, thought Bolli had "made a sorry repayment for his fostering" (*sár fóstrlaunin*) (*Lax*. 51:159).

26. With Boswell (1988, 286–94), compare Clover (1988).

27. Such may have been a contributing motive in the fosterings mentioned in *Ljós.* 22:63 and *Glúma* 17:57. In one instance a young man is raised by a powerful maternal kinsman to protect him from the aggressions of another man (*Bjarn.* 1:112).

28. The number of servants seems excessive, but given the number of servants, the number of cows is not excessive. In this regard note that the minimal property requirement obliging a farmer to pay the *þingfararkaup* was a cow free of debt or the value of a cow for each of his dependents (*ahuldahjún*) (see above p. 15 and Jóhannesson 1974, 289–90).

29. Jochens (1985, 107) would attribute the existence of this complex household to the dramatic purposes of an author who needed to have these people residing together so that they could be burned together as per the demands of the plot. Even if we concede that the extent and complexity of Njal's household may be somewhat aberrational (but see *Sturla* 7:69), the fact that it is extended or complex is not. Moreover, people who do not live together can still burn together as invitees to a feast (see, e.g., *Íslend.* 170–73:481–92).

30. One young *bóndi*'s daughter found living in a tent some distance from the farmhouse less tedious than life inside with her father. Her living arrangement facilitated her meetings with a young man not to her father's liking (*Hœn.* 16:42).

31. "Neolocalism," in the jargon of anthropology, refers to the practice of a newly married couple setting up on their own, and living by themselves, not with either set of parents (Laslett 1983, 531). A rule of neolocality tends to imply, therefore, simple households.

32. Cleasby and Vigfússon's gloss, s.v. *hjún*, I: "a married couple should get a house" is less ambivalent but hard to justify grammatically.

33. Jochens (1985, 100) describes three marriage models typical of *Sturlunga saga*. In one, men are twenty and women eighteen or younger. In a second a young man marries an older women, usually a widow with children. The third is the inverse of the second, an old man marries a young woman. The second and third type would do little to raise the average age of *first* marriages, given that the older women had usually been married or in fertile concubinage previously and assuming that the younger men who took older women take younger women at a later stage in their life cycles. The models are derived from a handful of cases and there is no way of determining their typicality. We also have no way of determining the number of celibates or illegitimacy rates. Jochens' models are taken from the later sagas of *Sturlunga*, a source perceptibly skewed to the most wealthy and powerful families, and only for the most wealthy and powerful of these are the accounts sufficiently circumstantial to allow for even a moderately accurate determination of marriage age. Nevertheless, it should also be noted that the laws envisage the possibility, at least, of very early marriages for women. Consider *Grágás* Ia 225, II 69: "If a woman is married when she is sixteen or younger...," "If she is widowed when she is younger than sixteen..." and such marriages are confirmed by the experiences of the main female characters in *Lax.* (34:93) and *Njála*. If we add to this information the fact of some servant marriage, we would have to assume a

fairly stiff mortality rate to keep the population within bounds. Some would find this in a systematic infanticide of female infants well into the twelfth and thirteenth centuries (Clover 1988). Our demographic information is so poor, however, that there is no way of knowing. It would seem unlikely that the general age of women at marriage was anywhere near as low as the laws and the few upper-class cases would suggest. Very late evidence from the census of 1703 yields "staggeringly" low nuptiality rates of 27.8 percent for women ages 15–49 (cf. Hajnal [1965, 137] who disbelieves the numbers with Gunnarsson [1980a, 7–15] who finds the rates credible). Needless to say, this is of doubtful relevance to the twelfth and thirteenth centuries. The laws, however, evince frequent anxiety about the fertile poor and excessive numbers of children (e.g., *Grágás* Ib 38–39, II 167; see above p. 122 and below chapter 4, n. 52.

34. In a stationary population, roughly twenty percent of all married couples will produce no children surviving their parents and another twenty percent will produce only daughters who survive their parents (Wrigley 1978, 139–44).

35. A sale of land would likely involve a loss of status for the seller since straitened circumstances, fertility failure, or insufficient strength to stand up to the would-be purchaser would be the usual reasons the land would be available in the first place; see, e.g., *Lax.* 75:218–21; *Sturla* 15–16:81–84 (cases of Erlend prest and Ozur's inheritance) and 23:96.

36. As noted in chapter 1, there were 4,560 farmers eligible to pay the *þingfararkaup* in the enumeration made by Bishop Gizur in 1095 (*Íslb.* 10:23). A count made in 1311 of tax-paying farmers totaled about 3,800 (*DI* II 374–75). The amount of property needed to qualify, it should be noted, was the same in *Jónsbók* (III.1), the law code in effect at the time of the second census, as it had been in *Grágás* (Ia 159).

37. Jochens' examples of neolocal marriage (1985, 98–101) involve only the wealthiest chieftain families.

38. There is no indication of the marital status of the sons, but it should be noted that Eyjolf intended them to have one establishment together, at least until his death when the paternal farm would become available.

39. The presence of the householders' siblings was a marked feature of the households enumerated in the 1703 census, marked, that is relative to roughly contemporaneous figures for England, Geneva, and Norway (Wall 1983a, 53).

40. In the last case, the brothers mismanage their affairs and must sell the farm shortly thereafter.

41. E.g., *Gísli* 4:16; *G.dýri* 11:181; *Heið.* 41:326; *Íslend.* 46:294; *Lax.* 32:86, 46:144; *Ljós.* 20:54, 22:62; *Njála.* 47:120; *Sturla* 3:65; *Vatn.* 47:126, 127; *Þorg. sk.* 14:123. The marital status of the brothers is not always determinable.

42. See *Grágás* Ia 246–49, II 85–87 (setting aside transfers of ancestor); Ib 76–77, II 410–14 (setting aside transfers of guardian); see also Ib 17–18, II 128. Successful reclamations were made in blood rather than at law (*Eyrb.* 32–37:87–102; *Háv.* 14:337–41).

43. Jochens' analysis (1985) suffers for taking a phase to represent the whole. Households have developmental cycles. Even societies that prefer a complex householding type will have at any one moment many simple households either on their way to becoming complex or being frustrated by mortality and infertility from getting there (see Berkner 1975, 729–32; Wheaton 1975, 606–8).

44. The notion of individually owned property must be qualified to some extent to take account of the claims of heirs and dependents. I do not wish to enter here into a technical discussion as to the precise indicia of something called individual ownership. See the discussion in White (1988, 133–43). I mean only to contrast the difference in how title is held to a particular piece of property that determines whether all or only some fraction of it will be subject to the owner's direction or be considered an asset of his estate when he dies.

45. Thus it is that the hostility between the Njalssons and Hoskuld Thrainsson does not erupt until he is independently established. The same holds true for the hostility of Bolli and Kjartan in *Lax.* See also *Eyrb.* 30:81ff.; *Ljós.* 2–4:6–15; and generally the dealings of the Sturlusons in *Íslend.*

46. An occasional notice in the sagas suggests that disputes between homeman and householder need not remain repressed. A certain Grim is given an end consonant with his name in this brief notice: "he was killed by his housecarls" (*Hafl.* 11:30).

47. See, e.g., *Eyrb.* 14:24–26; *Lax.* 19:45–47; but cf. *Hrafn Sv. St.* 13:214; *Sturla* 26:100. The property of minors (below the age of sixteen for males and twenty for females) was administered by a guardian called the *fjárvarðveizlumaðr*. In the absence of a father, the role was filled by a brother who had reached majority; see *Grágás* Ia 225–26, II 69–70.

48. The value of *Gísla saga's* evidence for householding should perhaps be discounted somewhat because householding type figures more integrally in the plot than the general run of saga householding evidence and hence is more likely to suffer fictionalizing distortions. That said, there is nothing in the description of householding arrangements in the saga that is inconsistent with the accounts derived from safer contexts.

49. Gisli, for example, had killed Thorkel's best friend in Norway before they emigrated. The two brothers were frequently at odds over controlling sexual access to their sister Thordis.

50. Instances of uxorilocal marriage are not uncommon; see, e.g., *Lax.* 35:96–97, 43:130, 69:203, 70:207; *G.dýri* 5:169. Couples could also relocate to provide care for aging parents; see, e.g., *Lax.* 10:20.

51. See the second marriage of Gudrun (*Lax.*) and Hallgerd's second and third marriages (*Njála*). Wealthy widows had a hard time staying unattached and often entered into or were constrained to enter into joint householding arrangements or loose marriages with men intent on their property (e.g., *Sturla* 2:64; *Íslend.* 52:302).

52. Gísli Gunnarsson (1980a, 15–19) doubts excessive illegitimacy. As has become the frequent refrain in this chapter, we just don't know. If we

count the children of concubines as illegitimate, then the sagas and gene-alogies suggest the rate was quite high among chieftains. The people most concerned with keeping the rates low were those upon whom the burden of support ultimately rested, that is kinsmen or members of the *hreppr*. Thus *Grágás* Ib 26, II 150: "No one is obliged to accept more than two illegitimate third cousins fathered by one man *unless the father of the children is cas-trated*" and further (Ib 28, II 150–51) where it is provided that the kin of vagabonds are not liable for the vagabonds' children unless the parents at-tach themselves to a household.

53. The provisions are brutally unsympathetic. Besides being liable for full outlawry (*Grágás* Ia 139–40), vagrants and those who showed them charity were subject to a number of legal disabilities. For example, fornica-tion with a beggarwoman was unactionable (Ib 48, II 178); it was lawful to castrate a vagabond, and it was unactionable if he were injured or killed in the process (Ib 203, II 151); one could take in beggars only to whip them (Ib 179, II 258); nor was one to feed or shelter them at the Thing on pain of lesser outlawry; their booths could be knocked down, and if they happened to have any property with them, it could be taken from them without li-ability (Ib 14, II 123).

## Chapter Five

1. I take time with Phillpotts' thesis because it is still adopted without argument, often without attribution, and without re-evaluation of the bases on which it was made. See, e.g., Searle (1988, 162) who adopts Phillpotts' position indirectly via the mediation of Byock (1988, 126), who in turn pre-sents it without reference to its source. For a discussion of Phillpotts' views, see Murray (1983, 24–26). Informed discussions of the formal structures of early Icelandic kinship can be found in Hastrup (1985, 70–104) and briefly in Vestergaard (1988). This chapter is the first attempt at a fairly compre-hensive treatment of practical kinship.

2. Kindreds are groups formed in reference to a person (ego) who is not a common ancestor of the people recruited to the group. All ego's kin are members of his kindred, but they are not all kin to each other. Only full blood siblings have the same kindreds. The group cannot be corporate be-cause it does not survive ego. It cannot be exclusive since one can belong to as many different kindreds as one has kin. A society made up of kindreds, in other words, cannot oppose discrete groupings of closed membership to each other as a society made up of unilineal descent groups can (see Fox 1967, 164–65; also Goody 1983, 222–39).

3. The history of debate on the nature of Germanic kinship is presented in an excellent account by Alexander Murray (1983, 11–38). Murray's pains-taking review of the evidence shows that there is no basis for supposing a unlineal foundation for early Germanic kinship structures. The evidence, such as it is, suggests that early Germanic kinship was bilateral or cognatic. Nevertheless, the debate was characterized by able performances on all

sides. For patrilineality, there was Sir Henry Maine (1861; 1917, 88–89), Sir Paul Vinogradoff (1911) and, more recently, Charles-Edwards (1972) and Meinhard (1975); for matrilineality, Phillpotts (1913) and Chadwick (1912); and for cognation, Maitland (1898), Bullough (1969), and Murray (1983). These kinds of formal kinship studies have been out of favor for some time in anthropology. Historians, too, have been getting more sophisticated about the interrelations of kinship theory and practice, about the play in the joints of kinship systems and how serviceable the categories of kinship are to people. See, for instance, Duby's studies documenting the shift from loose cognatic groupings to narrow agnatic lines of filiation in eleventh-century France (1980, 67–75, 149–57; Goody 1983, 228) and White's careful and insightful reconstruction of formal and practical kinship from the recalcitrant evidence of the *laudatio parentum* (1988, 86–129).

4. See Susan Reynolds generally (1984, 59–64) for a systematic critique of the dangers of measuring medieval collectivities and groupings by subsequently developed legal theories of corporations.

5. Even in many of those societies that do recognize unlineal descent groups, behavior seldom matches lineage theory. Descent groups might often serve more as tropes for the way people talk about rights and other things than as actively functioning units. See, e.g., Eickelman (1981, 105–34) and the discussion in White (1988, 126–27).

6. The ratio is reproduced on a much smaller scale by the four genealogies of the bishops that conclude Ari's *Íslendingabók* (26–27), three of which contain female links. Males outnumber females 23:6, almost twice as imbalanced as the sample from *Landnámabók*; see also Meulengracht Sørensen (1977, 35).

7. Carol Clover (1988) believes the skewed representation of males and females is some evidence of abnormally high sex ratios. A twelfth-century genealogy discussed by Duby (1980, 139) shows a 3:1 male bias that he attributes to a preference for male links as part of a process of kinship constriction and lineage construction.

8. See, for instance, Ari's own genealogy, tracing his descent from the legendary kings of Sweden through thirty-six generations (*Íslb.* 27–28). The genealogy of the Sturlungs, beginning with Adam, lists twenty-four males before reaching a daughter of Priam and then another forty-seven links, one of which is a fictitious female, before reaching Vigdis, the mother of Hvamm-Sturla, the father of Snorri and Sighvat Sturluson (*DI* I 504–6). Anthropologists have recognized the extent of fictionalizing involved in genealogical construction for nearly fifty years (see Evans-Pritchard 1940, 199). Historians have come to this knowledge somewhat later (see, e.g., Dumville 1977, 85–89 and literature cited therein). Genealogies are constructed primarily to explain and validate present relations and to assert present claims to land, title, or preeminence; see variously Sveinbjörn Rafnsson (1974); Jakob Benediktsson (1975–76, 315–18).

9. The inheritance law provides that people are called to succession in the following order:

1. So, freeborn and legitimate
2. Da
3. Fa
4. Br of same father
5. Mo
6. Si of same father
7. Br of same mother
8. Si of same mother
9. illegitimate So
10. illegitimate Da
11. illegitimate Br of same father
12. illegitimate Si of same father
13. illegitimate Br of same mother
14. illegitimate Si of same mother

From this point on all takers must be legitimate—

15. FaFa, MoFa, SoSo, DaSo
16. FaMo, MoMo, SoDa, DaDa
17. FaBr, MoBr, BrSo, SiSo
18. FaSi, MoSi, BrDa, SiDa

If none of the above then,

19. first cousins "shall take equally except if one man is from the mother's side or the father's side but more people are on the other side, then he takes half,"
20. then the nearest kinsman, "but if several people are equally close, then it shall be divided equally among the different branches [i.e., a *per stirpes* distribution]. . . . Men shall always take ahead of a woman of the same degree, but if women are closer, then the inheritance is divided among them." (*Grágás* Ia 218–20, II 63–63)

Earlier enumerated categories took to the exclusion of later ones. If a decedent was thus survived by a legitimate son, daughter, and brother, the son would take all.

10. In Icelandic the Old Norse term *ætt* could mean, depending on context, the kin group, genealogy, or pedigree. There is no suggestion at all in the Icelandic sources that *ætt* referred to a patrilineal group, the wishes of some scholars notwithstanding. Hastrup (1985, 73) writes that "the *ætt* had obvious connotations of a patrilineal kin group, as illustrated for example by the notion of 'coming into *ætt*'; this meant that one became a member of the paternal *ætt*, and the expression was used in connection with affiliating illegitimate children to the paternal kin group" (see also *KLNM* 20:591). Her example, it should be noticed, shows no evidence whatsoever of patrilinealism as opposed to patrilateralism. A child filiated to a father's

*ætt* also became, by virtue of that filiation, a kinsman of his father's mother's kin. There was a term for patrilineage (*langfeðgar*), but it does not appear in the laws. The enumeration of a *langfeðgar*, the *langfeðgartal*, was primarily constructed for Scandinavian royal lines. Ari's genealogy (above chapter 5, n. 8) is a rare Icelandic example. Even the ambitious Sturlungs admit female links in their lengthy genealogy. In Norwegian law, however, the *ætt* did indicate a three-generation minimal patrilineage (see Vestergaard 1988).

11. Second cousins were also disqualified from serving as a *lygkennandi*, a person charged with judging title to disputed animals (*Grágás* II 235). The laws recognize that in some procedures a rule disqualifying second cousins may be excessively burdensome. Only a brother, father, and son are thus improper summons witnesses (Ia 126–27) or ineligible to sit on a panel of neighbors in disputes involving common pasture (Ib 114, II 487). To these three are added the "three near affines" (SiHu, DaHu, MoHu) as people who may not sit on a debt court (Ib 149, II 226).

12. A further gradation of feeling or obligation seems indicated by the term *náfrændi* ("near kinsman"), which is used in one instance to designate without irony someone as distant as a first cousin (MoSiSo, *Hafl.* 2:13; also *Lax.* 79:230).

13. The same rules prohibited marriage with affines and sponsorial kin although on a slightly more lenient basis. Full outlawry was limited to marriages with affines only through the first-cousin level (Ib 60, II 181–82). These rules were revised in 1217 to accord with Lateran IV (1215), allowing fourth cousins to marry on payment of one-tenth of one's property (Ia 37, II 157; *DI* I 385).

14. The source says certain "clerics" were responsible for banning the ménage. Thorlak was undoubtedly the moving force since these events occurred during his episcopate and they were within his jurisdiction.

15. How they were related is not known.

16. A "person" can be either male or female, but to save myself the awkwardness of "he or she" and the imprecision of the third person plural I adopt the impersonal masculine form except when gender needs some special emphasis.

17. Only one debt-slave is known in the sagas. He shows great loyalty to the causes of his householder and is treated to a gift of sufficient value at the saga's end that he is able to set up a household (*Ljós* 24:77, 80; 31:105). Other information on the lot of the debt-slave is no less spare (see Foote 1977a, 55–57, 59). Debt-slaves and thralls, that is, simple slaves, are lumped together in *Grágás* in various provisions. A debt-slave is to be treated like a thrall for Sabbath violations (Ia 26, II 33); each is an exception to the general rule that a bear belongs to the man who killed it (Ia 31, II 40); cases involving harboring them go to the Fifth Court (Ia 78); both debt-slave and thrall are to be tortured and maimed for killing their master or mistress (Ia 189, II 401); and money they win on account of killing an outlaw is due to their creditors (II 399). It would appear, however, that there were differences between debt-slavery and thralldom. Debt-slavery endured only so long as

the debt and it does not appear that the debt-slave was freely transferable as chattel. And fornication with a woman debt-slave is more strictly punished than with a woman slave. The former merits lesser outlawry, the same as with a freedman's wife, the latter a three-mark fine (Ib 48, II 177–78; see also Ia 171, II 336–37).

18. The obligation is all the less attractive to B since the value of the debt with which he can charge A is limited to the value A would have if "he were a thrall" (*Grágás* Ib 4, II 104). Presumably this is intended to prevent the debt-slave's status from being theoretically lower than that of a thrall who might have been able to buy his freedom at the going rate. In this regard see the obscure provision at *Grágás* Ia 192.

19. "Child" refers to generational placement, not to the age of the debt-slave.

20. A stray clause of more general scope in the *Staðarhólsbók* version of the laws gives a corresponding right to the kinsman (B) to whom a dependent person (A) is assigned to make A a debt-slave if B so chooses. "He [B] is to announce his decision to five of his neighbors and at the Thing and forbid his employment elsewhere" (*Grágás* II 145). This provision is not concerned with the triadic arrangement of the child's obligation to support his parents by debt-slavery, but with the dyadic arrangement of a dependent kin and his maintainer. The provision is quite troubling, appearing as it does in only one manuscript, and then allowing the somewhat contradictory possibility that a person could make a debt-slave of his kin but was absolutely prohibited from doing the same to dependents of the Quarter (see p. 152) and paupers of the *hreppr* (*Grágás* Ib 172, II 250). In fact these were to be treated "as well as his servants and be provided clothing." We are unfortunately without saga cases on point and since saga cases on *ómagar* are infrequent there is no way to interpret the silence confidently.

*Ómagabálkr* also did its best to take some of the sting out of the obligations imposed, providing the maintainer other remedies to recoup his outlay. Detailed sections give the person who has maintained an *ómagi* the right to recover the amount of his expenditure, albeit without interest, against the dependent if the latter should come into any property (II 136–38). The right extended not only to property that the dependent might earn or inherit, but to any wealth that was derived from wrongs he had suffered. Thus the maintainer's claim for reimbursement could be satisfied out of any compensation that was due for injuries to or death of his ward, or from fornication payments if the dependent was a woman. The claim was superior to that of the person who might otherwise be entitled to receive such payment (II 136–37), and it survived the period of dependency. Imagine the case of a woman fostered in her youth as a dependent by kinsman X; she later marries Y and then has intercourse with Z. Z would be liable for a payment called *réttr* to the proper plaintiff, who would be Y, the woman's husband (Ib 48, II 177), but X would have a right to as much of the *réttr* as needed to make up his claim. The maintainer not only had a claim against the dependent himself but also against anyone who was more obligated to support the dependent should that person subsequently acquire the means to discharge the obligation (Ib 10, II 116). There is one saga example on point. When Ozur the Rich died there ensued a scramble for his estate. Einar, a chieftain, forced one of the possible claimants to sell his right to Einar. But a certain Alf objected, claiming that he had expended wealth on behalf of Ozur's *ómagar* and that he was thereby entitled to a portion of Ozur's estate (*Sturla* 15:81, 16:83).

21. Wealthy women may have been able to relegate nursing chores to foster-mothers, an option of limited availability to poorer women. Breast-feeding practices are lost to us. We get a glimpse of a mother in an impoverished household raking hay with a child she nursed strapped to her back (*Hrafn Sv. St.* 17:221). The law governing dispensations from Lenten fasting also purported to regulate breast-feeding. A woman is allowed to breast-feed a child until the third Lent after it is born, but she is only to be excused from fasting for the first Lent (*Grágás* Ia 35, II 44). There is little else (see further Þorláksson 1986, 82–84).

22. In *Vápn.* (6:36), the thirteenth-century narrator says that it was a custom in saga times, that is, the late tenth century, for a sick wife to offer to leave the household. The custom is mentioned nowhere else.

23. Divorce pitted household integrity against extrahousehold kin obligations in other ways. Upon divorce the woman was entitled to her dowry, and if the husband was responsible for the divorce, she was also entitled to the *mund*, the husband's contribution to her endowment at the time of marriage (*Grágás* Ib 42–43, II, 170–71). Saga descriptions of divorce show women, not men, leaving the marital household, although presumably if the marital household had been located among the wife's kin it would have been the husband who moved out. It then became her and her kinsmen's responsibility to reclaim her property. The loss of the wife's contribution to the marital property could doom the marital household as a viable economic enterprise; it is thus not surprising to find that husbands resisted the woman's attempt to reclaim her property (*Drop.* 8:156, 9:158–59; *Eyrb.* 17:31; *Heið.* 32:311; *Vápn.* 6:36–38; and cf. *Lax.* 35:96). Her kin, of course, had more than a passing interest in it. They were entitled to be her guardian, and if the marriage was without children, they were her prospective heirs. Moreover, the woman's property allowed her to fund her subsequent marriages herself, without further outlays from her kin. She could thus remain an attractive marriage partner.

24. A new law (*Grágás* Ib 37, II 157; *DI* I 372–92) adopted in 1217, reflecting the influence of the narrowing of kinship reckoning for purposes of marriage prohibition adopted in Lateran IV in 1215, repealed the need to contribute sixty ells to maintain fourth cousins. The *Staðarhólsbók* version of the laws (II 140) seems to reflect the new arrangement by raising to eight half-years the minimum property requirement needed to establish liability for caring for second cousins once removed and third cousins.

25. In a suit for determining liability for maintenance of the dependent, the accuracy of the kinship enumeration had to be sworn to by two men (*Grágás* Ib 11, II 118). The provision governing the challenging of judges for interest gives more detail. The person making the enumeration was to begin

with "brothers, or with a brother and sister, or with sisters, and enumerate the 'knees' until he reaches the man who sits in the court and the man who is the principal in the prosecution or defense" (Ia 47). The passage is somewhat obscure, but it seems to suggest starting with the children of the common ancestor and then counting down the generations until the two people whose kinship is at issue is reached. This would be consistent with the Germanic mode of kinship computation (see Hastrup 1985, 78). For a discussion of this and a comparison with the Roman and parentelic systems, see Goody (1983, 136–41). A false enumeration was to be punished with full outlawry.

26. I am uncertain what the exact arrangement for sending those flawed persons abroad would be. The verb suggests slavery—*selja af landi brott*—literally, to "sell" abroad, but probably simply "to deliver." These people hardly seem of fair merchantable quality. The law in fact allows them to be sent abroad because their value as forced workers in Iceland is so low. It seems fair, however, to see here a limited privileging of the repudiation of annoying kin (see pp. 174–77) or, perhaps, a form of abandonment.

27. Old Icelandic kinship terminology within the first-cousin range was descriptive, that is, relationships were specified by primary terms—mother, father, sister, brother, son, daughter—combined in genitive constructions to indicate the precise nature of the kinship connection. A father's sister was thus *fǫðursystir*, a mother's brother *móðurbróðir*, a sister's son *systursonr*, etc. The descriptive power of the terminology weakened at the first-cousin level with the failure of an individual term for cross cousins and was abandoned completely thereafter where relational distance was still indicated but without regard to the sex of intervening links (see Rich 1980, 476–79 and Barlau 1981, 196–98).

28. Heinrichs (1972) suggests apposition in the saga style is a marker of heightened emotion. This is consistent with the fact that the bulk of appositives are primary kinship terms.

29. There is also a possible connection between 'to cousin' in the sense of to beguile, deceive, and "cozen;" see OED, s.v. cousin 8.

30. Readers of *Njáls saga* have been troubled by two instances in which characters are referred to as *frændi*, and there is no demonstrable blood connection between them (*Njála* 59:150; 67:167). Both occur in contexts in which favors are being requested, and this fact suggests that the kinship term marks the style of request-making and is not a matter of authorial carelessness.

31. An occasional proverb does appear. We saw Gisli recite one to his brother in the preceding chapter about it being best for brothers to keep their property together. "One's back is bare without a brother" occurs in at least two places (*Grett.* 82:260; *Njála* 152:436). And one proverb declares that men are inclined to resemble their mother's brothers (*Pál.* 8:134). It should be noted here that aside from this proverb I have found no clear evidence that practical relations with a mother's brother were specially marked in Iceland the way they appear to have been elsewhere in Germania (see Bremmer 1976).

32. The remarkable thing in this case was that Sæmund's slowness may have been at least partially a consequence of his having been caught in the

middle. His nephew Loft needed support because he had killed the husband of Sæmund's niece. When Loft sought Sæmund for aid, Sæmund said that he was reluctant "to contend with [the victim's father], his *mágr*" (*Íslend.* 39:283). Loft reproached him strongly. Those composing the verses must have thought Sæmund's duty clearer than Sæmund thought it was. Or perhaps they felt that Sæmund's real reason was fear of the victim's father.

33. For classic anthropological treatments of structurally mandated social conflict, see Turner (1957) and Gluckman (1955b). Collaterals are those kin who are neither descendents nor ascendants to each other, such as one's siblings and cousins and the siblings of one's ascendants. No collateral derives being from another collateral as a descendent does from an ancestor.

34. The classic treatment of medieval impatient "youth" is Duby's (1980, 112–22). Compare Schach who treats the antagonisms of fathers and sons as a saga literary theme illustrating the transition from "the savage culture of the Viking Age to the farming community of the Icelandic Commonwealth," from "paganism to Christianity" (1977, 373).

35. In this regard, note that the killing of a foster-brother does not escape mention and is grounds for insults directed the killer's way years later (*Njála* 26:72, 139:371).

36. The sources are in disagreement as to exactly how they are related. *Drop.* (3:143) has Hrafnkel as Helgi A's brother's son, but *Landnámabók* and *Njála* have them as first cousins. Which variant we accept does not affect our discussion.

37. The text is mildly corrupt at this point. My reading follows the one adopted in Andersson and Miller (1989, 244n213).

38. The expectation could occassionally be brutally betrayed, if we extend the following example between friends to be equally likely to include kin: when Arni Bjarnason and Arni Bassason happened to meet in a battle sought by the principals they were attached to, Bjarnason proposed that they not fight each other "because we have undertaken a formal friendship." He then lowered his shield only to find Bassason taking the opportunity to use both hands to swing an ax at his head (*Sturla* 21:93).

39. For an extended discussion of the way in which Hrut admonishes and instructs Hoskuld about better observing his responsibility to consult with him on important matters, see Miller (1984, 120–25).

40. Orlygsstead was the location of a battle (1238) in which Thord kakali's father and brother, who were also kin to Asgrim, were killed.

41. Kolbein was one of the leaders of the opposition at Orlygsstead, who after the defeat of Thord's kin, was the most powerful man in the north of Iceland.

42. The laws, in one place, seem to equate the strength of the affinal bond with the blood bond one "knee" more distant (Hastrup 1985, 92). Thus marriage within the prohibited degrees was punished by full outlawry through second cousins, but only through first cousins if with affines. But I seriously doubt that this gradation was abstracted from practice into the laws, or that it was carried over in any consistent way from the laws into practice. The distinction has an utterly schoolish look.

43. It would appear that in practice *námágr* was applied somewhat less

precisely. In one instance (*Eyrb.* 10:16), a wife's brother is so designated. This should hardly be surprising since it merely accords a mutuality to the relationship of WiBr and his SiHu, that is, they are both in practice, if not in the law, perceived as *námágar* to each other. See the discussion on p. 162.

44. In modern Icelandic people connected by two marriage links are called one's *svili* or *svilkona* (f.). These terms are not, to my knowledge, used in the sagas, but Cleasby and Vigfússon cite an example in the *Snorra Edda* in which the husbands of two sisters are called *svilar*.

45. We may be entitled to see further confirmation of the regularity of such claims by an instance in which a bond of affinity is claimed ironically as part of a cruel joke by a guest who had killed his host's servant and slept with his daughter (see *Njála* 87:212).

46. There is no reason to think that affinal avengers were motivated more by their relation to the corpse than by their relation to the women who connected them to the corpse. Husbands helped their wives avenge her kin, brothers and fathers helped their sisters and daughters avenge their husbands.

47. Snorri's case amply demonstrates that in the world of big politics, when the stakes were high enough, political alliances might shift in spite of having been secured by affinity. Marriages were fragile. They could end in divorce or death. Snorri, in fact, was killed in a surprise attack led by two of his former sons-in-law.

48. The terms are reciprocal, applying both to the foster-parent and the fosterling.

49. The price of Hoskuld's protection was thus the right to the fosterer's entire estate in the future and the cost of raising his child in the present. The assignment of the right to inherit one's estate (*arfsal*) resembles in some ways the commendations of the continent. The sagas preserve several accounts of *arfsal* in consideration of protection, some also involving fostering (see, e.g., *Hœn.* 2:7; and also see p. 289 and below, chapter 7, n. 34).

50. A friend of the unwilling fosterer soon delivered the child to his mother's kinsman, with whom the boy had previously stayed. The friend incurred the wrath of Sturla as a result.

51. A child being fostered to be trained in letters could expect to be "beaten to the books" as was the future Bishop Gudmund (*Prest.* 4:123), something he appeared to have resented for some time (25:151). And children could be beaten for giving offense to visiting guests by the guests themselves, as was a pauper child maintained by the host (*Njála* 8:29)

52. See Miller (1988a, 208–11) for a fuller discussion and bibliography.

53. Primesigning (*primsigning*) was a preliminary baptism. The sagas tell that pagan Icelanders would become catechumens by having the sign of the cross made over them; they were thus allowed easier access abroad to Christian markets and benefactors. Some were primesigned as a way of hedging their bets. Primesigning did not disappear once Iceland converted to Christianity; it still served as a preliminary to baptism. The laws make frequent reference to it. Children who died primesigned but not baptized were to be

buried at the border between hallowed and unhallowed ground (*Grágás* Ia 7, II 6); the sponsors of a litigant's primesigning were disqualified to be judges or sit on a panel of neighbors in their sponsorial kin's case (Ia 47, 62, II 318); and the sponsor at primesigning was forbidden to marry his sponsorial kin (Ib 31, II 158).

54. Divorce and death have their ambiguities too, at least to the extent that the affinal connections that the marriage produced might linger on somewhat longer.

55. This is subject to the exception that a child born of a slave male and a free woman was not an heir of the mother's kin (*Grágás* Ia 224, II 68).

56. Sometimes the leading men of the district might get together and kill a troublemaker or thief before bothering to secure an outlawry judgment (see *G.dýri* 4:166–67; *Íslend.* 142:443).

57. *Grágás* (Ia 173, II 339–40) provides that a foreigner lodged in Iceland should not be quite so vulnerable. If he was killed while lodged with a householder, the householder had the right to prosecute. If he was killed by the householder, the case belonged to the householder's chieftain; if these two were the same person, as they were here, the case belonged to the other chieftains of the local Thing. The realities of the matter, however, were that no other chieftains were going to risk confrontation with Hrut and Hoskuld over someone as unpopular as Thjostolf.

58. It is to be doubted, however, that repudiations were normally a part of positive law, even in pagan times. The anti-Christian enactment has the look of a very special measure, not only because it was attempting to deal with a threatening innovation, but also because it adopted the extraordinary means of putting the enforcement power in the offender's kin. It seems that the law took this idea from a general custom of repudiation for *frændaskǫmm*. The repeal of this measure did not mean that extralegal customary repudiations still might not have taken place in a manner similar to Hrut's repudiation of Thjostolf. But as is readily apparent from my discussion, the evidence is thin indeed.

## Chapter Six

1. Among European historians, the most influential work has been Wallace-Hadrill (1962). For an especially able and thorough recent work see White (1986). Other more particular studies to be consulted are Brown (1986), R. R. Davies (1969), Miller (1983a; 1983b; 1984; 1986a; 1986b), and J. Wormald (1980).

2. The starting point for anthropological discussions of feud remains Evans-Pritchard (1940, 162). Other important and useful works I have consulted and have been influenced by are Black-Michaud (1975), Boehm (1984), Bourdieu (1966; 1977, 1–71), Colson (1953), Hasluck (1954), Gluckman (1955b), Koch (1974), Middleton and Tait (1958, 16–22), Moore (1978), and Peters (1967).

3. Boehm (1984, 218) considers alternating between offense and defense to be one of the defining criteria of feud. This view does not adequately

allow for the effects of ambiguity in the criterion. It was not always obvious whose turn it was, and one of the tasks of the skillful disputant was to convince others that it indeed was his turn to assume the offensive. Practice was considerably richer than the model can account for. Nevertheless, native practice in the feud was still conceptualized as if it were part of an exchange cycle. Cf. Bourdieu (1977, 10–12).

4. Those societies in which feud figures prominently tend to be characterized by a weak or nonexistent state. Early Iceland is a case in point. Historians have shown, however, that the state, at least in the earlier stages of state formation, need not necessarily be hostile to feud; see, e.g., Wallace-Hadrill (1962) and J. Wormald (1980). On state formation in the early medieval period, see Cheyette (1978) and the works cited therein; see also Crone (1986).

5. Some Rechtsschule scholars tried to make distinctions between revenge and feud on the basis of the degree of right the society accorded the wronged party to retaliate. Revenge was seen as an early manifestation of public order, feud as disorder (see, e.g., Wilda 1842, 189–90). Some made no such distinction but talked of both feud and revenge in the language of rights and public order. The Peace Theory, which provides the underpinnings of this work, is reviewed and subjected to an effective polemic by Goebel (1937, 7–25) who, relying heavily on the work of Beyerle (1915), understood feud and revenge as social rather than narrowly legal phenomena. It should be noted that much of Goebel's critique was anticipated by Heusler (1911, 119–23, 235). See generally the discussion in von See (1964, 139–73) confirming, in the Scandinavian context, the inapplicability of the Peace Theory.

6. The absence of a precise native term, it should be noted, deterred neither Maurer nor Gottzmann from talking about marriage as an institution, even though there is no Old Icelandic nominal term indicating the institution (Hástrup 1985, 90). As one consequence of their decision to substitute revenge for feud, neither Maurer (1910) nor Gottzmann (1982) did very well comprehending the disputing process as process, although Maurer's compendious work is still the starting point for many discussions of legal concepts.

7. The break in the line connecting Skarphedin and Sigmund is meant to indicate that, as a formal matter, the killing of Sigmund did not take place in the construct of the prior killings. The reason proffered for the killing at the time it occurred was not that Sigmund had killed Thord, but that he had, subsequent to the settlement for Thord, composed slanderous verses against Skarphedin, his brothers, and father. Nonetheless, the settlement for the killing shows that Sigmund's corpse, if not the act that made him a corpse, was integrated into the earlier series of killings in order to give that series formal closure. Some further relevant events in this dispute are discussed at p. 215, and for a detailed presentation, see Miller (1983a).

8. Disagreements arose as to when the balance was struck. Considerations other than the worth of the victims might figure into the balance also, as, for example, the distance one needed to travel to exact revenge. Thus,

when Bardi announced himself quit with his enemies after taking a "man for a man," his companions disagreed claiming the men were not equally balanced and that "it was insufficiently done to kill only one man considering how far they had traveled to do it" (*Heið*. 27:296). It should be noted, that although exactly when the balance was struck might be disputed, no one rejected the propriety of balancing itself.

9. One saga account shows a disputant consciously setting out to finance the compensation he expects he will have to pay for killing his enemy by collecting compensation from others in the settlement of claims he brings against them (*Ljós*. 5:20; 13:20).

10. There was little cultural precedent for having women participate directly in formal settlements. They were constrained by law and custom to being represented by males. One exceptional woman, however, was formally empowered by the disputants to act as an arbitrator in a case (*Þórð*. 8:17; see also *Vatn*. 44:120). There is more than a suggestion in our source that Njal acquiesced to Bergthora's wishes and indeed gave her subtle indications that he would not prevent her from carrying them out. For a discussion of this matter, see Miller (1986b, 106–7).

11. See chapter 6, n. 7.

12. A servant who killed his master for having fired his father on suspicion of having stolen hay was expeditiously hunted down and killed in *Íslend*. 141:440–42.

13. On the variations in the severity and types of law and social control as a function of differences in social strata, see Black (1976, 11–36; 1984).

14. See Miller (1983a) for a more detailed presentation of how prior events were recalled and reinterpreted; see also p. 217 in the text.

15. Some dying men tried to excuse their kin from taking vengeance on their behalf, but the honor of the living tended to outweigh the desires of the dead (see *Reyk*. 16:201, *Vatn*. 22:61, 47:129). Under certain circumstances the greater honor might lie in accepting compensation (see *Njála* 145:411–14 and *Íslend*. 40:285; see further chapter 8).

16. On *vígt*, see Heusler (1911, 54; also Ingvarsson 1970, 68–76). A man who had been killed justifiably was said to have fallen *óhelgaðr* ("unhallowed") or to have been in an unhallowed state, *óhelgi*. The issue of justification could arise procedurally as a defense and also as an independent action. In the latter procedure the dead man was summoned to *óhelgi* (e.g., *Grágás* Ia 165). In this action, the corpse's wrong was the central issue. Alternatively, the matter could be raised as a defense in a killing case brought by the corpse's kin. The question of justification was put to a panel of five selected by the defendant from the panel of nine neighbors who acted as a jury (Ia 157–58). If they found in favor of the defense submission, the plaintiff's case failed and he was without further recourse at law. See the discussion in Heusler (1911, 62–68, 114–20) and Maurer (1910, 61–75).

17. It is mentioned in *Vápn*. 14:53 that one avenger intended to take advantage of his adversary's trust that there would be no attack during the fall roundup.

18. The location of the vengeance killing could in some circumstances

confer honor on the corpse being avenged and the avenger. One of three reasons Grettir was considered unequaled among outlaws was that he was avenged in Byzantium, something that no other Icelander could claim (*Grett.* 93:290; see also *Fóst.* 24:258–59).

19. The norm is uttered in almost proverbial form in a heated argument: "All know that burners are the most vile of outcast, both in God's law and in man's" (*Þorg. sk.* 57:199). Yet Bishop Heinrek can still manage to justify the actions of his allies, who are the burners referred to in the preceding sentence: "You tell of what they did as burners, but you are silent about what was done to them before, the losses they suffered and other humiliations."

20. Assassination, interestingly, figures much more frequently in the family sagas, where we would expect some sanitization of the record, than in *Sturlunga saga* (Heusler 1912, 42). I suggest the following explanation for the variation: in both *Sturlunga saga* and the family sagas, assassins are disreputable men. They are outlaws, foreigners, destitute, or shipwrecked (*Eyrb.* 35:97; *Hafl.* 13:30; *Reyk.* 21:217, 22:218; *Sturla* 12:78; *Vatn.* 39:101, 40:103). Their usual method is to enter service in the target's household and wait for an opportunity to carry out the mission. While the evidence from the contemporary sagas suggests that this may indeed have been how assassinations were carried out, the formulaic and repetitive manner in which assassination is treated in the family sagas (see, especially *Reyk.* 21:217, 22:218; *Vatn.* 39:101, 40:103) would seem to indicate that the accounts are manifestations of householder fears of the servant class. The assassin is the image of all the dangers that lurk in the annual hiring of people during Moving Days. The assassin is the embodiment of the anxieties associated with the ambiguities of the stranger, who may be guest, servant, or assassin, but who in thirteenth-century Iceland was more likely to be a member of the impoverished class, forced by poverty into itinerancy and the necessity of seeking household attachment among strangers.

21. See, e.g., *G.dýri* 14:190–91, where the task of executing four men is parceled out among four different followers of Thorgrim, the group leader.

22. I am here assuming that it is more likely that thirteenth-century writers were idealizing their account of the Saga Age than that the people of the tenth century had especially refined sensibilities regarding mutilation. It is hard to believe that second- and third-generation descendents of Vikings would have been more averse to hewing off a leg or two than ninth- and tenth-generation descendents a couple of centuries later. The accounts of mutilation in the family sagas show no sign that these actions were in any way unusual, and we see one party nonchalantly negotiate with a hired assassin either to handhew or leghew his opponent, whichever he could manage (*Vatn.* 40:104).

23. See also *Grett.*, where striking a "half-dead" man formed the basis of an outlawry action (84:268).

24. Reykjaholt was Snorri Sturluson's chief residence and where he was killed in 1241.

25. See, e.g., the case of Sturla Barðarson (*Hrafn Sv.* St. 19:226, *Íslend.* 46:294). Regarding corpses: it was not proper to strike a corpse for the sake of humiliating it (*Grett.* 82:262). Decapitations of corpses were dealt with less directly, but the evidence suggests that it was not always appropriate. Thus, the decapitators were usually opposed to the saga hero (e.g., *Bjarn.* 32–33:203–5; *Fóst.* 17:210; *Grett.* 82:262; but cf. *Njála* 45:117). In one case the decapitators decided to amuse themselves by mocking the head, but ended up being so frightened by its grisly aspect that they immediately buried it (*Fóst.* 18:212). Two especially cruel mutilators displayed the heads to the mothers of the corpses (*Bjarn.* 33:205; *Grett.* 83:265–66). Yet there are cases that suggest that decapitation was less a matter of humiliation than a mode of proving death, especially in the case of outlaws (see, e.g., *Þorst. stang.* above chapter 2). The manner of burial of a victim could provide the avengers of the corpse with added grievance (*Þorg. sk.* 44:174) as could the refusal to allow the kin to recover the corpse (*Vápn.* 7:41). For a discussion of stripping and plundering corpses, see Gade (1988).

26. There is an enormous literature on this saga, none of which has cared to make the points to be made here. It is primarily around *Hrafnkels saga* that the Icelandic school of saga scholarship has centered its debate on saga historicity. With Sigurður Nordal (1940, 1957) compare Óskar Halldórsson (1976) and Hughes (1980); see most recently Andersson (1988).

27. The Old Norse name is *Sámr*, meaning dark complexioned, and it bears no connection to Hebrew Samuel.

28. Besides giving Eyvind a heroic end, the author supplies a gratuitous detail in order to establish Eyvind's generous spirit. Eyvind is accompanied by a servant boy, a kinsman of his, whom he had rescued from poverty and provided for in the same way he provided for himself (8:126). The author also constructs a remarkably tense chase scene that Hollywood has not yet improved upon, solely, it seems, to make the tragedy of Eyvind's failure to get away all the more frustrating to the reader.

29. Even in those cases in which a person was killed with sufficient legal justification, the community's perceptions of justice might still call for that person to pay some compensation for those people he lawfully killed. In cases in which people were killed justifiably, it is not unusual to find arbitrators awarding some compensation for the victims. The general feeling was that the prospect for future peace required some assuaging of the victims' kin; see especially *Bjarn.* 20:171, 27:187 and the discussion in the text on p. 282.

30. The plural "those" is original and is used as a mild indirection that is made direct in the following clause. The referent is still clearly Helgi.

31. Notice in the context of the preceding discussion (above p. 203) that there is no question but that only one of the several people who have engaged in liability-creating conduct would be killed.

32. People at times went to some length to distinguish themselves from groupings they were otherwise part of. Their measures could be directed legalistically to avoid giving rise to a specific cause of action. Some mem-

bers of Gizur's vengeance muster, for example, took care to provision themselves from their own property so as not to make themselves liable for the raiding that accompanied the blood-taking (*Íslend.* 175:495). Or their measures might be more designed to avoid giving general offense, which might make them the butt of nonlegal reprisal. The farmer, who sought to warn the men of Hvamm that their enemies were at the baths, felt it necessary to disguise his assistance by driving his cows toward the Hvammsmen and punctuating his warnings with cattle calls so that the other side would not observe him assisting its enemies (*Sturla* 19:87–88). *Grágás* too, as noted above chapter 4, n. 16, provided a formal procedure for one of two joint householders to deny liability if the other gave shelter to an outlaw (Ia 126). At some point conduct produced liability for what we would call an attempt. Thus Eyjolf did not inform the group of men he mustered of the mission's purpose until they were about ten miles from their destination, at which point his followers "considered it as bad to turn back as to continue on. And no one who had come that far turned back" (*Íslend.* 171:485). Devotees of the presently fashionable discourse of incentives might note that the law gave these men no great incentive to adopt the peaceful course. But it was less a matter of the legal liability incurred than of certain practical disadvantages to breaking off that urged them onward. It simply made no sense to abort an attack once someone had already done enough to apprise the other side of his aggressive designs. Abortive action, no less than completed action, justified the other side in taking reprisal (see *Grágás* Ia 183, II 377).

33. See generally *Þórð.*, and for a synopsis of the events, see Jóhannesson (1974, 257–59).

34. The victim's wrong need not excuse vengeance on his behalf, but it could very well provide his killer with a valid affirmative defense if the response were made at law rather than in blood (see chapter 6, n. 16).

35. Just as women were not appropriate expiators in the feud, they were not appropriate avengers. The sexual division of labor was at its strictest on this point. Nevertheless, there are women in the family sagas who play the role of the avenger. One, Breeches-Aud, is a crossdresser and suffers ridicule on that account from both the saga writer and his characters as indeed her cognomen clearly indicates (*Lax.* 35:95–98). The revenge she takes on the husband who divorced her merits a brief comment because of the ingenious way in which the saga (ironically) reintegrates her vengeance to acceptable gender activity, transforming her cutting flesh into tailoring a figurative shirt for her husband. Aud's husband, Thord, had divorced her, alleging as grounds her crossdressing. He had been provoked into doing so by his mistress, Gudrun. Gudrun had divorced her husband on identical grounds after she, following Thord's advice, had made him a lowcut shirt, considered appropriate only to women. When Aud managed to gash Thord with a knife across both his nipples she, in effect, cut him a shirt of the same low neckline that Gudrun had cut for her first husband. Thord is thus the object of artfully balanced requitals at the hands of both of his women: Gudrun

forced him to divorce his wife on the same grounds he had advised her to divorce her husband, and Aud forces him to suffer the consequences of that advice in, figuratively, the same way in which he had humiliated Gudrun's husband. The disapproving commentary on the other well-known female avenger is subtler and must be found only in her failure to kill her target (Gísli 37:116). Presumably part of the unspoken justification for Sturla's exceptionally high self-judged award for the gash in the cheek he suffered from Pal's wife (see pp. 158–59 and p. 255) was in part compensation for the humiliation of having been wounded by a woman (Sturla 31–32: 110–11). Women, however, did participate in fighting in order to defend their men and their households without any opprobrium whatsoever attaching to their actions (Íslend. 2:230, 199:531; Gísli 34–35:112–13; Sturla 8:72; Vatn. 44:118). On the interesting case of female avengers in the Albanian bloodfeud, see Whitaker (1981, 151) and Shryock (1988); see also Miller (1983b) and Clover (1986, 173–75), and for a review of the literature on women in the sagas, see Clover (1985, 256–59).

36. The sagas, in fact, do show a shaming ritual in every way analogous to sitting dharna. People requesting to be taken in and given protection threaten not to move: "and I shall be killed here to your great disgrace" (Vatn. 24:64). See also Njála 88:216, Ljós. 18:49, and Andersson and Miller (1989, 190n121).

37. Clover (1986, 174) argues that the vengefulness of women is directly related to the fact that they were excluded from the arbitrational and legal arenas "and hence from whatever agonistic satisfaction was to be had from the successful prosecution of a case (and according to the sagas this could be considerable; if legal revenge was a second-class revenge even for men, it must have been no revenge at all for women . . . )." But this argument proves too much since women were no less excluded from actual vengeance-taking by norms every bit as powerful as the legal rules that excluded them from the courts. Even when she goaded, she acted through men, just as she was constrained to do at law or in arbitration.

38. "the general view was" (var ok ekki þat orð á): My translation might be a little tendentious. Equally plausible are "there was no mention that" and "it was not said that." In whatever case, the Old Icelandic refers to people commenting on the fact of there having been no goading.

39. We have met Thoralf earlier but not by name. It was he who told Kalf to move the crucifix lest it be splattered with his blood when he was executed (see above p. 192).

40. It has been a common feature of saga studies that once the literary relations or qualities of a theme have been demonstrated that that determines negatively the issue of whether it also has social significance. Repetition, stylization, and conventionalization of form take place in the world of action as well as in the world of letters. And when it takes place in the world of letters alone, that too is not without social significance, if only because it is a social universe that is being depicted.

41. I discuss the role dreams play in the dispute-processing system in

some detail in Miller (1986b), where one can also find the relevant bibliography.

## Chapter Seven

1. The question of how to define law for purposes of cross-cultural comparison is a vexed one that at one time elicited enormous amounts of scholarly energy among legal anthropologists in the fifties and sixties. No one succeeded in proposing a definition that won a large following and eventually the struggle to find one petered out in exhaustion and a tacit admission that the question was not all that interesting. Precise definitions invariably suffered from the vice of ethnocentrism, usually finding law only where the investigator could discern people acting like western judges and lawyers. Some tried to overcome the ethnocentrism of their definitions by imagining wigs, robes, and three-piece suits in the strangest of places: for some, Eskimo song duels punctuated as they were by occasional head butts and performed to audience applause satisfied the requisites of primitive law (Hoebel 1954, 67–99). Still others favored such broad definitions that all social norms became law (Malinowski 1926, 31–32). See Roberts (1979, 17–29, 184–206) for a useful discussion of the debate. There is a tacit consensus now among those interested in legal anthropology that what is interesting are rules and how rules are socially constituted, not whether a particular rule can form the basis of a claim that can be heard by a court. But if the question of what is law is not all that interesting, the questions of why certain rules are institutionalized as laws, and what effect such institutionalization has on how people behave, is interesting.

2. For a thorough philological discussion of the etymology and semantics of Old Norse *lǫg*, see von See (1964, 174–95).

3. My colleague, Frederick Schauer, suggests a further distinction. Of those cultures that articulate their rules, some might take them more seriously than others. Compare, for example, American and English queuing practices or the varying effectiveness of American and North European jaywalking prohibitions. But it would be dangerous to generalize about attitudes toward rules as rules from such anecdotal evidence. Some rules are taken more seriously than others in any culture, and most all of us take a dim view of those who make no distinctions in the level of seriousness of different rules, although we are all familiar with such people. In early Iceland not every breach of every rule engendered dispute or loss of reputation.

4. On the various ways of commencing a lawsuit, see below chapter 7, n. 24.

5. Heusler (1911, 223) makes the same point using as his example of *Grágás'* tendency to overregulate and oversanction a provision that stipulates a three-mark fine for knocking a hat off someone's head, lesser outlawry if the hat has a chinstrap and is knocked off toward the front, but full outlawry and the right to kill if the hat has a chinstrap that holds fast and the hat is knocked toward the back (*Grágás* II 381).

6. I print a portion of the provision as another example of the *Grágás* style; it also gives some sense of the important role that neighbors were expected to play in the resolution of minor disputes:

> When the sea, water, or storms drive more than one person's hay together, then the one who has hay mixed with another's hay or in another's land should go to the home of the man who owns the land on which the hay is and call him for a hay-division on a weekday three days or more before the division if he speaks with the landowner himself, but in a week or more time if he does not speak with him directly. He shall call the neighbors who live nearest the hay that is the subject of the division and who have no interest in the hay. Five neighbors are to be called three days before the division in order to determine his share of that hay; they are to arrive before midday. The neighbors shall be challenged as they would for a "meadowcourt" [see Ib 85, II 457]. If the other obstructs the division, that is punishable by a three-mark fine. If he converts the hay to his own use, that is a minor theft [the penalty for which is double damages and a three-mark fine (Ib 162)]. Now if the man does not ask for a division before the other has taken the hay home, then the latter has so much recompense in hay as the neighbors estimate was the value of the hay he stacked. These people should dry their hay on the land in which it was driven; they are not to carry it off before it is divided . . . (*Grágás* Ib 106–7, II 460–61)

7. I mean restitution in the legal sense of making good actual material losses. In a broader sense, all punishment meted out pursuant to the law had a restitutional aspect because it was understood to restore the honor lost by the moving party (Grønbech 1932, 80–83).

8. This provision occurs in a chapter devoted to sorcery and idolatry. *Berserksgangr*, a berserk fit, was associated with heathen practices.

9. *Baugatal* (see above p. 144) seems to have been one such provision. It is necessary, nevertheless, to note that the sheer pleasure in the formulation of laws might not always carry over into a sheer pleasure in applying them or obeying them when they gave results that offended more general norms of justice and right.

10. On the transition from an oral to a written legal culture and its connection to the process of state formation, see the provocative article by Fredric Cheyette (1980).

11. We have no way of knowing the general extent of literacy. Anecdotal evidence suggests that the ability to read the vernacular may not have been unusual for a chieftain or farmer of means. The very existence of the sagas seems to indicate as much. A letter composed by a priest is sent to a *bóndi*

who reads it (*Íslend.* 94:365–67). Sturla Sighvatsson is shown singing a prayer (almost certainly in Latin) that he reads from a scroll (*Íslend.* 138:430). And the chieftains Brand and Gizur discussed feuding strategy in a letter (*Þórð.* 40:72). These passing notices are not without their problems. Do we know for sure that when someone is said to look at a letter or read it that it is not being read to him? (See Clanchy 1979, 175–230). The letter from Brand to Gizur could have been written by a priest in Brand's following and read to Gizur, but the first two examples seem fairly secure. Two oft-told anecdotes about the bishop's school at Hólar show that Latin literacy was not just confined to monks and priests. A woman named Ingunn taught Latin there and a certain builder employed by Bishop Jon was able to become very skilled at Latin simply by eavesdropping on the lessons of the young clerics while at his work (*Jóns saga* 23:235, 27:241).

12. The Gulathing law was generally applicable in southwest Norway, the region from which a large number of the settlers to Iceland originated.

13. The skill required seems to have been a general one. The *lǫgmenn* were expected to have a knowledge of the laws and to be skilled strategists and good pleaders. There do not appear to have been specialties within the law and no evidence suggests that special status was accorded the different aspects of legal wisdom and skill.

14. On the Lǫgrétta, see p. 18. Each chieftain who sat there, it will be recalled, was to select two advisers who then sat in the body. These advisers may have been drawn from the ranks of those legal experts who were not chieftains. If such were the case, the Lǫgrétta would provide an annual convocation of most all men skilled in law in the country. See *Grágás* Ia 211–17; Jóhannesson (1974, 63–66).

15. Not all legal experts were chieftains, however. The best known legal expert in the sagas, Njal, was a simple *bóndi*; see also, e.g., *Hafl.* 3:14.

16. The source says somewhat obscurely that "the women found the verdicts of the mock court rather strong. They could not make valid defenses and were not at liberty to come and go as they pleased."

17. The ultimate sanction, full outlawry, also had its symbolic aspects, but in Iceland the symbol was more social than legal inasmuch as the Old Icelandic word was not constructed with "law" as an element. The Icelandic term for full outlawry, *skóggangr*, meant forest-going, referring presumably to the haunts of the wolf, the outcast from human society, the wanderer, the exile. The reflex of "outlaw" in Old Icelandic, *útlagr*, referred only to a three-mark fine, not to full outlawry, except in late texts showing Norwegian influence.

18. The exception to this rule, as in the section on bone removal, is when special provision is made for the cause of action to belong to anyone who wanted it.

19. The same casuistic style informs nearly all of *Grágás'* provisions, whatever their original motivation may have been. In the absence of other evidence, complexity of expression and conception is not in itself always sufficient reason to doubt that the rule informed practice or affected actual

disputes. Although complexity of conception coupled with saga evidence showing no sign of the law's existence in situations to which it would have applied should raise serious doubts about the particular law's viability (see further p. 231).

20. This proverb appears in several early Scandinavian codes: the Norwegian Frostathing law and Járnsíða, the Norwegian code introduced into Iceland in 1271, as well as the Swedish Hednalagen. Von See (1964, 88, 188, 191) believes the proverb dates from the thirteenth century, cf. however Magnús Olsen (1946, 78–80), who finds indirect evidence of it much earlier in Thorgeir the Lawspeaker's speech at the Allthing, anno 1000. No other relevant proverbs appear to take law as their subject; see Jónsson (1914, 111), Gering (1915), and von See (1964, 87–88).

21. In another case the defendant, Glum, forcibly disrupted the court. The judges were eventually able to reconvene elsewhere, but once they started summing up the cases prior to giving judgment, Glum formally banned the judgment because the prescribed time for completing the cases had passed (Glúma 24:83–84). Even the violent disrupter did not claim the suspension of all law. The very act of disruption admitted the belief in the legitimacy and force of a proceeding that needed to be disrupted.

22. Grágás does not speak precisely to the point raised by this episode, but it takes care to legalize some moral obligations that third parties might have been expected to owe those who had to bury their dead. One stricture obliged a bóndi to provide hospitality to a man and up to four of his companions who bore a body for burial. The law backed the obligation by giving the man denied hospitality an action for a three-mark fine (Ia 8). Another scene in Eyrbyggja saga (51:143–45) suggests that the real sanction was the fear of what the corpse might do to the inhospitable man. After a farmer had denied food to the men who were taking Thorgunna's corpse for burial, Thorgunna rose from her coffin and prepared a meal for her bearers to the terror of the bóndi and his wife. The saga mentions that for the rest of the trip they were provided with good hospitality by all who heard of the strange event.

23. As long as the old provisions remained in the manuscripts, determinations of obsolescence are problematic for the researcher unless the new law's status as new was explicitly marked.

24. There were two ways a legal action could be commenced: (1) by summoning at the domicile of the defendant or (2) by publishing the case at the Thing for prosecution. In the former case the panel of neighbors was recruited from those neighbors who happened to be at the Thing, in the latter the neighbors were called to attend the Thing before the publication. In the publication procedure it was possible that the defendant might never receive notice of the action against him (see, e.g., Bjarn. 19:164 where a ruse depends upon a man believing he might not know if he was prosecuted the previous summer). Such lack of notice is consistent with the rule denying access to the Thing to those who have wounds or killings charged against them (Grágás Ia 174–75, II 351); the defendant wasn't supposed to be there

anyway. According to the law, a defense could be made by anyone present at the Thing if the defendant was not in attendance and if he had not transferred the defense to another (Ia 47). Those defenses based on pleading errors arising from the presentation of the case would presumably be noticeable by any number of reasonably competent observers. Cases specified as summoning cases had to be commenced by summons, but publishing cases could be initiated by either means (Ia 178–79, II 359). It seems likely that the summoning procedure was the earlier form to which publication was added. In killing cases, the publication procedure eliminated one confrontation between the victim's kin and the killer that summoning entailed.

25. Forcible disruptions or general affrays among disputants at the Allthing occur in *Hafl.* 18:34–35; *Íslend.* 5:233; *Njála* 145:402–8; and at local Things in *Glúma* 24:83–84; *Ljós.* 11:135; *Vápn.* 6:38; see further Heusler (1912, 67–68). According to saga chronology, years and even decades might pass between cases involving forcible disruption or general affrays at the Thing. And these are just the kind of incidents that were likely to have penetrated the saga record if they had occurred. But disruption of cases need not have been a frequent occurrence for the possibility of it occurring to have greatly influenced behavior. In any significant case people always planned around the possibility: "Gizur and Orm rode with their forces to the beginning of the Thing. They arrived there on Thursday and so arranged the Thing that they would be able to carry forward their legal actions" (*Íslend.* 157:466). Even the possibility of disruption, however, could not realistically have existed unless at least one of the disputants was very powerful. All the recorded cases of disruption were serious political disputes usually involving parties with longstanding feuds. The legal arena was simply not adequate to contain the nonlegal components driving the dispute. Presumably nicely confined lawsuits between people who were incapable of pursuing the feud or had no wish to do so did not always necessitate extensive support mustering.

26. *Grágás* (Ia 109) mentions two lesser grades of outlawry: (1) *fjǫrbaugsgarðr*, the so-called lesser outlawry providing for expulsion from Iceland for three years and forfeiture of property; (2) as in number 1, except that the term of expulsion is for life. The difference between number 2 and full outlawry or *skóggangr* is that the former privileged the outlaw to find passage abroad at specified harbors for a limited period of time. Punishments patterned after the lesser grades of outlawry appear regularly pursuant to arbitrated settlements. The family sagas do not show the lesser grades of outlawry being imposed as a consequence of legal judgments, although *Sturlunga saga* shows a few examples. See Heusler (1911, 124–90, esp. 158–63, and 1912, 81–83) for a full discussion of the forms of penalty in the sagas and laws.

27. Gudmund's anguish occurs in 1183. Ten years earlier the Norwegian archbishop, in a letter to the Icelanders, forbad any member of the clergy to celebrate services if he had killed a man; in the same letter, the clergy was likewise not allowed to prosecute cases except on behalf of orphans, desti-

tute women, or decrepit kinsmen (*DI* I 222). Gudmund seems to have been
more troubled by the first of these provisions than by the second.

28. The number of those cases that actually did result in legal judgments
do not reflect the possibility that the judgment would be formally released
or renegotiated in a subsequent arbitration proceeding. It should be noted
that the fact that most lawsuits did not go to judgment accords rather well
with what we know about dispute settlement on the continent in the
medieval and early modern period. See, e.g., Clanchy (1983), Sharpe (1983),
J. Wormald (1986), and below chapter 8. In some medieval settings, where
law itself was more amenable to bargain and negotiation and less coherent
as an independent body of rules, the distinction between legal judgment and
compromise settlement is not analytically very significant (see, e.g., White
1978). In other settings where law was, if not exactly autonomous, still distinguishable from other social norms, compromise settlements were often
"regarded as a necessity" (Wickham 1986a, 123; 1986b).

29. A paradigmatic example of the expandibility of disputes is discussed
extensively in Andersson and Miller (1989, 32–43).

30. If we see the feud as a process, in Iceland law was integral to it no less
than blood or arbitration. The Icelandic feud was not subculture dispute
processing. In this respect the Icelandic feud compares with the Merovingian feud (Wallace-Hadrill 1962) and contrasts with the feud as it is
practiced in twentieth-century Albania, Sardinia, or Sicily (Hasluck 1954,
Ruffini 1978). In those countries the feud was opposed to a hostile state law.
When a feuding party in Sardinia opted to use the court system, he opted
out of the feuding system. The decision to do so was a virtual repudiation
of the values of the community, a breach of the solidarity that bound the
hostile parties together in feud. The style of feuding did not, however, remain unaffected by the presence of state authorities claiming a monopoly
on justice, but there is no way to predict the effects without a knowledge of
local variables. The state may make its presence felt just enough to discourage the more violent forms of feud, or, by foreclosing meaningful access to
law, it may end up promoting the violent resolution of claims that in its
absence would have been settled out.

31. Typical of *Grágás'* fascination with intricate ordering, the outlaw's
status was upgraded one step for each outlaw he killed until he was fully
reprieved after three killings. He was entitled to passage abroad after the
first killing; after two killings he became a lesser outlaw. This opportunity,
however, was not allowed to those outlawed for theft or killing (II 399–400;
cf. Ia 187). A non-outlaw who killed outlaws was able to accord a living
outlaw the benefit of his actions by announcing before five neighbors that
the killing was for the reprieve of a certain outlaw (Ia 187–88, II 399–400).

32. The identity of the *aðili* followed the ordering of the inheritance law
with minor exceptions and with the total exclusion of women and minors
(see above chapter 5, n. 9).

33. The assignment could be made for actions arising in the future.
People who went abroad could thus transfer to another the defense or prose-

cution of any claims that might involve them (see *Ljós.* 22:65; *Sturla* 9:73).

34. Assignments of the right to inherit were made by the ancestor to the dispossession of his heirs. These could be set aside by the heir if they were not judged fair by five neighbors, but to the extent that the purchaser of the right was a powerful chieftain, the heirs right of reclamation was not worth much. The *arfsal*, or inheritance transfer, was, according to saga evidence, a common way big men expropriated the property of littler men needing protection. See *Grágás* Ia 247–49, II 85–87; *Eyrb.* 31:84–85; *Hœn.* 2:7; *Lax.* 16:37; *Vápn.* 7:38.

35. Occasionally the transferee was sought more for his skills as pleader or legal strategist than solely for his power, although most chieftains knew their law well enough to discharge the legal tasks their positions thrust upon them. Pleading was not the safest of jobs. The agent soon earned the enmity directed toward his principal. Fear of violent reprisal made some chieftains and pleaders reluctant to take up the claims pressed upon them (*Njála* 135:355–56, 138:364), not, it might be added, without some justification (e.g., *Njála* 141:377ff.).

36. On venue, see p. 17 above. As a general rule, all cases could be tried at the Allthing. Cases tried at the local Thing required that both litigants belong to that Thing, except a plaintiff could prosecute a defendant in the defendant's local Thing if both parties agreed to it (see *Grágás* II 356).

37. The role the household played in lawsuits and arbitrations was relatively minor. It was easier, some would say more efficient, to seek support from those who could transport and feed themselves because they were obliged to attend the Thing anyway than to provide horses, fodder, and food for one's servants and slaves in order to get them to the Thing.

38. Thorbjorn's response succinctly captures the cultural preference for activity rather than passivity when one felt aggrieved. The preference did not mean, however, that all old men acted. But when they felt incapable of action, they languished in despair until reminded, usually by their women, of the unmanliness of inaction (*Háv.* 5:308; *Íslend.* 97:370–71). Norse fatalism, unlike the Mediterranean variety, was not supposed to lead to stoic quiescence. To do something was better than to do nothing. Moreover, Thorbjorn had little to lose. His status and honor were so far beneath Hrafnkel's that he really risked no further loss of esteem for trying to sue him. And the very act of doing something assuaged the sense of loss and satisfied some of the desire for vengeance.

39. Flight was often more effective than law, surely from the weak defendant's point of view, but also from the weak grievant's. Testimony to the effectiveness—for a weak defendant—of simply leaving the Quarter can be deduced from a passing observation that it was considered a noteworthy feat that a prosecutor from one Quarter was able to outlaw and then kill his opponent in another Quarter (*Lax.* 82:236). Among equals, avoidance need not mean moving, but would manifest itself by withdrawing from gift and feast exchanges, athletic contests, and other social contact (e.g., *Eyrb.* 31:84).

40. Traditional legal history has consistently overemphasized the formal and irrational in early legal systems. The emphasis is partly a function of legal sources more likely to preserve rules of procedure than the actual processes of resolution and partly a function of researcher fascination with exotica, which in turn reinforced the evolutionary bias of much of this scholarship. The evolutionists wished to find evidence of early benighted practice to help construct the apologetics for the merits of "rational" bureaucratic decision making. A much-needed corrective, not without its own vice of romanticizing primitive practices, has been supplied by historians who have benefited from anthropological studies of primitive dispute resolution and ritual. These studies show that there is more sense to things like ordeal and oath than earlier legal historians were willing to admit. See, e.g., Bartlett (1986), Brown (1975), Colman (1974), Davies and Fouracre (1986), Hyams (1981), Reynolds (1984), White (1978, 1986, 1988). On Icelandic ordeal, see Miller (1988a).

41. Some errors were very serious, but they were usually of the same sort that would lead to dismissals today. A case could thus be voided for having been brought in the wrong court. But even then the case could be brought again in the proper court if the applicable limitations period had not as yet run (see also *Grágás* Ia 52; *Ljós.* 11:134–35).

42. See below chapter 7, n. 48.

43. Generally the panel of neighbors numbered nine men for full or lesser outlawry actions and five men for actions involving damages or the evaluation of property (e.g., see above chapter 7, n. 6). For a detailed discussion of the size of the panel, see Maurer (1910, 569–78). The party seeking the clearing verdict, in effect, makes the panel his own, and its members are thus subject to challenge by the prosecution for interest, just as if the prosecutor were the defendant (*Grágás* Ia 65).

44. One saga case, however, suggests that contrary testimony was possible, although it is not quite clear from the brief account whether the case was being heard in court or was being argued before arbitrators. The case is given in two versions, one in the full text of *Hrafns saga Sveinbjarnarsonar* (15:665), the other in the abbreviated version of the saga in *Sturlunga saga* (*Hrafn Sv.* St. 16:220). The full text has a more circumstantial account, which suggests the case was most likely being tried outside of court. The *Sturlunga* compiler, however, edited out the details that indicate it was likely to have been heard before arbitrators. The compiler may only have been intent on abridgment, but it also may be that he was not dismayed by the possibility of contrary testimony in a court case. Unfortunately, his lack of dismay is not likely to be informed by his knowledge of commonwealth legal procedure, if, as is usually supposed, the compilation dates c. 1300.

45. I treat the techniques for the discovery of secret wrongs at some length in Miller (1986b).

46. The significance of the number of cases is hard to establish, but it seems to be exceptionally low when compared to the number of ordeals we would see offered, if not performed, on the continent, given a like sample of cases.

47. For example, a case of plotting was made out against someone by his simply having been with one of the proven wrongdoers shortly before the particular wrong was committed (Íslend. 180:506).

48. Njáls saga was written not earlier than the last two decades of the thirteenth century. The author's fascination with pleading and legal procedure is well known, but it has been demonstrated that his knowledge of Grágás is often faulty, showing occasionally the influence of post-commonwealth Norwegian law. A systematic presentation of the saga's deviations from a supposed Grágás orthodoxy is detailed in Lehmann and Carolsfeld (1883). But in many respects Njála tracks Grágás' language quite closely, and it seems that the author may have been copying from a manuscript of laws, or had committed to memory portions of the law of procedure (Lönnroth 1976, 248). In other words, in matters of pleading procedure, the saga does not really give us evidence independent of the laws, and even then the evidence may be contaminated by late Norwegian influence. Lehmann, however, overstated the case against Njála's usefulness on some legal matters. Once the saga concerns itself with processual structures and disputing style, rather than with procedural technicality, it falls well within the range of patterns described in earlier sagas. But in matters of courtroom procedure the saga is to be used with caution, if at all.

49. Although the citation law clearly contemplates the consultation of books, the sagas, to my knowledge, do not show any examples of litigants, their advisers, or judges actually consulting a written legal text. The sagas show people consulting living experts, notably the Lawspeaker (e.g., Grett. 27:93, Njála 142:388–90). But as we have had occasion to note (above p. 225), other texts, Hungrvaka and The First Grammatical Treatise, suggest an intimate connection between literacy and law. Patrick Wormald notes the extreme rarity of any references to judges actually consulting written laws in western Europe in the ninth, tenth, and eleventh centuries (1977a, 119–25; 1977b, 105–7). There is no reason to believe that Icelandic judges used written texts to inform themselves of the law, but there is good reason to believe that the legal culture of the experts had become intimately connected to reading and writing by the twelfth century.

50. To summon the dead Sigmund to óhelgi (see chapter 6, n. 16) Glum first dug him up. The same procedure is also mentioned in Njála (64:161). If this were ancient practice, Christianity would presumably have assisted in its demise (Lehmann and Carolsfeld 1883, 71). The only provision for digging up corpses in Grágás is in the passage quoted in the text at the beginning of this chapter regarding the relocation of church cemeteries. A freshly slain corpse was to be viewed by witnesses called for that purpose by the aðili before being interred (Grágás Ia 152, II 310). On the legal life of corpses see Miller (1983b, 188–90).

51. One judge of the panel of judges was responsible for summing up the plaintiff's case prior to judgment, another the defendant's case. Lots were to determine to whom the responsibility fell if none of the judges volunteered (Grágás Ia 71). The procedure was necessary as an aid to the judges because

judgment was delivered in more than one case at the same time. The man who did the summing up was to "recount the formal means of proof that were presented and say to whose disadvantage they were, whether prosecution or defense" (Ia 72).

52. Von See (1964, 225–28) would attribute a concern for truth as opposed to law to be no earlier than the thirteenth century and ultimately attributable to Christian influence. I am suspicious only because I think that view is but another reflex of the traditional legal historical overevaluation of the pervasiveness of an earlier supposed mindless and magical formalism (see above chapter 7, n. 40).

53. Icelandic legal development seems to have taken place without significant influence from the changes in legal style and the rise of an interpretive jurisprudence that took place in Italy in the eleventh and twelfth centuries. And some of Charles Radding's description of the "prescientific," pre-eleventh-century style rings true for Iceland: Law was conceived primarily as a collection of rules rather than as a structure of categories; legal learning and "judicial expertise consisted not of interpretation, analysis, and argumentation but of knowing the myriad of rules and forms to be invoked as occasions warranted" (1988, 18–19). The Icelandic juristic style is mostly consistent with this, but Radding underestimates the degree of complexity that the casuistic style could accommodate, especially in matters of argumentation. It would seem that not all legal sophistication need prefer the extraction of underlying principle to the proliferation of rules. There is nothing necessarily inconsistent with a preference for the casuistic style and the existence of an interpretive jurisprudence.

54. As far as I know we have no example of a new rule being applied to the very case that raised the new problem in the manner of the English common law. If no such practice existed it meant that either the case would have to be dismissed as not being a proper subject of a legal claim, or that a rule that yielded the "wrong" result would be applied in the face of contrary social norms. It would seem, however, that there was a good possibility that new rules could be applied in the case that raised the issue. Presumably the Lǫgrétta would have to be convened in the same way as when litigants disagreed as to exactly what the law was when the law books did not resolve the matter (see above p. 225):

> Then those men who have matters in dispute are to rehearse
> the article of the law on which they differ and report what
> causes the rift between them. After that men must assess what
> they have said and make up their minds on the matter, and
> then all the Lǫgrétta men who sit on the middle bench are to
> be asked to explain what each of them wants accepted as law
> in the case. Then each chieftain is to say what he will call law
> and whose side he will take in the matter and it is decided by
> majority. . . . It is also prescribed that one man is to rehearse
> with witnesses the article of the law for which there is a ma-

jority, but all the Lǫgrétta men are to give their assent to it. Afterwards it is to announced at the Law Rock. (*Grágás* Ia 214, 216)

There is nothing in this procedure that would prevent the articulation of a new rule under the guise of determining what the true rule had been all along. But the subterfuge and delusion might not have been necessary. A new rule would become provisionally effective for three years if it were announced at the Law Rock the summer it was enacted (*Grágás* Ia 37; cf. III 443), and there is nothing in the *Grágás* texts that would prevent its being applied in a dispute that same summer (see further Líndal 1984, 138–41).

## Chapter Eight

1. Most local feuds seldom required mobilizations that endured beyond a week, although people expecting a return blow might augment the size of their households for a season (*Heið.* 32:311). The last decades of the commonwealth saw the first attempts to maintain standing forces by the big players in the scramble for power. Some of these retainers were self-supplying and maintained themselves on their own farms (e.g., *Íslend.* 142:442–43; see Sveinsson 1953, 11–12). But the scale of activities was larger than in the century preceding 1220. Sturla and Hrafn, for example, anticipating hostilities from Gizur, lodged a force of eighty men over the winter. Provisioning such a force was a burden for the little people of the region: "They swept widely for provisions; that was not, openly at least, claimed to be plundering" (*Íslend.* 165:478).

2. Not all women servants goaded their masters to acts of violence. What this incident reveals is that women servants reminded their masters of honorable courses of action, whether these happened to involve vengeance or peacemaking (see pp. 212–14).

3. Again exception must be made for the territorial battles of the last decades of the commonwealth period. But, as we have already had occasion to note, these confrontations were more in the manner of war than feud (see p. 218).

4. The laws also subjected the peacemaker intervening in an affray to liability if his actions could be construed as aiding a wrongdoer (see *Grágás* Ia 146, II 300 and above p. 250).

5. On the qualification to the orthodox model of arbitration needed to accommodate the dyadic arbitration of self-judgment, see p. 285.

6. Although compensation and various degrees of banishment were the basic features of arbitrated settlements, there were also other remedies. Arbitrators enjoined certain actions, such as the repetition of libelous verses (*Bjarn.* 15:154; *Njála* 45:118). And in disputes narrowly confined to specific pieces of property, they could adjust and declare rights to possession, a remedy, however, also available at law (*Drop.* 4:149; *G.dýri* 25:212). But

awards that provided neither for compensation nor for some form of exile were rare; see further below n. 27.

7. It is to be noted that those ultimately selected to arbitrate a dispute need not be those who had come forward urging and convincing the parties to agree to arbitration. Intervenors were said to *leita um sættir*, "to seek settlements," or *ganga í milli*, "to intervene," "to go-between" and these actions were distinguished from deciding the case, *gøra um málit* (Heusler 1911, 79). The disputants had more direct control over the identity of the arbitrators than of the intervenors, although disputants had some say in who was likely to play the intervenor's role (see p. 265). I distinguish the role of intervenor/peacemaker, on one hand, from that of arbitrator on the other (cf. Abel 1973, 247ff., who would include both roles in his use of intervenor). It was not unknown, in rare instances, for women to be selected as arbitrators; see chapter 6, n. 10.

8. The model of the self-interested and sharp-operating intervenor is Snorri goði, who consistently maintains his persona across several sagas; see, e.g., *Lax.* 71:209–11; *Njála* 139:372–73, 145:408.

9. Such men as Askel (*Reyk.*), Olaf the Peacock (*Lax.*), and Hall of Sida (*Njála*) are consistently represented as men of peace who use great skill and energy in attempts to keep the districts in which they live free of disruptive turmoil.

10. See, e.g., Holmstein (*Drop.* 4:149) and Ketil (*Njála* 93:235) and Einar Konalsson (*Reyk.* 16:202).

11. Virtually all feuds had some people linked to both sides. Marriage patterns in a small rural society would have made it impossible for it to be any other way. As a result, it is only too easy to find examples of feuds in which crosscutting ties were not adequate to the stress put upon them. The links established by marriage and fosterage in *Njáls saga* are a well-known case in point. In that case, the fosterage bond linking the two factions may even have exacerbated the trouble (see Miller 1983a).

12. Marriages contracted as part of a settlement of hostilities are known in the sagas, but are hardly so frequent as to be deemed conventional practice (see, e.g., *Eyrb.* 10:18; *Reyk.* 24:227; *Íslend.* 167:480). Marriages were usually arranged between groups not yet opposed to each other. Part of the purpose of contracting the marriage was to ally the two groups. The structures of bilateral kinship meant that after one generation the groups would have significant points of congruence.

13. See also Skegg-Broddi (*Ljós.* 26:85, 27:89–92), Snorri (*Lax.* 71:209), and Thorstein Sidu-Hallsson (*Ljós.* 11:135). The process of the emergence of conciliators from among the principals' supporters is discussed generally in Gulliver (1973, 687). Whether such people should be seen as negotiators or mediators, that is, as first and second parties or third parties, is unclear and reveals the limits of the standard classificatory definitions.

14. See Llewellyn and Hoebel (1941), Gulliver (1963), Evans-Pritchard (1940), and Barton (1919). For a convenient introduction to dispute-processing styles in stateless societies, see Roberts (1979).

15. See, e.g., clerics as peacemakers in *Hafl.* 19:36–37, 22:40, 24:42–43, 28–29:47; *Íslend.* 5:233; *Þórð.* 1:2, 41:74; as arbitrators *G.dýri* 4:168, 6:171 and see examples listed in Grímsdóttir (1982, 50–57) and Heusler (1912, 51–52).

16. Notice that the victorious defendant still sees fit to offer compensation, even though he has won at law; see further p. 282.

17. The clear implication is that Ketil would not have thought a sufficiently large compensation disgraceful at all. It's not compensation rather than legal victory that Ketil found humiliating, but that the other side was in the position of being able to dictate the amount.

18. It appears that Gudmund outdid Ketil in earthly support mustering. Ketil, it is to be noted, simply continues the support-mustering process on a different level. He, in effect, makes God his *goði*, assigning his claim to Him.

19. The wrongdoer's honor was not as easily jeopardized when he offered settlement, yet even then decorum required that he not look too eager to settle lest it be taken as a sign of fearfulness. The general significances of offers to settle could be manipulated and orchestrated to mean their opposite if the circumstances or skills and blunderings of the players conspired to do so. Thus Hall of Sida was able to acquire great honor by waiving his claim for his dead son (*Njála* 145:408–14). And there are other noteworthy examples of men of rank with apparent selflessness putting aside private claims for the benefit of communal order (*Prest.* 2:119–20; see also *Íslend.* 40:285). But as a general rule, the demands of honor would seldom allow forbearance to be the initial posture of the wronged party. After all, forgiveness was the mode forced upon the weak. And even the strong ran the risk of looking weak when they chose to ignore wrongs done them; see, e.g., *G.dýri* 12:185.

20. The Gulathing law of Norway was much less conciliatory than Icelandic practice. A person who made it a habit of settling for compensation was irrebuttably presumed to have been improperly motivated: "No one, either man or woman, has a right to claim atonement more than three times, unless he has taken revenge in the meantime" (tr. Larson 1935, 140, c. 186). Elsewhere in Scandinavia we hear of the "leveling oath" in which, as part of the settlement, the wrongdoer had to swear that he too would have taken compensation if he were in the claimant's position (Foote and Wilson 1970, 428). In Iceland as well, honor was at risk if a person looked too willing "to carry his kin in his purse," too willing to profit from his losses. Making concessions while maintaining honor was an art.

21. Lehmann and Carolsfeld (1883, 49–64) discuss various discrepancies between the saga's account of this case and the rules in *Grágás*, arguing thus the unreliability of the saga account. None of their technical points, some of them quite well taken, affect the point being made here, which depends on broader structural features of the integration of the legal process with arbitration (see chapter 7, n. 48).

22. *Grágás* does not provide for postjudgment release of outlawry by the judgment holder. In fact, he was subject to penalty if he did so (see above

p. 234). The laws did, however, provide for a mitigation of the full force of the judgment by allowing passage abroad, but only if the mitigation was permitted by the Lǫgrétta (Ia 95–96, 212). The sagas are consistent in painting another picture, and a convincing one at that. Release of an outlawry judgment seems to have been the norm in those cases in which big men were outlawed (e.g., *Hafl.* 31:48; *Íslend.* 51:301; see also 75:335). Two sagas preserve accounts of a formal procedure for "in-lawing" an outlaw by bringing him to three autumn assemblies (*leiðar*); if no one spoke against him, he regained his legal immunity (*Reyk.* 20:215; also *Ljós.* 2:7). Otherwise, it seems that an outlawry judgment could be released on making some kind of restitution for the outlaw's wrong (e.g., *G.dýri* 20:203). There are also accounts of a formal forgiveness ceremony in which the wrongdoer offered his head to the man who outlawed him by placing it on his knee (*Hrafn Sv. St.* 14:218; *Prest.* 3:122; *Þorst. hv.* 7:17). Few wrongdoers, presumably, trusted to their opponent's good will without prior negotiation before undertaking to perform this ceremony (cf., e.g., *Íslend.* 33:265; see further Miller 1983b, 202–3).

23. The litigant perspective had its vogue in legal anthropological scholarship of the 1970s. It is presently in vogue among many legal and social historians (see Helmholz 1982, 723–34).

24. Njal, Hall of Sida (*Njála*), Olaf the Peacock (*Lax.*), Askel (*Reyk.*) are typical "settlers"; Gisli (*Gísli*), Skarphedin and Kari (*Njála*) are of the uncompromising heroic school.

25. E.g., Einar Thorgilsson and Sturla (*Sturla*); Gudmund the Powerful (*Ljós.*); Helgi Droplaugarson (*Drop.*); see also Snorri and Gizur (*Íslend.*), who raise funds and provision themselves by arbitrated settlement.

26. Although Gluckman and Gulliver's readings of their data have been questioned, their basic claim provides a useful entry point for our discussion. Even in small face-to-face communities, the likelihood of conciliatory resolutions is contingent on things like power differences between the disputants, the exact subject matter of the dispute, and the goals of the litigants themselves (see Starr and Yngvesson 1975 and Cain and Kulcsar 1981–82).

27. Even when lifelong exile was decreed by an arbitrator, the person was allowed passage out of the country and immunity while abroad. Full legal outlawry did not contemplate any safe zones for the outlaw. Nor did exile necessarily mean total property confiscation, although the size of some of the monetary awards must have had the same effect.

28. The laws allowed for monetary atonements of forty-eight ounces, called the *réttr*, in serious cases, but it does not appear that it could be sued for separately; it was simply charged against the outlaw's estate in the court of confiscation (*Grágás* Ia 85; see *Grágás* III 661–62, s.v. *réttr*). The sagas barely mention *réttr* and then only in fornication cases; see Miller (1988a, 214n15) and Heusler (1911, 123, 202). In property and contract claims restitution, damages, or specific performance were available, but these kinds of disputes seldom penetrate the saga record until they have been transformed or subsumed into other claims providing for outlawry.

29. Snorri, in fact, shares the top spot for having been the most expensive corpse in *Sturlunga saga*. But in the case of Hall Kleppjarnsson, the total amount was actually paid over (*Íslend.* 29:259; see Ingvarsson 1970, 367).

30. Heusler (1912, 56) notes that the balancing style of settlement appears less frequently in *Sturlunga saga*, where he counts nine cases, than in the family sagas, where there are some thirty instances. The weighted difference is not as great but is still noteworthy. The difference may be due simply to authorial preferences of the family sagas for images of balance or they may reflect the more openly acquisitive and exploitive designs of some of the bigger moving parties in the late period, who used arbitrations as a way of collecting mulcts (see, e.g., *Íslend.* 140:440, 145:446; *Þórð.* 48:85).

31. Consider, e.g., the brief account in *G.dýri* 16:194:

> There was a man named Erlend, nicknamed the Red, who was in residence at Skjaldarvik. One time he happened to meet with Illugi from Hlad. Their conversation soon turned into a *mannjafnaðr*. Erlend said that no one was as noble and manly as Kalf Guttormsson (he had just recently returned to Iceland). But Illugi claimed that Thorgrim alikarl was no less manly. The conclusion of their conversation was that Erlend killed Illugi for no more cause than that.

The *mannjafnaðr* could also take the form of competitive verse exchanges (see Clover 1980; Bax and Padmos 1983).

32. Broad-based funding of compensation awards is frequent fare in the sagas and it rarely leads to any expressions of annoyance that the true debtor might not be the main source of the payment. I know of only one fairly explicit example, although not arising in the context of an arbitrated settlement, of a creditor refusing a third party's offer to discharge a debt on the grounds that the true obligor would get off too easy.

> Grim prepared to set out, saying he had a debt to claim from a man named Thorgrim. . . . "It's now been proven," said Grim, "that he has no intention of paying."
> "Don't go; I will discharge the debt," said Jorunn, [the wife of the man sheltering Grim].
> "But then he doesn't pay," said Grim, and he left taking with him some provisions for the journey. (*Drop.* 12:168)

Other less explicit examples, however, suggest that the source of payment might indeed matter at times; see also *Þorg. sk.* 30:158, discussed above p. 160, and *Reyk.* 10:175.

33. In the event the principal obligor failed to perform, the obligation fell to the sureties. But a surety's performance was often no more certain than the defaulting principal's. When, for example, Sturla refused to pay an award assessed against him, he ordered one of his sureties not to perform either.

The second surety then excused himself also "because he thought the settlement would not be saved should he pay one-half and the other half remain unpaid." Both these sureties, however, felt it prudent to relocate shortly thereafter, although moving did not succeed in insulating one of them from reprisal in the form of a sheep raid (*Sturla* 20:88–89).

34. One wonders why the initial award was set at an amount that was so high that concessions had to be made immediately. Reducing the award by half upon immediate payment of half the announced amount might have been envisaged as a way of "selling" the judgment to the party being ordered to pay damages by making complying look like a bargain, while at the same time assuaging the honor of the other side by nominally judging its wrong at a high value.

35. *Grið,* "peace," "truce," + *níðingr.* A *níðingr* was a quasi-formal status term. It was a catchall designation for the most offensive types of duplicity and scurrility in the culture. The *níðingr* was the coward, the kin-killer, the traitor, and when coupled with *grið,* the truce-breaker. *Grettis saga* (72:232) preserves an elaborate formal truce speech in which the *grið-níðingr* is anathematized; see also *Heið.* 33:312–13 and *Grágás* Ia 205, II 403, in which the truce-breaker is called a *griðbítr,* "truce-biter."

36. On the sanctions for breach of settlements, see further Heusler (1911, 95–97 and 1912, 58).

37. The virtues of separating the disputants as a means of keeping the peace are expressly stated to justify arbitrations in which one of the parties is required to relocate (see *Reyk.* 27:237; also *Finnb.* 38:323).

38. One of the functions, then, of arbitration was to avoid the undesired effects of certain legal rules. Arbitration thus served an equitable function. Even an outlaw's death could be compensable, or his corpse could figure in the arbitrational balancing act (see, e.g., *G.dýri* 4:168; *Njála* 80:196; *Reyk.* 6:169).

39. It is to be noted that the ideals of peaceful relations were not referred to by arbitrators at the time of announcing the award, but were invoked at earlier stages of the disputing process by those trying to convince the parties to submit to arbitration (Heusler 1911, 86). See, e.g., *Hafl.* 19:36–37, 22:39–40, and especially 28–29:47–48, for eloquent and full presentations of the peacemaking position.

40. I have found only one other ethnographic example of self-judgment. The tribes of North Yemen have a regularized practice of conferring the right of judgment on one of the principals much in the manner of Icelandic self-judgment (see Dresch 1989).

41. He describes himself as a plowman who is unattached to a household (36:95); Bergthora calls him a *húskarl* (36:96), suggesting that he is free, while to Skarphedin Njalsson he is a slave (37:98). The discussion that follows in the text indicates that in the community's eyes he was a slave (but cf. Wilde-Stockmeyer 1978, 126–28). Whatever Atli's precise status, he is effectively manumitted by the compensation Njal is able to get on his behalf. This case occurs in the course of the author's construction of the balanced-exchange model of feud (see p. 183) and Atli's equivocal status,

between slave and free, fits exactly the author's carefully constructed incremental escalation of the dispute.

42. This arrangement was apparently made during the *fardagar*, or Moving Days, during which people could change household attachments; it further deepens the confusion surrounding Atli's status since the options Moving Days allowed were clearly unavailable to slaves (see *Grágás* Ia 128–29).

43. An *arfsal* could also be an *arfskot*, a wrongful disinheritance, and arguably it was so in this case since, according to the law, the manumitter or his heirs were called first to the inheritance of a childless freedman (*Grágás* Ia 227, 247–49; II 72, 85–87; see also *Lax.* 16:37; *Vápn.* 7:38).

44. This transaction was also, in Arnkel's opinion (35:95), an *arfskot*: see preceding note.

45. *Grágás* does not confirm the existence of Snorri's limitation as to the place of an arsonist's *óhelgi*-status; it states simply that "they fall *óhelgir*," that is, their killers were fully justified (Ia 185, II 378).

46. There is also indication that this lawsuit was but one small skirmish in a larger conflict involving several households that were competing for certain tracts of land and power in the district. It was not just Thorolf who had an eye to Ulfar's property, nor Arnkel, who took it by formal transfer from Ulfar, but the sons of Ulfar's manumitter. And the woodland that Thorolf conveyed to Snorri would later become a source of serious contention between Snorri and Arnkel (see Byock 1982, 150–54).

47. According to *Grágás*, an action for the killing of a slave carries a punishment of lesser outlawry (Ia 190, II 395); two lesser outlawry actions brought by the same complainant against the same man are treated as a full outlawry action (Ia 110). Since Arnkel was liable for killing six slaves, he was liable for full outlawry (see also *Egil* 81:282).

48. For dispute models that hypothesize a correspondence between the procedural mode in which a dispute is likely to be processed and the orientation of the disputants' goals, see Aubert (1963, 30–31); also Comaroff and Roberts (1981, 110–31).

49. Presumably each side selected one arbitrator. *Grágás* provides that when a two-man panel cannot come to an agreement, they are to decide by drawing lots, the winner receiving the right to make the award (Ib 190, II 285); another procedure allows for the appointment of an "oddman," who is given the power to decide, conditioned on the failure of an arbitration panel of any size to come to agreement (II 279). The selection of two brothers as arbitrators must have been made, at least partially, with the expectation that they would be able to reach a reasonable compromise and not have the matter fall by lot to one very partisan arbitrator. The latter outcome occurs in *Sturla* 23:96; the oddman procedure is also confirmed by one saga case (*Íslend.* 167:479–80).

50. *Grágás* does not preserve the law which, as both saga sources note, reflected an earlier, pre-thirteenth-century practice.

51. There is manuscript support for both readings (see Kålund 1906–11, 169). Either original could have easily generated the other variant, given the

graphemic similarity of an abbreviated Gudmund and Gudrun. It would seem Gudmund is the preferable reading, if only because the saga went into substantial detail to name the parties present at the negotiation and Gudrun was not one of them. The fact that she was a woman would have operated to exclude her from the peacemaking process even though she was complicit, although this does not prevent Thord from arguing that Gudrun should pay half the settlement. It is noteworthy, however, that his suggestion is not followed up on. If indeed the proper reading is Gudmund his unwillingness to have Gudrun's complicity officially acknowledged suggests a certain indelicacy in holding women to account for their wrongs if there were men who were also complicit. The laws, it should be noted, made no sex-based distinctions in liability for wrongdoing. The sagas paint a different picture. Wounds inflicted by women are compounded for pursuant to self-judged arbitrations (*Gísli* 37:116; *Sturla* 31–32:109–11) or are lumped (*Gísli* 32:101; *Lax.* 15:36, 35:98). They do not lead to legal action. The one nonwitchcraft case in which a woman was summoned had disastrous consequences for the summoning party (*Njála* 50:129). According to saga evidence, only witchcraft accusation offers a legitimate basis for prosecuting and/or killing women, although they do not appear any more likely to be the object of witchcraft accusations than men.

52. Note that here again the source of compensation was not the wrongdoer or his nuclear family unit; see above chapter 8, n. 32.

53. Closure as to the original disputants might have also been attainable if the particular claim became unbounded and was subsumed into the feuding strategies of bigger people. The original grievance could get lost in the shuffle.

54. Chagnon (1988, 990) records the anxieties of one of his Yanomamö informants about living in a culture of revenge:

> A particularly acute insight into the power of law to thwart killing for revenge was provided to me by a young Yanomamö man in 1987. He had been taught Spanish by missionaries and sent to the territorial capital for training in practical nursing. There he discovered police and laws. He excitedly told me that he had visited the town's largest *pata* (the territorial governor) and urged him to make law and police available to his people so that they would not have to engage any longer in their wars of revenge and have to live in constant fear. Many of his close kinsmen had died violently and had, in turn, exacted lethal revenge; he worried about being a potential target of retaliations and made it known to all that he would have nothing to do with raiding.

The Icelandic example, I suspect, would temper Chagnon's and his informant's views of the virtues of the power of law, which they seem to be confusing with conquest and the power of the state.

## Conclusion

1. This seems to indicate that the tit-for-tat strategy that game theoreticians find so admirably suited for the evolution of cooperation is not quite as elegantly simple as simulated computer models suggest (see Axelrod 1984). Axelrod's analysis of computerized strategies for the Prisoner's Dilemma game is remarkably suggestive, but does not seem to be readily applicable to the Icelandic feud without considerable qualification. In those interactions which do approximate Prisoner's Dilemmas, there is rarely a possible unambiguous move that would promote greater amounts of cooperation societywide. The problem is that the same act is seldom, if ever, a move in just one game. The very act which may be a cooperative move in game A is often a defection in game B, which is simultaneously being played with another person or group. Moreover, as we have suggested and even shown, moves in any one game are subject to redefinition over time. What at first looked like cooperation can later be understood as a defection. It is thus that even completed games between the same players are never absolutely complete. I am not a student of game theory, so the points I am making here may well have easy answers I do not know about.

2. Elster (1989b) suggests a necessary psychological link between honor and revenge. I am not willing to universalize the connection between honor and vengeance by psychologizing it, but the interesting similarities in disputing styles among "heroic" peoples suggest at the least a close social connection between heroic styles of honor and feud. Further study, however, is needed. The content of honor is by no means the same cross-culturally and it can show significant variation even within a linguistic and cultural community (see Herzfeld 1980).

# WORKS CITED

## I. Primary Sources

A. The family sagas and *þættir* (short narratives), *Landnámabók*, and Ari Þorgilsson's *Íslendingabók* are cited to editions in the Íslenzk Fornrit series (hereafter ÍF) published in Reykjavík by Hið Íslenzka Fornritafélag as follows:

*Auðunar þáttr Vestfirzka*. 1943. In *Vestfirðinga sǫgur*, edited by Björn K. Þórólfsson and Guðni Jónsson. ÍF 6: 359–68.

*Bandamanna saga*. 1936. In *Grettis saga Ásmundarsonar*, edited by Guðni Jónsson. ÍF 7: 291–363.

*Bjarnar saga Hítdœlakappa*. 1938. In *Borgfirðinga sǫgur*, edited by Sigurður Nordal and Guðni Jónsson. ÍF 3: 109–211.

*Brennu-Njáls saga*. 1954. Edited by Einar Ól. Sveinsson. ÍF 12.

*Draumr Þorsteins Síðu-Hallssonar*. 1950. In *Austfirðinga sǫgur*, edited by Jón Jóhannesson. ÍF 11: 321–26.

*Droplaugarsona saga*. 1950. In *Austfirðinga sǫgur*, edited by Jón Jóhannesson. ÍF 11: 135–80.

*Egils saga Skalla-Grímssonar*. 1933. Edited by Sigurður Nordal. ÍF 2.

*Eyrbyggja saga*. 1935. Edited by Einar Ól. Sveinsson and Matthías Þórðarson. ÍF 4: 1–184.

*Finnboga saga*. 1959. In *Kjalnesinga saga*, edited by Jóhannes Halldórsson. ÍF 14: 251–340.

*Fóstbrœðra saga*. 1943. In *Vestfirðinga sǫgur*, edited by Björn K. Þórólfsson and Guðni Jónsson. ÍF 6: 119–276.

*Gísla saga Súrssonar*. 1943. In *Vestfirðinga sǫgur*, edited by Björn K. Þórólfsson and Guðni Jónsson. ÍF 6: 1–118.

*Gísls þáttr Illugasonar*. 1938. In *Borgfirðinga sǫgur*, edited by Sigurður Nordal and Guðni Jónsson. ÍF 3: 329–42.

*Grettis saga Ásmundarsonar*. 1936. Edited by Guðni Jónsson. ÍF 7.

*Grœnlendinga þáttr*. In *Eyrbyggja saga*, edited by Einar Ól. Sveinsson and Matthías Þórðarson. ÍF 4: 271–92.

*Gunnars þáttr Þiðrandabana*. 1950. In *Austfirðinga sǫgur*, edited by Jón Jóhannesson. ÍF 11: 193–211.

*Gunnlaugs saga ormstungu*. 1938. In *Borgfirðinga sǫgur*, edited by Sigurður Nordal and Guðni Jónsson. ÍF 3: 49–107.

*Hallfreðar saga.* 1939. In *Vatnsdœla saga,* edited by Einar Ól. Sveinsson. ÍF
8: 133–200.
*Hávarðar saga Ísfirðings.* 1943. In *Vestfirðinga sǫgur,* edited by Björn K.
Þórólfsson and Guðni Jónsson. ÍF 6: 289–358.
*Heiðarvíga saga.* 1938. In *Borgfirðinga sǫgur,* edited by Sigurður Nordal and
Guðni Jónsson. ÍF 3: 213–328.
*Hœnsa-Þóris saga.* 1938. In *Borgfirðinga sǫgur,* edited by Sigurður Nordal
and Guðni Jónsson. ÍF 3: 1–47.
*Hrafnkels saga Freysgoða.* 1950. In *Austfirðinga sǫgur,* edited by Jón Jó-
hannesson. ÍF 11: 95–133.
*Íslendingabók.* 1968. Edited by Jakob Benediktsson. ÍF 1, pt. 1: 1–28.
*Landnámabók.* 1968. Edited by Jakob Benediktsson. ÍF 1, pts. 1 and 2:
29–397.
*Laxdœla saga.* 1934. Edited by Einar Ól. Sveinsson. ÍF 5.
*Ljósvetninga saga.* 1940. Edited by Björn Sigfússon. ÍF 10: 1–139.
*Njáls saga.* See sub. nom. *Brennu-Njáls saga.*
*Ǫlkofra þáttr.* 1950. In *Austfirðinga sǫgur,* edited by Jón Jóhannesson. ÍF
11: 81–94.
*Reykdœla saga.* 1940. In *Ljósvetninga saga,* edited by Björn Sigfússon. ÍF
10: 149–243.
*Sneglu-Halla þáttr.* 1956. In *Eyfirðinga sǫgur,* edited by Jónas Kristjánsson.
ÍF 9: 261–95.
*Valla-Ljóts saga.* 1956. In *Eyfirðinga sǫgur,* edited by Jónas Kristjánsson. ÍF
9: 231–60.
*Vápnfirðinga saga.* 1950. In *Austfirðinga sǫgur,* edited by Jón Jóhannesson.
ÍF 11: 21–65.
*Vatnsdœla saga.* 1939. Edited by Einar Ól. Sveinsson. ÍF 8: 1–131.
*Víga-Glúms saga.* 1956. In *Eyfirðinga sǫgur,* edited by Jónas Kristjánsson.
ÍF 9: 1–98.
*Víglundar saga.* 1959. In *Kjalnesinga saga,* edited by Jóhannes Halldórsson.
ÍF 14: 61–116.
*Þorsteins saga hvíta.* 1950. In *Austfirðinga sǫgur,* edited by Jón Jóhannes-
son. ÍF 11: 1–19.
*Þorsteins saga Síðu-Hallssonar.* 1950. In *Austfirðinga sǫgur,* edited by Jón
Jóhannesson. ÍF 11: 297–326.
*Þorsteins þáttr stangarhǫggs.* 1950. In *Austfirðinga sǫgur,* edited by Jón Jó-
hannesson. ÍF 11: 67–79.

B. The sagas and *þættir* of the *Sturlunga* compilation are cited from the
edition of Jón Jóhannesson, Magnús Finnbogason, and Kristján Eldjárn:
*Sturlunga saga,* 2 vols., Reykjavík: Sturlunguútgáfan, 1946. These are:

*Ættartölur* I: 51–56.
*Guðmundar saga dýra* I: 160–212.
*Haukdæla þáttr* I: 57–62.
*Hrafns saga Sveinbjarnarsonar* I: 213–28.
*Íslendinga saga* I: 229–534.

*Prestssaga Guðmundar góða* I: 116–59.
*Sturlu saga* I: 63–114.
*Svínfellinga saga* II: 87–103.
*Þórðar saga kakala* II: 1–86.
*Þorgils saga ok Hafliða* I: 12–50.
*Þorgils saga skarða* II: 104–226.

Two remaining secular contemporary sagas that do not appear in the *Sturlunga* compilation proper are:
*Arons saga Hjörleifssonar.* In *Sturlunga saga* II: 237–78.
*Hrafns saga Sveinbjarnarsonar. Biskupa sögur.* Copenhagen, 1858: 639–76.
(This text is the complete unabbreviated version of the text that appears abridged and revised in *Sturlunga*).

C. The following sagas are traditionally cited to the collection of bishops'
sagas and other narrative sources concerning the Icelandic church in
*Biskupa sögur*, 2 vols. Copenhagen: Hinu Íslenzka Bókmentafélagi, 1858–
1878:

*Árna biskups saga. Biskupa sögur* I: 677–786.
*Hungrvaka. Biskupa sögur* I: 57–86.
*Jóns biskups saga.* (Gunnlaug's version). *Biskupa sögur* I: 213–60.
*Kristni saga. Biskupa sögur* I: 1–32.
*Oddaverja þáttr. Biskupa sögur* I: 280–93.
*Páls biskups saga. Biskupa sögur* I: 125–148.
*Þorláks biskups saga. Biskupa sögur* I: 87–124.

D. Other narrative sources cited are:

*Hákonar saga.* 1887. *Icelandic Sagas and Other Historical Documents Relating to the Settlements and Descents of the Northmen in the British Isles,* vol. 2, edited by Gudbrand Vigfússon. London.
*Heimskringla.* 1979. Snorri Sturluson. 3d ed. Edited by Bjarni Aðalbjarnarson. In 3 vols: ÍF 26–28.

E. Law Texts and other non-narrative sources:

*Diplomatarium Islandicum: Íslenzk Fornbréfasafn,* vol. 1, 834-1264. Edited by Jón Sigurðsson. Copenhagen: Hinu Íslenzka Bókmentafélagi, 1857–76.
———. Vol. 2, 1253–1350. Edited by Jón Þorkelsson. Copenhagen: Hinu Íslenzka Bókmentafélagi, 1888–93.
*Grágás* Ia, Ib. 1852. *Grágás. Islændernes Lovbog i Fristatens Tid, udgivet efter det Kongelige Bibliotheks Haandskrift,* edited by Vilhjálmur Finsen. Copenhagen: Berlings Bogtrykkeri. Reprint: Odense: Odense University Press, 1974. (Ia 1–217 translated by Andrew Dennis, Peter Foote, and Richard Perkins. *Laws of Early Iceland: Grágás.* Winnipeg: University of Manitoba Press, 1980.)

———— II. 1879. *Grágás efter det Arnamagnæanske Haandskrift Nr. 334 fol.*, *Staðarhólsbók*, edited by Vilhjálmur Finsen. Copenhagen: Gyldendal. Reprint: Odense: Odense University Press, 1974.

———— III. 1883. *Grágás. Stykker, som findes i det Arnamagnæanske Haandskrift Nr. 351 fol., Skálholtsbók, og en Række andre Haandskrifter*, edited by Vilhjálmur Finsen. Copenhagen: Gyldendal. Reprint: Odense: Odense University Press, 1974.

*Gulathing-Lov.* 1846. In *Norges gamle love*, vol. 1 of 5, edited by R. Keyser and P. A. Munch. Oslo, 1846–95.

*Ine.* In Felix Liebermann. *Die Gesetze der Angelsachsen.* Halle: Max Niemeyer, 1903. I: 88–123.

*Jónsbók.* 1904. *Jónsbók: Kong Magnus Hakonssons Lovbog for Island*, edited by Ólafur Halldórsson. Reprint: Odense: Odense University Press, 1970.

## II. Secondary Sources

Abel, Richard L. 1973. "A Comparative Theory of Dispute Institutions in Society." *Law and Society Review* 8: 217–347.

Aðalsteinsson, Jón Hnefill. 1978. *Under the Cloak: The Acceptance of Christianity in Iceland with Particular Reference to the Religious Attitudes Prevailing at the Time.* Uppsala: Acta Universitatis Upsaliensis.

von Amira, Karl. 1895. *Westnordisches Obligationenrecht.* Vol. 2 of *Nordgermanisches Obligationenrecht.* Leipzig: von Veit.

Andersson, Theodore M. 1964. *The Problem of Icelandic Saga Origins: A Historical Survey.* Yale Germanic Studies 1. New Haven: Yale University Press.

————. 1967. *The Icelandic Family Saga: An Analytic Reading.* Harvard Studies in Comparative Literature 28. Cambridge: Harvard University Press.

————. 1984. "The Thief in *Beowulf.*" *Speculum* 59: 493–508.

————. 1985. "Kings' Sagas (*Konungasögur*)." In *Old Norse-Icelandic Literature: A Critical Guide*, edited by Carol J. Clover and John Lindow, 197–238. Vol. 45 of Islandica. Ithaca: Cornell University Press.

————. 1988. "Ethics and Politics in *Hrafnkels saga.*" *Scandinavian Studies* 60: 293–309.

Andersson, Theodore M., and William Ian Miller. 1989. *Law and Literature in Medieval Iceland: Ljósvetninga saga and Valla-Ljóts saga.* Stanford: Stanford University Press.

Aubert, Vilhelm. 1963. "Competition and Dissensus: Two Types of Conflict and Conflict Resolution." *Journal of Conflict Resolution* 7: 26–42.

Axelrod, Robert. 1984. *The Evolution of Cooperation.* New York: Basic Books.

Barði Guðmundsson. See Guðmundsson.

Barlau, Stephen B. 1981. "Old Icelandic Kinship Terminology: An Anomaly." *Ethnology* 20: 191–202.

Barth, Fredrik. 1965. *Political Leadership Among Swat Pathans*. London School of Economics Monographs on Social Anthropology 19. London: Athlone Press.

Bartlett, Robert. 1986. *Trial by Fire and Water: The Medieval Judicial Ordeal*. Oxford: Clarendon Press.

Barton, R. F. 1919. "Ifugao Law." *University of California Publications in American Archaeology and Ethnology* 15: 1–186. Berkeley: University of California Press.

Baumgartner, M. P. 1984. "Social Control from Below." In *Toward a General Theory of Social Control*, 2 vols., edited by Donald Black, 1: 303–45. New York: Academic Press.

Bax, Marcel, and Tineke Padmos. 1983. "Two Types of Verbal Dueling in Old Icelandic: The Interactional Structure of the *senna* and the *mannjafnaðr* in *Hárbarðsljóð*." *Scandinavian Studies* 55: 149–74.

Beck, Heinrich. 1987. "Kaufungen, Kaupangr und Köping(e)." *Untersuchungen zu Handel und Verkehr der vor- und frügeschichtlichen Zeit in Mittel- und Nordeuropa*. Pt. 4: *Der Handel der Karolinger- und Wikingerzeit*. Edited by Klaus Düwel, et al. Abhand. d. Akad. d. Wiss. in Göttingen. Philol.-hist. Klasse. Series 3, no. 156: 358–73. Göttingen: Vandenhoeck & Ruprecht.

Benediktsson, Jakob. 1968. "Formáli." *Íslendingabók, Landnámabók*. Vol. 1 of ÍF. v–cliv.

———. 1969. "*Landnámabók*: Some Remarks on Its Value as a Historical Source." *Saga-Book of the Viking Society* 17: 275–92.

———. 1975–76. Rev. of *Studier i Landnámabók*, by Sveinbjörn Rafnsson. *Saga-Book of the Viking Society* 19: 311–18.

Berger, Alan J. 1976. "Old Law, New Law, and *Hœnsa-Þóris saga*." *Scripta Islandica* 27: 3–12.

Berkner, Lutz. 1975. "The Use and Misuse of Census Data for the Historical Analysis of Family Structure." *Journal of Interdisciplinary History* 5: 721–38.

Beyerle, Franz. 1915. *Das Entwicklungsproblem im germanischen Rechtsgang*. Deutschrechtliche Beiträge, Forschungen und Quellen zur Geschichte des deutschen Rechts, vol. 10, no. 2. Heidelberg: C. Winter.

Bjarni Einarsson. See Einarsson.

Björn Sigfússon. See Sigfússon.

Björn K. Þórólfsson. See Þórólfsson.

Black, Donald. 1976. *The Behavior of Law*. New York: Academic Press.

———. 1984. "Crime as Social Control." In *Toward a General Theory of Social Control*, 2 vols., edited by D. Black, 2: 1–27. New York: Academic Press.

Black-Michaud, Jacob. 1975. *Feuding Societies*. Oxford: Basil Blackwell. Also published sub. nom. *Cohesive Force: Feud in the Mediterranean and the Middle East*. New York: St. Martin's Press.

Bloch, Marc. 1961. *Feudal Society*, 2 vols. Translated by L. A. Manyon. Chicago: University of Chicago Press.

Bloch, Maurice. 1971. "The Moral and Tactical Meaning of Kinship Terms."
*Man* 6: 79–87.

Bø, Olav. 1969. "*Hólmganga* and *einvígi*: Scandinavian Forms of the Duel."
*Mediaeval Scandinavia* 2: 132–48.

Boehm, Christopher. 1984. *Blood Revenge: The Anthropology of Feuding
in Montenegro and other Tribal Societies*. Lawrence: University Press of
Kansas.

Boswell, John. 1988. *The Kindness of Strangers: The Abandonment of Children in Western Europe from Late Antiquity to the Renaissance*. New
York: Pantheon.

Bourdieu, Pierre. 1966. "The Sentiment of Honor in Kabyle Society." In
*Honour and Shame*, edited by J. G. Peristiany, 191–241. Chicago: University of Chicago Press.

———. 1977. *Outline of a Theory of Practice*. Translated by Richard Nice.
Cambridge: Cambridge University Press.

Bragason, Úlfar. 1986. "On the Poetics of *Sturlunga*." Ph. D. diss. University
of California, Berkeley.

Bremmer, Jan. 1976. "Avunculate and Fosterage." *Journal of Indo-European
Studies* 4:65–78.

Brown, D. J. J. 1979. "The Structuring of Polopa Feasting and Warfare." *Man*
14: 712–33.

Brown, Keith M. 1986. *Bloodfeud in Scotland, 1573–1625: Violence,
Justice and Politics in an Early Modern Society*. Edinburgh: James
Donald.

Brown, Peter. 1975. "Society and the Supernatural: A Medieval Change."
*Dædalus* 104: 133–51.

Brunner, Heinrich. 1906. *Deutsche Rechtsgeschichte*, 2d ed. Leipzig:
Duncker and Humblot.

Bullough, D. A. 1969. "Early Medieval Social Groupings: The Terminology
of Kinship." *Past and Present* 45: 3–18.

Byock, Jesse L. 1982. *Feud in the Icelandic Saga*. Berkeley: University of
California Press.

———. 1988. *Medieval Iceland: Society, Sagas, and Power*. Berkeley: University of California Press.

Cain, Maureen, and Kalman Kulcsar. 1981–82. "Thinking Disputes: An Essay on the Origins of the Dispute Industry." *Law and Society Review* 16:
375–402.

Campbell, J. K. 1964. *Honour, Family, and Patronage*. Oxford: Oxford University Press.

Chadwick, H. Munro. 1912. *The Heroic Age*. Cambridge: Cambridge University Press.

Chagnon, Napoleon A. 1988. "Life Histories, Blood Revenge, and Warfare in
a Tribal Population." *Science* 239: 985–92.

Chapman, Anne. 1980. "Barter as a Universal Mode of Exchange."
*L'Homme* 20.3: 33–83.

Charles-Edwards, T. M. 1972. "Kinship, Status, and the Origins of the
Hide." *Past and Present* 56: 3–33.

———. 1976. "The Distinction between Land and Moveable Wealth in Anglo-Saxon England." In *Medieval Settlement: Continuity and Change*, edited by P. H. Sawyer, 180–87. London: Edward Arnold.

Cheyette, Fredric L. 1978. "The Invention of the State." In *Essays on Medieval Civilization: The Walter Prescott Webb Memorial Lectures*, edited by Bede Karl Lackner and Kenneth Roy Philp, 143–78. Austin: University of Texas Press.

Ciklamini, Marlene. 1963. "The Old Icelandic Duel." *Scandinavian Studies* 35: 175–94.

Clanchy, Michael T. 1979. *From Memory to Written Record*. Cambridge: Harvard University Press.

———. 1983. "Law and Love in the Middle Ages." In *Disputes and Settlements: Law and Human Relations in the West*, edited by John Bossy, 47–67. Cambridge: Cambridge University Press.

Cleasby, Richard, and G. Vigfússon. 1957. *An Icelandic-English Dictionary*, 2d ed., edited by Wm. A. Craigie. Oxford: Clarendon.

Clover, Carol J. 1980. "The Germanic Context of the Unferþ Episode." *Speculum* 55: 444–68.

———. 1982. *The Medieval Saga*. Ithaca: Cornell University Press.

———. 1985. "Icelandic Family Sagas (*Íslendingasögur*)." In *Old Norse-Icelandic Literature: A Critical Guide*, edited by Carol J. Clover and John Lindow, 239–315. Vol. 45 of Islandica. Ithaca: Cornell University Press.

———. 1986. "Hildigunnr's Lament." In *Structure and Meaning in Old Norse Literature: New Approaches to Textual Analysis and Literary Criticism*, edited by John Lindow, Lars Lönnroth, and Gerd Wolfgang Weber, 141–83. Odense: Odense University Press.

———. 1988. "The Politics of Scarcity: Notes on the Sex Ratio in Early Scandinavia." *Scandinavian Studies* 60: 147–88.

Codere, Helen. 1950. *Fighting with Property: A Study of Kwakiutl Potlatching and Warfare, 1792–1930*. New York: Augustine.

Collier, Jane F. 1973. *Law and Social Change in Zinacantan*. Stanford: Stanford University Press.

Colman, Rebecca V. 1974. "Reason and Unreason in Early Medieval Law." *Journal of Interdisciplinary History* 4: 571–91.

Colson, Elizabeth. 1953. "Social Control and Vengeance in Plateau Tonga Society." *Africa* 23: 199–212.

Comaroff, John L., and Simon Roberts. 1981. *Rules and Processes: The Cultural Logic of Dispute in an African Context*. Chicago: University of Chicago Press.

Cover, Robert M. 1986. "Violence and the Word." *Yale Law Journal* 95: 1601–29.

Crone, Patricia. 1986. "The Tribe and the State." In *States in History*, edited by John A. Hall, 48–77. Oxford: Basil Blackwell.

Dalton, George. 1975. "Karl Polanyi's Analysis of Long-Distance Trade and his Wider Paradigm." In *Ancient Civilization and Trade*, edited by Jeremy A. Sabloff and C. C. Lamberg-Karlovsky, 63–132. Albuquerque: University of New Mexico Press.

Davies, R. R. 1969. "The Survival of the Bloodfeud in Medieval Wales."
*History* 54: 338–57.

———. 1986. "The Administration of Law in Medieval Wales: the Role of
the *Ynad Cwmwd (Judex Patrie)*." In *Lawyers and Laymen: Studies in
the History of Law presented to Prof. Dafydd Jenkins on his seventy-fifth
birthday*, edited by T. M. Charles-Edwards, Morfydd E. Owen and D. B.
Walters, 258–73. Cardiff: University of Wales Press.

Davies, Wendy, and Paul Fouracre, eds. 1986. *The Settlement of Disputes in
Early Medieval Europe*. Cambridge: Cambridge University Press.

Degler, Carl N. 1980. *At Odds: Women and the Family in America from
the Revolution to the Present*. New York: Oxford University Press.

Dennis, Andrew, Peter Foote, and Richard Perkins. 1980. *Laws of Early Iceland: Grágás*. University of Manitoba Icelandic Studies 3. Winnipeg: University of Manitoba Press.

Dresch, Paul. 1989. *Tribes, Government and History in Yemen*. Oxford:
Oxford University Press.

Duby, Georges. 1974. *The Early Growth of the European Economy: Warriors and Peasants from the Seventh to the Twelfth Century*. Translated
by Howard B. Clarke. Ithaca: Cornell University Press.

———. 1980. *The Chivalrous Society*. Translated by Cynthia Postan. Berkeley: University of California Press. This is a collection of previously published articles. I cite "Lineage, Nobility and Knighthood," pp. 59–80;
"Youth in Aristocratic Society," pp. 112–22; "The Structure of Kinship
and Nobility," pp. 134–48; "French Genealogical Literature," pp. 149–57.

Dumont, Louis. 1970. *Homo Hierarchicus: The Caste System and Its Im-
plications*. Translated by Mark Sainsbury. Chicago: University of Chicago
Press.

Dumville, David N. 1977. "Kingship, Genealogies and Regnal Lists." In
*Early Medieval Kingship*, edited by P. H. Sawyer and I. N. Wood, 72–104.
Leeds: School of History.

Ebel, Else. 1977. "Kaufmann und Handel auf Island zur Sagazeit." In *Han-
sische Geschichtsblätter*, 1–26. Cologne: Böhlau.

Edgerton, Robert B. 1985. *Rules, Exceptions, and Social Order*. Berkeley:
University of California Press.

Eickelman, Dale F. 1981. *The Middle East: An Anthropological Approach*.
Englewood Cliffs: Prentice-Hall.

Einar Ól. Sveinsson. See Sveinsson.

Einarsdóttir, Ólafía. 1964. *Studier i kronologisk metode i tidlig islandsk
historieskrivning*. Bibliotheca Historica Lundensis 13. Lund: Gleerup.

Einarsson, Bjarni. 1974. "On the Status of Free Men in Society and Saga."
*Mediaeval Scandinavia* 7: 45–55.

Eldjárn, Kristján. 1961. "Two Medieval Farm Sites in Iceland and Some Remarks on Tephrochronology." In *The Fourth Viking Conference: 1961*,
edited by Alan Small, 10–19. Edinburgh: Oliver and Boyd.

Elster, Jon. 1983. *Sour Grapes: Studies in the Subversion of Rationality*.
Cambridge: Cambridge University Press.

———. 1989a. *The Cement of Society: A Study of Social Order*. Cambridge:
Cambridge University Press.

———. 1989b. "Norms of Revenge." Unpublished MS.

Evans-Pritchard, E. E. 1940. *The Nuer: A Description of the Modes of Livelihood and Political Institutions of a Nilotic People.* Oxford: Oxford University Press.

Feil, Daryl Keith. 1979. "From Negotiability to Responsibility: A Change in Tombema-Enga Homicide Compensation." *Human Organization* 38: 356–65.

Felstiner, William L. F. 1974. "Influences of Social Organization on Dispute Processing." *Law and Society Review* 9: 63–94.

Fichtner, Edward G. 1979. "Gift Exchange and Initiation in the *Auðunar Þáttr Vestfirzka.*" *Scandinavian Studies* 51: 249–72.

Finley, Moses I. 1973. *The Ancient Economy.* Berkeley: University of California Press.

Finnur Jónsson. See Jónsson.

Firth, Raymond. 1959. *Social Change in Tikopia.* New York: Macmillan.

Foote, Peter. 1977a. "Þrælahald á Íslandi: Heimildakönnun og athugasemdir." *Saga* 15: 41–74.

———. 1977b. "Oral and Literary Tradition in Early Scandinavian Law: Aspects of a Problem." In *Oral Tradition, Literary Tradition: A Symposium,* edited by H. Bekker-Nielsen, et al., 47–55. Odense: Odense University Press.

———. 1984. *Aurvandilstá.* Edited by Michael Barnes, et al. Vol. 2 in *The Viking Collection: Studies in Northern Civilization,* edited by Preben Meulengracht Sørensen and Gerd Wolfgang Weber. Odense: Odense University Press. This is a collection of Foote's previously published articles. I cite variously "*Sturlusaga* and Its Background," pp. 9–30; "The Audience and Vogue of the Sagas of Icelanders—Some Talking Points," pp. 47–55; "*Sagnaskemtan:* Reykjahólar 1119," pp. 65–83; and "Some Lines in *Lǫgréttuþáttr,*" pp. 155–64.

Foote, Peter, and David M. Wilson. 1970. *The Viking Achievement.* London: Sidgwick and Jackson.

Foucault, Michel. 1980. *Power/Knowledge: Selected Interviews and other Writings, 1972–1977,* edited by Colin Gordon. New York: Pantheon.

Fox, Robin. 1967. *Kinship and Marriage.* Harmondsworth: Penguin.

Frank, Roberta. 1973. "Marriage in Twelfth- and Thirteenth-Century Iceland." *Viator* 4: 473–84.

Friedman, David. 1979. "Private Creation and Enforcement of Law: A Historical Case." *The Journal of Legal Studies* 8: 399–415.

Frier, Bruce W. 1985. *The Rise of the Roman Jurists.* Princeton: Princeton University Press.

Gade, Kari Ellen. 1986. "Homosexuality and Rape of Males in Old Norse Law and Literature." *Scandinavian Studies* 58: 124–41.

———. 1988. "The Naked and the Dead in Old Norse Society." *Scandinavian Studies* 60: 219–45.

Garmonsway, G. N., ed. and trans. 1953. *The Anglo-Saxon Chronicle.* London: Dent.

Geary, Patrick. 1986. "Échange et relations entre les vivants et les morts dans la société du Haut Moyen Age." *Droits et Cultures* 12: 3–17.

Gelsinger, Bruce E. 1981. *Icelandic Enterprise: Commerce and Economy in the Middle Ages.* Columbia, SC: University of South Carolina Press.

Gering, Hugo. 1915. "Altnordische Sprichwörter und sprichwörtliche Redensarte." *Arkiv för nordisk filologi* 32: 1–31.

Gestsson, Gísli. 1976. "Fjórar Baðstofur." In *Minjar og Menntir: Afmælisrit helgað Kristjáni Eldjárn,* edited by Guðni Kolbeinsson, et al., 190–207. Reykjavík: Bókaútgáfa Menningarsjóðs.

Gísli Gestsson. See Gestsson.

Gísli Gunnarsson. See Gunnarsson.

Gísli Pálsson. See Pálsson.

Gluckman, Max. 1955a. *The Judicial Process Among the Barotse of Northern Rhodesia.* Manchester: Manchester University Press.

———. 1955b. "The Peace in the Feud." *Past and Present* 7: 1–14.

———. 1956. *Custom and Conflict in Africa.* Oxford: Basil Blackwell.

Goebel, Julius, Jr. 1937. *Felony and Misdemeanor: A Study in the History of Criminal Law.* Reprint: Philadelphia: University of Pennsylvania Press, 1976.

Goody, Jack. 1983. *The Development of the Family and Marriage in Europe.* Cambridge: Cambridge University Press.

Gottzmann, Carola L. 1982. *Njáls saga: Rechtsproblematik im Dienste sozio-kultureller Deutung.* Frankfurt: Peter Lang.

Gouldner, Alvin W. 1965. *Enter Plato: Classical Greece and the Origins of Social Theory.* New York: Basic Books.

Green, Thomas A. 1985. *Verdict According to Conscience: Perspectives on the English Criminal Trial Jury, 1200–1800.* Chicago: University of Chicago Press.

Gregory, C. A. 1980. "Gifts to Men and Gifts to God: Gift Exchange and Capital Accumulation in Contemporary Papua." *Man* 15: 626–52.

———. 1981. "A Conceptual Analysis of a Non-Capitalist Gift Economy with Particular Reference to Papua New Guinea." *Cambridge Journal of Economics* 5: 119–35.

Grímsdóttir, Guðrún Ása. 1982. "Um afskipti erkibiskupa af íslenzkum málefnum á 12. og 13. öld." *Saga* 20: 28–62.

Grímsson, Þorkell. 1976. "Miðaldabyggð á Reyðarfelli." In *Minjar og Menntir: Afmælisrit helgað Kristjáni Eldjárn,* edited by Guðni Kolbeinsson, et al., 565–76. Reykjavík: Bókaútgáfan Menningarsjóðs.

Grønbech, Vilhelm. 1932. *The Culture of the Teutons.* 3 vols. London: Humphrey Millard. Translation of Danish orig. 1909–12.

Guðmundsson, Barði. 1958. *Höfundur Njálu: Safn ritgerða,* edited by Skuli Þórðarson and Stefán Pjetursson. Reykjavík: Bókaútgáfan Menningarsjóðs.

Guðmundsson, Valtýr. 1893. "Manngjöld-hundrað." In *Germanistische Abhand. zum 70 Geburtstag Konrad von Maurers,* edited by Oscar Brenner, 523–54. Göttingen.

Guðmundur Ólafsson. See Ólafsson.

Guðrún Ása Grímsdóttir. See Grímsdóttir.

Gulliver, P. H. 1963. *Social Control in an African Society: A Study of the Arusha, Agricultural Masai of Northern Tanganyika.* Boston: Boston University Press.

———. 1973. "Negotiations as a Mode of Dispute Settlement: Towards a General Model." *Law and Society Review* 7: 667–91.

Gunnar Karlsson. See Karlsson.

Gunnarsson, Gísli. 1980a. *Fertility and Nuptiality in Iceland's Demographic History*. Meddelande från Ekonomisk-Historiska Institutionen Lunds Universitet 12.

———. 1980b. *A Study of Causal Relations in Climate and History with an Emphasis on the Icelandic Experience*. Meddelande från Ekonomisk-Historiska Institutionen Lunds Universitet 17.

Gurevich, A. Ya. 1968. "Wealth and Gift-Bestowal among the Ancient Scandinavians." *Scandinavica* 7: 126–38.

Hajnal, J. 1965. "European Marriage Patterns in Perspective." In *Population in History: Essays in Historical Demography*, edited by D. V. Glass and D. E. C. Eversley, 101–43. Chicago: Aldine.

———. 1983. "Two Kinds of Pre-industrial Household Formation System." In *Family Forms in Historic Europe*, edited by Richard Wall, et al., 65–104. Cambridge: Cambridge University Press.

Hale, Christopher S. 1981. "Modern Icelandic Personal Bynames." *Scandinavian Studies* 53: 397–404.

Halldórsson, Óskar. 1975. "Sögusamúð og stéttir." *Gripla* 1: 92–104.

———. 1976. *Uppruni og þema Hrafnkels sögu*. Rannsóknastofnun í Bókmenntafræði við Háskóla Íslands. Fræðirit 3. Reykjavík: Hið Íslenzka Bókmenntafélag.

Hammer, Carl. I. Jr. 1983. "Family and *familia* in Early-Medieval Bavaria." In *Family Forms in Historic Europe*, edited by Richard Wall, et al., 217–48. Cambridge: Cambridge University Press.

Hart, H. L. A. 1961. *The Concept of Law*. Oxford: Clarendon Press.

Hasluck, Margaret. 1954. *The Unwritten Law in Albania*, edited by J. H. Hutton. Cambridge: Cambridge University Press.

Hastrup, Kirsten. 1982. "Establishing an Ethnicity: The Emergence of the 'Icelanders' in the Early Middle Ages." In *Semantic Anthropology*, edited by David Parkin, 145–60. ASA Monographs 22. London: Academic Press.

———. 1984. "Defining a Society: The Icelandic Free State Between Two Worlds." *Scandinavian Studies* 56: 235–55.

———. 1985. *Culture and History in Medieval Iceland*. Oxford: Clarendon Press.

Haugen, Einar, ed. 1972. *First Grammatical Treatise: The Earliest Germanic Phonology*. 2d ed. London: Longman.

Heinrichs, Anne. 1972. "The Apposition: A Signal for Emotion in Saga-Writing." *Scandinavica* 11:21–30.

Helgi Þorláksson. See Þorláksson.

Heller, Rolf. 1958. *Die literarische Darstellung der Frau in den Isländersagas*. Halle: Kreuz.

Helmholz, R. H. 1982. "Advances and Altered Perspectives in English Legal History." *Harvard Law Review* 95: 723–34.

Herlihy, David. 1985. *Medieval Households*. Cambridge: Harvard University Press.

Hermann Pálsson. See Pálsson.

Herzfeld, Michael. 1980. "Honour and Shame: Problems in the Comparative Analysis of Moral Systems." *Man* 15: 339–52.

Herzog, Don. 1989. *Happy Slaves: A Critique of Consent Theory.* Chicago: University of Chicago Press.

Heusler, Andreas. 1911. *Das Strafrecht der Isländersagas.* Leipzig: Duncker & Humblot.

———. 1912. *Zum isländischen Fehdewesen in der Sturlungenzeit.* Abhand. d. königl. -preuss. Akad. d. Wiss. Phil.-hist. Klasse, Nr.4. Berlin. 1–102.

Hobbes, Thomas. 1651. *Philosophical Rudiments concerning Government and Society.* Vol. 2 of *The English Works of Thomas Hobbes,* edited by William Molesworth. London, 1841.

Hoebel, E. Adamson. 1954. *The Law of Primitive Man: A Study in Comparative Legal Dynamics.* New York: Atheneum.

Hughes, Shaun F. D. 1980. Review of Óskar Halldórsson, *Uppruni og þema Hrafnkels sögu. Scandinavian Studies* 52: 300–308.

Hyams, Paul R. 1981. "Trial by Ordeal: The Key to Proof in the Early Common Law." In *On the Laws and Customs of England: Essays in Honor of Samuel E. Thorne,* edited by Morris S. Arnold, et al., 90–126. Chapel Hill: University of North Carolina Press.

Ingvarsson, Lúðvík. 1970. *Refsingar á Íslandi á Þjóðveldistímanum.* Reykjavík: Bókaútgáfa Menningarsjóðs.

Jakob Benediktsson. See Benediktsson.

Jochens, Jenny M. 1980. "The Church and Sexuality in Medieval Iceland." *Journal of Medieval History* 6: 377–92.

———. 1985. "En Islande médiévale: A la recherche de la famille nucléaire." *Annales ESC,* no. 1: 95–112.

———. 1986. "The Medieval Icelandic Heroine: Fact or Fiction?" *Viator* 17: 35–50.

Jóhannesson, Jón. 1950. "Formáli." In *Austfirðinga sǫgur.* ÍF 11: v–cxx.

———. 1974. *A History of the Old Icelandic Commonwealth.* Translated by Haraldur Bessason. University of Manitoba Icelandic Studies 2. Winnipeg: University of Manitoba Press.

Jónas Kristjánsson. See Kristjánsson.

Jones, Gwyn. 1933. "Some Characteristics of the Icelandic '*Hólmganga.*'" *Journal of English and Germanic Philology* 32: 203–24.

Jón Hnefill Aðalsteinsson. See Aðalsteinsson.

Jón Jóhannesson. See Jóhannesson.

Jónsson, Finnur. 1914. "Oldislandske Ordsprog og Talemåder." *Arkiv för nordisk filologi* 30: 61–111, 170–217.

Kålund, Kristian. 1906–11. *Sturlunga saga.* Copenhagen: Guldendalske Boghandel.

Karlsson, Gunnar. 1972. "Goðar og bændur." *Saga* 10: 5–57. Summarized in "*Goðar* and *Höfðingjar* in Medieval Iceland," in *Saga-Book of the Viking Society* 19 (1977): 358–70.

———. 1975. "Frá þjóðveldi til konungsríkis." In *Saga Íslands,* edited by Sigurður Líndal, 2: 3–54. Reykjavík: Hið Íslenzka Bókmenntafélag, Sögufélagið.

——. 1980. "Völd og auður á 13. öld." *Saga* 18: 5–30.

Karras, Ruth Mazo. 1988. *Slavery and Society in Medieval Scandinavia.* New Haven: Yale University Press.

Ker, W. P. 1908. *Epic and Romance: Essays on Medieval Literature.* 2d. ed. Reprint: New York: Dover 1957.

Kertzer, David. 1989. "The Joint Family Household Revisited: Demographic Constraints and Household Complexity in the European Past." *Journal of Family History* 14: 1–15.

KLNM. 1956–78. *Kulturhistorisk leksikon for nordisk middelalder.* 22 vols. Copenhagen: Rosenkilde og Bagger.

Koch, Klaus-Friedrich. 1974. *War and Peace in Jalémó: The Management of Conflict in Highland New Guinea.* Cambridge: Harvard University Press.

Kristján Eldjárn. See Eldjárn.

Kristjánsson, Jónas. 1986. "The Roots of the Sagas." In *Sagnaskemmtun: Studies in Honor of Hermann Pálsson,* edited by Rudolf Simek, et al., 183–200. Vienna: Hermann Böhlaus.

Kronman, Anthony T. 1983. *Max Weber.* Stanford: Stanford University Press.

Kuhn, Hans. 1980. "Das Schenken in unserem Altertum." *Zeitschrift für deutsches Altertum und deutsche Literatur* 109: 181–92.

Larson, Laurence M. 1935. *The Earliest Norwegian Laws, Being the Gulathing Law and the Frostathing Law.* New York: Columbia University Press.

Laslett, Peter. 1972. "Introduction: The History of the Family." In *Household and Family in Past Time,* edited by Laslett and Richard Wall, 1–89. Cambridge: Cambridge University Press.

——. 1983. "Family and Household as Work Group and Kin Group: Areas of Traditional Europe Compared." In *Family Forms in Historic Europe,* edited by Richard Wall, et al., 513–63. Cambridge: Cambridge University Press.

——. 1987. "The Character of Familial History, Its Limitations and the Conditions for Its Proper Pursuit." *Journal of Family History* 12: 263–84.

Lehmann, Karl. 1893. "Kauffriede und Friedenschild." In *Germanistische Abhand. zum 70 Geburtstag Konrad von Maurers,* edited by Oscar Brenner, 49–64. Göttingen.

Lehmann, Karl, and Hans Schnorr von Carolsfeld. 1883. *Die Njálssage insbesondere in ihren juristischen Bestandtheilen: Ein kritischer Beitrag zur altnordischen Rechts- und Literaturgeschichte.* Berlin.

Lévi-Strauss, Claude. 1943. "Guerre et commerce chez les Indiens de l'Amérique du Sud." *Renaissance* 1: 122–39.

Little, Lester K. 1978. *Religious Poverty and the Profit Economy in Medieval Europe.* Ithaca: Cornell University Press.

Líndal, Sigurður. 1984. "Lög og lagasetning í íslenzka þjóðveldinu." *Skírnir* 158: 121–58.

Llewellyn, K. N., and E. Adamson Hoebel. 1941. *The Cheyenne Way: Conflict and Case Law in Primitive Jurisprudence.* Norman: University of Oklahoma Press.

Lönnroth, Lars. 1976. *Njáls Saga: A Critical Introduction*. Berkeley: University of California Press.

Lúðvík Ingvarsson. See Ingvarsson.

Luhmann, Niklas. 1982. "The Autonomy of the Legal System." In *The Differentiation of Society*, translated by Stephen Holmes and Charles Larmore, 122–37. New York: Columbia University Press.

MacFarlane, Alan. 1978. *The Origins of English Individualism*. Cambridge: Cambridge University Press.

McGovern, Thomas, et al. 1988. "Northern Islands, Human Error, and Environmental Degradation: A View of Social and Ecological Change in the Medieval North Atlantic." *Human Ecology* 16: 225–70.

Magnússon, Magnús, and Hermann Pálsson. 1969. "Introduction." In *Laxdæla Saga*, 9–42. Baltimore: Penguin.

Magnús Stefánsson. See Stefánsson.

Maine, Henry S. 1861. *Ancient Law*. New York: Dutton, Everyman, 1917.

Maitland. See Pollock and Maitland.

Malinowski, Bronislaw. 1922. *Argonauts of the Western Pacific*. Reprint: New York: Dutton, 1961.

———. 1926. *Crime and Custom in Savage Society*. London: Routledge and Kegan Paul.

Maurer, Konrad. 1871. "Ueber die *Hænsa-Þóris saga*." *Abhand. d. philosophisch-philologischen Klasse der königl. bayerischen Akad. d. Wiss.* 12, no. 2: 157–216.

———. 1874. "Das Gottesurtheil im altnordischen Rechte." *Germania* 19: 139–48.

———. 1893. Rev. "Fóstbræðralag," by Valtýr Guðmundsson. *Zeitschrift des Vereins für Volkskunde* 3: 100–107.

———. 1909. *Das Staatsrecht des isländischen Freistaates*. Vol. 4 of *Vorlesungen über altnordische Rechtsgeschichte*, 1907–10. Leipzig: A. Deichert.

———. 1910. *Altisländisches Strafrecht und Gerichtswesen*. Vol. 5 of *Vorlesungen über altnordische Rechtsgeschichte*, 1907–10. Leipzig: A. Deichert.

Mauss, Marcel. 1967. *The Gift*. Translated by Ian Cunnison. New York: Norton.

Meinhard, H. H. 1975. "The Patrilineal Principle in Early Teutonic Kinship." In *Studies in Social Anthropology: Essays in Memory of E. E. Evans-Pritchard*, edited by J. Beattie and R. Lienhardt, 1–29. Oxford: Clarendon.

Meulengracht Sørensen, Preben. 1977. *Saga og samfund: En indføring i oldislandsk litteratur*. Copenhagen: Berlingske Forlag.

———. 1983. *The Unmanly Man: Concepts of Sexual Defamation in Early Northern Society*. Translated by Joan Turville-Petre. Odense: Odense University Press.

Middleton, John, and David Tait. 1958. "Introduction." In *Tribes Without Rulers: Studies in African Segmentary Systems*, 1–31. London: Routledge and Kegan Paul.

Miller, William Ian. 1983a. "Justifying Skarpheðinn: Of Pretext and Politics in the Icelandic Bloodfeud." *Scandinavian Studies* 55: 316–44.

———. 1983b. "Choosing the Avenger: Some Aspects of the Bloodfeud in Medieval Iceland and England." *Law and History Review* 1: 159–204.

———. 1984. "Avoiding Legal Judgment: The Submission of Disputes to Arbitration in Medieval Iceland." *American Journal of Legal History* 28: 95–134.

———. 1986a. "Gift, Sale, Payment, Raid: Case Studies in the Negotiation and Classification of Exchange in Medieval Iceland." *Speculum* 61. 18–50.

———. 1986b. "Dreams, Prophecy and Sorcery: Blaming the Secret Offender in Medieval Iceland." *Scandinavian Studies* 58: 101–23.

———. 1988a. "Ordeal in Iceland." *Scandinavian Studies* 60: 189–218.

———. 1988b. "Some Aspects of Householding in the Medieval Icelandic Commonwealth." *Continuity and Change* 3: 321–55.

———. 1988c. "Beating Up on Women and Old Men and other Enormities: A Social Historical Inquiry into Literary Sources." *Mercer Law Review* 39: 753–66.

Milsom, S. F. C. 1981. *Historical Foundations of the Common Law.* 2d ed. Toronto: Butterworths.

Moore, Sally Falk. 1978. *Law as Process: An Anthropological Approach.* London: Routledge and Kegan Paul.

Murray, Alexander. 1978. *Reason and Society in the Middle Ages.* Oxford: Clarendon Press.

Murray, Alexander Callander. 1983. *Germanic Kinship Structure: Studies in Law and Society in Antiquity and the Early Middle Ages.* Studies and Texts 65. Toronto: Pontifical Institute of Mediaeval Studies.

Nadel, S. F. 1947. *The Nuba.* London: Oxford University Press.

Nader, Laura, and Harry F. Todd, Jr. 1978. "Introduction." In *The Disputing Process: Law in Ten Societies*, 1–40. New York: Columbia University Press.

Netting, Robert McC., Richard R. Wilk, and Eric J. Arnould. 1984. "Introduction." In *Households: Comparative and Historical Studies of the Domestic Group*, xiii–xxxviii. Berkeley: University of California Press.

Njarðvík, Njörður P. 1973. *Birth of a Nation: The Story of the Icelandic Commonwealth.* Translated by John Porter. Iceland Review History Series. Reykjavík: Iceland Review.

Njörður Njarðvík. See Njarðvík.

Nordal, Sigurður. 1938. "Formáli: Hænsa-Þóris saga." In *Borgfirðinga sǫgur*. ÍF 3: vii–xxxviii.

———. 1940. *Hrafnkatla.* Studia Islandica 7. Translated by R. George Thomas. *Hrafnkels saga Freysgoða.* Cardiff: University of Wales Press, 1958.

———. 1957. *The Historical Element in the Icelandic Family Sagas.* Glasgow: Jackson for Glasgow University Press.

Nozick, Robert. 1974. *Anarchy, State, and Utopia.* New York: Basic Books.

Ólafía Einarsdóttir. See Einarsdóttir.

Ólafsson, Guðmundur. 1980. "Grelutóttir: Landnámsbær á Eyri við Arnarfjörð." Arbók hins Íslenzka Fornleifafélags, 25–73.

Ólason, Vésteinn. 1987. "Norrøn Litteratur som Historisk Kildemateriale." In Kilderne til den tidlige middelalders historie. Rapporter til den XX nordiske historikerkongres Reykjavík 1987, Bind I, edited by Gunnar Karlsson, 30–47. Reykjavík: Háskóla Íslands.

Olsen, Magnús. 1946. "Með lögum skal land byggja." Maal og Minne, 75–88.

Ortner, Sherry B. 1973. "On Key Symbols." American Anthropologist 75: 1338–46.

Óskar Halldórsson. See Halldórsson.

Pálsson, Árni. 1932. "Um lok þrældóms á Íslandi." Skirnir 97: 191–203.

Pálsson, Gísli. 1989. "Language and Society: The Ethnolinguistics of Icelanders." In The Anthropology of Iceland, edited by E. Paul Durrenberger and Gísli Pálsson, 121–39. Iowa City: University of Iowa Press.

Pálsson, Hermann. 1971a. Art and Ethics in Hrafnkel's Saga. Copenhagen: Munksgaard.

———, trans. 1971b. Hrafnkel's Saga and Other Stories. Harmondsworth: Penguin.

Peters, E. L. 1967. "Some Structural Aspects of the Feud Among the Camel-Herding Bedouin of Cyrenaica." Africa 37: 261–82.

Phillpotts, Bertha Surtees. 1913. Kindred and Clan in the Middle Ages and After. Cambridge: Cambridge University Press.

Pitt-Rivers, Julian. 1977. The Fate of Shechem or the Politics of Sex: Essays in the Anthropology of the Mediterranean. Cambridge: Cambridge University Press.

Polanyi, Karl. 1944. The Great Transformation: The Political and Economic Origins of Our Time. Reprint: Boston: Beacon, 1957.

Pollock, Sir Frederick, and Frederic William Maitland. 1898. The History of English Law Before the Time of Edward I. 2d ed. Cambridge: Cambridge University Press. Reprint: 1968.

Radding, Charles M. 1988. The Origins of Medieval Jurisprudence: Pavia and Bologna, 850-1150. New Haven: Yale University Press.

Rafnsson, Sveinbjörn. 1974. Studier i Landnámabók. Bibliotheca Historica Lundensis 31. Lund: Gleerup.

Reynolds, Susan. 1984. Kingdoms and Communities in Western Europe, 900-1300. Oxford: Clarendon.

Rich, George W. 1980. "Kinship and Friendship in Iceland." Ethnology 19: 475–93.

Roberts, Simon. 1979. Order and Dispute: An Introduction to Legal Anthropology. New York: St. Martin's.

Rosenwein, Barbara H. 1989. To Be the Neighbor of Saint Peter: The Social Meaning of Cluny's Property, 909-1049. Ithaca: Cornell University Press.

Ruffini, Julio L. 1978. "Disputing Over Livestock in Sardinia." In The Disputing Process: Law in Ten Societies, edited by Laura Nader and Harry F. Todd. Jr., 209–46. New York: Columbia University Press.

Sahlins, Marshall. 1972. *Stone Age Economics*. New York: Aldine.

Sawyer. Peter H. 1982a. *Kings and Vikings: Scandinavia and Europe, AD 700–1100*. London: Methuen.

———. 1982b. "The Vikings and Ireland." In *Ireland in Early Mediaeval Europe: Studies in Memory of Kathleen Hughes*, edited by Dorothy Whitelock, et al., 345–61. Cambridge: Cambridge University Press.

———. 1987. "The Bloodfeud in Fact and Fiction." In *Tradition og Historie-Skrivning*, 27–38. Acta Jutlandica 63.2. Humanistisk serie 61. Aarhus: Aarhus University Press.

Schach, Paul. 1977. "Some Observations on the Generation-Gap Theme in the Icelandic Sagas." In *The Epic in Medieval Society: Aesthetic and Moral Values*, edited by Harald Scholler, 361–81. Tübingen: Max Niemeyer.

———. 1984. *Icelandic Sagas*. Boston: Twayne.

Schelling, Thomas C. 1984. *Choice and Consequence*. Cambridge: Harvard University Press.

Searle, Eleanor. 1988. *Predatory Kinship and the Creation of Norman Power, 840–1066*. Berkeley: University of California Press.

von See, Klaus. 1964. *Altnordische Rechtswörter: Philologische Studien zur Rechtsauffassung und Rechtsgesinnung der Germanen*. Tübingen: Max Niemeyer.

Sharpe, J. A. 1983. "'Such Disagreement betwyx Neighbours': Litigation and Human Relations in Early Modern England." In *Disputes and Settlements: Law and Human Relations in the West*, edited by John Bossy, 167–87. Cambridge: Cambridge University Press.

Shryock, Andrew J. 1988. "Autonomy, Entanglement, and the Feud: Prestige Structures and Gender Values in Highland Albania." *Anthropological Quarterly* 61: 113–18.

Sigfússon, Björn. 1960. "Full goðorð og forn og heimildir frá 12. öld." *Saga* 3: 48–75.

Sigurður Líndal. See Líndal.

Sigurður Nordal. See Nordal.

Smith, R. M. 1979. "Some Reflections on the Evidence for the Origins of the 'European Marriage Pattern' in England." In *The Sociology of the Family: New Directions for Britain*, edited by C. Harris, 74–112. Sociological Review Monograph 28. Keele.

Starr, June, and Barbara Yngvesson. 1975. "Scarcity and Disputing: Zeroing-in on Compromise Decisions." *American Ethnologist* 2: 553–66.

Steblin-Kamenskij, M. I. 1973. *The Saga Mind*. Translated by Kenneth H. Ober. Odense: Odense University Press.

Stefánsson, Magnús. 1975. "Kirkjuvald eflist," translated by Björn Teitsson, in *Saga Íslands*, edited by Sigurður Líndal, 2: 55–144. Reykjavík: Hið Íslenzka Bókmenntafélag, Sögufélagið.

Steffensen, Jón. 1967–68. "Aspects of Life in Iceland in the Heathen Period." *Saga-Book of the Viking Society* 17: 177–205.

Strömbäck, Dag. 1975. *The Conversion of Iceland*. Translated by Peter Foote. London: The Viking Society.

Sveinbjörn Rafnsson. See Rafnsson.

Sveinsson, Einar Ól. 1933. *Um Njálu*. Reykjavík: Bókadeild Menningarsjóðs.

———. 1953. *The Age of the Sturlungs: Icelandic Civilization in the Thirteenth Century*. Translated by Jóhann S. Hannesson. Vol. 36 of Islandica. Ithaca: Cornell University Press.

———. 1958. *Dating the Icelandic Sagas: An Essay in Method*. Viking Society for Northern Research, Text Series, 3. London: Viking Society for Northern Research.

Thorarinsson, S. 1970. "Tephrochronology and Medieval Iceland." In *Scientific Methods in Medieval Archaeology*, edited by Rainer Berger, 295–328. Berkeley: University of California Press.

Thurnwald, Richard. 1932. *Economics in Primitive Communities*. London: Oxford University Press.

Turner, V. W. 1957. *Schism and Continuity in an African Society: A Study of Ndembu Village Life*. Manchester: Manchester University Press.

Úlfar Bragason. See Bragason.

Valtýr Guðmundsson. See Guðmundsson.

Verdon, Michel. 1980. "Shaking Off the Domestic Yoke, or the Sociological Significance of Residence." *Comparative Studies in Society and History* 22: 109–32.

Vésteinn Ólason. See Ólason.

Vestergaard, Torben Anders. 1988. "The System of Kinship in Early Norwegian Law." *Mediaeval Scandinavia* 12: 160–93.

Vinogradoff, Paul. 1911. *The Growth of the Manor*. 2d ed. New York: Macmillan.

Vries, Jan de. 1961. *Altnordisches Etymologisches Wörterbuch*. Leiden: E. J. Brill.

———. 1967. *Altnordische Literaturgeschichte*, vol. 2. 2d ed. Berlin: Walter de Gruyter.

Wall, Richard. 1983a. "Introduction." In *Family Forms in Historic Europe*, edited by Richard Wall, et al., 1–63. Cambridge: Cambridge University Press.

———. 1983b. "The Composition of Households in a Population of 6 Men to 10 Women: Southeast Bruges in 1814." In *Family Forms in Historic Europe*, edited by Richard Wall, et al., 421–74. Cambridge: Cambridge University Press.

Wallace-Hadrill, J. M. 1962. "The Bloodfeud of the Franks." In *The Long Haired Kings*, 121–47. London: Methuen.

———. 1975. "War and Peace in the Earlier Middle Ages." *Transactions of the Royal Historical Society* 5th ser. 25: 157–74.

Weber, Max. 1968. *Economy and Society*, edited by Guenther Roth and Claus Wittich. New York: Bedminster.

Wheaton, Robert. 1975. "Family and Kinship in Western Europe: The Problem of the Joint Family Household." *Journal of Interdisciplinary History* 5: 601–28.

———. 1987. "Observations on the Development of Kinship History, 1942–1985." *Journal of Family History* 12: 285–301.

Whitaker, Ian. 1981. "'A Sack for Carrying Things': The Traditional Role of Women in Northern Albanian Society." *Anthropological Quarterly* 54: 146–56.

White, Stephen D. 1978. "*Pactum . . . Legem Vincit et Amor Judicium*: The Settlement of Disputes by Compromise in Eleventh-Century Western France." *American Journal of Legal History* 22: 281–308.

———. 1986. "Feuding and Peace-making in the Touraine Around the Year 1100." *Traditio* 42: 195–263.

———. 1988. *Custom, Kinship, and Gifts to Saints*. Chapel Hill: University of North Carolina Press.

Wickham, Chris. 1986a. "Land Disputes and their Social Framework in Lombard-Carolingian Italy, 700–900." In *The Settlement of Disputes in Early Medieval Europe*, edited by Wendy Davies and Paul Fouracre, 105–24. Cambridge: Cambridge University Press.

———. 1986b. "Dispute Processes and Social Structures." Part 3 of Conclusion in *The Settlement of Disputes in Early Medieval Europe*, edited by Wendy Davies and Paul Fouracre, 228–40. Cambridge: Cambridge University Press.

Wilda, Wilhelm Eduard. 1842. *Das Strafrecht der Germanen*. Vol. 1 of *Geschichte des deutschen Strafrechts*. Halle.

Wilde-Stockmeyer, Marlis. 1978. *Sklaverei auf Island*. Heidelberg: Carl Winter.

Wormald, C. Patrick. 1977a. "*Lex Scripta* and *Verbum Regis*: Legislation and Germanic Kingship, Euric to Cnut." In *Early Medieval Kingship*, edited by P. H. Sawyer and I. N. Wood, 105–38. Leeds: School of History.

———. 1977b. "The Uses of Literacy in Anglo-Saxon England and its Neighbors." *Transactions of the Royal Historical Society*, 5th series, 27: 95–114.

———. 1982. "Viking Studies: Whence and Whither?" In *The Vikings*, edited by R. T. Farrell, 128–53. London: Phillimore.

Wormald, Jenny. 1980. "Bloodfeud, Kindred and Government in Early Modern Scotland." *Past and Present* 87: 54–97.

———. 1986. "The Sandlaw Dispute." In *The Settlement of Disputes in Early Medieval Europe*, edited by Wendy Davies and Paul Fouracre, 191–205. Cambridge: Cambridge University Press.

Wrigley, E. A. 1978. "Fertility Strategy for the Individual and the Group." In *Historical Studies of Changing Fertility*, edited by Charles Tilly, 135–54. Princeton: Princeton University Press.

Yanagisako, Sylvia Junko. 1979. "Family and Household: The Analysis of Domestic Groups." *Annual Review of Anthropology* 8: 161–205.

Young, Michael W. 1971. *Fighting with Food*. Cambridge: Cambridge University Press.

Þorkell Grímsson. See Grímsson.

Þorláksson, Helgi. 1978. "Comments on Ports of Trade in Early Medieval Europe." *Norwegian Archaeological Review* 11.2: 112–14.

———. 1979. "Stórbændr gegn goðum: Hugleiðingar um goðavald, konungsvald og sjálfræðishug bænda um miðbik 13. aldar." In *Söguslóðir: Afmælisrit helgað Ólafi Hanssyni*, 227–50. Reykjavík: Sögufélag.

———. 1982. "Stéttir, auður og völd á 12. og 13. öld." *Saga* 20: 63–113.

———. 1986. "Óvelkominn börn?" *Saga* 24: 79–120.

Þórólfsson, Björn K., and Guðni Jónsson. 1943. "Formáli." In *Vestfirðinga sǫgur*. ÍF 6: v–cxi.

# INDEX

Icelandic school of saga scholarship,
45, 50, 316n9, 317n10
Illegitimacy, 136, 339n52
Inheritance: households and, 128;
law, 144, 149, 150, 231–32,
341n9; slavery and, 26–27; transfer of rights (*arfsal*), 289, 348n49,
362n34, 372n43; women and, 27
Insult (*níð*), 61, 63, 66, 72, 233,
322n28, 323n42. *See also* Honor
Isleif Gizurarson, first bishop of Iceland (1056–80), 35
*Íslendingabók*, 13, 15, 35, 224, 226,
338n36, 341nn6,8, 343n10. *See
also* Ari Thorgilsson
*Íslendinga saga:* arbitrators and,
372n49; clerics in combat and,
39; Christianity in, 192; combat
and, 325n58; compensation for
accidents, 66; dependents and,
152; end of commonwealth and,
40, 41, 219; fosterage and, 173;
goading and, 212–14; honor, 32,
33; household and, 118, 120,
127–29, 338n41; inheritance and,
144; kinship relations and, 146–
47, 159, 160, 164–70 *passim*,
339n45, 347n32; kinship terms
and, 157; lawsuits and, 247,
360n25, 362n38, 364n47; literacy
and, 357n11; old age and, 210;
outlawry and, 238, 369n22;
peacemaking and, 259–60, 267,
270, 277–81 *passim*, 286,
351n15, 367n12, 368nn15,19,
369n25, 370nn29,30; raids and,
100; sale of land and, 332n49;
selling goods and, 79, 88,
329nn27,28, 330n35; servants
and, 334n10, 336n23, 351n12;
style of, 51; tithe laws and, 231;
vengeance and, 194, 196, 197,
206–8, 349n56, 353nn25,32,
366n1; women and, 335n17,
339n51, 355n35
*Íslendingasögur. See* Family sagas

*Íslenzk fornrit* (editions of family
sagas), 44, 316n9

Jochens, Jenny, 317n10, 337nn29,
33, 338n37, 339n43
Jon Loftsson, 32–33, 38, 143, 172,
266, 279
Jon Ogmundarson, Bishop of Hólar
(1106–21), 37
*Jónsbók* (Norwegian law code), 98,
331n38, 338n36
*Jóns saga*, 358n11
Judges, 17–18, 227, 235, 240, 251,
253–54 *passim*, 312n8
Judicial system. *See* Courts; *Grágás*; Law; Lawsuits

Ker, W. P., 316nn3,5
Ketil Thorsteinsson, Bishop of Hólar (1122–45), 268–70
Kindred: definition of, 340n2; leadership of, 155–56; Phillpotts'
views of, 140–42; practical organization of, 155–56, 178
Kings' sagas (*konungasögur*), 316n4
Kinship: generally, 139–78; fictive,
171–74; fosterage and, 123, 171–
72; groupings of kin, 119, 155;
household and, 111; laws and,
221; recruitment for feud and,
164–67, 210; servants and, 122;
formal structures of, 142–45 *pas-
sim*, 340nn2,3, 341nn4,5; termi-
nology of, 157–58, 346nn27–31.
*See also* Fosterage; Marriage;
Sponsorial kin
Kinstrife, 160. *See also* Feud;
Kinship
Klæng Thorsteinsson, Bishop of
Skálholt (1152–76), 146, 272
*Konungsbók*, 43, 315n1. *See also*
*Grágás*
*Kristni saga*, 16, 35, 97, 177, 312n4

Land, 107–8, 332n49, 338n42. *See
also* Households

Printed and bound by CPI Group (UK) Ltd, Croydon, CR0 4YY

09/06/2025

14685694-0004